Imagining Multilingual Schools

Imagining Multilingual Schools

Languages in Education and Glocalization

Edited by
Ofelia García, Tove Skutnabb-Kangas
and María E. Torres-Guzmán

Orient BlackSwan

IMAGINING MULTILINGUAL SCHOOLS: Languages in Education and Globalization

ORIENT BLACKSWAN PRIVATE LIMITED

Registered Office
3-6-752 Himayatnagar, Hyderabad 500 029 (A.P.), INDIA
e-mail: centraloffice@orientblackswan.com

Other Offices
Bangalore, Bhopal, Bhubaneshwar, Chennai, Ernakulam, Guwahati, Hyderabad, Jaipur, Kolkata, Lucknow, Mumbai, New Delhi, Patna

First Published in India by
Orient Blackswan Private Limited, 2009

ISBN 13: 978 81 250 3654 8

Printed in India at
S.D.R. Printers
Delhi

Published by
Orient Blackswan Private Limited
1/24 Asaf Ali Road
New Delhi 110 002
e-mail: delhi@orientblackswan.com

Dedication

The three of us, and most of our authors, are teachers/educators ourselves. Over the years we have worked with teachers. We have observed classrooms and interacted with thousands of teachers in all types of imaginable contexts. In many countries, teachers are poorly paid, work in unsatisfactory and often desperately bad conditions, with harsh and often impossible demands. Teachers are made invisible most of the time, but get all the blame when schools are seen 'not to deliver'. Despite this, most teachers persist, 'deliver', and are real change agents.

We admire your hard work, your energies and efficiency, your professionalism, your love and care, your reflection, analysis and openness to change, your devotion, and your imagination in finding ways to show children (and parents) that other worlds are possible!

We want to dedicate this volume to you and to the all the world's teachers of multilingual children. We want to thank you for inspiration and for believing and showing through your daily work that change is possible.

Admiramos tu duro trabajo, tu energía y eficiencia, tu profesionalismo, tu amor y cuidado, tu reflexión, análisis y apertura al cambio, tu devoción, y tu imaginación al buscar maneras de enseñarle a los niños (y a sus padres) que hay posibilidad de otros mundos.

Queremos dedicarte este volumen, a ti, y a todas las maestras del mundo de niños multilingües. Queremos agradecerte tu inspiración y tu compromiso, mostrado a través de tu trabajo diario, de que el cambio es posible.

Me ihailemme teidän kovaa työtänne, tarmoanne ja tehokkuuttanne, ammattitaitoanne, rakkauttanne ja huolenpitoanne, harkitsevaa ja erittelevää ajatteluanne ja muutosalttiuttanne, työllenne omistautumista ja mielikuvitustanne löytäessänne keinoja osoittaa lapsille (ja vanhemmille) että toisenlaisetkin maailmat ovat mahdollisia!

Haluamme omistaa tämän teoksen teille ja kaikille maailman monikielisten lasten opettajille. Haluamme kiittää teitä innostavasta esimerkistä ja siitä että uskotte ja näytätte päivittäisellä työllänne että maailmaa voi muuttaa.

New York and Trønninge Mose
Ofelia García, Tove Skutnabb-Kangas, María E. Torres-Guzmán

Contents

Editors' Preface

The contributions in this volume give evidence to how, especially in education, local languages and cultures resist homogenizing tendencies, either global or national. The chapters herein also present ways in which the imagination opens spaces for the local in the global, enabling the co-presence of both universalizing and particularizing tendencies in multilingual schools.

Some of the chapters end with a summary in languages other than English. For some authors, a voice in languages other than English has been a way to ensure a space for local languages within an English language book. In placing these summaries within the context of this book in English, we, as editors, give testimony to these languages, the people who speak them, and the teachers who use them to educate.

The editors wish to gratefully acknowledge the help given to us by graduate students at Teachers College, Columbia University, in the preparation of this volume. In particular, we want to thank Leah Mason for her prompt searching and enthusiasm, Tammy Arnstein for her attention to detail, Christal Burnett and Victor Quiñones for their help with the indexes and Cambria Russell for her thorough reading of the entire manuscript.

OFELIA GARCÍA,
TOVE SKUTNABB-KANGAS,
MARÍA E. TORRES-GUZMÁN

Part 1

Introduction

Chapter 1

Weaving Spaces and (De)constructing Ways for Multilingual Schools: The Actual and the Imagined

OFELIA GARCÍA, TOVE SKUTNABB-KANGAS and
E. MARÍA TORRES-GUZMÁN

To imagine is to begin the process that transforms reality.
bell hooks, 1990: 9

If we're seriously interested in education for freedom as well as for the opening of cognitive perspectives, it is also important to find a way of developing a praxis of educational consequence that opens the spaces necessary for the remaking of a democratic community. For this to happen, there must of course be a new commitment to intelligence, a new fidelity in communication, a new regard to imagination. It would mean the grant of audibility to numerous voices seldom heard before and, at once, an involvement with all sorts of young people being provoked to make their own the multilinguality needed for structuring of contemporary experience and thematizing lived worlds
Maxine Greene, 1988: 127

Introduction

The United Nation's 2004 Human Development Report links cultural liberty to language rights and human development (http://hdr.undp.org/reports/global/2004/) and argues that there is

> ... no more powerful means of 'encouraging' individuals to assimilate to a dominant culture than having the economic, social and political returns stacked against their mother tongue. Such assimilation is not freely chosen if the choice is between one's mother tongue and one's future. (UNDP, 2004: 33)

The press release about the UN report (see web address above) exemplifies the role of language as an exclusionary tool:

> Limitations on people's ability to use their native language – and limited facility in speaking the dominant or official national language – can exclude people from education, political life and access to justice. Sub-Saharan Africa has more than 2500 languages, but the ability of many

> people to use their language in education and in dealing with the state is particularly limited. In more than 30 countries in the region, the official language is different from the one most commonly used. Only 13% of the children who receive primary education do so in their native language. (UNDP, 2004: 33)

How do we imagine schools that would build on and support the multiplicity of languages and literacies in our globalized world, and where people can 'use their native languages' (see above)? How can we 'unstack' the 'economic, social and political returns' that are at present stacked against most mother tongues in the world? What are the issues that educators, linguistically diverse[1] children and youth and their parents, educational authorities and politicians must face if they/we want schools where people can have both their mother tongues and a future, rather than needing to make a false, impossible and unethical choice between them? What are the multilingual educational options available? How do factors beyond the school itself impact the design and implementation of such multilingual education programs?

The chapters that make up this volume give multiple perspectives on these questions. Spanning different multilingual situations of individuals, ethnolinguistic groups and peoples, states and global connections, they collectively give us a vision of the complex ecology of multilingual education in the 21st century, emphasizing a situated view of languages and language varieties in different sociolinguistic, sociopolitical, and sociohistorical contexts. We start in Section 1 by presenting, in the appropriate Part and order in which they appear in the book, the English-language summaries for each chapter, written by the authors themselves. In that way the reader, when reading this Introduction, will understand the main points of each contribution, in the words of the authors themselves, rather than summarized by us. Section 2 of this Introduction identifies our positions as researchers, and our standpoint on multilingual schools. Section 3 poses and discusses important questions contained in this volume, while Section 4 reflects on the five threads identified in the contributions. We close the chapter with a Conclusion.

Section 1: Summaries

Part 2: Pedagogies, Values and Schools

Chapter 2: *Identity Texts: The Imaginative Construction of Self Through Multiliteracies Pedagogy (Jim Cummins)*

The chapter highlights the centrality of the interpersonal space (or *zone of proximal development*) created in the interactions that teachers orchestrate with their students. Optimal academic development within this interpersonal space occurs only when there is both maximum cognitive engagement and maximum identity investment on the part of students. The products of student work carried out within this pedagogical framework are termed *identity texts* insofar as students invest their identities in these texts (written, spoken, visual, musical, or combinations in multimodal form) that then hold a mirror up to the students in which their identities are reflected back in a positive light. When students share identity texts with multiple audiences (peers, teachers, parents, grandparents, sister classes, the media, etc.) they are likely to receive positive feedback and affirmation of self in interaction with these audiences. Several examples of identity texts created by students in culturally and linguistically diverse classrooms are presented and discussed in relation to transmission, social constructivist, and transformative approaches to pedagogy.

Chapter 3: *Imagining Multilingual Education in France: A Language and Cultural Awareness Project at Primary Level (Christine Hélot and Andrea Young)*

This chapter presents a *language awareness* project in a primary school in Alsace, France where, over three years, children aged 6 to 9 have been introduced to 18 languages and their associated cultures. The aims of the project were twofold – to legitimate the regional and immigration languages of some of the pupils in the eyes of all learners (monolinguals and bilinguals alike), and to educate children to the wealth of linguistic and cultural diversity before they start to learn one foreign language at primary school.

The language awareness approach developed in the project is analyzed in terms of an alternative model of language education that can transform the traditional monolingual habitus of most schools and sow the seeds of multilingual education. The educational partnership developed by the teachers with the parents is an example of a collaborative approach through which speakers of minority languages can be empowered.

Chapter 4: *Reimagining Multilingual America: Lessons from Native American Youth (Teresa L. McCarty, Mary Eunice Romero, Ofelia Zepeda)*

This article examines the role of Native languages in the lives and aspirations of Native American youth. Drawing on a five-year, multi-method study of Native language shift and retention in five tribal communities, we analyze language ideologies that suggest the evolving contemporary causes of language shift among the young. Native youth narratives suggest three overarching themes that influence their language choices: concern about the future of their heritage language, the politics of shame and caring, and the constraints of larger standardizing regimes. We conclude by discussing examples of Indigenous counter-initiatives to the pressures that limit youths' language choices: Native charter schools, counter-standards for culturally-responsive schooling, and Native-language immersion programs.

These bold education practices wedge open spaces of possibility, creating new arenas in which to reimagine multilingual schools.

Chapter 5: *Attitudes Towards Language Learning in Different Linguistic Models of the Basque Autonomous Community (Feli Etxeberría-Sagastume)*

This chapter focuses on the language learning attitudes and motivations of the first student cohort to graduate from high school in one of three linguistic models (A, B, and D) under the 1983 Spanish bilingual law within the Basque Autonomous Community. The qualitative analysis of students' written responses to open-ended questions shows that students are positively disposed to language learning, and variations in attitudes are associated with the different languages being learned (Euskara, Spanish, and English) and the linguistic school models the students attended. It is concluded that in imagining multilingual schooling, researchers must account for the role of values associated with language learning and the social contexts.

Part 3: Extending Formal Instructional Spaces

Chapter 6: *Back to Basics: Marketing the Benefits of Bilingualism to Parents (Viv Edwards and Lynda Pritchard Newcombe)*

This chapter examines the central role of parents in language transmission and argues that the ultimate success of any attempt to imagine multilingual schools depends on the extent to which advocates of bilingual education are able to communicate their case to families. Using the example of *Twf*, a highly innovative project that promotes the benefits of bilingualism to parents and prospective parents in Wales, the chapter explores the ways in which modern marketing strategies can be used to challenge myths about bilingualism. While recognizing that the linguistic issues vary from one setting to another, it proposes that the central marketing messages of *Twf* – that bilingualism is something that parents should aspire to for their children, that the ability to speak another language increases children's life chances and makes the family proud – are ones that are likely to resonate not only in Wales but in a wide range of other settings.

Chapter 7: *Popular Education and Language Rights in Indigenous Mayan Communities: Emergence of New Social Actors and Gendered Voices (Karen Ogulnick)*

Formal public education for indigenous children consists primarily of passive learning from authoritarian teachers who transmit cultural and linguistic values that are markedly distinct from those of the communities in which they are teaching. Within this system, children are taught to reproduce the cultural capital of the dominant class, thus complying with their own subjugation. Many obstacles face indigenous people in realizing a free, public education that respects and promotes their rich linguistic diversity and cultural heritages. Nonetheless, the perseverance and deeply-held belief in the right to learn and maintain one's native language, or *batsi'kop* (literally, 'true language' in Tsotsil) is keeping the dream of multilingual education alive, and indeed making it a reality for many children and adults in Chiapas, Mexico, where one-third of the population is indigenous and 11 indigenous languages are spoken, many of which are endangered.

Beginning with the historical and sociopolitical context of indigenous native language rights and bilingual education in Mexico, this chapter describes two main models through which the indigenous people of Chiapas have organized their resistance to the enforced acculturation process in public schools for indigenous peoples. One of these models is the autonomous school movement created by the *Zapatistas*. Another one is the popular education programs of two Chiapas-based Mayan non-governmental organizations – *Sna Jtz'ibajom* (House of the Writer) and *Fortaleza de la Mujer Maya* (Empowering Mayan Women). This chapter demonstrates how these grassroots organizations are succeeding in reviving and promoting the native languages for the indigenous people in Chiapas. In addition, with the support of national and international organizations, the work of these grassroots organizations is influencing national language policies in Mexico, and inspiring people across the Mexican borders to promote similar movements for social justice and linguistic human rights in their own communities.

Part 4: Tensions between Multiple Realities

Chapter 8: *Imagined Multilingual Schools: How Come We Don't Deliver? (Elana Shohamy)*

The chapter begins by portraying the 'imagined multilingual schools' where it is legitimate to use and develop multilingual languages, fusions and hybrids, even beyond languages and towards multimodalities, and where languages are used in free and creative ways beyond monolingual boundaries, purity and correctness. By identifying specific mechanisms that prevent the fantasies from becoming realities, the chapter then proceeds to describe reasons why such goals remain fantasies. Specifically, it claims that it is through a number of powerful mechanisms, used to promote ideologies of nation states, that monolingualism and standards for language correctness continue to be perpetuated. Presenting empirical data on academic achievements of immigrants in schools, as well as appropriate test modifications, the chapter argues that different language policies, language educational policies and especially high-stake language testing policies (e.g. the *No Child Left Behind* Act in the US) mean that the messages that are delivered and perpetuated are those of de-legitimacy and suppression of other languages, and promotion and perpetuation of criteria based on 'native' varieties and language correctness. The chapter also identifies other mechanisms, such as language in the public space, language myths and propaganda. It is by examining the mechanisms that operate behind *de facto* language policies that we can reach some understanding of why 'we don't deliver'. The author calls for increasing understanding of these issues through language awareness and activism.

Chapter 9: *Monolingual Assessment and Emerging Bilinguals: A Case Study in the US (Kathy Escamilla)*

This chapter presents a case study examining the implementation of large-scale programs for testing emerging bilingual students. US schools have become increasingly diverse linguistically. However, assessment systems to determine student academic achievement have become more monolingual in their focus. Second language learners are frequently blamed for any perceived under-performance on these exams. In a few states, including Colorado, Spanish/English emerging bilinguals are allowed to take assessments in Spanish. Data collected in this case study compared academic achievement in reading and writing between students who took the Colorado CSAP test in Spanish and English. Findings indicated that students taking the assessments in Spanish outperformed students taking the CSAP in English, and in the schools studied, Spanish outcomes exceeded district-wide English averages. Findings support the need to assess emerging bilinguals in both their languages.

Chapter 10: *The Long Road to Multilingual Schools in Botswana (Lydia Nyati-Ramahobo)*

At independence, the government of Botswana imagined a monolingual society in which English would be the only language of education, the judiciary, and all other social domains. The government also imagined that Setswana would be the only language used in national life when dealing with the general population. The language-in-education policy and related legal instruments were put in place to create an ordinary citizen who is monolingual in Setswana and an educated one who is bilingual in Setswana and English.

In contrast to this view, the situation on the ground was that 99% of the population spoke one of the 26 unrecognized languages (Walter & Ringenberg, 1994). This population imagined a multilingual society and multilingual schools, thus creating a backlash between the Tswana political leaders and the numerical majority non-Tswana. This chapter describes government efforts in creating monolingualism and societal movements that counteracted this position and developed multilingualism and multiculturalism. Etsha 6 Primary School serves as an example of a school environment that represents the battlefield for and against monolingualism and reflects how this tension impacts on learning and social integration.

Part 5: Negotiating Policies of Implementation

Chapter 11: *Nichols to NCLB: Local and Global Perspectives on US Language Education Policy (Nancy Hornberger)*

In the anniversary year of landmark US Supreme Court decisions affirming the right to equal educational opportunity for all children irrespective of race or language origin, it behooves us to take a look at how well we are fulfilling the mandates of *Brown v. Board of Education* (1954) and *Lau v. Nichols* (1974). In an attempt to understand both what is happening and what could happen to promote and build on the multilingual resources present in US schools, this chapter takes a historical and comparative look at US language education policy at the federal level since 1974 and draws on ethnographic work locally in one urban school district and globally in multilingual contexts.

Chapter 12: *Cultural Diversity, Multilingualism, and Indigenous Education in Latin America (Luis Enrique López)*

This chapter re-evaluates some underlying principles of intercultural bilingual education (IBE) in Latin America, based on a brief overview of the sociolinguistic contexts in which this type of education is implemented. Emphasis is placed on the cases of Bolivia and Guatemala, countries where indigenous peoples constitute real national majorities. Although intercultural bilingual education has evolved as a recognized national model, attention is paid to the emergence of recent alternative proposals, which according to their authors – indigenous leaders and organizations – search for even more cultural pertinence. The discrepancy results from the low importance given to indigenous knowledge in school curricula.

Thus, the new proposals of *educación propia* (own education) or endogenous education, in spite of its denomination also includes interculturalism and multilingualism under indigenous control and management. In the midst of such discrepancies, intercultural bilingual education is periodically reinvented through bottom-up indigenous proposals.

Chapter 13: *Multilingualism of the Unequals and Predicaments of Education in India: Mother Tongue or Other Tongue? (Ajit K. Mohanty)*

Analysis of the nature of Indian multilingualism shows that, despite the strong maintenance norms, the hegemonic role of English gives rise to a socially legitimated and transmitted hierarchical pecking order in which mother tongues are gradually marginalized and pushed into domains of lesser power and resource in what can be characterized as a self-defensive anti-predatory strategy. Caught in the process of unequal power relationship between languages and lacking a clear multilingual framework, education in India is unable to balance the demands of the societal multilingualism and the dominant status of English.

The place of languages in Indian education and the various nominal forms of multilingual education are analyzed to show the cost of neglecting the mother tongues and tribal languages in education. Some studies interrogating the myth of English medium superiority and showing the benefits of mother-tongue-based multilingual education are discussed. It is argued that education must cater to the social needs of every child to develop from mother tongue to multilingualism and provide equality of opportunity through a language-shelter type of multilingual education that begins in mother-tongue medium and introduces other languages after at least three to five years of primary schooling.

Section 2: Positioning as Researchers on Multilingual Schools and Questioning of Issues

Our multivision positioning as researchers: What is and what ought to be, the actual and the imagined

Homi Bhabha (1990, 1994) and Walter Mignolo (2000) have emphasized that 'the place of enunciation' makes a difference in our construction of knowledge. Gloria Anzaldúa (1987), Bhabha (1994) and Edward Said (1993) remind us of one of the resources of immigrants, exiles, refugees, and other 'transnationals'; namely, their/our ability to have 'double vision' or to 'be in the middle', so as to be able to have a critical orientation towards the many places in which they/we have lived.

If this is so, then those of us whose life experience – often, not schools – has made us bilingual or multilingual also have multiple ways of using our languages to voice an alternative worldview and a critical perspective. We have multiple associations, visions and voices, developed through our ability to be in the middle.

Many of the authors in this volume describe educational and language-related struggles of marginalized indigenous peoples or minorities and challenges they/we face. Many do it both from the inside and from the outside. Is this biased or less than 'objective'? All views, in fact, are subjective. The dominant views, which are unmarked and appear as non-biased, correspond to the dominant special interest, while at the same time enjoying the privilege of appearing as 'objective'. Thus, standpoint theorists criticize 'the claims of objectivism that insist that the only alternative to a "view from nowhere" (a positivistic 'objective' view posing as neutral) is a special interest bias – which leads to value relativism' (Skutnabb-Kangas, 2000: xxix–xxx). In contrast, according to Sandra Harding (1998: 159), 'standpoint epistemologies propose that institutionalized power imbalances give the act of starting off from marginalized lives a critical edge for formulating new questions that can expand everyone's knowledge about institutionalized power and its effects'.

The age-old debate about the role of researchers is whether we should state only what is, or also suggest and study what ought to be. As editors of this book, we hope that the text invites readers to build on what Myles Horton (founder of the earliest Center for Civil Rights work in the US) has called 'a divided vision'. In *The Long Haul* (1997), Horton explains that, during his work with Martin Luther King Jr and others, he kept a divided vision – one eye on where people were at the time, and one eye on where he thought it was possible for them to go. Maxine Greene (2000) holds that the role of all educators, namely to enable transformation, is about the interaction of the actual and the imagined. Transformation is about staying in touch with the world as it is, while calling for the possibility of naming alternatives to the given. Transformation is also about bringing the virtual into existence by going beyond ordinarily accepted limits.[2] With these multivisions and multilingual voices, our texts support people and peoples who struggle for societal equity, and want multilingual educational programs as a building block on the way to social justice. We situate our vision in the hope of possibilities and of creating spaces for dreams to come forth, and in the hope of making the struggle of indigenous and minority peoples to achieve equity through an appropriate education, a reality. Thus, we stand as scholar activists (Crawford, 1999; Nagengast & Vélez-Ibañez, 2004) and assume the standpoint of what DuBois called the 'two-ness' or double consciousness (cited in Aldridge, 2003). Upholding the right to multilingualism, we denounce the mechanisms through which society and schools oppress less powerful groups into shame and silence.

Our positions on education and schools as control agents

This book recognizes that education is not solely about formal schools. Education is social action, and all families, peers and other social groupings attempt to transform themselves and their 'consociates' through everyday teaching and learning (Varenne, forthcoming). As social action, education occurs in informal contexts, outside of school. The chapter by Edwards and Pritchard Newcombe on the educational efforts with health professionals on behalf of the bilingualism of Welsh children is an example of an effort to create a supportive out-of-school educational context that impacts families, children, educators, and schools.

Other out-of-school examples are alternative educational programs for adults who have been failed by state schools and remain formally 'uneducated'. The latter is the case of the popular education programs in Latin America described by both Ogulnick and López in this volume.[3] Out-of-school programs could be important vehicles for alternative certification, for the labor market, and for the individual and society in general.

Sometimes ethnolinguistic groups are able to create and develop parallel educational sites that build on their own language and literacy practices. When these groups have sufficient financial resources and political clout, these alternative educational sites function alongside the established state schools, and provide a true alternative to the education state-schools provide. That is the case of many of the programs for indigenous education described by McCarty, Romero, and Zepeda in this volume.

One could imagine that bringing such programs permanently into the folds of the formal education system, as Etxeberría reports to be the case with Model D in the Basque Country, could result in mutual gain and benefits. Easier state financing might be one of the benefits for the programs.

On the other hand, becoming part of the formal state system might also suffocate some of the freedom and flexibility these educational programs enjoy as alternatives. Schools, and especially state schools, are subjected to external control – educational state agencies that, under the pretense of supporting accountability, prescribe top-down curricula, books, testing, and even language of instruction and assessment. Escamilla, Hornberger, McCarty *et al.*, and Shohamy, among others in this volume, discuss this control.

In some states, education systems are very centralized and hierarchical. This is the case of, for example, the French system described by Hélot and Young, where decisions are taken at ministerial level in Paris and circulated down to teachers through a monthly official bulletin. Some other education systems are more decentralized, with more control by local educational authorities. This is the case with the Finnish system. In the international comparisons in the PISA (Programme for International Student Assessment) of the OECD studies (http://www.pisa.oecd.org/pages/0,2987,en_32252351_32235731_1_1_1_1_1,00.html), Finns come out as the best readers in the world. The Finnish National Board of Education mentions on its website, in addition to several other factors, 'Supportive and flexible administration – centralised steering of the whole, local implementation' as one of the reasons for the success.[4]

But, regardless of more or less flexibility, all state schools participate in functioning as agents of imagined nationhood (in Benedict Anderson's sense, 1983). This often promotes the semblance of, or the idealized image of, *one* identity, *one* culture, and *one* standard language and literacy (even though these realities are much more complex), to which the individual partially attaches his/her sense of identity. Some of the chapters in this book 'uncover' some of the dominant hidden curricula of schools, and especially the role they have played in suppressing the diversity of language and literacy practices of children and youth – the most vulnerable in society.

The chapters in this volume go beyond describing parallel educational programs and uncovering or deconstructing the dominant hidden curricula. Even under oppressive regimes and conditions, human beings find ways of engaging in resistance, what Varenne (forthcoming) calls 'centrifugal, hidden and playful activity' that has the potential to transform their conditions, even if the educational activity itself is hidden. For example, within the United States, enslaved African Americans taught each other to read, even when their literacy was forbidden (Gundaker, forthcoming). Even in highly structured state schools, there is much centrifugal, hidden and playful activity that has the power to imagine and create new possibilities that transform the monolithic and monoglossic vision of these schools.

Building on the power of imagination and resilience, some of the chapters in this volume (for example, Cummins, Hélot and Young, McCarty *et al.*) describe practices and pedagogies that have the potential of transformation. Many of the pedagogies in the chapters build on indigenous and minority social and cultural contexts that are usually not thought of, are not acknowledged, or are prohibited within the hidden curricula in public schools organized by dominant groups (Ada, 1995; Trujillo, 1999). These alternative pedagogies proposed within this volume acknowledge that there are multiple ways of knowing and doing which are essential to fully educate indigenous and immigrant or autochthonous minority children.

Our positions on multilingual education and its complexity

We have often seen terms such as multicultural or intercultural education celebrated and used in ways that exclude multilingualism. We have also observed schools claim that they practice multilingual education when they, at the most, teach a few languages as subjects. Often this teaching has been outside ordinary school hours, organized by parents or some minority organization, and paid for by parents, embassies or the like, not the school. We do not want to water down the concept of multilingual education.

We adhere to Andersson and Boyer's (1978) classic definition of bilingual education as one in which two languages are used as languages of instruction in subjects other than the languages themselves. This means that the main criterion for multilingual education is the number of languages of instruction. Accordingly, multilingual education is education where more than two languages are used as languages of instruction in subjects other than the languages themselves.

It is manifestly not enough for a school that wants to offer multilingual education to be 'linguistically diverse' (i.e. to have students with many mother tongues) or to have a population that is linguistically different from a country's dominant majority (where this exists, as it does in most European countries and in North America, but not in many African or even Asian countries, which may not have any decided 'majorities'). It is not enough to have multilingual staff, or a situation where many languages are heard in the corridors or seen on the walls. All of this is positive, and necessary, but it is not sufficient for designating a program as multilingual education.

We adopt in this book the term 'multilingual school' to mean schools, which *exert educational effort* that takes into account and builds further on the diversity of languages and literacy practices that children and youth bring to school. This means going beyond 'acceptance' or 'tolerance,' to *cultivation* of children's diverse languages and culture resources and includes using the children's languages (whether dominant, indigenous, or immigrant or autochthonous minority) as teaching languages. This educational effort can be very different, depending on social, historical, political, economic and linguistic factors, and thus there are many ways of being a 'multilingual school.' A necessary ingredient, though, is using several teaching languages.

One of the challenges we have had in writing this Introduction stems from the richness of this variety in educational provision and, especially, from understanding the complexity of how far whose imagination can stretch in which sociopolitical and sociolinguistic contexts and in which country. On a global scale, what seems like an unrealistic dream for some countries and educators already takes place in other contexts; likewise, for some of us, what factually is happening in some other places seems like a nightmare. What follows are some examples.

Starting with small *dominant groups*, Icelandic-speakers in *Iceland*, we find that 94% of the population of 296,000 people (see Appendix, Table 1.3) have all their education, from day-care to kindergarten to school to university, through the medium of Icelandic. The whole society functions in Icelandic, a language with a written tradition stretching over a thousand years. Icelanders are very proud of their language, aware of its structure and vocabulary, interested in its planning; and it is self-evident for them that they can do everything in Icelandic. Despite few natural resources except fish, Iceland has one of the highest living standards in the world. In *South Africa*, however, the numerically largest group (over 10 million) is the *Zulu*, 23.8% of the population of some 44 million (see Appendix, Table 1.3). Despite being numerically 33 times the number of Icelanders, many Zulu say that their language is so small that it is impossible to develop higher education in Zulu, or to use it in most advanced formal functions. Note that Zulu is easily among the 100 largest languages out of the 6,912 languages in the world identified in the 15th edition of the *Ethnologue* (2005). Many Zulu children undergo subtractive English-medium education, which does not support high levels of multilingualism. Very few of them learn Zulu at a high formal level, or learn other African languages in school. Thus, 'small' and 'big' are not only functions of power relations, they are also functions of the eyes of the imaginer.

The terms *immersion, submersion, transition, maintenance* or *revitalization* – terms traditionally used to describe different kinds of bilingual education programs and approaches – are also terms that shift depending on whether one is speaking about the program itself or the power relationships of the language(s) of instruction in relation to the student. For example, to be 'immersed' into a language not your own, you need to be a power majority (such as an English-speaker in Canada taught through the medium of French, a Finnish-speaker in Finland taught through the medium of Swedish or an English-speaker in the US taught through the medium of Spanish in an immersion or two-way program). Alternatively, if you are not a power majority (in the way that the Zulus, for example, are not, despite their numerical strength), being taught through the medium of a foreign language is submersion – unless this language happens to be that of your ancestors', your grandparents' or parents' revitalizing language, as is the case in most Hawai'ian, Māori, Ojibway, Navajo or Anár Saami immersion programs. A concept interpretation that does not take into account the sociopolitical circumstances of groups can turn a dream into a nightmare and vice versa.

Some *indigenous peoples* do have 'dream' schools in which their own languages are used as the main media of education at least up to upper secondary education; some can also study a few subjects (at least their own language and culture, sometimes more) in their L1 at university level. This is true for some *Māori* children in *Aotearoa/New Zealand* (some 319,000 people, 7.9% of the population of around 4 million) and some *North Saami* in *Norway and Finland* (see Appendix, Table 1.3 for figures; there are altogether 10 Saami languages; the number of Saami is between 60,000 and 100,000, maybe half of whom speak Saami languages; see http://www.galdu.org/english/index.php?sladja=25&vuolitsladja=11; for the uncertainty of figures, see also Magga & Skutnabb-Kangas, 2003 and Aikio-Puoskari & Pentikäinen, 2001). All Saami children become minimally trilingual.

Bodo 'tribal' children in *India* have also, after a long struggle, managed to get mother-tongue-medium education in Assam, and Bodo is now one of the 22 official languages in India. Bodo children in mother-tongue-medium education are doing as well as Assamese children in Assamese-medium education, and much better than Bodo children in Assamese-medium education (see, Saikia & Mohanty, 2004). Eight other tribal group children in Andra Pradesh, India, have also started education through the medium of their own languages in 2005 (Rao, 2005).

Quotes from various studies in Ian Martin's reports (Martin, 2000a, 2000b) for the Nunavut government in Canada also characterize *Inuit* children, taught completely through the medium of English, in ways that articulate the disaster or nightmare that indigenous children face in the world as a result of the imposition of dominant languages.[5] The report *Keewatin Perspective on Bilingual Education* (by Katherine Zozula and Simon Ford, 1985) tells of Canadian Inuit students who are 'neither fluent nor literate in either language,' and presents statistics showing that students 'end up at only Grade 4 level of achievement after 9 years of schooling'. *The Canadian Royal Commission on Aboriginal Peoples 1996 Report* notes that 'submersion strategies which neither respect the child's first language nor help them gain fluency in the second language may result in impaired fluency in both languages'. *The Nunavut Language Policy Conference in March 1998* claims that 'in some individuals, neither language is firmly anchored'. The report *Kitikmeot struggles to prevent death of Inuktitut* (1998) tells of 'teenagers [who] cannot converse fluently with their grandparents'.

In an interview in PFII's (United Nations Permanent Forum on Indigenous Issues) *Quarterly* Newsletter *Message Stick 3:2*; (http://www.un.org/esa/socdev/unpfii/news/news_2.htm), PFII's first chair, Professor Ole Henrik Magga, sums up the connections between the concepts of human rights, language, language policy, and education. In his view, education is one of the three most important challenges for the world's indigenous peoples in the years to come (the other two are land and health issues). He sees linguistic human rights in education as a necessary prerequisite for the maintenance of indigenous languages and traditional knowledges, and demands much more work on languages and an end to the killing of languages caused by the educational systems in today's nightmarish education for indigenous peoples.[6] López (Chapter 12) makes the same case for the education of indigenous peoples in Latin America, showing how they fall behind in school precisely because of the lack of an education that acknowledges the need for the indigenous mother tongues.

The education of an *autochthonous minority*, like the *Swedish speakers* in *Finland* (some 5.7% of the population, under 300,000 people) also represents a dream for many. In this case all education, up to and including university, takes place in Swedish, and Swedish-speakers see Swedish as a medium of instruction and the value of their language as self-evident. Of course they learn the majority language, Finnish, in school; and those who also use it outside school, develop very high (often native-like) proficiency. In addition, one, two, or even three other languages can be studied as subjects in school. Few Swedish-speaking parents fear that the children might not learn Finnish and English well in their Swedish-medium school – and results show that there is no reason to fear. All Finnish-speaking children also study Swedish in school as a subject, and many are in Swedish-medium immersion programs (see www.uwasa.fi/hut/svenska/eside 1.html). *French-speakers* in *Quebec in Canada*, have a similar position. For most *African autochthonous minorities* (much smaller in numbers than the

Zulu, also in terms of percentages of the total population), the educational situation is a submersion and assimilationist nightmare, with results that remind us of the Inuit quotes about education above. Even here, both politicians and researchers/authors know well what should be done instead (see, for example, www.outreach.psu.edu/C&I/AllOdds/declaration.html for the Asmara Declaration on African Languages and Literatures).

Few *immigrant minority* children have good additive bilingual education. Nonetheless, there are examples of effective bilingualism and multilingualism in the education of immigrant minority children. One example would be *Spanish-speaking* children in the *United States* in some two-way programs (if these last long enough – see Lindholm-Leary, 2001; Thomas & Collier, 2002; Freeman *et al.*, 2005), or in more traditional bilingual education programs, such as Late Exit bilingual transitional education programs (Villarreal, 1999). Another example would be *Finnish speakers* in *Sweden* who are in one of the eight private Finnish-medium schools and get excellent results.

An example of a nightmarish educational situation for immigrants would be that of Denmark, as this country has the harshest assimilation policy in Europe. There are no mother-tongue-medium schools and next to no mother-tongue teaching as a subject, and the (only) important educational goal for immigrant children is the learning of Danish. The type of education described by Cummins in this volume (Chapter 2), for instance, would be a dream – it does not exist. Minority children's Danish is proposed to be tested from the age of three, and if they do not perform well, severe measures follow. At least half of these children leave school as so-called 'functional illiterates,' and fairly few get any further education after grade 9. In Denmark, immigrant minority youth is grossly overrepresented in criminality statistics. Sixty percent of the inmates in closed institutions for criminal youngsters have immigrant background (July 2005 figures). It is a basic economic issue – prevention may cost less than punishment. One place in these 'correctional' facilities costs the taxpayers (including, of course, immigrant minority taxpayers – even if immigrant minorities' unemployment figures are for many groups three times those of the Danes) 1,8 million Danish crowns, a bit under 250,000 Euros (around 300,000 US dollars) per year. With the cost of maintaining a young person in one of these institutions for one year, he (most are males) could have had a private bilingual teacher, through the medium of the mother tongue, during the whole nine years of comprehensive school.

Bilingual education also exists for other types of children who are not immigrant, autochtonous minorities or indigenous. The twelve *European (Union) Schools*, with over 16,000 students are a positive example (see Baetens Beardsmore, 1995; www.eursc.org/SE/htmlEn/IndexEn_home.html). These European (Union) Schools have subsections where each language is used as the main medium of education for many years, and the children learn at least two other languages, one of them at a near-native level. Many elite schools of this type exist in several countries; some international schools may also partially belong here, at least with respect to some of their students, even though for many students these schooling experiences represent *submersion* (see Carder, forthcoming). The shift in meanings with respect to who is experiencing the teaching language(s) does not preclude us from recognizing the ways of characterizing and categorizing multilingual schools.

We believe that William Mackey's old typology (1972) is still one of, if not *the* most elaborated one, and is perfectly valid even today. He uses four main dimensions, each with many subcategories:

(1) the relationship between the language(s) of the home and the schools;
(2) curriculum;
(3) the linguistic character of the immediate environment as compared with the wider national environment;
(4) the function, status and differences between the languages.

Those within the first two dimensions seem to loom large in the present text. In the first one, Mackey distinguishes between learners from unilingual and bilingual homes, with the home language (one or both) used or not used as school language. The curriculum dimension distinguishes between:

(1) medium of instruction (single or dual medium);
(2) pattern of development (maintenance of two or more languages or transfer from one medium of instruction to another);
(3) distribution of the languages (different or equal and the same);
(4) direction (towards assimilation/acculturation into a dominant culture or towards integration into a resurgent one, i.e. irredentism – or self-determination, as we might call it today);
(5) complete or gradual change from one medium to another.

Fishman and Lovas (1970), Gonzáles (1975), Skutnabb-Kangas (1981, 1990, 2000), Skutnabb-Kangas and García (1995), García (1997), and Baker and Prys Jones (1998), among others, have added various aspects and dimensions. Skutnabb-Kangas and García (1995) emphasized schooling as experienced by the student and the relationship he/she has with the language of instruction.

Most of the dimensions, which in several typologies are presented as opposites, are in fact continua, and all the developers of the typologies are aware of that. If we see most of Mackey's categories as continua (similar to Hornberger's continua of biliteracy, see Hornberger, 2003) rather than as discreet either/or points, most of the educational experience described in this book can in fact be placed within this over-30-year-old typology. Certainly some of the emphases today are different from 30 years ago, and more details are known about various situations around the world. But, despite all the changes that have come with corporate globalization, voluntary and enforced mobility, and global media access for some, the complexities, dynamisms, and hybridizations of multilingualism have been in existence, albeit not recognized or named, for a long time. To us, this emphasizes the fact that we know more than enough about how minority education should NOT be organized, and a great deal about how it could be organized under different circumstances to yield positive results. The main problem is not our lack of knowledge or shallow understanding of the old and new complexities. The problem is that the knowledge is not being acknowledged, not used nor implemented widely. Nyati-Ramahobo in this volume says, for instance, when speaking about the development of multilingual schools in Botswana, that there is a social choice, and that the major impediment is lack of political will.

Many indigenous peoples have known for a long time the genocidal consequences of the nightmarish, subtractive dominant-language-medium education. For example, 'The Code of Handsome Lake' ('The Good Message'), developed by Handsome Lake, a Seneca born in 1735, and contained in Chief Jacob Thomas's *Teachings from the Longhouse* (1994), describes the consequences of transferring their children to the 'white race'. The Code was meant to strengthen and unify the Iroquoian community 'against the effects of white society'. Handsome Lake says:

> We feel that the white race will take away the culture, traditions, and language of the red race. When your people's children become educated in the way of white people, they will no longer speak their own language and will not understand their own culture. Your people will suffer great misery and not be able to understand their elders anymore. We feel that when they become educated, not a single child will come back and stand at your side because they will no longer speak your language or have any knowledge of their culture. (Handsome Lake, quoted in Thomas, 2001/1994: 41–42)

Likewise, the results of additive teaching through the medium of the mother tongue (even if it is transitional) have been known for a long time. The USA *Board of Indian Commissioners* (here quoted from Francis and Reyhner) wrote in 1880:

> First teaching the children to read and write in their own language enables them to master English with more ease when they take up that study ... A child beginning a four years' course with the study of Dakota would be further advanced in English at the end of the term than one

> who had not been instructed in Dakota (page 77) ... It is true that by beginning in the Indian tongue and then putting the students into English studies our missionaries say that after three or four years their English is better than it would have been if they had begun entirely with English (page 98). (Francis & Reyhner, 2002: 45–46)

What all of this means is that multilingualism in education can be studied only from an ecological perspective centered on the dynamic and changing conditions of the complex historical, ideological, structural, and practical contexts in which people use different languages and different varieties of languages in society and schools. Multilingual practices are enmeshed within, and influenced by, social, historical, political, economic, and linguistic factors (Nieto, 2001). To design spaces and both deconstruct and then construct ways for multilingual schools requires a situated view of languages and their speakers and identities, and attention to these different conditions. But especially it requires attention to the power relations that maintain negative educational models, as well as the ensuing unequal social and political relations which represent linguicism; that is:

> [i]deologies, structures and practices which are used to legitimate, effectuate, regulate and reproduce an unequal division of power and resources (both material and immaterial) between groups which are defined on the basis of language (on the basis of their mother tongues). (Skutnabb-Kangas, 1988: 13)

This ecological view of languages in education recognizes that the threads of the multiple enmeshed continua are not independent of each other or of other factors. They are often tangled and intertwined.

Section 3: Important Questions and Issues for Reflection

Before we present, based on an ecological view of languages in education, some of the threads in this book, we want to introduce some of the important issues that are discussed and debated, often with strong emotional arguments, in many countries, including in this text – the segregation of minorities, the separation of languages, the need for bilingual teachers, the privileging of minority languages, and the need (or otherwise) for standardization. Questions emerging from these issues have to do with the types of reflection discussed below:

Question 1: To what extent is it necessary, beneficial and ethically acceptable to separate minority students into their own, linguistically homogenous groups, for some or all of the education?

Social reactions to old apartheid and other segregationist education experiences often seem to prevent people from seeing that it is not an issue of segregating or excluding anyone permanently. But at least initial physical segregation of minority students may be pedagogically necessary for them to be taught cognitively challenging material and learn their own language at a high level (for an example, see García & Bartlett, forthcoming). Students need to start from their own level of proficiency, in order for instruction to be organized most effectively.

Claiming that one wants the children to maintain their language and develop it further sounds hollow if the school system is not prepared to organize education that makes this possible. Unless the non-dominant language is used as the main medium of education for a number of years, competence in it necessarily remains shallow. Often many of the measures taken by schools are therapeutic, more social psychological 'feel good', 'proud of their heritage', 'enhance their self-confidence' type, rather than beneficial linguistically and educationally. A wish to 'integrate' minority students physically as early as possible with dominant group students overrides educational and linguistic concerns in most cases, particularly when teachers are not prepared linguistically and educationally to deal with the added complexity of a linguistically heterogeneous student group (Howard & Loeb, 1998). This results in the violation of children's educational and linguistic human rights (Magga *et al.*, 2005; Dunbar *et al.*, forthcoming). It has been pointed out, for example, that despite the good intentions of some two-way dual language education programs in the United States, language minority students' linguistic and educational needs are often ignored (for more on this, see García, 2006; Valdés, 1997). The reason, of course, is that the political agenda of states to socially integrate and homogenize is often more important than the educational needs of children.

As Rodolfo Stavenhagen (1995: 77) has put it: 'State interests thus are still more powerful at the present time than the human rights of peoples'. Amy Tsui's conclusion is similar:

> Medium-of-instruction policies are shaped by an interaction between political, social, and economic forces. However, among these agendas, it is always the political agenda that takes priority. Other agendas, be they social, economic, or educational, come to the fore only if they converge with the political agenda. Yet it is always these agendas that will be used as public justification for policy making. (Tsui, 2004: 113)

Allan Luke, having worked as a Deputy Director General of Education in addition to doing innovative educational research in several countries, states:

> The question is only in part about whether and how teachers and schools can change. The prior question is whether governments,

> bureaucracies and education systems themselves have the intellectual resources, the research infrastructure and capacity, and, indeed, the psychological maturity and electoral patience to understand, articulate and promote complex and multidimensional strategies needed to unprecedented educational, social and economic problems. And even then, they must stay the course. (Luke, 2005: 676)

We agree with these authors and believe that, because the education of linguistic minorities has been disastrous to date, policies need to be discussed more broadly and widely, bringing together the social issues of inclusion/exclusion, linguistic equity, and educational experiences and outcomes, as they relate to non-dominant language students. These discussions call for a wide distribution of what we know to date about the positive effects and benefits of multilingual education to the individual, to specific social groups, and to society at large.

Question 2: To what extent do the languages need to be fairly strictly separated in the classroom, allocating different functions, times, or spaces to each language?

Should classrooms concentrate on one language at a time, or are they allowed to mirror the realities outside schools where many mix and switch freely? Shohamy in this volume (Chapter 8) reminds us: '[L]anguages and their varieties need to be acquired, used, and developed harmoniously, for nothing else but to reflect the 'real world', as schools are meant to prepare students for the "real world".'

Usually the bilingual, trilingual or multilingual programs that separate languages have more prestige than the models that use languages interchangeably and that only use certain aspects of the two languages in education. Elite bilingual education programs tend to always separate languages. This is also the case of the models of ethnolinguistic groups like the Basque in Etxeberría's chapter, reclaiming their autochthonous languages and using them in education, thus transforming their roles and equalizing their value with that of dominant society. Yet, the transitional bilingual education programs organized for indigenous peoples in Latin America described by López (Chapter12), for many regional groups in India described by Mohanty (Chapter 13), and for African groups described by Nyati-Ramahobo (Chapter10), as well as those for immigrant minorities in the United States described by Escamilla (Chapter 8), tend not to separate the languages, at least not strictly. As Nyati-Ramahobo and Mohanty make evident, practices in the classroom are often quite multilingual, with the two languages being used simultaneously (Nyati-Ramahobo refers to this as the 'creeping in' of other languages and cultures). This may reflect the community language experiences of using more than one language in social interaction (Zentella, 1997; Torres, 1997) or the lack of consistency in language policy implementation at local levels (Garcia, M.E., 2004; Howard *et al.*, 2003; Torres-Guzmán *et al.*, 2005), despite the state's efforts to impose monolingual schooling or programmatic mandates of separating the languages.

Question 3: To what extent is it necessary to have bilingual or multilingual teachers who know the students' mother tongue(s)?

This is obviously most important where there are minority children from only one or at the most two linguistic groups in the same classroom (i.e. in transitional or maintenance models for minority students), in immersion models for dominant group students, and in two-way models for both groups (provided that neither group includes any students with other mother tongues than the two that are involved). But it is also important to have multilingual teachers who are knowledgeable of many languages and cultures in linguistically heterogeneous classrooms, such as the ones described by Cummins in Chapter 2 of this volume (see question 4 below).

An argument we often hear is: 'But I have 14 different mother tongues in my class – how can I possibly know all of them?' The number of languages in a classroom is not only a question of what kinds of students exist in the catchment area of the school, but it is also a challenge for the organization of schools. If we know that students benefit from linguistically-homogenous classrooms, these can be organized, maybe not for all, but at least for a large number of students, provided the political will exists. The teachers' bilingual competence is essential in these cases.

More importantly, if one wants bilingual teachers, the question would be whether to invest in linguistic and pedagogical training of many monolingual teachers or to ask the monolingual teachers how far teacher solidarity goes. Are monolingual teachers willing to learn a new language and new pedagogies, or are they willing to offer the jobs to bilingual teachers? The *Hague Recommendations Regarding the Education Rights of National Minorities* from OSCE's High Commissioner on National Minorities (http://www.osce.org/documents/html/pdftohtml/2700_en.pdf.html) are very clear on this point, as they recommend bilingual teachers for all minority students, including bilingual teachers in the dominant language as a second language. The recommendations, which sum up standards from international law, are also valid for immigrant minorities, and the USA and Canada are, in addition to most European countries, members of the OSCE.

Worldwide, the issues of teacher preparation and language proficiency of the teachers are critical variables associated with the quality of programs. Often, where teacher preparation programs exist, they suffer from lack of resources (Benson, 2004). The preparation of large numbers of bi/multilingual teachers is critical.

Question 4: To what extent does the minority language need to be spoken and written by many or all *high-status staff* in schools?

In schools where two or more languages are used as languages of instruction for several years (as outlined in the question above), high status staff must be bilingual. But is it enough if the students are 'allowed' to use their first languages amongst themselves, during the breaks, or in group work in the classroom, with or without support from parents and their own community (as in Cummins' chapter)? Is it enough that parents and community members are invited to school to present a minority language (as in Hélot and Young's chapter)? Is it enough that teachers' aids use it in class? Cummins and Hélot and Young describe integrated educational efforts that in some ways build on the students' multilingualism, and we believe this kind of education can certainly change attitudes towards minority languages and make all children (and teachers) more metalinguistically aware. Schools in which the latter practices take place have not traditionally been considered bilingual or multilingual schools. But increasingly today, as more than two languages are included in schools, these kind of practices characterize positive schools.

Many of the successful programs whose results include high levels of both bi- or multilingualism and school achievement, and positive identities (as in the Basque models described by Etxeberría in Chapter 5) go much further than the practices described above in their attempts at privileging the minority language and equalizing the status of the languages involved. Part of these efforts to equalize the status of the languages in schools involves employing high-status staff – principals, administrators, teachers – who are bilingual. Another part of these efforts involves the question of to what extent positive results for minority students include or even depend on linguistic mutuality; that is, dominant language students also learning at least some of the minority language(s).

Question 5: To what extent do the languages involved, especially the minority students' mother tongue, need to be standardized, and also have written literature (as opposed to only orature, oral literature)?

Language revitalization efforts are often, although not always, accompanied by the development of a written language and standardization. Some researchers see standardization as leading to disappearance of many languages (see Mühlhäusler, 1990, 1996) and many programs have worked well despite the lack of a standardized or even written language (see. e.g. McCarty, 2002, 2003, 2005a, 2005b; McCarty & Watahomigie (1999); and articles in McCarty, 2005c). Questions of standardization, and of inventing spaces for literacy in schools where there is no corresponding community need for literacy, as in the case of some of the United States indigenous communities, are extremely complex (for some of these issues see, for example, Hornberger and King, 1999).

Despite the dynamism of, and the variety of issues emerging from multilingualism that are evident in these five questions and in expanded forms within this volume, there are certain threads that pull our chapters together, AND apart – as expressed in the visions in the individual chapters. Many of the threads present paradoxes with tensions that mirror the multiple and/but often contradictory identities and ideologies at an individual level. Hence, in the next part of this Introduction we try, in addition to the questions posed above, to identify some of the threads that already go and might go into the designs of spaces where multilingual education is possible, threads that need both deconstruction and also pulling together.

Section 4: Weaving the Threads: Tangled Threads as Paradoxes in Multilingual Education

James Tollefson and Amy Tsui (2004) summarize some of the key issues in language in education policy:

(1) medium-of-instruction policies as ideological and discursive constructs;
(2) the gap between (pluralist) discourse and (monolingual) practice;
(3) the importance of resources;
(4) the relationship between ethnolinguistic diversity and social conflict;
(5) the potential impact of language rights in education;
(6) the tension between global and local concerns.

Most of these issues are also very present in this volume, despite the fact that the case studies Tollefson and Tsui include in their volume have little overlap with the ones here. The issues of language education policy are universal.

We identify and discuss below five threads that present paradoxes and tensions that surround multilingual schools and that are addressed by our contributors:

(1) linguistic diversity is more visible today, yet increasingly disappearing;
(2.) languages are equal, yet language hierarchies prevail;
(3) hybridities in multilingual practices and in identities are old, yet awareness of them has increased;
(4) tensions between state-imposed homogenization and real-life multilingualism can occasion the closing or carving out of spaces;
(5) English, English, everywhere...

Thread 1: Linguistic diversity is more visible, yet increasingly disappearing

We are continuously hearing that the world is increasingly linguistically diverse. Hélot and Young (Chapter 3) tell us: 'As in many other countries in the world, the linguistic landscape of France is undeniably becoming more diversified.' Traditionally, with bounded and territorialized languages and less mobility, many people from the East and, especially, the West, did not see, hear, or come into contact with as many languages, and as frequently, as we do now. Because of our technologically-enriched world, many of us are more aware of the world's linguistic diversity, as we hear different languages in the media, and see different scripts on the walls and on the web (those of us who are wired, meaning one sixth of the world's population). The diffusion of the world's languages, a product of the flow of people, goods, services, ideas and communications, caused by transnational capitalist exploitation, market societies, and new technologies, has led to the more dynamic and fluid plurilingualism of the present, with people not only speaking a particular language in one territory, but yielding multiple ways of using that language depending on the country and social context in which it is used. Increasingly, the languages of Nigeria, for example, are not just heard in rural villages, spoken by members of one ethnic nation, and often in combination with the languages of neighboring ethnic nations with whom they communicate. Nigerian languages are also heard today in New York City, London, Paris, and other urban centers that attract labor from around the world. Schools in these cities suddenly have to cope with the many languages of Africa that children bring into the classrooms. Many teachers have never heard the names of the languages and some have difficulty even placing the countries of origin of their students on a map. Urbanization in many African, Asian and Latin American countries likewise brings teachers in contact with languages and cultures earlier unknown to them.

These changes have been surprisingly difficult in those parts of the world where an ideology of (the desirability of) monolingualism has prevailed, mainly European and Europeanized countries. Old (Britain, France, Spain, etc) and New World (USA) empires have often reacted and continue to react with patronizing harsh assimilation policies. Just as they were – and still are – busy with killing off indigenous languages (Australia and the US have killed off more languages during the last 200 years than any other countries in the world),[7] their education systems make every effort to ensure that the new linguistic and cultural capital that has been injected into these countries in the form of immigrant minorities will disappear within three generations, and possibly sooner. Since Europe is the poorest part of the world in terms of native languages (see Appendix), followed by the Americas, and since both linguistic capital and the diversity of ideas, fostered by high levels of multilingualism, will be decisive for progress and economic well-being in knowledge societies (see Skutnabb-Kangas, 2000), these countries are, with the help of their education systems, following a dangerous and self-destructive course.

Despite the seemingly increasing linguistic diversification, the world's language diversity is increasingly at risk. Languages are lost as speakers shift to more dominant languages at the expense of their own. The discussion about language endangerment was spurred by Michael Krauss in 1992. It continues, not only among language researchers (e.g. Krauss *et al.*, 2004), but also and increasingly among indigenous peoples themselves and among international organizations (e.g. UNESCO) and NGOs (such as. Terralingua, www.terralingua.org and The Foundation for Endangered Languages, http://www.ogmios.org). Most disappearing languages are very small, and indigenous. Optimistic linguists estimate that half of today's spoken languages may be extinct or seriously endangered by the end of the present century (see http://portal.unesco.org/culture/en/ev.php-URL_ID=8270&URL_DO=DO_TOPIC&URL_SECTION=201.html or UNESCO's position paper *Education in a Multilingual World* http://unesdoc.unesco.org/images/0012/001297/129728e.pdf). Pessimistic but fully realistic estimates place 90-95% of the world's languages in this category (Krauss, 1998). UNESCO's Intangible Cultural Heritage Unit's Ad Hoc Expert Group on Endangered Languages uses this more pessimistic figure in their report, *Language Vitality and Endangerment* (http://portal.unesco.org/culture/en/ev.php-URL_ID=9105&URL_DO=DO_TOPIC&URL_SECTION=201.html).

Mohanty (Chapter 13) refers to the domain shrinkage of Indian languages and to the fact that nearly 80% of all Indian languages face endangerment. Schools, in their efforts to assimilate and homogenize, have played and continue to play a major role in annihilating languages and identities (see Magga *et al.*, 2005; articles in McCarty, 2005c).

The new research about not only a correlational, but very likely also causal, relationship between linguistic diversity and biodiversity (see Harmon, 1995, 2002; Maffi, 2000, 2001a, 2001b; Nettle, 1999; Nettle & Romaine, 2000; Posey, 1999a, 1999b; Skutnabb-Kangas, 2000; Skutnabb-Kangas *et al.*, 2003) has also attracted the attention of other organizations. By killing languages and cultures, we may in the end be destroying prerequisites for human life on Earth, since distinct knowledges about our environment and how to maintain it sustainably are also lost. International organizations such as UNEP (United Nations Environmental Programme) and ICSU (International Council for Science) have expressed this worry and have started suggesting measures to counteract it. The main international NGO working with these issues is Terralingua (www.terralingua.org). ICSU now acknowledges that indigenous and other local people's knowledge about their own environment is in many ways more detailed than that of (Western) scientists. And this is how ICSU (www.icsu.org) formulates the role of schools in this destruction in its 2002 report:

> Universal education programs provide important tools for human development, but they may also compromise the transmission of indigenous language and knowledge. Inadvertently, they may contribute to the erosion of cultural diversity, a loss of social cohesion and the alienation and disorientation of youth. [...] In short, when indigenous children are taught in science class that the natural world is ordered as scientists believe it functions, then the validity and authority of their parents' and grandparents' knowledge is denied. While their parents may possess an extensive and sophisticated understanding of the local environment, classroom instruction implicitly informs that science is the ultimate authority for interpreting 'reality' and by extension local indigenous knowledge is second rate and obsolete. [...] Actions are urgently needed to enhance the intergenerational transmission of local and indigenous knowledge. [...] Traditional knowledge conservation therefore must pass through the pathways of conserving language (as language is an essential tool for culturally-appropriate encoding of knowledge). (ICSU, 2002)

Thread 2: Languages are equal, yet language hierarchies prevail

It is evident throughout this volume that not all language groups have equal chances of having their languages or language varieties included in schools. This mirrors the situation outside – speakers of certain languages in certain situations have more power than others, and the power is partially connected to the languages they know and do not know. Mostly, as Mohanty describes in the case of India, hierarchies are institutionalized through statutory process. The VIII Schedule in India identifies 22 constitutional languages and English as associate language, leaving most of India's hundreds of languages relegated to an inferior position (see also Annamalai, 1998, 2001, 2003). Botswana, as described by Nyati-Ramahobo has only two official languages, English and Setswana, although at least 28 others are spoken. In most countries in the world, only one or two – or none – of the country's native languages are official, and this often endangers all the non-official ones.

However, linguistic hierarchies are not always and certainly never only statutorily established but are also developed through what Bourdieu (1991) calls 'symbolic violence.' This refers to the production and reproduction of the homogeneity of dominant values through systems such as schools and media. Nyati-Ramahobo, for example, in Chapter 10 describes how the curriculum and the textbooks in Setswana reflect only Tswana history, language and culture, thus giving the impression that the Tswana are the majority who have the right to impose their language on other groups in Botswana. Tanzania's over hundred languages are more or less invisible in textbooks and media – it is easy to get the impression that Swahili is almost everybody's mother tongue (Rubagumya, 1990). Many North Americans hear little about the linguistic and cultural genocide perpetrated by state representatives against indigenous peoples (even if the physical genocide may be described), and those who dare call it genocide (e.g. Churchill, 1997; Costo & Costo, 1987; Hernández-Chávez, 1994; Milloy, 1999) often get harsh treatment in the media

Edwards and Pritchard Newcombe (Chapter 6) refer to the well-known case in which a US District Court Judge in Amarillo, Texas, admonished a woman for speaking Spanish to her daughter, telling her that this would condemn the daughter to life as a maid (Baron, 2001). López reminds us that the 'illiteracy' rate for indigenous peoples in Latin America is 47% – double that of non-indigenous populations. Indigenous languages, spoken by a formally uneducated and poor population, have low status; in the best case, they are made invisible, in the worst, they are killed off.

A few 'European' languages, and English in particular, have been traditionally taught as foreign languages in school in European schools,[8] and thus have more power in educational settings than regional and indigenous languages, most of which have been excluded from schools. Even those regional and indigenous languages that are now taught as subjects or used as teaching languages suffer still from the long years of invisibility. One of the students in Etxeberría's study writes: 'I do not mind learning German and English because they are useful for my future, but Euskara does not seem very useful.'

Hélot and Young refer to the fact that in France a distinction is made between modern foreign languages (MFL), regional minority languages (RML) and immigrant minority languages (IML). Each of these types of language has a distinct and different value when used in schools, in descending order. But these categories are variable and flexible, responding to the context in which the language is studied. For example, as we saw in the example of the judge in Texas, 'European' languages do not hold the same value in different social contexts. In the United States, Spanish, which is an MFL in France, in most other European and some African countries, and in some North American contexts, is also an RML in the US southwest and some areas of the south and northeast. And certainly, Spanish is as an IML all over the United States.

One might imagine that the linguistic hierarchy follows numbers, and to some extent it does – the smaller the number of speakers, the less power and status the languages and their speakers have, and vice versa. But a look at the list of the 21 languages with the highest number of speakers in the world (see Appendix) invalidates this hypothesis. In the *Ethnologue's* 15th edition, English as a native language has been surpassed not only by Chinese, but also by Hindi and Spanish. As we saw earlier, Zulu with its over 10 million speakers has less status (as the language of media, higher education, administration, etc.) than Icelandic with its under 300,000 speakers. If we use the criterion that an indigenous language has to be used as a medium of education, at least 99% of the world's indigenous languages would be lower in the hierarchy than Anár Saami – it has fewer than 300 speakers; it has regional official status in Finland,[9] and it is used as the main medium of teaching in primary school and in 'language nests,' indigenous-medium day care centres, modelled after the Māori 'kohanga reo', with elders who know the language and culture joining in and teaching parents, pre-school teachers (who are not always fully competent in the language) and the children.

The linguistic hierarchy also depends on the social distances constructed for languages. Faced today with the Structural Adjustment programs of the International Monetary Fund (IMF) and the policies of the World Bank, many autochthonous languages are blamed for the ills of the developing world. Speaking of the indigenous peoples of Oaxaca, México, Pardo (1993: 114) points out that *'la presencia indígena ... es asumida como una de las causas del atraso y marginación socioeconómica'* ('indigenous presence ... is assumed to be one of the causes of backwardness and socioeconomic inferiority').

Schools, even multilingual ones, are partially responsible for maintaining and reproducing these language hierarchies. Schools structure the symbolic violence within their policies and curriculum, making them one of the worst direct culprits in maintaining language and socioeconomic hierarchies (see also Magga *et al.*, 2005; Torres-Guzmán, 2003; Dunbar *et al.*, forthcoming). As already mentioned, language choices for educational programs, curricula and instructional materials are important mechanisms to establish these hierarchies. How the languages are reflected in the school and in the positions of those who speak them also establish language hierarchies. The language of school announcements used on official bulletin boards, in grade reports, and in communication with parents becomes more dominant than the one that is relegated to a 'special' classroom in which the second language is used. Often the language of instruction in the morning holds more prestige than the language of instruction in the afternoon, since children are purported to pay more attention during the first few hours of attendance. Who speaks the language in the school also helps establish language asymmetries (Amrein & Peña, 2000) and, thus, language hierarchy. If the principal speaks both languages, there is more equality between languages, than if only the service staff speaks the minority language. And if all students speak both languages, there is less power differential between the languages than if just the ethnolinguistic minority group speaks both languages. It is often found that in the United States (and in Sweden) bilingual education programs are relegated to the basement, or to the corridor at the end of the school. Certainly the physical, social and temporal positioning of the two or more languages helps establish linguistic hierarchies.

Recently, as more languages are present and evident in many Western schools, either formally or informally, schools have insisted on another more forceful mechanism of control – tests. Although national education standards have always existed, attention to homogenous standards, controlled by testing, has intensified in many countries in the last decade. Shohamy and Escamilla insist on the increasing and dangerous power of tests to establish and perpetuate the language hierarchies in schools. McCarty *et al.* (Chapter 4) describe how bilingual teachers in the United States, faced by accountability standards that are measured by English standardized tests, have stopped using the non-English language. One of the teachers whom McCarty *et al.* interview says: 'We don't have time to teach Navajo – we've been told to teach to the standards.' And Escamilla in Chapter 9 describes how, despite the fact that Spanish-speaking students are becoming literate in Spanish at higher levels than their peers who are learning only in English, these results are discounted, for only knowledge of reading and writing in English counts. As Stephen Krashen's extensive research and overviews show, 'research in language and literacy development now tells us that wide, extensive, self-selected recreational reading is the most powerful means known to boost reading ability, writing ability, grammar, and vocabulary' (from Krashen's e-mail list http://sdkrashen.com/mailman/listinfo/krashen_sdkrashen.com; see also Krashen, 2003, 2004). But testing reading only in English negates children's literacy ability in a language other than English and the knowledge and understanding that they have in other languages.

It is clear that the use of languages in schools does not in itself equalize the power hierarchies in which languages exist in society. Many schools are happy to reproduce the *societal diglossia* (functional differentiation) that has traditionally existed, and that continues to exist. Although they may give languages that have been previously relegated to families and communities access to a new social domain, they see to it that these languages keep the status of lower prestige within the school. This is the case of the transitional bilingual education programs described in this volume by Mohanty in India, López in Bolivia and Guatemala, Nyati-Ramahobo in Botswana, and Hornberger and Escamilla in the United States, in which the non-dominant language is used to foster the rapid dissemination (though not always learning) of the/a dominant language.

Comparing the models described in this book makes it manifestly clear that a concise labeling of a program as immersion, transition, submersion, or maintenance depends on the power relations between speakers of the languages in each context. It depends on linguistic hierarchies, rather than solely on the formal characteristics of the model. Most authors in this volume agree that *transitional models* are language-shift models and reproduce inequality, even if they give children a better chance than submersion programs. Our authors would obviously want the transition to come either late, or not at all (with the exception of a few subjects possibly being taught through the medium of the dominant language; and not even this is done in the Finland Swedish schools described earlier).

On the other hand, some multilingual schools establish language practices that affirm and privilege the non-dominant language. For example, López (Chapter 12) expresses the belief that the diglossic use of languages with unequal status where primacy is given to the indigenous language is the only way to stabilize and equalize languages. For López, *intracultural* use of indigenous languages, which proposes to affirm and develop these languages while dealing with the existing asymmetries (Amrein & Peña, 2000) is an important stage of development in order to equalize the two languages. Once equalized, a more *intercultural* stage can follow.

Sometimes the language practices of schools are based on turning the tables – affirming and privileging the non-dominant language, with the purpose of re-establishing the lost equilibrium between two or more languages. These multilingual schools separate the two languages strictly, and work on equalizing their power, by maximizing the role of the earlier dominated language. As described by Etxeberría in Chapter 5, Models B and, especially, D are good examples of these language practices. In Model B, half of the instruction is in Spanish, and half in Euskara; in Model D (which tends to get the best results in terms of bilingualism) instruction is in Euskara, and Spanish is taught as a subject. It is instructive to realize that in this kind of revitalization case, the model itself does not make it *immersion or maintenance*, but it is the way in which students experience it that makes it so. In Model D, Spanish-language students are immersed in Euskara. For Euskara-speaking students, however, Model D is simply instruction through the medium of their mother tongue. Language practices in schools cannot be divorced from student (and teacher) characteristics, history of oppression and the sociopolitical context of those who are immersed in those practices.

Mohanty (Chapter 13) makes a distinction between multilingual practices in three different types of Indian schools – informal, formal with a single medium of instruction, and formal with multiple languages as medium of instruction. Under the *informal type*, the lesson can be presented in one language and explained in another, usually the students' mother tongue. The students can also interact with each other in their mother tongue while the whole classroom interaction is in another local mother tongue, but the teacher conducts the lesson in a more dominant language. Even if these may be more traditional teacher-centered classrooms, they show a great variety of multilingual practices. In the *formal types of schools with a single medium of instruction*, a dominant language (e.g. Hindi or a regional dominant language, or English) is the medium of instruction, while other languages are taught as subjects. Here too, from a student's point of view, it is not a question of which language is used as a medium. The main question is whether it is or is not (one of) the student's mother tongue(s). Or, stated in another way, what socio-historical and political relationship does this young person have with the language of instruction? Since the Indian states have been drawn and redrawn to follow linguistic lines as much as possible, there are smaller or larger minorities in every state, and for these, including 99% of the indigenous ('tribal') peoples, using a state's majority language (for instance Oriya in Orissa, or Hindi in the northern Hindi-majority states) as the main medium of instruction, is still submersion, while for Oriya or Hindi speakers it is a maintenance program. The *formal school types with multiple languages as media of instruction* are true multilingual schools (more than two languages are used as media of instruction). They could be good representatives of the specifically Indian 'three language formula'. They can support multi lingualism if all languages are, through being used as media and taught as subjects, maintained throughout the students' entire schooling years. But they can also, despite being multilingual schools, be early-exit or late-exit transitional programs, if the earlier languages (which are more likely to be the mother tongues of at least some of the students) are dropped as media of instruction, and even as subjects. In the latter case, these multilingual schools can also be agents for later monolingual practices within the school setting. Again, language practices must be seen in their socio-political context, and from the point of view of the language of instruction whether they are present and in what capacity (medium, subject, informal interaction) for what length of time, and whether they can be thoroughly learned.

Thread 3: Hybridities in multilingual practices and in identities are old, yet awareness of them has increased

Even though *language practices* in schools often seem to be neatly sorted into different times, subjects, teachers, students, etc., there is evidence of much hybridity in the language practices themselves. The concept of *hybridity* is important in understanding the multiplicity of language practices today. The concept is inspired by the work of Bakhtin (1981) on the hybridity of the dialogue of languages, by Anzaldúa (1987) on the hybridity of being in the 'borderlands,' and by Bhabha (1994) on the hybridity of postcoloniality. Gutiérrez *et al.* (2001: 128) have said 'hybrid language use is more than simple code-switching as the alternation between two codes. It is more a systematic, strategic, affiliative, and sense-making process ... ' The contributions in this book describe both language and literacy practices, as well as identities, that build on hybridity.

As Mohanty shows, it is precisely this hybridity of language practices that is responsible for the maintenance of the many languages of the Indian subcontinent. Sridhar (1996) posits that in 21st century plurilingual societies languages are not compartmentalized in a diglossic situation, but rather they overlap, intersect, and interconnect. This fluidity in multilingual interaction often characterizes communication in indigenous communities, as López shows for Guatemala and Bolivia, and in highly multilingual contexts, as Nyati-Ramahobo describes for Botswana. Shohamy (Chapter 8) reminds us: 'Immigrants and other groups continue to construct meanings in the most creative ways, holding multiple identities and using multiple varieties of languages, especially in the current era of a transnational world.' A fusion of languages, dialects, scripts, registers, and semiotic systems characterizes how people communicate today.

The increased variation in multimodal discourses that result from the new media has led to multiplicities of language and literacy practices. As political and economic alliances are shaped and technology advances, language and literacy practices and identities are variable and integrated. In the 21st century, with the increased variation in multimodal discourses that are result of new media, *multilingual literacies* are practiced, as Coste (2001) says, in an *integrated* fashion. García, Bartlett and Kleifgen (forthcoming) refer to a *pluriliteracies approach* that 'captures not only literacy continua with different interrelated axes, but also an emphasis on *literacy practices in sociocultural contexts*, the *hybridity* of literacy practices afforded by new technologies, and the increasing *interrelationship of semiotic systems*.'

Very few schools are building on the variability, hybridity, and sense-making processes that characterize out-of-school multilingual practices today, especially as languages that had been previously relegated to private domains access public domains, including the Web. In Chapter 2, Cummins gives some indications as to how these hybrid multilingual language and literacy practices are capable of weaving spaces for multilingual education, even in schools that do not formally use several languages as media of education. Cummins builds on the multiliteracies pedagogy of the New London Group – pedagogy that includes (1) situated, meaningful practice, (2) overt instruction to scaffold students' progress, (3) critical framing, and focus on historical, cultural, sociopolitical and ideological roots of knowledge and social practice, and (4) transformed practice in other cultural sites. Cummins adapts this pedagogy for multilingual students, building on the multilingual practices that children and youth use outside and inside school, and proposing that technology be used as the amplifier to expand practices with languages and literacies in developing *identity texts*. In the school described by Cummins, young students of diverse linguistic background create stories in English and, as far as they are able, in other languages. These are translated with the help of older students, parents, and teachers into the mother tongues of the minority students. These multilingual stories are then published on the web, accompanied by images, spoken, musical, dramatic renderings or combinations in multimodal form. Awareness of the hybridities of identities in classrooms is certainly enhanced, together with contrastive language awareness.

Recent scholarly work on language ideologies has made evident that *identity* is multidimensional and interrelated to its negotiation in different contexts (Pavlenko & Blackledge, 2004). Mohanty describes the multiplicity of linguistic identities in Indian and South Asian bilingualism, as well as the flexibility in the perception of languages and their boundaries. Multilingualism as a mother tongue may be the future. Even when multilingualism is a reality, the type of multilingualism will be determined by which languages are involved, and their location. In an information society, where reading and writing skills at a high level are essential for the socioeconomic mobility that many of today's ordinary multilinguals desire, an 'international' multilingual-postmodern-highly-formally-educated elite nomad can easily disclaim any specific mother tongue. The situation is altogether different for people with little formal education and mobility, who have learned several languages in the environment, but have never had an opportunity to learn to read or write any of them, let alone in a standardized form.

The chapters in this volume also make evident that different social contexts can prevent individuals from adopting certain identities (see Heller, 1982, 1995; Woolard, 1998). Etxeberría's chapter studies how the different school models in the Basque Country have shaped different language attitudes and identities. And McCarty *et al.* make evident how micro and macro processes inside and outside school interact to produce different language attitudes, language ideologies, and language choices. For the many Spanish and Native American students quoted in the chapters by Etxeberría and McCarty *et al.*, their languages are sometimes sites of discrimination. 'They just kind of feel dirty about the whole thing,' says one of the Native American students in McCarty *et al.*about their use of Native American languages. But languages are also often used as sites of resistance and solidarity (see Pavlenko & Blackledge, 2004). One of the students in Etxeberría's study says: 'To speak Euskara well has made me feel Basque. And, yet, to speak Spanish has never really made me feel Spanish. If I speak Euskara, I feel Basque and I like that because it is our language'. In Chapter 12, López describes a sad situation:

> Perhaps the most insidious obstacle to bilingual education is the situation of indigenous teachers who speak the same languages as their students but prefer to use Spanish due to ideological beliefs that the children will be left behind in Mexican society if they learn in their native languages.

Cummins posits that identity investment is a central component of learning, and that negotiation of identities is a primary determinant of whether students will engage cognitively. Cummins' negotiation of identities is related to the authentic caring in schools that McCarty *et al.* speak about in educating indigenous peoples.

Canagarajah (2005) claims that the relationship between language and identity may be more relevant today than ever because national identities are becoming fragmented with the weakening of 'nation'-states. An awareness of languages as an important (rather than 'contingent' and in most cases not important or necessary – see May, 2003: 141) part of the identities of many, if not most, people may be enhanced with this weakening, when people are looking for their roots in an increasingly threatening global environment. The *Language Awareness* pedagogy that Hélot and Young (Chapter 3) describe in the Didenheim school in Alsace is used in many European school contexts today to familiarize students with many different languages and to learn to value both them and the multilingual competence and identities of some of their peers – and themselves.

Hélot and Young also describe the difference between the *CLIL/EMILE pedagogy (Content and Language Integrated Learning*) being promoted in Europe and the bilingual education and immersion pedagogy of North America.[10] Using another language as medium of instruction for one or two school subjects, CLIL/EMILE allows for integrated competencies in different languages where some dominate.

The *popular education programs* described by Ogulnick are, by necessity, bilingual and multilingual, since the programs are based on the linguistic and cultural reality and perspectives of poor and marginalized people. In creating the term 'popular education' Paulo Freire (1973b) referred to grassroots literacy programs designed to create conditions for transformation and empowerment of the poor, illiterate peasants in Brazil. Popular education programs always teach *critical language awareness*, i.e. the need to understand the ways in which languages are used to exclude and discriminate. Often this education leads to language activism (Fairclough, 1992). In Chapter 7, Ogulnick describes in particular, how language and social activism occurs through the use of Agosto Boal's method of liberatory education, *Theater of the Oppressed.* Participants role play real-life incidents to reflect on their subjugated positions and to reverse them. Tove Skutnabb-Kangas used this pedagogy in the mid-1980s in Rinkeby, the Stockholm suburb that then had the highest percentage of foreign nationals in Sweden. The participants were Finnish parents, some with six years of formal education. In one role play, one side represented the Swedish National Board of Education, the other side represented immigrant minority parents, and they discussed Christina Bratt Paulston's report to the Board, which was at that point used by the Board against parents' demands for mother-tongue-medium education. Regardless of the extremely solid scientific arguments that the 'parents' used, the 'Board' dismissed their demands. Some of the participants spoke of their sudden discovery – when they played the Board, they did not even need to listen to the parents' arguments, let alone analyze them. They had, as 'the Board', the power, and could do exactly what they wanted. Arguments posed by others did not count. And likewise, the 'parent' side described their feeling of total powerlessness at meeting this attitude. The deep impact this made on the participants' critical (language) awareness encouraged them to more consciously change their strategies in real life.

Most of the chapters in this volume attest to the importance of community/parental support and participation in constructing good multilingual schools. Edwards and Newcombe point out that in South Africa, the United States, and Wales, parents are the moving force behind the imagining of multilingual solutions. It is for that reason that the program that Edwards and Newcombe describe – *Twf* – precisely targets parents to educate them about the advantages of their children's bilingualism.

Good multilingual schools always need to include critical (language) awareness as an important component of the curriculum. Multilingual students and parents need to understand the ways in which languages are used in undemocratic ways to exclude and discriminate, and what their alternatives are. The hybridity that emerges from the multilingual students and parents 'in between' or 'borderland' experiences must be brought out into the open and acknowledged as different and important world views, and as an important pedagogical tool.

Irvine (1998: 255) has, like many others, pointed out that attitudes, values and beliefs about language are always ideological, and involved in social systems of domination and subordination of different groups. Schools are, in their work of teaching the standard national languages, responsible for one of the most prevalent linguistic ideologies – constructing a unidirectional link between language and ethnicity. And so, language ideologies are also responsible for the closing of spaces for multilingual practices in schools. Language awareness and linguistic and social activism stemming from the position of borderlands will together create more spaces for a multilingualism that will contain the voices that have been silenced and will permit language minority communities to make visible their dreams of a better world.

Thread 4: Tensions between state-imposed homogenization and real-life multilingualism can occasion the closing or carving of spaces

When national policies start to support bilingual education, especially for formerly excluded groups, it is often because they are trying to make up for years of exclusion, racism and discrimination. In Guatemala and Bolivia (López), and in Wales (Edwards and Newcombe), it has been grassroots pressure that has yielded political concessions for language in education. And yet, the implementation of these policies often leaves much to be desired. For example, Ogulnick, speaking about Chiapas, says that 'the reality of public education for indigenous children in rural areas is far from the promises made in the San Andrés Accords.' Ogulnick quotes an educator who says:

> They say that education is bilingual and bicultural, but it really isn't. Only a little. Most teachers don't speak the languages of the students, so they teach in Spanish. They don't teach the native languages. (personal communication, July 2004)

Edwards and Newcombe, and Hornberger, suggest that both bottom-up and top-down activity is necessary. Citing Chick and McKay (2001), who suggested in the case of South Africa that ideological space opened up by top-down policies contributed to new discourses in implementational spaces at the grassroots level, Hornberger concludes:

> Ideological spaces can carve out implementational ones. I think that perhaps it is also possible that implementational spaces carved out from the bottom-up may reciprocally be a means for wedging open ideological spaces as they are being closed by top-down policies.

On the other hand, Hornberger also describes what she sees as the 'closing of ideological and implementational space for multilingual education in the US.' There is increasing tension between the ongoing homogenization (through the insistence on national curricula and testing, for instance; see our earlier discussion) and the heterogeneity that we find in today's schools (see García & Traugh, 2002). Sometimes, as Hornberger, McCarty *et al.*, and Escamilla make evident about the situation in the United States, the result of this tension is that 'linguistically different' students are excluded, resulting in increasingly alarming rates of failure and push-out rates among these groups. As Hornberger also points out, in this closing, however, spaces can and are being found and opened for new ways of thinking and acting that are only testimony to the resilience of the populations that face such linguistic oppression.

The more fluid situation of 21st century technology, economy and politics, the multiplicity of languages, literacies and identities in the classrooms, and the increased interest in acquiring the languages of power, and English in particular, puts multilingual schools and multilingual educational practices at the center of schooling today. In many contexts, there are strong forces, which are trying to turn multilingualism into English plus (maybe, just a little bit of) one other language.

Thread 5: English, English, everywhere ...

The unchecked, subtractive spread of English is responsible for much submersion education, push-out, and educational failure throughout the world. Parents demand access to English for their children because learning English is seen as gaining a resource that might lead to other social opportunities (Nical *et al.*, 2004; Craig, 1996). Braj Kachru's metaphor in his *The Alchemy of English* (1986) is still all too valid (see also Pennycook, 1994, 1998; Phillipson, 1992, 2003, 2005; Phillipson & Skutnabb-Kangas, 1994, 1996, 1999). Mohanty echoes this: 'Over the post-independence years, English has become the single most important predictor of socio-economic mobility.' Cummins tells us: 'The general population in contexts as disparate as Hong Kong, India, South Africa, and throughout Europe, accurately sees English as associated with upward social and economic mobility and demands that schools assign top priority to the teaching of English'. McCarty quotes a Navajo student: 'English ... that's always taking over ... It's just kind of hard to have anything really of a Native thing going on.'

In many parts of the world parents seem to be choosing English-medium education whenever it is available. But Hornberger quotes Neville Alexander's (2003) affirmation that South African parents are not choosing English, but rather they are choosing the 'superior resourcing and academic preparation offered by the English-medium schools.' In India, a decade ago, a colleague told of a friend, a Kannada-speaking parent – the choice was between the Kannada-medium school where there were a dozen textbooks for the whole class, and the English-medium school which, among other things, had two pianos. But in many cases, the contrast is not as stark, and if parents knew how the hopes of other parents and children in English-medium education have been shattered, they might choose differently. The false either/or ideologies and the forces behind them are the main culprit.

In South Africa, Kathleen Heugh (2000) conducted a countrywide longitudinal statistical study of final exam results for 'Black' students in South Africa. The percentage of 'Black' students who passed their exams decreased every time the number of years spent learning through the medium of the mother tongues decreased. Despite the resource-wise really inferior and partly racist apartheid education, the students did better when more of the education was through the medium of their own languages rather than English or Afrikaans. Another African study, that of Edward Williams (1998) of 1500 students in grades 1–7 in Zambia and Malawi, came up with similar results. Large numbers of Zambian pupils, who had had all their education in English, had little or no reading competence in two languages, Williams observed. On the other hand, in Malawi, the children were taught in local languages (mostly their mother tongues), during the first four years, while studying English as a subject; English became the medium only in grade 5. The Malawi children had slightly better test results even in the English language than the Zambian students. In addition, they knew how to read and write in their own languages. Williams (1998: 63–64) concluded: 'there is a clear risk that the policy of using English as a vehicular language may contribute to stunting, rather than promoting, academic and cognitive growth.' This, just like many of the other examples of submersion education, fits one of the United Nations genocide definitions of 'causing serious mental harm to members of the group.'[11]

In Australia, Anne Lowell and Brian Devlin (1999) clearly demonstrated that after Aboriginal students had been taught mainly through the medium of English, 'even by late primary school, children often did not comprehend classroom instructions in English'. Communication breakdowns occurred frequently between Aboriginal children and their non-Aboriginal teachers, with the result that 'the extent of miscommunication severely inhibited the children's education when English was the language of instruction and interaction'. In their conclusions the authors state: 'the use of a language of instruction in which the children do not have sufficient competence is the greatest barrier to successful classroom learning for Aboriginal Children' (Lowell & Devliin, 1999: 156).

Skutnabb-Kangas (2000) refers to English as a 'killer language.' Languages are today being killed faster than ever before in human history, and English is today the world's most important killer language, even if there are many other numerically large languages (see Appendix). Also many dominant official or national or regional languages, regardless of size, can and do function as killer languages (e.g. Oriya in relation to small indigenous languages in India; Hausa, Ibo and Yoruba in relation to the other 400-plus Nigerian languages; or Finnish in relation to Saami or Romany in Finland). As Skutnabb-Kangas has said: 'If dominant languages are learned subtractively, at the expense of other often smaller dominated languages, the dominant languages become killer languages.' 'Being' a killer language is NOT a characteristic of any language. It is a relationship, a question of how a language functions in relation to other languages. Any language can become a killer language in relation to some other language. Besides, 'languages' do not kill each other. It is the power relations between the *speakers* of the languages that are the decisive factors behind the unequal relations between the languages, which then cause people from dominated groups to learn other languages subtractively, at the cost of their own. Obviously other languages should (and can) be learned additively, in addition to one's own language(s), not instead of it or them (Skutnabb-Kangas, 2004c).

If minority or dominated group parents knew that their children could, in maintenance programs, both maintain and develop their own language(s) AND learn the dominant (or a second) language (often English) at least as well and often better than in dominant-language-medium submersion programs, most parents would obviously start demanding these kind of programs. Strong grassroot demands might also help steer resources to these additive programs, rather than to the often disastrous and in most cases genocidal submersion programs.

If we want to be charitable, we might accept that the threat from the spread of subtractive English has functioned and is functioning as a bell of warning, waking up many groups to the weakened and endangered status of their languages. The presence of English in education may carve out spaces for regional and indigenous languages, previously pitted against the monolingualism of an educational system in the national language only. Mohanty describes how it is precisely in order to fight the dominance of English that Indian policy makers have used the concept of *diversification,* attempting to make sure that there is a wide choice of languages available in the curriculum at all levels. In Europe, there are almost weekly conferences discussing the threat from English at all levels and in all quarters.

The spread of English has been facilitated by its initial virtual appropriation of new technologies in media, film, etc. But as Cummins here reminds us, new technologies also 'afford opportunities for less dominant languages to carve out virtual space.' In a few years' time, English will no longer be the most widely-used language on the Web. Indigenous peoples are also actively demanding that their languages be developed for purposes of the information society so that they can be used for all aspects of Information and Communication Technology (ICT), including computer software, database portals, and every possible type of digitizing these languages.[12] At the same time as there is linguistic colonization and self-colonization in education (Phillipson, 1992; Spring, 1998; see Karmani, 2005a, 2005b, and www.tesolislamia.org/language_policy.html for accounts of and discussions on some of the new forms this takes; for university level, see also topics at www.palmenia.helsinki.fi/congress/bilingual2005/program. asp), there is also a lot of resistance to subtractive language spread and endangering languages, all over the world and not only in education but also in the rest of society.

Conclusion: Between Dispossession, Anger and Hope

In a chapter called 'Accumulation by dispossession', David Harvey

(2005) first describes the old classic imperialism where empires accumulated capital and other resources through dispossession in the colonies, something that Hannah Arendt (1968: 28) called 'the original sin of simple robbery'. Harvey then, after discussing military invasions, especially that of Iraq, has the following description of present-day imperialism:

> Hegemonic state power is typically deployed to ensure and promote those external and international institutional arrangements through which the asymmetries of exchange relations can so work as to benefit the hegemonic power. It is through such means that tribute is in effect extracted from the rest of the world. Free trade and open capital markets have become primary means through which to advantage the monopoly powers based in the advanced capitalist countries that already dominate trade, production, services, and finance within the capitalist world. The primary vehicle for accumulation by dispossession, therefore, has been the forcing open of markets throughout the world by institutional pressures exercised through the IMF and the WTO, backed by the power of the United States (and to lesser extent Europe) to deny access to its own vast markets to those countries that refuse to dismantle their protections. (Harvey, 2005: 181)

Robert Phillipson (2005) notes that the domain losses that other languages suffer, because they are no longer used (or are not being developed for use) in prestigious areas (universities, research, business, IT, etc) or simply in/for primary and secondary education, can be described with Harvey's economic concepts. (Speakers of) English and other dominant languages accumulate power and resources through dispossessing other languages and their speakers; expropriating the creative human capital, ideas, and knowledges of indigenous peoples and minorities (in addition to the expropriation of material resources that is happening simultaneously at an accelerated speed). The 'carrots' given to consolidate the role of English (e.g. 'free' textbooks, grants for students, in-service training courses for teachers) are one way of 'forcing open the markets' in other countries for English-medium products and their concomitant ideologies. Everything seems to become gold once you touch it with your newly-acquired English competence – but there is no notice or realization of the seriousness of having lost your own linguistic capital in the process.

The Swedish-medium school had taught the Saami researcher Johannes Marainen that Swedish was his 'mother tongue', and he became a 'mother tongue' teacher, i.e. a teacher of Swedish for Swedish children. At some point, Marainen gave a speech about the Saami, in Swedish. His father, a Swedish citizen, happened to visit him and heard the speech but did not understand all of it. After experiencing that he was not able to translate the speech for his father into Saami, Marainen said:

> It was then that I got my life's greatest shock! I realized that 'mother tongue' had taken over my *eatnangiella* ['mother tongue' in North Saami]. I realized in horror that *I could no longer relate the most common and everyday matters in my own language!* That was the first time since I grew up that I realized the negative sides of my becoming Swedish. I started to comprehend that the Swedish educational system had robbed me of something valuable, yes, perhaps the most valuable thing I had owned – my language. I could no longer talk to Father! This fact made me shiver. I became desperate, despondent. And then I became angry.[13] (Marainen, 1988:183)

We hope that many other people become angry in this sense, angry at the dispossession that schools are involved in daily, and that this anger is then used to start not only demanding but finally implementing the multilingual imaginings that this book also describes, not only for the hitherto dispossessed and already multilingual indigenous peoples and minorities and dominated groups, but also for those who do not know that monolingualism has dispossessed them.

Notes

1. In the rest of the chapter, we use 'minority', to stand for 'indigenous and minority'. The North American expression 'linguistically diverse children' is a positive replacement for degrading terms that make the children's knowledge of their own language(s) invisible and/or characterize them, negatively (LEP, NEP) or 'positively" (English learners) only in terms of the dominant language that they do not yet know fully. In addition, 'linguistically diverse students' are a non-entity in international law, whereas indigenous children and minority children have at least some rights.
2. We're grateful to Cecelia Traugh for calling our attention to this positioning in the work of Horton and Greene.
3. Hereafter we refer to chapters in this volume only with the author names, without a year. All other references also have a year.
4. The factors contributing to the Finnish success are, according to the Finnish National Board of Education:

   > Equal opportunities for education irrespective of domicile, sex, economic situation or mother tongue; regional accessibility of education; education totally free of charge; comprehensive, non-selective basic education; supportive and flexible administration-centralised steering of the whole, local implementation; interactive, co-operative way of working at all levels; idea of partnership; individual support for learning and welfare of pupils; development-oriented evaluation and pupil assessment – no testing, no ranking lists; highly qualified, autonomous teachers; socio-constructivist learning conception (http://www.oph.fi/english/page.asp?path=447,488, 36263). See also http://www.oph.fi/english/pageLastasp?path=447,488,36 263,36266; http://www.oph.fi/english/pageLast.asp?path=447,488,362 63,36268.
5. All the quotes are from Martin 2000a or 2000b; these reports do not have page numbers, and the references are not given in full.

6. See also e.g. Hamel, 1994, Hamel, 1997; May, 1999; McCarty, 2005c; Magga *et al.*, 2005, for some assessments of the situation.
7. The USA has, in Teresa McCarty's view (personal communication, August 2005) 'really had a "White USA" (like "White Australia") policy all along – just not formally acknowledged (or celebrated, historically as in the case of Australia).' We thank Teresa for valuable comments on this chapter.
8. See www.eurydice.org/Doc_intermediaires/indicators/en/key_data.html for the latest data on schools in Europea.
9. For the Finnish Language Act, see www.finlex.fi/fi/laki/kaannokset/2003/en20030423.pdf; for the Sámi Language Act, see www.finlex.fi/fi/laki/kaannokset/2003/en20031086.pdf.
10. For more on CLIL/EMILE, visit the following websites: http:// www.clilcompendium.com, http://www.cec.jyu.fi/tilauskoulutus/henk_keh/clil.htm, and http://www.guardian.co.uk/guardianweekly/story/0,12674,1395532,00.html
11. See Skutnabb-Kangas (2000) and many of her publications listed or available through her home page (http://akira.ruc.dk/~tovesk/) on linguistic genocide in education.
12. See *World Summit on the Information Society, The Report of the Global Forum of Indigenous Peoples and the Information Society*, 8–11 December 2003, Geneva, UN, ECOSOC, E/23 December 2003, at www.un.org/esa/socdev/pfii/PFII3/documents/FinalReportUNSPFII2003.pdf
13. Similar experiences are common. Teresa McCarty (personal communication, August 2005): 'It reminds me of a statement by a Navajo elder whose son spoke Navajo, but whose grandchildren (through the son) spoke only English (their Navajo mother had been dispossessed of her mother tongue through mission schooling): "I cannot communicate [with them] ... I live in silence." Yes, we should be outraged!'

Appendix

The *first Count column* in Table 1.1 gives the number of living languages (with at least one first language speaker) that originate in the specified area.[1] Each language is counted only once, under the area of its primary country. The *second Count column* gives the total number of people who use those languages as their first language, regardless of where in the world they may live. The total is somewhat less than the actual world population because the *Ethnologue* lacks population estimates for about 5% of the languages. The *Percent columns* give the share of the count for that area as a percentage of the total number listed at the bottom of the Count column. The *Mean column* gives the average number of speakers per language, while the *Median column* gives the middle value in the distribution of language populations (that is, half of the languages have more speakers than that number and half have that number or fewer). There is a huge disparity between the mean size of languages and the median size.

Table 1.2 summarizes the distribution of languages by size. The *Count columns* give the actual number of languages within the specified population range and the total number of first-language speakers of those languages. Where the language entry in Table 1.1 lists a range of values for

Table 1.1 Distribution of languages by area of origin

Area	*Living languages*		*Number of speakers*			
	Count	*%*	*Count*	*%*	*Mean*	*Median*
Africa	2,092	30.3	675,887,158	11.8	323,082	25,391
Americas	1,002	14.5	47,559,381	0.8	47,464	2,000
Asia	2,269	32.8	3,489,897,147	61.0	1,538,077	10,171
Europe	239	3.5	1,504,393,183	26.3	6,294,532	220,000
Pacific	1,310	19.0	6,124,341	0.1	4,675	800
Totals	*6,912*	*100.0*	*5,723,861,210*	*100.0*	*828,105*	*7,000*

Source: http://www.ethnologue.com/ethno_docs/distribution.asp?by=size

the population, the midpoint of the range is used for this tabulation. The *Percent columns* give the share of the count for that population range as a percentage of the total number listed at the bottom of the Count column. Note that there are still a few hundred languages for which the *Ethnologue* (15th edition), does not have a population estimate; the calculation of

Table 1.2 Distribution of languages by number of first-language speakers

Population range	*Living languages*			*Number of speakers*		
	Count	*%*	*Cumu-lative %*	*Count*	*%*	*Cumu-lative %*
over 100 m	8	0.1	0.1	2,301,423,372	40.208	40.208
10–100 m	75	1.1	1.2	2,246,597,929	39.250	79.457
100–10 m	265	3.8	5.0	825,681,046	14.425	93.882
100,000–1m	892	12.9	17.9	283,651,418	4.956	98.838
10,000–100,000	1,779	25.7	43.7	58,442,338	1.021	99.859
1,000–10,000	1,967	28.5	72.1	7,594,224	0.133	99.992
100–1.000	1,071	15.5	87.6	457,022	0.0080	99.9997
10–100	344	5.0	92.6	13,163	0.0002	99.9999
1–9	204	3.0	95.5	698	0.00001	100.0000
Unknown	308	4.5	100.0			
Total	*6,912*	*100.0*		*5,723,861,210*	*100.0*	

Source: http://www.ethnologue.com/ethno_docs/distribution.asp?by=size

percentages for speakers is therefore not able to take those languages into account. The Cumulative columns give the cumulative sum of the percentages going from top to bottom in the column.

Note that 347 (or approximately 5%) of the world's languages have at least one million speakers and account for 94% of the world's population. By contrast, the remaining 95% of languages are spoken by only 6% of the world's people.

Table 1.3 contains, for purposes of comparison, some data about countries described in this book or mentioned in the Introduction, from the website of the US Central Intelligence Agency (http://www.cia.gov/cia/publications/factbook/geos/pp.html – accessed 9 Aug 2005). There are errors in some of the data, but we wanted all the data to come from the same source and have therefore not corrected the errors. The lack of data in

Table 1.3 Some basic data about some countries mentioned in this chapter

Country	*Population*	*Ethnic groups*	*Languages*	*Literacy %*	*GDP in $ per capita*
Canada	32,805	French origin 23% Amerindian 2%	English 59.3%, French 23.2%, Other 17.5%	97	31,500
Finland	5,223	Finnish xx, Swedish 5,7	Finnish xx, Swedish 5,6, Saami 0.1	100	29,000
Iceland	296	Icelandic 94%		99.9	31,900
India	1,080,264		No figures, lots of errors	59.5	3,100
Israel					
New Zealand	4,035	Māori 7.9%		99	23,200
Norway	4,593	Sami 20.000		100	40,000
Papua New Guinea*	5,545		715 (not correct) English spoken by 1–2%	64.6	2,200
South Africa	44,344		Zulu 23.8%, Xhosa 17.6, Afrikaans 13.3, Sepedi 9.4, English 8.2	86.4	11,100
Sweden	9,001	No figures	No figures	99	28,400
USA	295,734	White 81.7	English 82.1, Spanish 10.7	97	40,100

certain columns is also telling. We have also ourselves left out several observations, especially in the column about Ethnic groups, because they are less relevant for the issues in the book. The reader is encouraged to find information for other countries mentioned in the Introduction that we haven't included in this table.

Note to Appendix

1. The texts for Tables 1.1 and 1.2 are modified from the original *Ethnologue* texts. Table 1.2 uses the *Ethnologue* data but we have simplified some of the figures. For clarification on how figures were derived, please visit the *Ethnologue* site: http://www.ethnologue.com/ethno_docs/distribution.asp?by=size

Part 2

Pedagogies, Values and Schools

Chapter 2

Identity Texts: The Imaginative Construction of Self through Multiliteracies Pedagogy

JIM CUMMINS

Introduction

Three pervasive influences on education systems around the world frame this chapter. These influences are:

(1) the increasing linguistic and cultural diversity of urban education systems as a result of greater population mobility than at any time in human history;
(2) the escalating demand for English-medium education based on the perception of parents and policy-makers that English is key to economic and social advancement;
(3) the late 20th century change from an Industrial Age economy to an Information Age economy brought about by rapid technological development.

These changes raise fundamental educational questions: How should schools address the multilingual realities of their student populations? Do students from linguistically diverse backgrounds have ethical and/or legal rights to support within the school for maintenance of their home languages? If so, how should these rights, and the obligations of educators to respect these rights, be realized in school contexts characterized by multiple languages and literacies? If no legal rights to home language support are recognized by national governments, how can educators challenge the exclusion of students' linguistic and cultural capital from the life of the school?

With respect to the spread of English as a global language, and the demand for ever more intensive English-language teaching programs, educators and policy-makers are faced with the need to communicate well-validated research findings regarding the limitations and potential pitfalls of early intensive English teaching to a skeptical public. The general populations in contexts as disparate as Hong Kong, India, South Africa, and throughout Europe accurately see English as associated with upward social and economic mobility, and demand that schools assign top priority to the teaching of English. This orientation also characterizes some immigrant parents in English-speaking countries who devalue the development of home language literacy in comparison to literacy in English. In some cases, parents try to switch to speaking English in the home and refuse to place their children in bilingual programs designed to develop literacy in both English and the home language on the grounds that only English is relevant to their children's academic and social advancement. Under these circumstances, how should educators create programs that will develop strong English language and literacy skills that build on, rather than replace, students' home language and literacy skills? How can educators communicate to parents and policy-makers that the research supports a *both/and*, rather than the *either/or*, orientation to the development of home language and English literacy?

Clearly, the spread of English has been facilitated by the current dominance of English in many forms of popular culture that are easily accessible through modern communications technology. The late 20th century change from an Industrial Age economy to an Information Age economy has brought about instantaneous global communication that English was well-positioned to appropriate (see Phillipson & Skutnabb-Kangas, 1996). However, new technologies represent more than just a new vehicle for English imperialism; they also afford opportunities for less-dominant languages to carve out virtual space that does not depend on geographical proximity. Within schools, we can ask how new technologies might be harnessed to reinforce the development of home-language literacies and make them less subject to the destructive influence of English. Can new technologies also be harnessed as tools for the development of critical literacy that would enable students to gain access to alternative perspectives and resist dominant discourses?

This chapter addresses these questions. The term *identity texts* is introduced to highlight the importance of identity negotiation and societal power relations in understanding the nature of classroom interactions. Working collaboratively with educators in the Greater Toronto Area as part of a Canada-wide project entitled 'From literacy to multiliteracies: Designing learning environments for knowledge generation within the new economy' (Early *et al.*, 2002), we have been exploring how to create interpersonal spaces within the classroom that support the development of literacy in both English and the home language. The following sections discuss constructs that form the core of the emerging pedagogical framework. These include the concept of *multiliteracies*, general orientations to pedagogy including *transmission*, *social constructivist*, and *transformative* orientations, and the research consensus from cognitive psychology regarding *how people learn*. These constructs set the stage for description of a framework for the development of *academic expertise* (Cummins, 2001). This framework differs from many others that have been proposed in postulating *identity investment* as a central component of learning for deep understanding and *the negotiation of identities* as a primary determinant of whether or not students will engage cognitively in the learning process. Our collaborative work with educators in the Greater Toronto Area has shown how the creation of *identity texts* can fuel sustained biliteracy development and simultaneously challenge the exclusion of students' cultural and linguistic capital from curriculum and instruction.

Each of these concepts is reviewed briefly below, and the emerging pedagogical framework is illustrated with examples from the Multiliteracies project.

Multiliteracies

The term *multiliteracies* was introduced by The New London Group (1996) to highlight the relevance of new forms of literacy associated with information, communication, and multimedia technologies and, equally important, the wide variety of culturally-specific forms of literacy evident in complex pluralistic societies. From the perspective of multiliteracies, the exclusive focus within schools on linear text-based literacy in the dominant language of the society represents a very limited conception that fails to address the realities of a globalized, technologically sophisticated knowledge-based society. In urban contexts across North America and Europe, the student population is multilingual and students are exposed to, and engage in, many different literacy practices outside the school (Gregory & Williams, 2000; Jiménez, 2003; Pahl & Rowsell, 2005). Within schools, however, the teaching of literacy is narrowly focused on literacy in the dominant language and typically fails to acknowledge or build on the multilingual literacies or the technologically-mediated literacies that form a significant part of students' cultural and linguistic capital.

At a very basic level, multiliteracies pedagogy involves building on the cultural and linguistic capital that students bring to school, and using technology as an amplifier to expand students' literacy practices beyond linear text-based reading and writing. The New London Group proposed a pedagogical framework that highlighted the importance of four dimensions of instruction:

- *Situated practice* involves immersing students in meaningful practice and experience within a community of learners.
- *Overt instruction* involves explicit instruction on the part of the teacher to demystify skills and content and scaffold learner progress; its goal is systematic, analytic, and conscious understanding.

- *Critical framing* entails a focus on the historical, cultural, sociopolitical, and ideological roots of systems of knowledge and social practice; students step back from the meanings they are studying and view them critically in relation to their social and cultural context.
- *Transformed practice* aims to put transformed meanings and knowledge gained from previous situated practice, overt instruction, and critical reflection to work in other contexts or cultural sites.

The essence of this framework is that students should be given opportunities to engage in meaningful experience and practice within a learning community, and explicit instruction should support the development of concepts and understanding as required. Students should also have opportunities to step back from what they have learned and examine concepts and ideas critically in relation to their social relevance. Finally, they should be given opportunities to take the knowledge they have gained further – to put it into play in the world of ideas and come to understand how their insights can exert an impact on people and issues in the real world.

The relevance of this framework can be appreciated in light of the fact that transmission approaches to learning (e.g. teaching content primarily from textbooks) predominate in most educational contexts around the world, particularly in the case of low-income students (e.g. Warschauer *et al.*, 2004). The New London Group's multiliteracies framework assigns a legitimate role to overt instruction (transmission pedagogy) but only as one component of a more inclusive and comprehensive framework for learning. The next section reviews the relationship between transmission approaches to instruction and alternatives that take into account how learners construct knowledge and how this knowledge relates to social realities.

Pedagogical Orientations

The themes articulated in the New London Group's (1996) multiliteracies pedagogical framework can also be viewed in the context of three pedagogical orientations, variations of which have been discussed by many authors (e.g. Skourtou, Kourtis *et al.*, in press). These orientations are labeled *transmission, social constructivist*, and *transformative.*

As illustrated in Figure 2.1, the three pedagogical orientations are nested within each other rather than being distinct and isolated from each other. Transmission-oriented pedagogy is represented in the inner circle with the narrowest focus. The goal is to transmit information and skills articulated in the curriculum directly to students. Social constructivist pedagogy, occupying the middle pedagogical space, incorporates the curriculum focus of transmission approaches, but broadens it to include the develop-

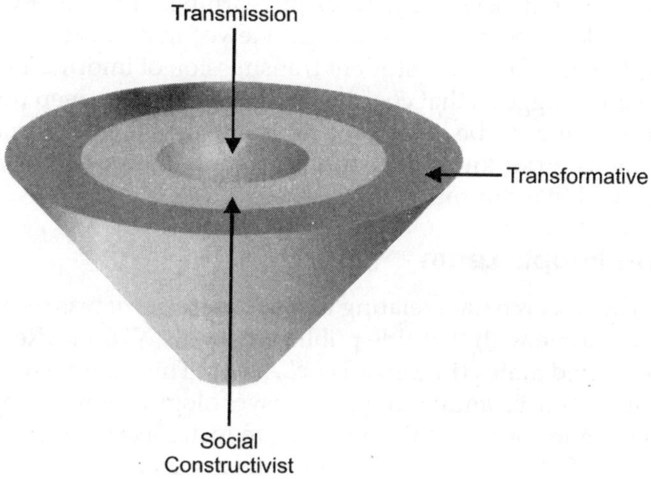

Figure 2.1 Nested pedagogical orientations
Source: Skourtou *et al.* (in press)

ment among students of higher-order thinking abilities based on teachers and students co-constructing knowledge and understanding. Finally, transformative approaches to pedagogy broaden the focus still further by emphasizing the relevance not only of transmitting the curriculum and constructing knowledge, but also of enabling students to gain insight into how knowledge intersects with power. The goal is to promote critical literacy among students to encourage them to read between the lines of societal discourses rather than to skim along their surface. In other words, the goal is deep understanding.

The development of critical literacy is particularly relevant in an era of global propaganda where skillfully-crafted multimedia messages broadcast by privately-owned media conglomerates dramatically influence public perceptions and attitudes. Witness the fact that more than 40% of the US population continues to believe that Saddam Hussein was instrumental in the 9/11 attacks despite the universal acknowledgement, even grudgingly by the Bush administration, that this was not the case. Thus, there is an urgent necessity to teach for deep understanding and critical literacy, not so much because the economy demands it, but because the survival of democratic institutions in our societies may depend on it.

It is clear that the nested pedagogical orientation framework intersects with the themes articulated in the New London Group's multiliteracies framework. In both cases, a legitimate role is assigned to overt instruction (transmission pedagogy), but only as one component of a more inclusive and comprehensive framework for learning. In a similar way, the cognitive psychology research on learning reviewed in the next section highlights the limitations of teacher–student transmission of information and skills. This research suggests that cognitive engagement and deep understanding are more likely to be generated in contexts where instruction builds on students' prior knowledge and learning is supported by active collaboration within a community of learners.

How People Learn

The research data relating to *How People Learn* was recently synthesized in a volume with that title published by the National Research Council in the United States (Bransford *et al.*, 2000). This volume represents a significant consensus among cognitive psychologists in relation to how learning occurs and the optimal conditions to foster learning. The authors emphasize the following conditions for effective learning:

- *Learning with deep understanding:* Knowledge is more than just the ability to remember; deeper levels of understanding are required to transfer knowledge from one context to another. This implies that instruction for deep understanding involves the development of critical literacy (reading between the lines) rather than simply literal comprehension of text.
- *Building on pre-existing knowledge:* Prior knowledge, skills, beliefs, and concepts significantly influence what learners notice about their environment and how they organize and interpret it. This principle implies that in classrooms with students from linguistically-diverse backgrounds, instruction must explicitly activate students' prior knowledge and build relevant background knowledge as necessary. The implied acknowledgment and affirmation of students' language and cultural backgrounds is not sociopolitically neutral. Rather it explicitly challenges the omission and subordination of students' culture and language within typical transmission-oriented classrooms.
- *Promoting active learning*: Learners should be supported in taking control of, and self-regulating, their own learning. When students take ownership of the learning process and invest their identities in the outcomes of learning, the resulting understanding will be deeper than when learning is passive.
- *Support within the community of learners:* Learning takes place in a social context and a supportive learning community that encourages dialogue, apprenticeship, and mentoring. Learning is not simply a cognitive process that takes place inside the heads of individual students; it also involves socialization into particular communities of

practice. Within these learning communities, or what Gee (2001) terms *affinity groups*, novices are enabled to participate in the practices of the community from the very beginning of their involvement. Lave and Wenger (1991) describe this process as *legitimate peripheral participation*. The learning community can include the classroom, the school, the family and broader community, and also virtual communities enabled through electronic communication.

This account specifies some minimal requirements for effective learning. It also brings into immediate focus the lack of scientific credibility of approaches that rely on simple transmission of knowledge and skills from teachers to learners. Exclusive reliance on transmission pedagogy is likely to entail memorization rather than learning for deep understanding, minimal activation of students' prior knowledge, and passive rather than active learning. Since active and creative use of language by students is typically regarded as 'off-task' within a transmission approach, there is no community of learners.

Transmission approaches typically entail one-size-fits-all learning objectives and whole class instruction. These approaches are unable to accommodate the diversity of language and cultures that represents the new mainstream in many European and North American urban schools. For example, within a transmission approach it is virtually impossible to enable recently-arrived immigrant students to participate effectively in the life of the classroom when their knowledge of the language of instruction is initially minimal. By contrast, a multiliteracies approach that attempts to incorporate students' language and culture into the curriculum is much more capable of including all students productively within the learning community. Recently-arrived students can express their intelligence, imagination, and literary/artistic talents through writing in their home language and then working with peers to create bilingual texts in the home language and the language of instruction. The theoretical constructs that underlie this type of pedagogical approach have been articulated in the Academic Expertise framework.

The Academic Expertise Framework

The academic expertise framework (Figure 2.2) incorporates the same emphasis on critical literacy, active learning, deep understanding, and building on students' prior knowledge articulated in the pedagogical approaches discussed above.

However, the academic expertise framework also argues for the centrality of *identity negotiation* and *identity investment* in any conception of teaching for deep understanding. These constructs are implied but not

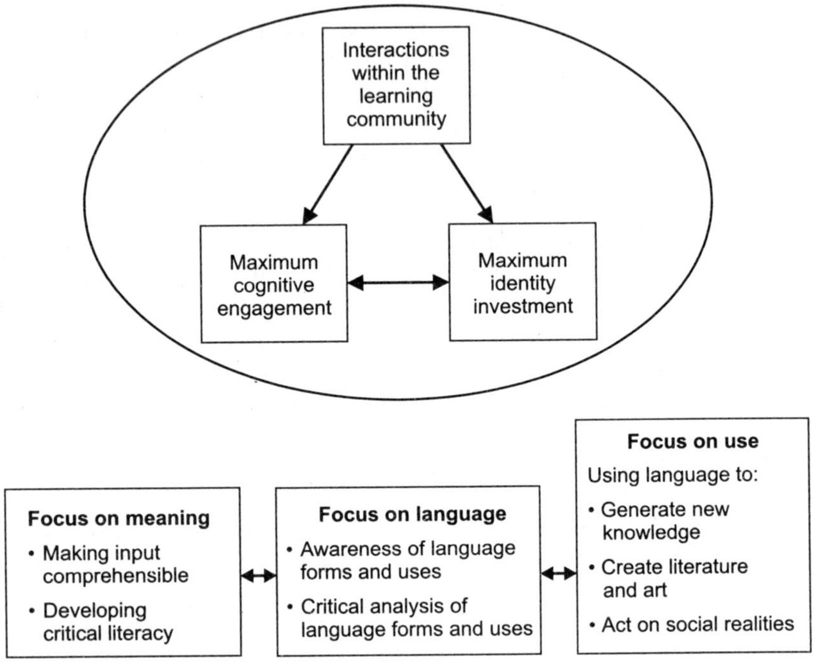

Figure 2.2 The academic expertise framework
Adapted from Cummins (2001)

made explicit in either the New London Group multiliteracies framework or the Bransford *et al.* (2000) discussion of how people learn. Teacher–student interactions, and other interactions within the learning community, create an interpersonal space within which knowledge is generated and identities are negotiated. Learning will be optimized when these interactions maximize both cognitive engagement and identity investment (Cummins, 2001).

The framework (Figure 2.2) attempts to express in a very concrete way the kinds of instructional emphases and language interactions required to build students' academic expertise. Optimal instruction will include a *focus on meaning*, a *focus on language*, and a *focus on use*. The focus on meaning entails the development of critical literacy rather than surface-level processing of text. Within bilingual/trilingual programs students have the opportunity to apply their critical literacy skills in two or more languages, thereby enhancing the possibility of cognitive transfer.

The focus on language involves promoting, not just explicit knowledge of how the linguistic code operates, but also critical awareness of how language operates within society. If students are to participate effectively within a democratic society they should be able to 'read' how language is used to achieve social goals: to elucidate issues, to persuade, to deceive, to include, to exclude, etc. The focus on language takes on additional dimensions within bilingual/trilingual programs because students can actively compare and contrast how each language constructs reality (e.g. comparison of idioms or proverbs across languages).

The focus on use parallels the New London Group's transformed practice, but expresses in much more concrete ways what this might look like within the classroom context. It argues that optimal instruction will enable students to generate knowledge, create literature and art, and act on social realities. Again, coordination of these projects across languages is highly appropriate within bilingual/trilingual programs. For example, students might write a story or poem for publication in one of their languages and then translate it into the other languages for publication in a book and/or the World Wide Web, thereby showcasing their bilingual or trilingual skills for multiple audiences.

The academic expertise framework also makes explicit the fact that classroom instruction always positions students in particular ways that reflect the implicit (or sometimes explicit) image of the student in the teacher's mind. How students are positioned either expands or constricts their opportunities for identity investment and cognitive engagement.

Although the construct of identity investment has not received much attention in the cognitive psychology or educational reform research literature, it has emerged as a significant explanatory construct in the educational anthropology and second language learning literature (e.g. Fordham, 1990; McCarty, 1993a, 1993b; Norton, 2000; Pavlenko & Norton, 2006; Peirce, 1995; Toohey *et al.*, 2006). In the sections that follow, the role of *identity texts* in developing academic expertise is discussed.

Identity Texts

The relevance of what we are calling *identity texts* can be appreciated by visiting the Dual Language Showcase site created by educators at Thornwood Elementary School in the Peel District School Board near Toronto, Canada (http://thornwood.peelschools.org/Dual/). Grades 1 and 2 students from culturally- and linguistically-diverse backgrounds created stories initially in English (the language of school instruction). They illustrated these stories and then worked with various resource people (parents, older students literate in L1, some teachers who spoke a variety of the students' languages) to translate these stories into their home languages. The stories and illustrations were then entered into the computer through word processing and scanning. The Dual Language website was created to enable students' bilingual stories to be shared with parents, relatives or friends in both Canada and the students' countries of origin who had Internet access (Chow & Cummins, 2003). Our more recent work has extended this initiative to older students who write bilingual or trilingual stories that reflect their experiences (e.g. of immigration) or are intended for younger audiences (Leoni & Cohen, 2004).

The academic expertise framework proposes that optimal academic development within the interpersonal space of the learning community occurs only when there is both maximum cognitive engagement and maximum identity investment on the part of students (Cummins, 2001). The products of students' creative work or performances carried out within this pedagogical space are termed *identity texts* insofar as students invest their identities in these texts (written, spoken, visual, musical, dramatic, or combinations in multimodal form) that then hold a mirror up to students in which their identities are reflected back in a positive light. When students share identity texts with multiple audiences (peers, teachers, parents, grandparents, sister classes, the media, etc.) they are likely to receive positive feedback and affirmation of self in interaction with these audiences (Chow & Cummins, 2003). Although not always an essential component, technology acts as an amplifier to enhance the process of identity investment and affirmation. It facilitates the production of these texts, makes them look more accomplished, and expands the audiences and potential for affirmative feedback.

The process can be illustrated in the English/Urdu story created by three students in Lisa Leoni's grade 7 class in Michael Cranny Public School in the York Region District School Board (Leoni & Cohen, 2004). The students had arrived from Pakistan at different ages: Kanta and Sulmana had been in Canada since grade 4 (3 years) while Madiha had been in the country for less than a year. Madiha's English was minimal, but her Urdu was fluent; Sulmana was fluent and literate in both Urdu and English. Kanta's home language was Punjabi and she had attended an English-medium school in Pakistan. Much of her Urdu acquisition had taken place since arriving in Toronto as a result of participation in the social and religious life of her community and she had become highly skilled in switching back and forth between Urdu and English. In composing the story, the three girls discussed their ideas primarily in Urdu but wrote the initial draft in English. Sulmana participated somewhat less in the discussion but was very skilled in turning the ideas into written text. She served as scribe for both languages. They collaboratively wrote the story entitled *The New Country* (see Figure 2.3) based on their collective experiences. It was written in the context of a unit on the theme of migration that integrated social studies, language and ESL curriculum expectations.

Over the course of several weeks, the three girls discussed the general

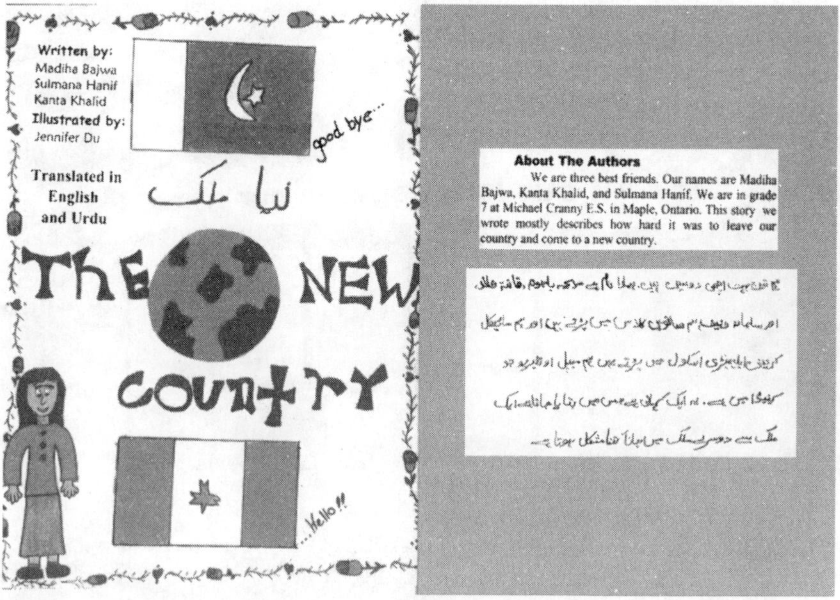

Figure 2.3 Pages from the English/Urdu bilingual book authored by Madiha, Sulmana, and Kanta, grade 7 students in Michael Cranny Elementary School

content of their story using both Urdu and English. As they were writing the story, there were many points where they discussed appropriate translations from one language to the other, as well as aspects of the grammar of each language. The fact that the story was written in both languages enabled all three students to participate fully in the creative process and to contribute their experiences to the text. For Kanta, whose Urdu literacy was less well developed than that of the other two girls, it reinforced Urdu and brought it into contact with English, her stronger literate language. Sulmana was the most bilingual and biliterate of the three girls and she took major responsibility for scribing in both languages. Madiha's English proficiency was not sufficient for her to write anything substantive in that language or to participate fully in class discussions that took place only in English. However, as a result of the collaborative creation of the bilingual identity text, she became a proud author of a lengthy book in both Urdu and English. In Lave and Wenger's (1991) terms, her role in the class was transformed from one of legitimate peripheral participation to legitimate central participation. This transformation of her academic and personal identity was made possible by the teacher's willingness to re-structure the interpersonal space of classroom interaction such that instruction could truly build on students' prior experience and engage them actively in the creation of

Figure 2.4 Wall display from Perminder Sandhu's grade 4 class in Coppard Glen Public School

literature and art. Legitimizing the use of students' home language within the classroom is an essential component of this process.

In other classrooms that are participating in the Multiliteracies project, we have observed similar processes of increased identity investment and cognitive engagement brought about by the introduction of students' home languages into the normal life of the classroom. In Perminder Sandhu's multilingual grade 4 classroom in Coppard Glen Elementary School in the York Region District School Board, for example, students worked in pairs to create bilingual or trilingual books. Early in the school year, language became a topic for discussion within the classroom. Many students initially expressed embarrassment in relation to their home languages and did not see them as appropriate for use within the school context. However, over time and with encouragement from their teacher, students came to realize the legitimacy of their languages and became more aware of the rich culture expressed through these languages. Gradually, pride replaced shame and students wrote about their languages and shared with each other their knowledge of writing systems, dialects, and the meanings of specific words. Visitors to the class would invariably be taken by several students to the wall display where students had written about their languages. Students would elaborate not only about their own language but also about other languages represented in the class (see Figure 2.4).

Emerging Claims

In our work in various highly diverse classrooms where students have worked collaboratively to write and publish bilingual/multilingual identity texts, we have found evidence for the following claims:

(1) students' home language (L1) knowledge is an educationally significant component of their cultural capital;
(2) even in an English-medium instructional context, teachers *can* create an environment that acknowledges, communicates respect for, and promotes students' linguistic and cultural capital;
(3) newly-arrived students whose knowledge of English is minimal are enabled to express their artistic and linguistic talents, intelligence and imagination through the creation of identity texts written initially in their L1. In this way, they quickly join the classroom and school learning community as valued members rather than remaining at the periphery for an extended period.
(4) students' attitude towards and use of L1 changes positively in L1-supportive classroom contexts;
(5) parent–student communication and collaboration increase when dual language literacy projects such as book authoring are initiated;
(6) technology can increase the audience for students' books and provide reinforcement for students' literacy practices;
(7) dual language initiatives can serve to normalize linguistic diversity within the school and result in more coherent and effective school policies with respect to (a) affirming students' linguistic and cultural identities, (b) parental involvement, and (c) technology use within the school.

These claims may appear almost mundane to those who are aware of the research on bilingual and trilingual programs and the potential power that schools have to promote strong literacy skills in three or more languages (e.g. Skutnabb-Kangas, 2000). However, bilingual and trilingual programs are not accessible to the vast majority of bilingual students in countries around the world. One reason frequently advanced by educators and policy-makers is that such programs are impossible to implement in school contexts characterized by multiple languages. Large school systems across North America and many parts of Europe have more than 100 languages represented among their student body, and individual schools may have 30 or more languages represented.

The attitude that students' home languages can be ignored in curriculum and instruction because bilingual programs are not feasible has given rise to a normalized 'default option' that violates many of the basic principles of learning articulated above (e.g. Bransford *et al.*, 2000). Specifically, the following assumptions and practices have become normalized in ways that constrict both the identity options for culturally-diverse students and their cognitive and academic engagement:

- literacy is assumed to equal English literacy;
- there is minimal acknowledgement or promotion of students' cultural/linguistic/imaginative capital;
- the involvement of culturally and linguistically-diverse parents is limited and passive;
- technology use is sporadic and unconnected to coherent pedagogical philosophies and practices.

The claims that are emerging from our research become relevant for policy and pedagogy in the context of this normalized 'default option.' We are suggesting a very different starting point for the creation of curriculum and the implementation of instruction than that which currently exists in most multilingual school contexts. This 'deep structure' of learning and teaching is articulated in the next section.

Multiliteracies Pedagogy Revisited

A radically different image of the child is implied in the classrooms we have observed than in more typical transmission-oriented classrooms. Within the framework of multiliteracies pedagogy, broadly defined, educators expand the opportunities for children to express themselves – their intelligence, imagination and linguistic and artistic talents. When this kind of expression is enabled, children come to see themselves as intelligent, imaginative and talented. In some cases, identity texts will involve children's home languages; in other cases, the school language(s) may be the medium. Similarly, technology has the power to amplify and enhance the 'peak experience' (Maslow, 1968/1999) that the identity text represents.

On the basis of the collaboration with educators in the project schools, we can articulate in a very concrete way five central components of a multiliteracies pedagogy that prioritize the role of identity investment in learning for deep understanding.

- Multiliteracies pedagogy constructs an image of the child as intelligent, imaginative, and linguistically talented; individual differences in these traits do not diminish the potential of each child to shine in specific ways.
- Multiliteracies pedagogy acknowledges and builds on the cultural and linguistic capital (prior knowledge) of students and communities.
- Multiliteracies pedagogy aims explicitly to promote cognitive engagement and identity investment on the part of students.
- Multiliteracies pedagogy enables students to construct knowledge,

create literature and art, and act on social realities through dialogue and critical inquiry.
- Multiliteracies pedagogy employs a variety of technological tools to support students' construction of knowledge, literature, and art and their presentation of this intellectual work to multiple audiences through the creation of identity texts.

Although entirely consistent with the empirical research on how people learn, the form of multiliteracies pedagogy outlined above represents a radical departure from the normalized assumptions that characterize many North American and European classrooms serving culturally and linguistically-diverse students. The funds of knowledge (Moll *et al.*, 1992) represented in the community form the foundation for knowledge building within the school. Instruction is oriented explicitly to enable students to express and expand their linguistic and cultural capital. These principles of multiliteracies pedagogy are clearly consistent with the Academic Expertise framework. They entail a somewhat different emphasis from the New London Group's framework and from the work of Bransford *et al.* (2000) insofar as the construct of *identity investment* is viewed as a core element whereas this construct is only implicitly acknowledged in alternative frameworks.

In the final section, the implications of multiliteracies pedagogy for bilingual and trilingual school programs are discussed.

Strategies for Implementing Multiliteracies Pedagogy

The following list is intended to show the range of powerful applications of multiliteracies pedagogy in schools with large numbers of culturally- and linguistically-diverse students. The list is illustrative rather than exhaustive and most of the suggestions have been implemented in various projects at one time or another. All these projects reflect either a social constructivist or transformative orientation to pedagogy. They are also readily interpretable within the context of the Academic Expertise framework and consistent with the principles for learning and literacy development that have been discussed in previous sections.

- *From kindergarten on, students bring in words (in L1, L2, or L3) to class to explore with peers and teacher and they incorporate these words into technology-supported bilingual/multilingual dictionaries.* These words can be discussed in the class and entered into Google image searches to find images that depict the meanings. Students can also look up the words in electronic dictionaries and create their own multimedia glossaries (print, image, audio). This kind of 'language detective' work reflects the *focus on language* component of the Academic Expertise framework. Pilot work involving the creation of multimedia dictionaries by bilingual students has proved to be highly motivating for students (Dennis Sayers, personal communication).

- *Students write creatively in L1 and L2 and amplify these identity texts through technology (as in the Dual Language Showcase); audio can also be integrated into the texts that appear on the web.* For example, students can read their stories (in L1 and/or L2) and enable the sound to be turned on or off by those who visit the web page. If the student is not fully literate in his or her L1 (or L2), a parent, teacher, or peer might read the story in that language.
- *Students create movies, audio CDs, and/or web pages to communicate the outcomes of their projects aimed at generating new knowledge, creating literature and art, and acting on social realities.* Durán *et al.* (2001) and Hull and Schultz (2001, 2002) have described how low-income minority students created various kinds of multimedia resources on substantive topics of relevance to their lives in the context of after-school technology-mediated initiatives. Bilingual students can utilize both their languages in creating these identity texts. Currently, in some contexts characterized by rigid testing requirements (e.g. the United States), it seems to be more feasible to engage in this kind of project in after-school programs; however, the powerful learning that appears to characterize these projects highlights the lack of powerful learning associated with technology in the schools attended by these students.
- *Newly-arrived students write in L1 and work with peers, teachers, older students, community volunteers, and technology (Google or Babel Fish translations) to create bilingual identity texts.* For example, a newly-arrived student in grade 5 might write a story or a personal account of some aspect of his/her experience in Spanish. Students and/or the teacher can then cut and paste this text into Google or Babel Fish for automatic translation into English. The resulting translation will likely be somewhat garbled but sufficiently comprehensible to give the teacher (and other students) the gist of what the new arrival is trying to communicate. A group of students can then be assigned to work with the newly-arrived student to edit the English version of the text and to 'teach the computer proper English.' Then the dual language text can be entered into the class or school website as a bilingual identity text. Thus the newly-arrived student very quickly attains the status of a published bilingual author.
- *Students engage in technology-mediated sister class exchanges using L1 and L2 to create literature and art and/or to explore issues of social relevance to them and their communities (e.g. Social History of Our Community, Voices of our Elders, Working Conditions of Farm Workers).* These sister-class exchanges can provide powerful motivation for students to engage in

language learning and/or language maintenance activities. One example is the *DiaLogos* project (Kourtis-Kazoullis, 2002; Skourtou *et al.*, in press) that linked students in Greece and Canada and enabled them to engage in extensive collaborative writing as well as a variety of other collaborative inquiry activities. For example, students completed a story begun by a very popular Greek children's writer and generated more than 80 versions of the story in Greek and English on the project web site.

- *Bilingual students can develop critical literacy and language awareness by examining media reports on contemporary issues and comparing the way events and controversies are reported in different languages.* For example, are there differences in the way controversial current events are reported in newspapers from different parts of the world? Access to newspapers around the world is easily available through the World Wide Web and thus technology makes this kind of analysis possible. Obviously, this kind of activity would not be possible within a program that conceived of literacy only as literacy in the dominant language.

Conclusion

As sketched above, multiliteracies pedagogy draws on transmission, social constructivist, and transformative orientations to teaching and learning. Although entirely consistent with the empirical research on how people learn, it represents a radical departure from the normalized assumptions that characterize classrooms around the world that serve culturally and linguistically diverse students. The funds of knowledge (Moll *et al.*, 1992) represented in the community form the foundation for knowledge building within the school. Instruction is oriented explicitly to enable students to express and expand their linguistic and cultural capital. By contrast, the normalized approach that ignores students' cultural and linguistic capital fails to acknowledge students' pre-existing knowledge, and is thus significantly less capable of teaching for deep understanding.

This chapter has proposed that within the broad context of multiliteracies pedagogy, the construct of *identity investment* represents an important tool for planning curriculum and instruction in multilingual school systems. If we want students to take ownership of their languages and feel proud of their growing linguistic talents, then surely it makes sense to encourage them to create a variety of multimedia identity texts in all their languages. Ownership and identity investment in literacy practices requires active use of the language.

Similar considerations apply within bilingual or trilingual programs. Typically, the languages of instruction are kept rigidly separate within these programs, with the result that the process of transfer across languages and explicit comparison of languages is left haphazard. Paradoxically, these programs aim to develop bilingual and trilingual proficiency, but they often fail to teach explicitly for transfer across languages. When the languages of instruction are left in isolation from each other, monolingual instructional strategies are applied rather than the potentially much more powerful bilingual instructional strategies articulated above. The multiliteracies pedagogy proposed in this chapter would create frequent opportunities for students to transfer knowledge and cognitive strategies across languages through the creation of bilingual identity texts and other cognitively-challenging collaborative activities. Application of these pedagogical strategies would strengthen bilingual and trilingual programs by enabling teachers to teach explicitly for transfer of concepts and skills across languages. Thus, the pedagogical framework proposed here represents an underlying structure that has relevance regardless of whether the instructional program is ostensibly monolingual or bilingual/trilingual.

Acknowledgement

I would like to acknowledge all members of the OISE/UT Multiliteracies Project team and partner teachers in the York Region District School Board and the Peel District School Board who have contributed to the ideas in this chapter.

Summary

This chapter highlights the centrality of the interpersonal space (or *zone of proximal development*) created in the interactions that teachers orchestrate with their students. Optimal academic development within this interpersonal space occurs only when there is both maximum cognitive engagement and maximum identity investment on the part of students. The products of student work carried out within this pedagogical framework are termed *identity texts* insofar as students invest their identities in these texts (written, spoken, visual, musical, or combinations in multimodal form) that then hold a mirror up to the students in which their identities are reflected back in a positive light. When students share identity texts with multiple audiences (peers, teachers, parents, grandparents, sister classes, the media, etc.) they are likely to receive positive feedback and affirmation of self in interaction with these audiences. Several examples of identity texts created by students in culturally and linguistically diverse classrooms are presented and discussed in relation to transmission, social constructivist, and transformative approaches to pedagogy.

Chapter 3

Imagining Multilingual Education in France: A Language and Cultural Awareness Project at Primary Level

CHRISTINE HÉLOT and ANDREA YOUNG

Introduction

Imagining multilingual schools in France is both a challenging question and one that should not be considered as utopian. Nowadays, a growing number of children in French schools are indeed multilingual, but this does not mean our classrooms have become multilingual. We would define a multilingual school as a place where linguistic and cultural diversity is acknowledged and valued, where children can feel safe to use their home language alongside the school language (French in this case) to learn and to communicate, where teachers are not afraid and do not feel threatened to hear languages they do not know, and where multilingualism and multilingual literacies are supported. In other words, a multilingual school is not just a place where pupils can learn one or two foreign languages or be taught through two or more languages. It is also a place where the plurilingual repertoire of bilingual/multilingual pupils is recognised and viewed as a resource to be shared and built upon, rather than as a problem.

Is it possible to envisage such schools in the French educational context? Elsewhere, we have shown how language education policy in France is another example of the way language is used to maintain unequal power relationships (Hélot, 2005). We have described the ideology at work behind bilingual education (Hélot, 2003) and we have explained why the bilingualism of minority-language-speaking children remains ignored or is seen as a handicap for the acquisition of the French language (Hélot & Young, 2002).

In this chapter, we focus on the obstacles that still make it difficult for our schools to move away from their traditional monolingual *habitus* and we point to the tensions within an education system based on top-down policies designed to make our pupils efficent multilingual European citizens, while at the same time neglecting or simply ignoring the linguistic and cultural diversity of many of its bilingual/multilingual pupils.

With this in mind, we will describe how a *language awareness project* that involved the participation of parents made it possible for three teachers in a primary school in Alsace to adopt an inclusive approach to all the languages spoken by their pupils, to transform the linguistic and cultural diversity of their pupils into a learning resource, and to change their attitudes towards multilingualism. We will insist on the political dimension of the project that has helped this particular school deal with problems of racism by laying the foundations for a form of multilingual education aimed at very young learners, minority- and majority-language speakers together, bilinguals and monolinguals alike. As an example of good practice, the project also illustrates how parents and teachers can support one another to develop multilingual resources for today's classrooms and new pedagogical approaches to intercultural understanding. It also shows how, in the process, minority languages and cultures can be legitimised and minority language speakers empowered.

Language Education in France

To allow readers to grasp the full import of the language awareness project that we describe in this chapter, we need to mention some features of the French sociolinguistic context. As in many other countries in the world, the linguistic landscape of France is undeniably becoming more diversified, and this is proving to be a challenge not only for politicians, policy-makers and researchers, but for teachers as well. Indeed, it is not easy for teachers to deal with the increasing complexity of the linguistic situations of their pupils, particularly when they have to implement a top-down curriculum which, as far as languages are concerned, focuses on improving provision for the learning of dominant European languages at the expense of the great variety of languages spoken by many children at home which remain virtually ignored.

Fighting the hegemony of English

In the face of increasing globalisation and mobility of populations, the French education system has developed its own answers: by trying on the one hand to resist the overwhelming hegemony of the English language, and on the other, by looking for more efficient approaches to foreign language teaching (FLT). In order to fight the dominance of English, policy-makers have used the concept of diversification – i.e. making sure a wide choice of languages is available in the curriculum at all levels. For instance, at primary level, children can theoretically choose between the following eight languages: Arabic, Chinese, English, German, Italian, Russian, Spanish and Portuguese (BO n°4, 2002). But, in fact, most schools offer only English and sometimes a second language. On the whole, this policy has not prevented the English language from being the favourite choice of most pupils, and this is also the case in secondary schools, universities and teacher education colleges.

The wide gap between policies that insist on diversification and the reality of provision at grass roots level, where the choice of languages is restricted, means that English dominates language education in France and leaves little space for other languages. But diversification was defended again recently (*Le Monde*, 2004) by the President against the plans of the Minister of Education to make English the only language available at primary school. The political tensions of the national context that underlie the choice of languages available in schools are mirrored at the local level with most parents wanting their children to learn English and policy-makers trying under governmental pressure to combat its hegemony.

Republican values and cultural diversity in France

This battle should also be understood within a political context where the protection of French in France, in Europe, and in the world is a priority and more of an issue than the protection of minority languages. This is not surprising. Bourdieu's analysis (1991) of the process of language domination, in which he traces the emergence of French as the 'national' language of post-Revolutionary France, is most useful to understand the specificity of the French sociolinguistic context. Bourdieu explains how the dominance of French was based on the vitiation of minority languages and how the French state education system has been one of the main agents for the spreading of the ideals of the French Revolution: uniformity and the extinction of particularism. This has meant that linguistic diversity not only had to be fought, but that the French language should be the single national language upon which the Republic was founded.

These Republican principles are still very central to the French State and to its education system. Most teachers are attached to these principles. Many of them believe that integration can take place only through the acquisition of the national language and that speaking minority languages at home slows down this process, thus hindering social cohesion.

It is only very recently that France has taken stock of the multiplicity of languages being spoken within its borders. In 1999 a national census (INED, 1999) revealed that one person in four had heard their parents speak a language other than French at home. In 2001, the 'General Delegation for the French Language', one of several organisations set up to protect the French language was renamed the 'General Delegation for the French Language *and the Languages of France*'.[1] In 2003 a report entitled *The Languages of France* (Cerquiglini, 2003) was published which conceded that French was no longer the only recognised language of the Republic. Another example of the breach into the myth of monolingualism in France is the declaration by former Minister of Education Jack Lang (2001) that 'Contrary to widespread belief, France is not a monolingual country.' Fifteen years earlier, several studies by French sociolinguists (Vermes & Boutet, 1987) provided descriptions of multilingualism in France, but until now they have had little impact on educational policies.

Readers should also be reminded that the French education system is very centralised and hierarchical. Decisions are taken at ministerial level in Paris and circulated down to teachers through a monthly official bulletin. General and regional inspectors are responsible for the implementation of new policies. While teachers do have pedagogical freedom in their classrooms, the very ambitious curriculum leaves little room for innovation. Pedagogical innovations at grass roots level tend to remain confidential, and state-funded innovative programmes are often bogged down by bureaucracy. Most teachers are used to implementing top-down policies since they work under the authority of inspectors whose job it is to make sure such policies are put into practice.

This explains to a certain extent why French schools are still so entrenched in their monolingual and monocultural *habitus*. It has only very recently been recognised that the French model of integration has failed and that discrimination is widespread, including in schools. But teachers should not be blamed for their attitudes towards multilingualism: official texts and reports insist on the priority of the French language in every educational reform, and on the notion of integration, when in fact it is assimilation that has been taking place. Moreover, linguistic policies dealing with minority languages are rather ambiguous (Hélot, 2003).

As late as 1990, many primary teachers were very ambivalent towards the introduction of European foreign languages in the primary curriculum. Most of them felt that, in the case of minority language speakers, more time should be given to the acquisition of French rather than to a foreign language (FL). Telling them that France is no longer a monolingual country today is saying something that is self-evident; but asking them to change attitudes towards minority languages is going to take time, particularly when no extra measures or funding are provided to help them support the multilingual pupils in their classroom.

Even if more and more young student teachers are expressing a need for classes in French as a second language to support pupils whose home language is not French, we would argue that this is not enough to address the problems of intolerance and racism at the classroom level. It also means envisaging an approach aimed at supporting minority language pupils within the compensatory model, whereas what is needed is for teachers to acknowledge the special strengths of young bilingual learners (Bourne, 2003). In France, the latest curriculum for primary schools (MEN, 2003) hardly mentions the issue of increasing linguistic and cultural diversity, not even in the section entitled 'Living Together' which is about socialisation through schooling. Furthermore, even if one page (MEN, 2003: 90) deals for the first time with 'the case of pupils for whom French is not a mother tongue', the content of the directives are so ambiguous and confusing that it can only reinforce negative attitudes towards bilingualism (Hélot, 2003).

The ambiguity of the curriculum regarding bilingual pupils is an illustration of the hesitancy of policy-makers to envisage multilingualism as an asset rather than a handicap, especially when minority language speakers are concerned. In our opinion, it is also a refusal to take stock of the very real problems of discrimination and racism towards certain sectors of the population. For instance, third-generation immigrant children are still often referred to as 'children of foreign origin', when in fact many of them were born in France and hold French nationality. Varro (2003) is right when she questions the persistent and discriminatory use of this terminology and shows how it keeps these children outside of the mainstream and separate from their peers. Varro's analysis of the ambiguous terminology used in official educational documents and in the discourse of teachers, and of the way this points to the almost automatic association between learning difficulties and foreign origins makes a very strong point. Immigrant languages are still seen as a handicap for the acquisition of the school language, and therefore as a source of learning difficulties.

Extensive Language Learning

Table 3.1 gives a summary of the provisions for extensive language teaching, that is, the teaching of languages other than French in the curriculum. A distinction is made between modern foreign languages (MFL), regional minority languages (RML) and immigrant minority languages (IML). It is not the purpose of this chapter to discuss the denominations used in French, but it is clear that they reflect ideological choices and reinforce a hierarchy that weighs in favour of dominant European languages.

Despite what looks like a wide choice of languages in theory, most pupils take one MFL at primary level and a second one at secondary. Very few of them choose a RML or an IML – for instance, recent figures show that only 0.9% of primary pupils take a regional language (RERS, 2003) so that the strong rhetoric of diversification in language learning translates very weakly on the ground.

Some effort has been made recently (MEN, 2003) to give better status to some minority languages by including them in the primary curriculum alongside European languages. However, this has had a counter-productive effect: these languages are now in competition with dominant European languages, since only very committed parents will choose Breton or Arabic before English. While these measures do have some symbolic value

Table 3.1 Extensive language teaching in France (public sector)

Type of language	*MFL*	*RML*	*IML*
Provision for *extensive model*	**Primary:** 1 MFL compulsory **Secondary:** 2nd MFL compulsory 3rd MFL optional	**Primary:** 1 RML optional (pupils must take either an MFL or an RML) **Secondary:** 1 RML optional	**Primary:** 1 IML optional **Secondary:** 1 IML optional (often outside regular timetable)
Target pupils	All pupils	All pupils	IML speakers only
Name of languages	*Langues vivantes: LV1, LV2, LV3*	*Langues et cultures régionales*	*Langues et cultures d'origine*
Examples of languages	English, Spanish, German, Italian, Portuguese,*Arabic**	Basque, Breton, Corsican, Catalan***	Arabic, Turkish, Polish, Serbo-Croat ***

* These five are the most common MFLs, but there are many others.
** Arabic was included in the MFL provision at the primary level in 1995, but has not been implemented. Only classical Arabic is offered at secondary level.
*** These are examples of the most common RML/IML languages, but there are others.

for minority languages, the recommended methodological approach shows a strong monolingual bias: for example, Arabic is supposed to be taught at beginners' level to all learners, which means the knowledge of children who speak this language at home is negated. Why should the model for the teaching of MFLs be the dominant model applied to RMLs and IMLs? If the notion of equality is behind such choices, it illustrates even more strongly that policy-makers envisage all learners as monolingual and that they are reluctant to acknowledge the multilingual repertoire of many of our pupils.

Furthermore, in the case of Arabic, implementation at the ground level has been so limited that one doubts the impact of the curriculum change on attitudes of teachers and parents. Hardly any classes of Arabic as a foreign language have been established in primary schools and few in secondary schools.

The status of IMLs and the provision for their teaching can be understood only in the light of our colonial past and the reluctance to deal with it. The Algerian war of independence in particular has left many wounds which are only slowly being healed today, half a century later (Stora, 2004). The very wide controversy around the recent law forbidding obvious religious signs in public schools is part of the same phenomenon. It reflects the failure to integrate people belonging to minorities from former French colonies (Dewitte, 1999). And one could also argue that collective amnesia is one of the reasons for the failure to come up with new policies concerning IMLs.

It is striking that, in the midst of so many proposals to improve the teaching of MFLs over the past 14 years, so little progress has been achieved concretely for IML speakers in our schools. While new curricula for MFLs have been drawn up at primary and secondary level, and the importance of supporting RMLs has finally been recognised, IMLs have been left in limbo. The Senate report on FL teaching (Legendre, 2004) is another example of the way IMLs are marginalised: the report is 115 pages long and only 5 pages deal with IMLs, and only 3 languages are mentioned – Portuguese, Arabic and Berber.[2] The report states in bold type that knowledge of these languages is important for integration and to fight 'the humiliation felt by young speakers of Arabic' (Legendre, 2004: 61). But then, it also insists on the economic advantages for France of its relationship with Arab countries. It quotes a previous report (Berque, 1985) which came to the same conclusions 20 years ago, yet very little has been done to improve the status of Arabic in our schools, and Berber does not figure anywhere.

Bilingual Education in France

As we have explained elsewhere (Hélot, 2003) bilingual education in France is viewed mainly as a way to improve foreign language learning for monolingual pupils and not as a means to support bilingual children to cope with the curriculum in their second language.

The same language categorisation shown in Table 3,1 applies to the different models of bilingual education available. Of course these models have a different history, but again, the main focus today is on dominant European languages for which the approach known as *Content and Language Integrated Learning* (CLIL) has been developed. CLIL is viewed as innovative because the FL is used as medium of instruction for one or two school subjects (Gajo, 2001; Baetens Bearsdmore, 1999). The appellation 'European section' stresses the fact that such classes are also meant for pupils to develop a stronger sense of European identity. The main problem with the implementation of this model is that it is élitist since children are assessed to enter such a programme. This means that only high achievers can avail themselves of bilingual education.

Table 3.2 shows that some progress has been made concerning RMLs[3] but it is only under European pressure that they have become better protected in legal terms and by affirmative educational policies. Moreover, the immersion model of bilingual education as it is known in Canada (Rebuffot, 1993) is available to all pupils in theory but only as partial immersion and only in regional minority languages. The total immersion model that was demanded by parents in order to redress the very low level of family transmission of RMLs was twice rejected by the Constitutional Court because it contradicts the priority guaranteed to the French

Table 3.2 Bilingual education in France (public sector)

Type of Language	*MFL*	*RML*	*IML*
Type of bilingual education	One or two subjects taught through the foreign language *CLIL*	Half curriculum in French/ half in RML *Partial immersion*	Possible to have one or two subjects taught through the IML, but very rare. *CLIL possible in theory*
Languages	English (dominant) German, Spanish, Italian	Corsican, Breton, Basque, Catalan, Creole Occitan, etc.	Arabic, Russian, Chinese, Vietnamese
Target pupils	All pupils	All pupils in theory	All pupils in theory
Level	Secondary only	Primary & secondary levels	Secondary only. Very rare
Name of programme	*Sections européennes*	*Classes bilingues*	*Sections orientales*
Entry requirements for bilingual programmes	Assessment in maths and French	No assessment. Must join programme at kindergarten level	No information available

language. And immersion education is not available in MFLs because most parents would choose English first.

As to IMLs, the situation reflects again the wide gap between the rhetoric of official texts and the reality at school level. While 'Oriental Sections' were created at the same time (in 1992) as 'European Sections' for the so-called 'Oriental languages', such classes are very rare and few teachers and parents even know that they exist.

This situation is not very different from what prevails in other European countries. Extra and Yagmur's (2004: 18) research shows that 'At the European level, guidelines and directives regarding IMLs are scant and outdated.' Indeed, IMLs are still too often considered by speakers of dominant languages and by policy-makers as obstacles to integration. This is particularly true in France where the Republican ideals of integration have played such an important part in educational policies and in the central role given to the French language at school.

It is against this background that we would like to present a school project where an alternative model of language education was developed. In this model languages were not categorised but envisaged in an inclusive approach, the knowledge of minority language speakers (pupils and parents) was valued and transformed into a learning resource for all, and monolingual pupils and teachers learned from bilingual children.

The Didenheim School Project

The project in Didenheim, in the region of Alsace, was not started with the idea of improving language teaching. While the teachers were aware of the lack of motivation for learning German as a foreign language among primary school students,[4] their aims were much broader. Firstly, they wanted to address the linguistic and cultural diversity present in their class in order to improve the climate in the school. Secondly, they wished to use diversity as a means to face and go beyond differences in order to built a common classroom culture of tolerance and openness towards others. Therefore, the objectives of the project were not language learning but learning to live together. The pupils' differences were no longer meant to be ignored or hidden but brought forward and shared with pupils, teachers and parents.

The project's objectives

The teachers' objectives were:

> To bring the children into contact with other languages and to sensitise them to the use of languages, to familiarise the children with other cultures through the presentation of festivals, traditions, costumes, geography ... and last but not least to promote the acceptance of differences, to learn about others and to attempt to break down stereotypical misconceptions. (Minutes from school project meeting, 7/10/00; our translation)

Both dimensions of the project have been innovative in the French context, and especially the combined objectives of education about linguistic and cultural diversity for the development of tolerance and openness to others. We present it here as an example of good practice in the domain of anti-racist education in France, where the revival of ethnic or religious intolerance is being felt in schools as well as in society at large.

The project was set up in 2000 for three years and rubber stamped by the local inspector since all primary schools must propose school projects on various topics that are part of educational priorities. The teachers were aware that tackling problems of intolerance also involved reaching outside the school, and therefore based their project on parents' participation. All parents were simply asked whether they would like to come and present their language and culture to three classes of children aged six to nine, during Saturday morning sessions. Over a dozen parents volunteered and the children encountered 18 different languages and their related culture, through a very wide number of pedagogical activities prepared by parents in collaboration with teachers. As the project grew, exchange students from the local teacher education institute came to present Russian and Finnish for example, and sign language was offered by a hearing-impaired teacher and her interpreter.

It should be made clear that the project was started by the teachers themselves, and was not an experiment that we set up ourselves. Our analysis is based on participant observation, notes and video films taken over three years. Apart from suggesting the inclusion of sign language, and giving some legitimacy to the project because of our presence as researchers, the teachers and parents ran their project according to their own agenda.

Language diversity in Didenheim: The home and school contexts

Table 3.3 shows the discrepancy between the number of languages presented to the children through the project and the number of languages that, according to the primary curriculum, can be taught in the school. The middle column shows that even in a small school like Didenheim (approximately 90 children), the number and variety of languages spoken at home is much greater than what the school offers. It should also be explained that among the taught languages, only German is compulsory and taught to all children, although it is not spoken at home (Alsatian is). English was offered for one year only because it threatened the position of German in a region where the official policy is to give priority to the German language.

Table 3.3 Languages in Didenheim

Presented in the project	*Spoken at home*	*Taught at school*
Turkish	yes	yes
Moroccan Arabic	yes	yes
English	yes	(yes)
Polish	yes	yes
German	no	yes
Spanish	yes	no
Berber	yes	no
Brazilian Portuguese	yes	no
Serbo-Croat	yes	no
Mandarin	yes	no
Italian	yes	no
Alsatian	yes	no
Vietnamese	yes	no
Malay	yes	no
Japanese	no	no
French sign language	no	no
Russian	no	no
Finnish	no	no

As to the teaching of Moroccan Arabic, Turkish and Polish, the classes are optional and restricted to children whose parents belong to these 'origins'.

In the school project, on the other hand, languages were not used to separate children: all the pupils were presented with the 18 languages, whether they spoke them at home or not. Indeed one of the objectives of the project was to legitimise home languages, to give all languages equality of status. Teachers went beyond the categorisation imposed by the curriculum and took an unusual stance: they decided on their own language policy for the three classes involved in the project.

Language awareness: An alternative and complementary approach to language learning

It should be made clear, however, that the model of language education implemented in Didenheim is very different from models whose aim is language learning. The model described here is known under the English label of 'language awareness' (Hawkins, 1984) and in French as *'éveil aux langues'* (Candelier, 2003a) or *'éducation et ouverture aux langues'* (Perregaux *et al.*, 2003).

Language awareness (LA) does not mean learning a multiplicity of languages, but coming into contact with many different languages in order to understand the way language works and the function of languages in society. Thus it is not language learning, it is not bilingual education, and it is not mother-tongue teaching; but it has implications for bilingual pupils and for pupils who speak minority languages because it gives a place and a space to languages which are usually ignored in the mainstream classroom. LA is based on the principle that monolingual pupils should be exposed to linguistic and cultural diversity, and not just through learning one dominant FL. They should also come to understand that some of their peers speak more than one language and know different cultures, and that multilingualism is much more of an asset than a disadvantage.

The way the teachers in Didenheim implemented the LA approach was of course influenced by their original objective – parents' participation was crucial to the project. This had many positive consequences. First of all, it meant the languages were presented in their social settings and linked to the culture of the speakers who use them, as well as to their personal history (for example, the reasons why they migrated were discussed). Understanding cultural diversity was as important as discovering linguistic diversity. We have explained elsewhere how stereotypes can be overcome through meeting real people and engaging in dialogue with them (Young & Hélot, 2003).

What happened during the language awareness lessons?

The children loved the activities and looked forward to their Saturday morning sessions with great curiosity. 'Which language is it this morning?' they were heard to ask in the schoolyard. They were very curious and very keen to discover languages they had never encountered before. They had no difficulties repeating tones in Mandarin Chinese and really enjoyed using the language in songs with actions. They were quick to notice the same ideograms being used in different contexts (the *Happy* Birthday song and *Happy* New Year written on the board). They loved practicing new sounds like the /r/ phoneme in Spanish, or repeating new words such as the Spanish 'azul' whose sound they took great delight in reproducing. While hesitant at first to use Alsatian, the local German dialect, in the classroom, they went on to sing enthusiastically, and when asked which words they liked in that language they showed no hesitation in producing all the words or expressions they knew. One pupil also asked why Alsatian was called a 'dialect' and not a language.

After watching a film about a school in Finland, the children wanted to know whether there were class reps in that country, as there are in their school in France. During the Vietnamese sessions they were not afraid to ask the Vietnamese mother why the colour of her skin was different, and why she had come to France. They also questioned her about the war. Sign language was met with awe, an impressive silence and full attention. Many very pertinent questions were asked: 'Is the same sign language used all over the world?' 'How do you answer the telephone when you are deaf?' 'How does one learn sign language?' 'Who taught you sign language?' etc. Pupils also manifested an almost immediate desire to learn some of the signs in order to communicate with the hearing-impaired teacher.

Berber presented the opportunity for one child to state with pride that it was the language of his absent father. Moroccan Arabic was discovered by the pupils to the sound of Moroccan music accompanied with mint tea and special cakes prepared by the Moroccan mother. The Italian lesson consisted in making pizzas from a recipe in Italian and working out the meaning of words through comparison with French. Turkish had a particular impact on the Turkish-speaking children who witnessed a Turkish mother in the role of teacher, their own teacher learning their home language and their peers learning about everyday life in Turkey. One child heard his name being pronounced correctly for the first time in front of his peers and his teacher. The teacher became aware that serious mispronunciation of a first name can rob a pupil of his identity.

The video recordings show how much the Turkish children's behaviour in the class changed after the sessions of Turkish language and culture. The words of one of the teachers are significant: 'Now they exist in the class, before they did not really exist.' What she meant was that the children made their presence felt, that they had their hands up and participated much more in class activities. In other words that they found their voice in French once their home language had been acknowledged in their school. The project was also much talked about in the Turkish community, who welcomed it because such collaboration is still very rare in French primary schools.

More generally, most pupils were interested in knowing how the adults in front of them had learnt French, for example 'Is it difficult to learn French when you are Chinese?' They were very quick to make comparisons with French. When it was explained to the children that in Finnish all written letters are pronounced, one child concluded that, unlike French, it must be very easy to learn to read in Finnish. Told about reading in Arabic from right to left, they asked about Berber and whether it was the same for that language. Shown the alphabet in Russian, the children had no problems picking the identical letters to the Latin alphabet and working out the different ones. One pupil asked how to say 'I love you' in Russian, and the whole class at once wrote it down in their copybooks, in order to be able to use the expression.

Again and again their questions showed their thirst for knowledge about language and languages once the programme had started, as well as about the people who speak these languages. During the week, the teachers made sure to include in other school subjects some aspects of the language and culture presented the previous Saturday. For example, bilingual tales were read in French with the original language shown to the children. And art lessons included calligraphy work in Cyrillic or Arabic script.

The variety and richness of the activities prepared by the parents provide an example of what a language awareness curriculum for young children can include – from singing to cooking, to learning different rules of politeness, to human geography, history of migration, reading and writing, learning to listen to new sounds to differentiate them, finding clues to understand a language close to French, and, last but not least, feeling respect for languages spoken by one's peers.

Teachers and parents co-constructing knowledge about multilingualism and cultural diversity

Our evaluation so far has concentrated on the social dimension of the project and how relationships have changed in the school and even outside the school. While not all problems of intolerance between the children are solved, the teachers have noticed marked progress in the attitudes of their pupils towards the minority language speakers, as well as a readiness in all children to use the languages they can remember whenever a special event takes place. A child's birthday, for example, now means that *Happy Birthday* is sung in several languages, including sign language, which the children rarely forget. An outing on a pedagogical farm will give rise to questions about language and language use of the farmer. As a Turkish mother explained during the final interviews:

> Before, my children had problems with other children, but since I have given the class about Turkish, everytime we meet children from the class, they say to me, they want to speak to me, but before it was different, now they even say the word, they say 'merhaba', some of them say hello, I'm happy.

These examples show that not only has the *habitus* of the school changed but children also show more open attitudes outside the school. Up to a certain point, the school has begun 'to sow the seeds of multilingualism' (Skutnabb-Kangas, 2004b). It has become inclusive of linguistic and cultural diversity, teachers and pupils are now aware that multilingualism is part of our world and that one should learn to value it. But it should be stressed that this transformation came about as a result of the collaboration between teachers and parents. While knowledge about various languages and cultures could be laid out in a book, a recording, pictures or film, in Didenheim the parents' participation made all the difference. The meals prepared and shared together, the personal photographs and objects brought in, the traditional clothes the children tried on, the sand from the Moroccan desert which the children could touch, the personal testimonies of migration, meant that the pupils and their teachers had a direct experience of diversity. We know how important this is at primary level where new knowledge needs to be contextualised.

Moreover, the parents' participation was decisive for other reasons. It showed the teachers that a collaborative approach could be developed, and it showed the parents that the teachers needed them and that they could take part in their children's education. Through the project, the parents' linguistic and cultural knowledge and heritage became a source of learning in the eyes of all the children, as well as in the eyes of the teachers. In the final interviews, some children commented on the role of parents: 'It's good that other people come to our class because the teacher does not come from other countries'; 'We understand better when it's outside people who come to present their languages'; 'My mother, she knows more than the teacher'.

Parents' are also very positive about their own participation and they testify to the change of attitudes in their children towards their home language. For example, a Berber mother told us:

> It's clear my son is very proud that his mother came into the class. He does not say it, but he asked, would I go back, and was disappointed when I said no ... but now he looks at books of poetry in Arabic at home, he did not do that before.

Through the teachers' trust and support, many parents felt empowered and changed their relationship to the school. They invested a lot of time and energy on their preparations, attended evaluation meetings after their sessions, and supported the parents who had to present the next session. They also learned to overcome their fear of being in front of a group of children, as well as being watched by teachers and filmed by researchers. In the final interviews they all said how much better they understood the workload of teachers and their professionalism.

As a result of the close collaboration with teachers, the gap between home cultures and the school culture was reduced. Parents who were previously reluctant to approach the school became part of a real pedagogical project that is quite different from an after-school or end-of-term activity. In the words of one of the teachers 'the walls of the school have come down,' and so have the barriers of the national language and culture. The languages spoken at home became a collective resource for all: pupils, teachers, parents and researchers. But beyond the celebration of diversity, something else was constructed. As explained by the Year 2 teacher:

> I think we tried to take the differences, to focus on them, on the good aspect of differences and how enriching it can be ... the cultural aspects were so different from our culture, but there is also everything we live together, we build the history of the class together with the children who are rich from their own experiences, their personal culture, but we put all this together to build a common history for our class.

What is particularly interesting in this comment is the fact that the teacher is able to envisage differences and universality in a complementary fashion. On the one hand, she questions the basic principles of our education system by focusing on differences, but on the other, she strengthens the common ground on which she wants the children to learn. She sees her class as a small community of learners who need to understand what it means to live and work together. In other words the project is not about singling out particular pupils because of their home background, but is aimed at integrating linguistic and cultural differences into the construction of a common history for the class.

This aspect of the project shows that the process of socialisation at school can include a plurilingual dimension. Even if not all children speak a language other than the school language, the acknowledgement of their peers' home languages and the pedagogical activities carried out in a wide choice of languages transform the class into a multilingual space that is shared by everybody and where no one feels excluded because of his language or her culture. This is fundamentally different from FLT classes where everyone learns one dominant language and no reference is made to the other languages known by some of the pupils.

In Didenheim, before the project started, the children left their home language outside the school gate. Now they see it as part of the school curriculum. It is important to state once more that LA activities target all pupils, not just bilingual pupils, because monolingual children also need to distance themselves from their own language – which is also the school language. This was expressed in a felicitous way when a first year Didenheim pupil asked after several sessions of different languages, 'Is French also a language then?'

We are well aware that bilingual learners need much more support than LA activities to develop their competence in both their languages in order to cope with the cognitive demands of the primary curriculum (Cummins, 1981, 1984; Skutnabb-Kangas 1981; Skutnabb-Kangas and Cummins, 1988). But how can we have bilingual education programmes when there are so many different languages in a class? We agree with Bourne (2003) who argues that mainstream teachers must address the question of linguistic and cultural diversity.

The inclusion of bilingual books in the school library is an example of the way multilingualism is now concretely present. The project could be taken further and encompass support for bilingual literacy with the help of parents. For, although the Didenheim teachers cannot help their pupils to learn to read in their first language, they have now given their bilingual pupils resources to work with at home. This is all the more feasible because the teachers now value parents' support and have changed their attitudes towards their bilingual pupils' L1. The Year 2 teacher explains her position thus:

> I have to admit my position has changed on this subject: one is quick to think that speaking French at home means the child will learn French faster. Well, it's true that this year, through the project and everything that was put into place in this school, we became aware of the importance of knowing one's mother tongue before acquiring anything else, so, yes, my opinion has changed on this matter.

In France, where the priority of the national language is so central, and where it is seen as the major instrument of integration, most teachers are hesitant to make it possible for the home languages of their pupils to be legitimised. In Didenheim, the teachers decided to go beyond the top-down curriculum (which imposes one foreign language at primary) in order to embrace the linguistic diversity of their pupils. In this way they created possibilities for many languages rather than restricting them. And, within the LA approach, the more languages the better, because the more diversity, the more the children can be motivated to learn – not only dominant languages, but the languages of their family, their neighbours, or distant people. LA activities are also particularly suited to classrooms where a multiplicity of languages is present because, the more languages are in contact, the more comparisons can be made and the more obvious the relativity of cultural practices becomes.

In their own way, these teachers questioned the power relationships at work in the education system. They gave equal place and equal status to all languages. They legitimised their pupils' home knowledge and the knowledge of their parents. They were not afraid to switch places with parents and put themselves in the situation of learners. They even went further in the sense that they were able to transform the common perception of minority languages and cultures from being a problem into being learning resources (Ruiz, 1984a).

Language Awareness and Teacher Education

The Didenheim experience gives us plenty to think about on the subject of teacher education. Firstly, we should remember that teachers are often constrained by the limits of their curriculum but, when faced with everyday problems such as racism, they are quicker to react and devise pedagogical solutions than policy-makers are. We believe, like Cummins (2000), that real changes happen at the school level, and that educators have a choice even within a constricted context. Therefore, it is most important for researchers to analyse the way teachers are coping with the linguistic and cultural diversity of their pupils and to report on projects such as the Didenheim school where, even in a strongly monolingual instructional context, the teachers were able to create an environment that not only acknowledged minority languages but legitimised them.

We should add that none of the three teachers involved in the Didenheim project felt they had the competence to teach a FL (neither English nor German). Even if FLT is an obligatory component of the curriculum, many primary teachers, well aware of the importance of offering a good phonological model to young learners, do not feel confident enough to teach a FL. While they have no choice but to take the FLT didactic courses when they are training, we believe that introducing them to the principles of LA would be more profitable to them. For whether they are going to teach a FL or not, teachers need to understand the complexity of linguistic situations some of their pupils are experiencing.

While the didactics of FLs deal with the learning of only one FL envisaged from a monolingual point of view, LA activities as they have been developed in the best-known European projects (Candelier, 2003b; Perregaux *et al.*, 2003), deal with as many as 70 different languages. Of course, the objectives of the two models are not the same, but they could be envisaged as complementary. How can one work on the cultural objectives of 'otherness' (Roberts *et al.*, 2001) set out in the FLT curriculum when only one FL is concerned and no one in the class speaks it? What about the knowledge of so many French pupils who already have their own personal experience of other cultures and other people? As shown in the Didenheim project, opening to others can begin with learning a few words from the home language of one's classmates. From the teachers' point of view, is it not self-defeating to talk about opening to others in the English class and at the same time to negate or ignore the otherness of one's own pupils?

In the French curriculum at present, no school subject deals with the question of linguistic and cultural diversity, not even the section entitled 'Living together' (MEN, 2003: 97–104). Therefore, as language educators, we feel that more than one pedagogical model should be presented to future primary teachers, and that it is not enough today in our globalised world to learn one or two dominant languages. Just like the protection of the environment is now part of the science curriculum, young children should be made aware of the wealth of languages spoken by human beings and of the value of their own, whether they are monolingual, bilingual or multilingual.

In the domain of teacher education, language awareness activities can be a basis for a first introduction to sociolinguistics. It can help future teachers to reflect on their own language-learning experiences and to change their attitudes towards the traditional ideal criteria – the model of the native speaker, the 'perfect' bilingual, the priority of the national language, the relationship between L1 and L2 for minority speakers at school. The materials developed for the EVLANG and JALING European projects (Candelier, 2003a, 2003b) and the Swiss EOLE project (Perregaux *et al.*, 2003) give examples of what a curriculum in LA can include. The activities designed for children can easily be used with teachers and are also accompanied by teachers' manuals which address many issues related to language and languages. It can also make them aware that 'when linguistic diversity is the norm, it is no longer acceptable for mainstream teachers to believe that supporting second language learners is not an essential part of their responsibility' (Bourne, 2003: 29).

Thus the competence needed by teachers for LA is of a different nature from FLT competence. It focuses on attitudes rather than on aptitude, and it should lead to reflection on the relationship between language and power, on the lack of equality towards different languages in our curriculum (Heller, 2002; Hornberger, 2003), as well as to awareness of the way power operates in a classroom.

As to integrating parents into pedagogical projects, the Didenheim experience could be cited as an example of good practice. The teachers were very supportive and open to the parents' varied suggestions, appreciative of their efforts, sensitive to their needs. Teachers were also very motivated to learn from parents. This was particularly important again for the parents of minority backgrounds who usually find it rather intimidating to approach teachers. What was built over the three years was a relationship of mutual trust and respect without which the project could not have taken place and which led to a real educational partnership (Cummins, 2000).

Conclusion

As a model of language education, LA fills a gap in teacher education and includes objectives that go far beyond those of FLT. It builds bridges between languages themselves, between various school subjects, between home and school, and between school and the wide world where multilingualism is the norm. We would say that it represents a first attempt at 'accommodating the greater language and cultural hybridity of the 21st century' (García, 2006).

Admittedly, more research needs to be carried out to evaluate exactly what children learn through LA activities and how much of an impact it can have on their attitudes and motivation to learn languages. The LA model is not a panacea. Recent research at European level (Genelot, 2002) indicated that the approach benefited children with learning difficulties as well as children from multilingual background, but only when they had been exposed to at least 35 hours of LA activities. The work of De Goumoëns *et al.* (1999) in Switzerland showed that teachers responded very positively to the LA model and believed it was important not only for minority language speakers but for monolingual pupils as well. The Didenheim project shows convincingly that young learners are very keen to know more about the wealth of languages spoken in their environment and in the world. Thus it questions the early FLT model where the learning of one dominant language such English tends to dampen pupils' curiosity for other languages.

Finally, and most importantly, the LA model is neither a model for monolinguals nor is it a compensatory approach for minority speakers. It is an inclusive model, aimed at all learners, integrating the languages and cultures of all pupils, based on learners' knowledge of any and every language, including the school language. For these very reasons, it can be a first step towards making our schools multilingual.

The Didenheim project shows that teachers are able to devise 'radical' programmes (Bourne, 2003), that they could adapt their mainstream classroom to respond to the needs of their bilingual pupils, and through this process educate their monolingual pupils. Furthermore, teachers can learn to develop cooperative, team-teaching strategies with parents, which have the effect of empowering parents from minority backgrounds. If multilingualism is about 'how people relate together' (Skutnabb-Kangas, 2004a), the Didenheim project is an illustration of a learning community coming together to learn together to live together in harmony.

Language awareness websites

Austria:

- Kiesel: www.zse3.asn-graz.ac.at

Belgium:

- http://www.mag.ulg.ac.be/eveilauxlangues/

California:

- Language Awareness for Education: Leo Van Lier's personal site about LanguageAwareness at http://maxkade.miis.edu/Faculty_Pages/lvanlier/language.html
- http://www.lmp.ucla.edu/

Canada:

- ELODIL: www.elodil.com
- Site sur l'aménagement linguistuque et les langues dans le monde http://www.tlfq.ulaval.ca/axl/: e

Finland:

- Metalinguistic Awareness and foreign language learning (Centre for Applied Language Studies, University of Jyväskylä) at www.solki.jyu.fi/english/research/

France:

- http://plurilangues.univ-lemans.fr/index.php

United Kingdom

- ALA: Association for Language Awareness at www.lexically.net/ala (Richard Aplin, Treasurer, School of Education, University of Leicester, 21 University Rd, Leicester, LE1 7RF, UK)
- *Language Awareness*: Journal of the ALA association, published by Multilingual Matters, Clevedon: UK (on-line magazine subscription required) at www.multilingual-matters.co.uk

Council of Europe:

- http://www.coe.int/T/E/Cultural_Co-operation/education/Languages/

Notes

1. These terms are our translation of *Délégation Générale pour la Langue Française (known as DGLF) and Délégation générale pour la Langue Française et les langues de France* (known now as DGLFLF). The emphasis is ours as well.
2. The term 'Berber' will be used throughout this chapter because it is the term used in France for the people and the language and was also the term used in the project discussed here by the Berber participant herself. It is not a derogatory term in France, where the umbrella term 'Amazigh' is used only by experts. Amazigh covers several dialects such as Kabyle, Tachelhit, Rifain, Chaoui and Touareg.
3. See Colinet & Morgen (2004: 261–275) for more details and recent figures.
4. There are many reasons for this: the historical situation of Alsace, and the fact that German is still perceived as 'the language of the enemy' (Mombert, 2001), the lack of choice of other languages particularly English, the pedagogical approach and its lack of links with the local dialect, Alsatian.

Summary

This chapter presents a *language awareness* project in a primary school in Alsace, France where, over three years, children aged 6 to 9 have been introduced to 18 languages and their associated cultures. The aims of the project were twofold – to legitimate the regional and immigration languages of some of the pupils in the eyes of all learners (monolinguals and bilinguals alike), and to educate children to the wealth of linguistic and cultural diversity before they start to learn one foreign language at primary school.

The language awareness approach developed in the project is analyzed in terms of an alternative model of language education that can transform the traditional monolingual habitus of most schools and sow the seeds of multilingual education. The educational partnership developed by the teachers with the parents is an example of a collaborative approach through which speakers of minority languages can be empowered.

Cet article relate une expérience d'éveil aux langues dans une école primaire en Alsace, France, expérience qui a duré trois ans et au cours de laquelle 18 langues et les cultures qui leur sont associées ont été présentées à des enfants de 6 à 9 ans. Le projet avait deux objectifs principaux: la légitimation des langues minoritaires régionales et de l'immigration auprès de tous les enfants, qu'ils soient monolingues ou bilingues, et l'éducation à la pluralité linguistique et culturelle avant le début de l'apprentissage d'une langue étrangère à l'école.

L'approche de l'éveil aux langues, telle qu'elle a été développée dans le projet, est présentée comme un modèle alternatif d'éducation linguistique qui pourrait transformer l'habitus monolingue traditionnel de nombre d'écoles et jeter les bases d'une éducation au multilinguisme. Le partenariat éducatif que les enseignantes ont su construire avec les parents est un exemple d'approche collaborative qui apermis aux locuteurs de langues minorées de voir leur langue, leur culture et leur savoir valorisés. (French)

Artikkelissa esitellään Ranskassa, Elsassin maakunnassa toteutettu projekti, jossa pyrittiin lisäämän oppilaiden kielitietoisuutta. Kolmen vuoden ajan perusasteen 6–9 – vuotiaille lapsille esiteltiin 18 eri kieltä sekä niihin kiinteästi liittyviä kulttuureja. Projektin tavoitteet olivat kahdenlaisia: ensinnäkin haluttiin legitimoida oppilaiden käyttämät – joko alueelliset tai maahanmuuttajaryhmien käyttämät – kielet kaikkien oppilaiden keskuudessa, olivatpa nämä yksi- tai kaksikielisiä. Toiseksi haluttiin kasvattaa lapset ymmärtämään kielellisen ja kulttuurisen rikkauden arvo ennen kuin he aloittavat ensimmäisen vieraan kielen opiskelunsa perusasteella.

Projektissa kehitettyä kielitietoisuutta lisäävää lähestymistapaa analysoidaan vaihtoehtoisen kielikasvatuksen pohjalta. Tämä malli voi muuttaa useimpien koulujen noudattaman perinteisen yksikielisen käytännön ja antaa ideoita monikieliseen opetukseen. Opettajien kehittelemä kasvatuksellinen yhteistyö vanhempien kanssa on esimerkki yhteisöllisestä lähestymistavasta, jonka avulla vähemmistökielten puhujat voivat voimaantua. (Finnish)

Der vorliegende Artikel beschreibt ein französisches Projekt zum Thema Sprachbewusstsein, das drei Jahre lang in einer elsässischen Grundschule mit Kindern von 6 bis 9 Jahren durchgeführt wurde. Die Ziele des Projektes waren einerseits die Legitimierung von Regional- und Einwanderersprachen: 18 verschiedene Sprachen und die damit verbundenen Kulturen wurden von der ganzen Klasse behandelt und dadurch im Klassenverband aufgewertet. Auch wenn sie zu Beginn nur für einige der Schüler Bezugswert hatten, wurden damit alle Schüler – ein- oder mehrsprachige in gleichem Maße – angesprochen. Andererseits sollten die Schüler allgemein für die sprachliche und kulturelle Vielfalt sensibilisiert werden, bevor sie dann in der Grundschule eine Fremdsprache lernten.

Hiermit wird ein alternatives Modell der Spracherziehung im Sinne der language awareness vorgestellt, welches den traditionellen monolingualen Habitus zahlreicher Schulen verändern und die Grundlagen einer Erziehung zur Mehrsprachigkeit legen könnte. Die erzieherische Partnerschaft, welche sich im Kontakt zwischen den Lehrerinnen und den Eltern entwickelt hatte, konnte bei den Sprechern von Minderheitensprachen das Selbstbewusstsein steigern und somit zu mehr sozialer Gerechtigkeit beitragen. (German)

Chapter 4

Reimagining Multilingual America: Lessons from Native American Youth

TERESA L. MCCARTY, MARY EUNICE ROMERO and OFELIA ZEPEDA

Introduction

When we were invited to contribute to this volume, we spent some time 'imagining multilingual schools.' Reminded of the many schools, teachers, students, and communities with whom we have been privileged to work, we realized that imagining their multilingualism or multiculturalism was not difficult at all. Our schools and society *are* multilingual and multicultural. The problem is that education policies and practices often deny that multilingual, multicultural reality, attempting to coerce it into a single, monolingualist and monoculturalist mold. The policies and practices are deviant, not the students and communities these schools serve.

In this chapter we take the normalcy of multilingualism and multiculturalism as our starting point, focusing specifically on Native American students, communities, and schools.[1] Multilingualism was always highly valued in Indigenous North American societies and indeed, was essential to trade and survival in one of the most culturally, linguistically, and ecologically diverse regions of the world. Prior to European contact, some 300 to 500 Native languages were spoken in what is now the United States and Canada (Krauss, 1998; Zepeda & Hill, 1992). To rephrase a metaphor suggested by Ofelia García (1992), this remarkable linguistic and cultural diversity makes Native North America one of the hemisphere's most colorful 'language gardens' (Baker & Prys Jones, 1998: 204–205).

Multilingualism and multiculturalism are still highly valued in Native North America. But the palette and variety of the 'language garden' are fading, and the garden itself is in grave danger of perishing within our lifetimes. Although more than 200 Indigenous languages are still spoken in the United States and Canada – testimony to the resistance and resilience of their speakers – only 34 are still being naturally acquired as a first language by children in the context of their families and communities (Krauss, 1998). Put another way, fully 84% of all Indigenous languages in the US and Canada have no new speakers to pass them on. Even those languages with a substantial number of speakers – Navajo in the US Southwest, for example – are slipping away, as the residue of a genocidal and linguicidal past and the modern influences of English media, technology, globalization, and schooling all take their toll.[2]

The troubling paradox is that even as more Native children come to school speaking English (or even English only), they are not, on the whole, doing better in school. A far greater proportion of Native children than their numbers warrant continues to be stigmatized as 'limited English proficient' – a label that subscribes them to remedial tracks and scripted, monolingual English reading programs. In 1999–2000, more than 10% of all Native pupils enrolled in US public schools – 55,000 students – were identified as limited English proficient. In schools overseen by the Bureau of Indian Affairs (BIA), the federal agency charged with administering education and social service programs for the 560+ Indigenous nations in the US, nearly 60% of Native pupils were identified as limited English proficient during the same period (Tippeconnic & Faircloth, 2002: 1).

What are we to make of this disturbing paradox? What are its consequences for Native children and their communities and schools?

Examining Native Languages in the Lives of Native Youth

Understanding the role of Native languages in language learning and the in-school and out-of-school lives of Native American youth is the focus of the Native Language Shift and Retention Project, a 5-year, federally-funded research project based in Arizona.[3] As principal investigators for this project, we have been listening to the voices of Native educators, parents, elders, and youth as they have reflected upon the role of the Native language in their lives. These are the questions we are asking:

(1) What role does the Native language play in the personal, familial, community, and school lives of Native American youth?
(2) How do language loss and revitalization factor into how well youth do in school?
(3) How might the findings from this study inform tribal language planning efforts?
(4) What are the lessons for state and national education policies and minority language rights?

Each of us comes to this work from our positions as educators, anthropologists, linguists, and activists in Indigenous education. We are both insiders and outsiders, Indigenous and non-Indigenous scholars who continuously negotiate tribal community, university, school, and larger societal contexts and relationships. To date we have conducted 229 in-depth, ethnographic interviews – 166 with adults and 63 with youth in grades 4 through 12 at each of five school-community sites in the US Southwest. The sites were selected for their representativeness in terms of tribal language groups – Navajo, Akimel O'odham (also called Pima), Pii Paash (Maricopa) and Tohono O'odham – and degrees of language vitality, and to obtain a cross-section of rural reservation and urban settings and of community, public, federal, and charter schools. This remains very much a work in progress. But the preliminary findings are intriguing, exciting, and troubling – and, we believe, informative of efforts by all language minorities to (re)assert their language rights. By illuminating language attitudes and ideologies, youth accounts in particular suggest the evolving *contemporary* causes of language shift among the young, and the role of Indigenous languages within their lives.

In the first part of this chapter we examine a select corpus of data from our Navajo school site, which we call 'Beautiful Mountain' (all names are pseudonyms), concentrating on interviews with Navajo youth. We begin with a brief overview of the Navajo language and Indigenous schooling in the US. We do this to situate the current status of Navajo and other Native North American languages, and to contextualize the research reported here.[4] We then describe the school–community setting and the interview protocols employed. We analyze the interviews according to three patterns or themes, showing how micro and macro processes inside and outside school interact to produce language attitudes (ideologies) and choices.[5] We conclude by offering illustrations of Indigenous educational 'counter-initiatives' – programs and practices that resist and subvert increasingly ascendant standardizing regimes – and their implications for reasserting linguistic and educational self-determination as a fundamental human right.

Sociolinguistic and Historical Background

A member of the huge Athabaskan language family that stretches from the Arctic to the US–Mexico border, Navajo is the most vital Indigenous language in the US today, with more than 170,000 speakers. Yet even this prominent language group is engulfed in the crisis of language shift. In 1969, Spolsky found that '90% of the Navajo children in [Bureau of Indian Affairs] boarding schools had no preschool experience of English' (Spolsky, 2002: 140). By 1990, 'the situation had virtually reversed, with six-year-old Navajo children beginning [school] suspected to have little if any knowledge of the language of their people' (Spolsky, 2002: 140; see also Spolsky, 1974). Spolsky attributes these changes to ease of access to schools and off-reservation towns, but the devastating and lingering legacy of colonization also must be acknowledged (Blanchard *et al.*, 2003). Like other Indigenous peoples, Navajos have been *dispossessed* of their language (see Nicholls,

2005: 166–167, for a similar discussion of Australian Aboriginal peoples and languages).

Following the American revolution, the new federal government turned its attention to pacifying and 'civilizing' Native peoples, 'so that they would live on small farms and, therefore, make available their hunting grounds to White settlers' (Spring, 1996: 12). Toward this end, the US Congress passed the 1819 Civilization Fund Act to support the work of missionaries on the (White) frontier. Education was synonymous with civilization, the overriding goal being the complete annihilation of Indigenous languages and lifeways. In the words of a missionary to the Lakota during the late 19th century:

> Uncle Sam [the federal government] is like a man setting a charge of powder. The school is the slow match. He lights it and ... in time it will blow up the old life, and of its shattered pieces will make good citizens. (Adams, 1988: 3)

Throughout the 19th and much of the 20th centuries, federal Indian education policy was one of almost zero tolerance for linguistic and cultural difference. 'There is not an Indian pupil …who is permitted to study in any other language than our own – the language of the greatest, most powerful, and enterprising nationalities beneath the sun,' wrote Commissioner of Indian Affairs J.D.C. Atkins in 1886 (Atkins, 1887/1992: 49). After cleanliness and obedience, 'No Indian Talk' was the first rule in many federal Indian schools (Spack, 2002: 24). The underlying agenda was the subjugation of Indian people and the confiscation of their lands (Adams, 1988). Although some important reforms were initiated during the 1940s and 1950s, including the introduction of bilingual instruction at selected reservation schools, the assimilationist goals and ideology of racial superiority were never threatened. It was not until the advent of the Civil Rights Movement and the concurrent movement for Indigenous self-determination that some schools for Native Americans came under Indigenous control. In the meantime, incalculable damage had been done to Indigenous children, families, and futures. 'What the boarding schools taught us,' one Navajo teacher reported, 'is that our language is second best.'

Methods and Setting

Perhaps because we come to this work as educators, but also because of the crucial role of schooling in shaping contemporary Indigenous life, schools have been points of entry and access to each of the five tribal community sites in our study. At each site, we have negotiated research protocols according to local, tribal, university, and federal norms – a labor-intensive process, but one that has been amply rewarded by a high degree of local participation in the research.

A key feature of the project is the involvement of Native co-researchers – teachers and paraprofessionals whom we call Community Research Collaborators or CRCs. The CRCs have been instrumental in all phases of the research, facilitating entrée and access through tribal councils and school boards, helping to design and validate research protocols, assisting in the conduct of in-depth interviews, and participating in university-based training on Native language immersion and ethnographic research methods. These individuals represent the critical change agents positioned to apply the findings of research to local practice once the project ends.

Our research methods have included participant observation, questionnaires, analysis of district-maintained achievement data, and ethnographic interviews. We focus on the interview data here. In structuring interviews, we have adapted an interview sequence proposed by Seidman (1998) containing four key elements:

(1) a focused life history;
(2) details of school experiences, particularly language learning in school;
(3) details of observed and personal language use inside and outside of school;
(4) and, for youth, aspirations and life goals.

Most interviews have lasted 60 to 90 minutes; some continued for more than two hours, and in some cases we returned to interview particular participants again. To identify participants, we have been guided by the recommendations of local CRCs, at the same time seeking a balance of native speakers and non-native speakers, males and females, and individuals of different ages (parents, elders, and youth) and professional backgrounds (teachers, school support staff, community workers, administrators, tribal-community leaders, and so on). In partnership with the CRCs, we and our graduate assistants conducted the interviews. Some were conducted in the Native language, and all were audio-taped. For interviews conducted in the Native language, we relied on Native-speaking CRCs and the skills of a bilingual, biliterate Native speaker to transcribe and translate the work.

The interviews that follow were all recorded at Beautiful Mountain, a small, kin-based community in the center of the Navajo Nation in northern Arizona, with a population of 1500. As is typical on the Navajo reservation, the local school constitutes the community center and the primary source of local employment. In 2003–04, approximately 700 students attended the pre-K–12 (pre-kindergarten to grade 12) Beautiful Mountain School. Family incomes at Beautiful Mountain remain well below national poverty levels (approximately $2500 per capita per year), lending economic as well as symbolic importance to the traditional economic pursuits of sheep herding and small-scale farming. Although the economic significance of these activities has diminished relative to wage labor, herding, farming, and ranching – along with the Navajo kinship system (*k'é*) and religious life – still constitute well-recognized 'traditional' contexts in which language socialization occurs.

We emphasize that our interpretation of data from Beautiful Mountain remains a 'work in progress,' and that it represents a single site. Beautiful Mountain is different in many respects from the other sites in our study, and is itself distinct among other Navajo school-community sites. Despite these limitations, the data we analyze here contain significant insights that merit analysis, discussion, and further investigation. We turn now to a consideration of the data and themes.

Themes

Theme 1: Intergenerational consensus and concern about the future of the heritage language

In analyses of Indigenous language loss, some researchers have suggested that Native speakers are in 'denial' about the fragility of their languages, and are unwilling 'to confront and voice the problem of language loss' (Krauss, 1998: 15). Acknowledging that '[a]ll of this is ... simply in accord with what the community has been educated and programmed to do in assimilationist schools' (Krauss, 1998: 15), explanation-by-denial nonetheless obscures the complex micro and macro dynamics that influence language ideologies and choices. In their interviews, both adults and youth at Beautiful Mountain explicitly recognized the vulnerability and critical importance of their language to their identities and the future of the Navajo people (*Diné*). As one parent told us, in Navajo:

> To this day I value what my people have taught me ... I value the language and culture. I wish for us not to lose the language, for our children's sake.

A 43-year-old Navajo mother stated:

> [T]here was only one language left for us [after Indigenous languages were divided among the peoples at the time of Creation], which is Navajo.

What has been especially impressive, however, is the consciousness that young people have of these issues. Navajo youth at Beautiful Mountain are remarkably thoughtful and mature articulators of the importance of their language and the threat of heritage language loss.

We introduce readers first to Samuel, a 17-year-old of Navajo, Apache, Hopi, and French ancestry who learned both Navajo and Apache at an early age. When asked about his language proficiencies, Samuel said he considered himself to be fluent in Apache and Navajo (both Athabaskan languages), and to know 'some Hopi' (a Uto-Aztecan language) and 'a little French.' When he was interviewed in the spring of 2004, Samuel was attending Beautiful Mountain Community High School. A tall, self-possessed young man with an easy smile and a quick intellect, he wore a T-shirt with the inscription, 'In the event of my demise ... I hope I die for a principle or belief that I had lived for.' In many ways, this inscription was emblematic of Samuel's young life. He aspired to become a medical doctor and to return to the Navajo reservation to treat diabetes, a condition that has reached epidemic proportions in Native American communities and which afflicted his beloved 'grandma.' Asked whether Navajo (his self-identified primary language) was important to him, Samuel replied that it was 'very important,' and explained:

> [b]ecause I get the best of both worlds. I mean I get to know how to communicate – I mean, I want to become a doctor. And to do that, I have to know how to communicate with patients in Navajo and ... English. And not just because I want to go into medicine, it's important because the language is dying out – not slowly, as it used to be, but it's going very vigorously now. There's a lot of people that aren't even being taught. Their parents can speak Navajo, but they don't do it inside the home. They would do it inside the chapter house [the local branch of tribal government], or somewhere else, but they wouldn't even teach their children Navajo at all. And that, in a way, kind of makes me angry, because I wasn't brought up that way. I mean, Navajo is supposed to be spoken at all times in the house, no matter what, and these parents, they shouldn't be treating things that way. I mean, they're Navajo, and they should be speaking Navajo ...

English, Samuel added, is also important 'because it's used a lot in America.' But, he insisted, 'you have to know your own language to succeed.'

Jonathan, a 16-year-old ninth grader at Beautiful Mountain, wore 'Gothic'-style attire when he was interviewed in 2004. Tall and intense, Jonathan was dressed in layers of black shirts printed with red and gray flames, a heavy black vest, and baggy black pants adorned with red stitching and numerous safety pins and zippers characteristic of the Gothic style. When asked if he spoke Navajo, Jonathan at first reported that he was 'learning it' in school. However, during a two-hour interview, he revealed that his first language was, in fact, Navajo. For years, he had been 'caught up in the confusion of learning English, having to form those words in my head.' His Navajo elementary teacher had belittled him for his accented and ungrammatical English, making his early goal in school 'just survival, how to cope in this colonial world.' About the importance of Navajo, Jonathan said:

> Yes, it helps me, having that as my first language spoken to me, you know, having to understand ... the kind of things, you know ... The Navajo, it helps separate the side ... of where all these teachings come in. That helps me not get too far in, not to lose the identity of who I am, of where I come from ...
>
> I have sheep at home, and I have horses and whatnot. I could just spend my whole life ... doing that, because I know where all the springs are, I know where to take my livestock and everything. I could just do that until the day I die. But the thing that holds me back from doing that is that I have some responsibility to see some change in how things work and everything, and to see how things are supposed to be, and instead of going backwards ... go forward and keep moving on ...

Despite his early traumatic school experiences as a Navajo first-language speaker, Jonathan viewed Navajo as integral to his identity and, moreover, as central to his ability to bring about positive change 'in this colonial world.'

Other students were more pragmatic about the value of their heritage language. Kelly, a petite female senior with a ponytail, said that Navajo helped her in school 'because you can compare the two different languages.' When questioned about a person she admired, Kelly revealed more about the value she attached to her language; she chose her school principal 'because he's a Navajo and he talks Navajo on the intercom.' (And indeed, our audiotape recordings from Beautiful Mountain High School are peppered with the principal's regular bilingual announcements to students and staff.)

There were exceptions to these expressed language attitudes. Jamie was 18 years old when we interviewed him in 2004. Having grown up in a reservation border town, Jamie's primary language was English. On the day of his interview, he wore Gothic-style clothing identical to Jonathan's; his black hair was shaved except for six dyed-purple spikes across the top of his head. Jamie insisted that Navajo language and culture were 'just the past.' At the same time, when asked if Navajo is important for the future of the Navajo people, Jamie reflected, 'Yeah, 'cuz it's their culture.' Jamie's responses are intriguing; he appeared disaffected from his Navajo-ness ('their' culture), yet he acknowledged that he was trying to learn Navajo in school. When asked if he thought there had been a decline in the use of Navajo, he replied: 'Yes, 'cuz kids don't really care anymore ... They don't want to turn out like their parents.'

Ambivalence such as this was echoed by adults and other youth at Beautiful Mountain. 'When we were talking [to students] in Navajo,' a culture teacher reported, the students 'were making fun of us.' Admonishing them, 'you are Navajo ... if you are laughing about your language ... you are laughing about your parents, you are laughing about your grandparents,' the teacher found, after administering a Navajo language assessment, 'that they knew the language but were just ashamed of it.' A teacher assistant stated that 'there are some students that have said ..."I'm not going to learn [Navajo]. Navajo's nothing. I hate it."'

This leads us to consideration of a second theme.

Theme 2: The politics of shame and caring

> No one speaks Navajo. They only speak English now.
> (female school employee whose native language is Navajo)

Interviewer: In school, what percentage of the kids are fluent speakers of Navajo?
Samuel: 80%.
Jonathan: Probably 75%.
Kelly: 75%.
Jamie: 80%.
Howard: Everybody knows Navajo out here.

Each of the adult and youth responses above was recorded in a separate, individual interview. The responses are typical of those to questions asking individuals to estimate the number and percentage of students at Beautiful Mountain School who are proficient speakers of Navajo. As the excerpts above reveal, there was wide divergence in the responses to this question by youth and adults, with teachers and administrators rating the percentage of Navajo-proficient students at 30–50%, and youth consistently providing much higher estimates. Recognizing that self-assessments of language proficiency are highly problematic, we do not take these estimates at face value. What these responses *do* indicate to us are local *perceptions* of language vitality. Such perceptions, in turn, have important implications for language choices. For example, a bilingual adult who believes the children to whom she or he is speaking have little knowledge of or interest in using Navajo is likely to address them in English. For their part, youth state that speaking Navajo is often viewed as an emblem of shame. Samuel's interpretation was typical:

Samuel: Well ... a lot of [youth] tend to hide [their Native language ability] ... they put a façade on, and they ... try to make teachers believe that they speak primarily [English] and weren't exposed to Navajo. But I can tell that they have been exposed just by the way they'll say a certain word, and then I'll know that they were brought up with Navajo.

Interviewer: How do you think kids at [Beautiful Mountain High School] feel about Navajo?

Samuel: They probably think it's important, but there's a time when they're put at a standpoint when they're judged by it by other people that speak English more clear than they do and they just kind of feel dirty about the whole thing, and that's why they put on the fake ... and try to make it sound like they speak more English than they do Navajo ... Because ... if you have that Navajo dialect (gives example) ... they'll be judged by that, and they'll say, 'Oh, you're Johnned out,' you know. And (laughs) Navajos don't like to be told they're Johnned out. The word itself is a put-down word.

Interviewer: And what does that mean to you?

Samuel: It means a person ... that's uneducated, and they haven't experienced anything in the world.

In this statement, Samuel uses powerful words to describe some of his peers' feelings about their heritage language: '[T]hey just kind of feel dirty about the whole thing.' Even more poignantly, Jonathan talked about what he called the 'Long Walk syndrome,' referring to the Navajos' enforced Long Walk – a death march undertaken at bayonet point across wintry New Mexico plains, that preceded the Navajos' four-year incarceration at Fort Sumner (*Hwéeldi*) from 1864 to 1868. This holocaust of Navajo history still brings to mind images of genocide and unspeakable loss. Recalling those painful images, Jonathan said:

> Like I said, this Long Walk syndrome ... we're afraid to be punished, we're afraid that someone will whip us in the back ... You know, you forsake who you are, you give up having to learn Navajo ... You're having to give all that up, in order to accommodate the mainstream life.

He asserted that shame and self-hate led many youth 'to give all that up':

> ... [M]any of these kids know how to speak Navajo, but many times they might be ashamed, or got that kind of self-hate, you know. It's been pumped into them. It's not something natural. It's being told Navajo is stupid ... to speak Indian is the way of the devil, that kind of thing. Like I said, it's a hereditary thing that's been pumped into you, and many times, the older people will encourage English so they [youth] can make it in the Whiteman's world ... Many of these children were taken away at an early age, to go to school ... Like I said, for me, it kind of confused me. Where was *I* in the world?

Jonathan and other youth viewed the presence of caring adults as a key factor capable of transforming self-doubt into self-empowerment. 'Well, the [school] administrators and teachers really don't have a one-on-one personal relationship with students,' Samuel said, leading youth to 'put on a façade' and 'hide' their knowledge of Navajo. According to Jonathan, adults were reluctant to take on 'that excess burden' of bonding with youth:

> There's a lot of kids here, they've grown up with the kinds of things I've grown up with, having nowhere to turn, you know ... they come here, they just barely struggle from class to class ... They [teachers/adults] don't want to take on that excess burden ... They don't want to form any kind of bond. So it's not surprising to hear [adults] say the kids don't speak Navajo in front of them, or with them.

There is a danger in reducing these responses to examples of simple intergenerational misunderstanding. We suggest instead a more complex and nuanced interpretation. The notion of caring surfaced repeatedly in our field notes and interviews at Beautiful Mountain. Here, Noddings' (1984, 1992) concept of 'authentic caring' – reciprocal, respectful relations between youth and adults – is useful. At Beautiful Mountain, many teachers (Native and non-Native) viewed students as not caring about the Navajo language ('You are laughing about your language') – a behavior that youth did, in fact, demonstrate. Youth, on the other hand, often viewed teachers and other adults as not caring about *them* ('Teachers don't want to take on that excess burden'). Our observations suggest that adults at Beautiful Mountain care deeply about their students. Native educators in particular repeatedly expressed the desire to support youth in using and valorizing their heritage language. In one Native administrator's words:

> And the language itself, it needs more takers, somebody to hold it up high ... I think it's getting back down to roots, getting back down to being proud of who you are, being able to say, 'Yes, I'm proud to say I'm Navajo.'

There were, nonetheless, divergent conceptions of caring among youth and adults that appeared to work at cross-purposes. This led some adults to dismiss or underestimate young people's knowledge of and interest in the Navajo language, at the same time inhibiting youth from presenting themselves as proficient Navajo speakers or engaged language learners. Much as Valenzuela (1999) reports for Latino students and their teachers in urban US public schools, the effect of these competing definitions of caring at Beautiful Mountain was to subtract opportunities within and outside the school in which adult–child interaction in Navajo might be nurtured.

It would be inadequate and misleading to end our analysis here, however. In a post-colonial context such as Beautiful Mountain, youth and adults continuously negotiate multiple and power-laden cultural worlds. Youth preferences in dress, hairstyle, and other aspects of their physical appearance attest to the attractiveness of mainstream pop culture. At the same time, neither youth nor adults are unconscious of or immune to the marginalization of Navajo language and culture within larger regimes of power. 'The world speaks English,' a 43-year-old father of four stated, explaining his decision not to teach his children or his students Navajo. Samuel described English as a necessary 'business language.' And Jonathan reflected, 'English ... that's always taking over ... It's just kind of hard to have anything really of a Native thing going on.'

This leads to our final theme.

Theme 3: Narrowing of the local context by the larger policy context

> The school can spend *some* time teaching Navajo, but we can't be bogged down ... we have so many requirements to meet. (High school teacher at Beautiful Mountain School)

Youth and adults at Beautiful Mountain (and, for that matter, at all of our school sites), are keenly aware of the pressures placed upon them by current Federal and state surveillance systems, legitimated by English-only standardized tests. Beverly Gordon, past vice president of the American Educational Research Association, writes (2001: 3): '[N]o other country in the world tests their children to the extent that we do.' What distinguishes the current standards movement from previous practices is both the quantity of standardized tests, and their high stakes. Under a new labeling system in the federal No Child Left Behind (NCLB) Act of 2001, standardized tests are administered not only to putatatively gauge student knowledge, but as a gate-keeping device, enabling or curtailing educational opportunity as never before. Students who fail to perform at a predetermined level are denied a high school diploma, and their schools – typically the most under-resourced in the nation – are denied Federal funding and remanded to for-profit management groups. Exacerbating these punitive policies is a burgeoning corpus of state constitutional amendments that make instruction in a language other than English illegal, despite students' language proficiency. Arizona's Proposition 203 is one of the most extreme English-only statutes. It criminalizes teachers and school administrators, threatening to rescind their certification for using English language learners' primary language in instruction.

According to both young people and adults at Beautiful Mountain, these pressures force Navajo language and culture instruction to take a 'back seat' in the school curriculum. '[W]e're run by the state, and we're told to do these tests and everything,' Jonathan pointed out. A Navajo teacher put it more bluntly: 'We don't have time to teach Navajo – we've been told to teach to the standards.'

As these statements indicate, the challenges inherent in reclaiming Indigenous languages – in envisioning and sustaining bi-/multilingual schools – are heightened considerably by the coercive politics of education 'reform.' Working with drastically reduced numbers of speakers, communities such as Beautiful Mountain face a gauntlet of obstacles to their efforts to support and sustain their language and culture in school. They must acknowledge and transform internalized images of the Native language as 'dirty,' 'backward,' or 'the way of the devil' – a task that requires consciousness-raising and hard, long, home- and community-based work. At the same time, they must confront the homogenizing juggernaut of standards, high-stakes tests, and English-only policies that, despite their rhetoric, threaten to leave Indigenous languages and cultures, once and for all, 'behind.'

It remains to be seen how Beautiful Mountain will address these challenges. 'These are desperate times,' Lily Wong Fillmore (2005) reminds us, 'and so there are desperate curriculum decisions.' At Beautiful Mountain School, one response has been the adoption of a scripted English phonics program mandated by NCLB. At the same time, the school's director and many teachers are determined to work around these mandates by implementing a Navajo immersion program in the primary grades. At other school sites in our study, Native teacher aides – the primary sources of expertise in the Native language – have been removed from instructional positions because they lack the two-year college degrees required by NCLB.

There *are* hopeful alternatives, however, which suggest new directions for language teaching and learning in Indigenous communities and schools. In the next section, we consider these alternatives. We identify them as education counter-initiatives because they resist, subvert, and contest the policies and practices that stifle bi/multilingualism and Indigenous linguistic and education rights.

Indigenous Education Counter-Initiatives

Native Charter Schools: Combining Native language, culture, and 'academic rigor'

As the pressures for standardization have mounted, with no evidence that the focus on standards and high-stakes testing improves educational outcomes for Native youth, some Indigenous communities have looked to alternative institutional arrangements as a means of retaining control over their schools and ensuring that the curriculum is infused with local linguistic and cultural content. Charter schools, linked through formal agreements to authorizing entities such as public school districts but chartered by a distinctive mission, have become an increasingly popular – if controversial – option. According to the US Department of Education, in 1997–98, nearly one-tenth of all American Indian/Alaska Native students were enrolled in charter schools (Tirado, 2001: 14).

One such school, Bahidaj High, is a particularly relevant case, as its mission is to serve as an academically rigorous, bicultural community-based high school for Native youth. 'By infusing all aspects of the educational experience with elements of Native language and history,' a school brochure reads, 'the school will nurture individual students, helping them become strong and responsible contributors to their communities.'

Bahidaj teachers, many of whom are Native American, describe their goals as 'helping kids really understand the things that they can do with their talents.' Authentic multicultural literature is widely evident at the school. English literature courses, for example, emphasize writers of color, including Native American authors. The US history text is Howard Zinn's (2003 [1980]) *A People's History of the United States*, which begins with this critique of the Christopher Columbus story: 'Even allowing for the imperfection of myths, it is enough to make us question ... the excuse of progress in the annihilation of races ...' (Zinn, 2003: 22). The predominant Native language is offered as a 'foreign' language (a brilliant response to Arizona statutes requiring foreign language teaching in public schools). Native and non-Native teachers take classes in the language. Other curricular areas include traditional Native basket weaving, ethnobotany, and permaculture.

In 2003-04, Bahidaj High was rated by the state education agency as 'meeting adequate yearly progress' according to NCLB. Every graduating senior had applied to at least one college or university, and some had won scholarships. Perhaps most important are students' perceptions of the quality of their education. 'I can always look forward to the future,' a student writes, 'while still looking back at the past to find out who I am. As long as I know my background, I can have some sense of pride, and can know that I won't get lost' (Juan, 2003a: 29).

We do not endorse charter schools as a panacea, and in general are concerned that the charter school movement may serve to undermine struggling public schools. For Indigenous communities who have experienced centuries of discrimination and mis-education, however, Native-operated charter schools represent one option for mediating the pressures of the standards movement and exerting local control. Charter schools cannot be the only option; BIA and public schools must also become more responsive to and accountable to the Indigenous communities they serve. In this regard, Alaska Native communities have taken a strong stand in developing 'counter-standards' and guidelines for culturally-responsive schooling – a story we turn to next.

Alaska Native counter-standards

The present standards movement is replete with the language of accountability. We agree that holding schools accountable for providing a healthy, uplifting, quality education is important. Yet we must ask: accountable to what or to whom?

In contrast to test-driven accountability, some Native nations are adopting formal approaches to assessment that hold schools and educators accountable to the children, Native nations, and the communities they serve. In Alaska, a statewide initiative has created a parallel set of 'cultural standards' and guidelines intended to extend and complement education standards adopted by the state. These cultural standards 'are predicated on the belief that a firm grounding in the heritage language and culture ... is a fundamental prerequisite for the development of culturally-healthy students and communities' (AANE, 1998: 2).

The *Alaska Standards for Culturally-Responsive Schools* were developed to ensure that students achieve state standards 'in such a way that they become responsible, capable and whole human beings in the process' (AANE, 1998: 3). 'The cultural standards are not intended to produce standardization,' the Assembly of Alaska Native Educators asserts, 'but rather to encourage schools to nurture and build upon the rich and varied cultural traditions that continue to be practiced in communities throughout Alaska' (AANE, 1998: 3–4). Accompanying these standards are *Guidelines for Strengthening Indigenous Languages* that call upon educators to '[m]ake effective use of local expertise, especially Elders' in local language teaching, for schools to set aside 'special times and places where students can ... practice their language skills in [a heritage language] immersion environment,' and for education agencies to provide sufficient funding and administrative support for heritage language immersion in Alaska schools (AANE, 2001: 15–17).

According to Barnhardt and Kawagley (2005), these initiatives have strengthened the quality of education and improved the academic performance of the nearly 20,000 Alaska Native students in 176 participating schools. In all of these efforts, elders have been recognized as key repositories of cultural and linguistic knowledge and expertise. 'In the course of implementing [these] initiatives,' Barnhardt and Kawagley (2005: 15) write, 'we have come to recognize that there is much more to be gained from further mining of the fertile ground that exists within Indigenous knowledge systems.'

Heritage language immersion

Indigenous language immersion programs are arguably the most effective approaches to heritage language revitalization (see, for example, Hinton & Hale, 2001). Here, we briefly highlight three immersion programs of note.

The first of these is Hawaiian immersion, begun in the late 1970s. After years of language repression that left only a few hundred Native speakers, the State of Hawai'i designated Hawaiian and English as co-official languages in 1978. At the same time, a new state constitution mandated the promotion of Hawaiian language, culture, and history (Warner, 2001). Encouraged by these developments and the example of the *Te Kohanga Reo* or Māori pre-school immersion 'language nests' in New Zealand (Bishop, 2003), a small group of parents and language educators began the *'Aha Pūnana Leo* ('language nest gathering') preschool (see Warner, 2001; Wilson, 1998, 1999). The family-run preschools (there were 11 in 2005) are designed to strengthen the Hawaiian *mauli* – culture, worldview, spirituality, morality, and social relations – and enable children to interact with fluent speakers entirely in Hawaiian. Through parental activism, the preschools grew into a pre-K–12 system that includes full-day Hawaiian-medium strands within English-medium public schools as well as a pre-K–12 total immersion school. The results of Hawaiian immersion have been impressive. In addition to producing a new generation of Hawaiian speakers (1800 in 1999–2000, according to Warner, 1999, 2001), Hawaiian immersion students have demonstrated achievement gains that equal or surpass the performance of students in English-medium schools, even in English language arts (Kamanā & Wilson, 1996; Wilson & Kamanā, 2001).

On the Navajo Nation, Arizona's only Navajo full-immersion program operates at Tsé Ho Tso' Diné Bi'olta', a school in the Window Rock Unified School District near the Arizona-New Mexico border. Founded in 1986 as a Navajo-medium option within an English-medium public school, Tsé Ho Tso Diné Bi'olta' is now a kindergarten through grade 8 Navajo immersion school in its own right. In grades K–2, instruction is entirely in Navajo; English-medium instruction is introduced and gradually increased in grades 3 through 8. The school places a heavy emphasis on critical thinking and 'accountable language' – that is, developing *academic* proficiency in Navajo and the content areas. Students in this immersion program have historically outperformed comparable peers in monolingual English classrooms (see, for example, Arviso & Holm, 2001; Holm & Holm, 1995; McCarty, 2003). Moreover, the district is challenging Arizona's English-only law, claiming that 'maintaining the language is the crux of maintaining the culture, which is central to maintaining self-government and tribal sovereignty' (Horstman & Jackson-Dennison, 2005; Johnson & Wilson, 2005).

Our third example comes from the Pueblos of New Mexico. Altogether, there are 20 Pueblo tribes, including the Hopis of northern Arizona, with the remaining 19 situated along the Rio Grande and Rio Puerco in northern New Mexico. Since the 1990s, the Keres-speaking Pueblos of Cochiti (population 700) and Acoma (population 5000) have been actively involved in community-based language planning. Recent language surveys in both Pueblo communities revealed a marked decline in Native-speaking ability among the young, but a strong desire by adults and young people to revitalize the heritage language (Pecos & Blum-Martínez, 2001; Romero, 2001; Sims, 2001). In 1996, Cochiti Pueblo launched an immersion program and, in 1997, Acoma held its first summer immersion camp. The focus in both programs is on strengthening oral skills rather than literacy. Oral tradition 'has been an important element in maintaining [community] values [and tribal] leaders know that writing the language could bring about unwanted changes in secular and religious traditions,' Pecos and Blum-Martínez explain (2001: 76). Recently, Cochiti expanded its efforts to year-round instruction in the public elementary school, where students receive daily Keres instruction in grades 1 through 5.

Preliminary program data show that on national assessments of English language arts, students who participated in immersion classes performed significantly better than those in English-only classes (Sims, 2001). More important to community members are the facts that children have gained conversational ability in Keres and that there is growing evidence of Native language use community-wide. 'Across the community,' Pecos and Blum-Martínez (2001: 81) write of Cochiti '... one can see closer, more intimate relationships ... as fluent speakers take the time to share their knowledge.' In short, 'the children's success is the community's success, and many people are now aware of the need to speak Keres publicly and consistently' (Pecos & Blum-Martínez, 2001: 81).

Concluding Thoughts

In this chapter, we have attended to the voices of Native youth as they have reflected upon the role of the heritage language in their lives. The majority of the Navajo youth in our study indicated that they value the Native language, view it as central to their identities, want and expect parents to teach it to them, and employ it as a strategic tool in learning English at school. At the same time, both youth and adults are keenly aware of the legacy of oppression that has marginalized their language in their own community – creating conflicting language ideologies and choices –

and of the language- and culture-negating pressures inherent in current standardizing regimes.

Yet, as Jonathan, one youth in our study, told us, young people believe that 'there is always hope.' Youth have much to teach us about the politics of hope and caring in schooling (Valenzuela, 1999). Their testimony calls upon adults to care even more deeply – to exercise their authority to resist standardization and to nurture the community language within the community and its school. In our brief examination of Indigenous education counter-initatives, we have seen such visions of self-empowerment in practice. These bold education practices wedge open spaces of possibility, asserting local control and creating new arenas in which to cultivate Native America's multilingual 'language garden.' Viewed in this light, Indigenous education counter-initiatives not only re-imagine multilingual schools, they remind us that linguistic and educational self-determination is an inherent human right.

Acknowledgement

The Navajo summary at the end of the chapter was written by AnCita Benally. The O'odham summary was written by Ofelia Zepeda. We thank AnCita Benally for her contribution to this chapter.

Notes

1. We use the terms American Indian, Native, Native American, and Indigenous interchangeably to refer to peoples indigenous to what is now the United States and Canada. We recognize that the pre- and post-colonial experiences of Alaska Natives and Native Hawaiians differ substantially from those of tribes in the 48 contiguous states, just as great diversity exists among the more than 560 American Indian tribes. Nevertheless, all Native peoples in the US share a singular legal-political status in terms of their relationship to the US government and their inherent rights as Indigenous peoples (Lomawaima & McCarty, 2002). It is this distinctive relationship and these rights that are invoked by the use of these terms.
2. The concepts of linguicide and linguicism have been developed by Tove Skutnabb-Kangas. Referring to languages that have been exterminated, she points out that they have died '*not* because this has been a 'natural' development, but because they have been 'helped' on their way. They have not 'died' because of old age or lack of adaptability – they have been murdered' (Skutnabb-Kangas, 2000: 222). The analogous concept is physical genocide (for more on this as it relates specifically to Indigenous peoples and language rights, see Dunbar *et al.*, 2005; Magga *et al.*, 2004).
3. We are grateful to the US Department of Education Institute of Education Sciences for funding the Native Language Shift and Retention Project. All data, statements, opinions, and conclusions or implications in this chapter solely reflect the view of the authors and research participants, and do not necessarily reflect the views of the funding agency, the tribes or their tribal councils, the Arizona Board of Regents, or Arizona State University, under whose auspices the project operates. This information is presented in the pursuit of academic

research and is published in this volume solely for educational and research purposes. Per our agreement with the Arizona State University Internal Review Board, this chapter may not be reproduced in any medium, transmitted or distributed, in whole or in part, without the authors' prior written consent. Parts of this chapter are adapted from McCarty (2003) and McCarty *et al.* (2006).

4. This is not the place to provide a detailed historical background on the history of Native American schooling or of language policies for Indigenous people in the US. For that background, readers are referred to Lomawaima and McCarty (2002, 2006), McCarty (1993a, 1993b, 2004) and Reyhner and Eder (2004). See also Churchill (1994) for a broader treatment of cultural annihilation and genocide.
5. The terms 'language attitudes' and 'language ideologies' are often conflated. The difference, in our view, lies in the explicit acknowledgement of power relations within the latter term. Here, we take language ideology to mean not language per se, but 'the very notion of the person and social group' (Woolard, 1998: 3). Thus, language ideology connotes ideas and attitudes about language that are inescapably infused with relations of power.

Summary

This chapter examines the role of Native languages in the lives and aspirations of Native American youth. Drawing on a five-year, multi-method study of Native language shift and retention in four tribal communities, we analyze language ideologies that suggest the evolving contemporary causes of language shift among the young. Native youth narratives suggest three overarching themes that influence their language choices: concern about the future of their heritage language, the politics of shame and caring, and the constraints of larger standardizing regimes. We conclude by discussing examples of Indigenous counter-initiatives to the pressures that limit youths' language choices: Native charter schools, counter-standards for culturally-responsive schooling, and Native-language immersion programs. These education practices wedge open spaces of possibility, creating new arenas in which to re-imagine multilingual schools.

Tsiłkéí bizaad bił danilį́įgo yaanitsídaakees lą. K'ad ashdla naahai Ał'ąą Dine'é ashdlago' dah yineełgo bizaad diishjį́įdí bił adahoot'ehígíí naalkaahgo ahoolzhiizh. Áko tsiłkéí yaanídaat'į́įgo taa'go t'áá'yísíí anahoot'į' daaníí lá: (1) saad daats'í naasgóó t'áá bá'adahwiizt'i'doo daanii lá? (2) saad naakih nilį́įgo baanitsíhákees lá, bayahasin doo yit'į́į la; anda ilį́į dóó nizhónígo ba'ahayą́ągo choo'įgo baanitsíhákees lá; (3) áadoo anda beehaz'áanii t'oo'ahayoigo nida'níłtl'a lą-ólta'dę́ę' dóó hadahwiisdzoodę́ę' doo Washindoondę́ę'. Ákondi Áł'ąą Dine'é hajooba'adéínízin lá. T'aa'ísii yinidaaldzilgo t'óó'ahayói t'aa la'ada'ileeh lá. Daałahgo ólta' t'áá bí daayiilyeed la. Naanii t'áábí saad dóó iiná bił haz'ą́ągi beehaz'áanii adéíle' lá. Binahjį' Áł'ąą Dine'é bizaad naasgóó t'áá bá'adahwiizt'igo adahale' lá. Ánda binahjį' ólta' baahoozhoonii, t'aa'ałtsoh haishįį dine'é yigaałii yee'adeení't'ooldįįł doo lą. Bizaad dóó bee'iina' ílį́įgo ba baanítsíhąkees doogo adahale' lá. Naasgoo ał'ąą saad t'áá baa'adahwiizt'i'doo lá. (Navajo)

Id 'eḍa 'o'ohana 'o 'am 'eḍa 'o'ohanas hegai matt mai 'ab ha-amjeḍ g wecij hemajkam. Heg 'att mai mo has masma 'ab 'i-ñeid g e-duakag c e-ki:dag g wecij hemajkam. Hetasp 'ahidag 'ac 'an 'oyopo kc 'an ha'icu ha-kakk'e 'ab ha-amjeḍ c 'ab ha'icu ma:cim. Heg 'ac 'ab si 'i-ñeñeid mo hab cu'ig hemu mo we:s g wecij hemajkam pi ma:c g O'odham ñi'okĭ c hab cu'ig mo mu'i heg 'a'i s-ma:c milga:n ñi'okĭ c heg 'a'i ñeok. Id 'eḍa 'o'ohana 'att 'am 'o'oha 'i:da mo ḍ wecij hemajkam ha-je:ñigida. I:da ha-jeñigida 'at 'ab 'amjeḍ 'i-wu:ṣ g has ha-elida. I:da 'at hab 'i-wu:ṣ mo hascu 'am 'i-cegito 'idam wecij hemajkam 'ab 'amjed g 'e-ñi'okĭ, mat has o ma:skad o mat has o cu'igk g ha-ñi'okĭ 'im b ha'ap. Heg 'am 'ep 'i-wu:ṣ mo hab 'e-wua g wecij hemajkam mo heba'ic s-e-elid mat o ñeokad g 'e-ñi'okĭ, c hegai e:p mo hemu hab cu'ig mo g milga:n ha-kownalig pi ha-hiwigid, 'an ha-ṣo:bid g O'odham c na:nko ma:s O:bĭ hemajkam mat o ñeñokad g e-ñi'okĭ o mat o ha-maṣcamad g 'e-ñi'okĭ 'am maṣcamakud c-ed. We:s 'idam ha'icu 'at 'ab 'amjeḍ 'e-je:ñig 'idam wecij hemajkam. Ñia, 'att 'amjeḍ heg 'ab 'ep 'i-oi mo hemu hab hahawa hab 'e-wua g O'odham c O:bĭ hemajkam mo hejel 'am 'i-e-nakogk c 'am 'i-himcud g 'e-ñi'okĭ. Hemu 'o mu'i g na:nko ma:s O:bĭ hemajkam hejel 'am melcud g 'e-mamṣcamakuḍ c heg 'eḍa 'an behĕ g ṣel mat 'am o ha-maṣcamad g 'e-ñi'okĭ. Hemu 'o hab cu'ig mo we:s g O:bĭ c O'odham hemajkam hab 'e-elid mo g ha-ñi'okĭ wuḍ si ha'icu c hab 'e-lid mo wuḍ ha-ma:kig 'at heg hekaj has i-masma 'o 'i-e-nakogk c s-gewkam 'an 'o 'u'ad c o ñeokad g 'e-ñi'okĭ. (O'odham)

Chapter 5

Attitudes Towards Language Learning in Different Linguistic Models of The Basque Autonomous Community

FELI ETXEBERRÍA-SAGASTUME

Introduction

In the historical territories of the Basque Autonomous Community,[1] the different linguistic models operating in the educational system (A, B, D) and the varying number of Basque language speakers in the different areas, affects the rhythm of the normalization process of Euskara,[2] the Basque language. The value in learning Euskara is widely recognised in bilingual schooling, but there is an alarming relatively low social usage of the language learnt at school. The fact that language plays a part in the configuration of social identity and positive attitudes towards the process of recuperating Euskara has been shown to positively influence the learning of the language. Nonetheless, there are other factors that limit its use. The minority status of Euskara and the linguistic behaviour of students outside the classroom seem to suggest that the need to use the language, in the case of Euskara, is limited to the academic space. This situation brings forth certain questions – What do students in their last year of compulsory education think of their language acquisition during their school life? Has there been a change in their perceptions as to their attitudes and motivations about the language and their language learning experience? Do they display different degrees of motivation with regard to the learning of different languages? How do they think about norms of linguistic behaviours when in mixed language groups? Do students schooled in models more heavily weighted in Euskara display greater affinity with the language as an identity marker?

This chapter sets out to provide the answer to some of these questions by drawing from a wider research project undertaken to study the perception and self-evaluation of bilingual acquisition amongst students in the second cycle of secondary education which was coordinated by the author (Etxeberría *et al.*, 2002).[3]

The Sociolinguistic Context

The Basque Country includes the Spanish Basque and the French Basque regions, which for political-administrative reasons are divided into three territories: the Autonomous Community of the Basque Country, the Autonomous Community of Navarra, and the Northern Basque Country located in the State of France.[4] The Basque language, Euskara, is the common language of these three territories, and is considered an element of unification of the Basque culture, which at the present time exists alongside Spanish and French.

The Basque Country has 2.5 million inhabitants, of which 24.7% can freely use either of the two languages; 16.3% are passive bilinguals, and 0.6% are monolingual Basque speakers. In the Comunidad Autónoma Vasca (CAV, also called the Basque Autonomous Community), 58.4% of the population is monolingual in Spanish, whereas in the French Basque area, 64.2% of the population is French monolingual (Encuesta Sociolingüística, 1996). Although there is a positive progression towards bilingualism, monolingual speakers of Euskara are socially compelled to become bilingual, whilst the speakers of the majority language can remain monolingual.

In the last few decades, Spain has undergone far-reaching political, social and cultural changes. An important expression of social and cultural transformation is the process of linguistic normalization in the autonomous communities of Catalonia, Galicia, and the Basque Country. Spanish is the official language of the state (Spain) and the other languages – Catalan (*catalan*), Galician (*gallego*) and Basque (*euskara*) – are recognized as languages in their own right, and share official status with Spanish in their respective communities.

In the context of the Basque Autonomous Community (which is the specific Basque area that is the context for the study), the Law for the Normalization of Euskara (1982) together with the Decree of Bilingualism (1983) are fundamental for the development of the Basque language and culture. The linguistic policy of normalization adopted in the Basque Autonomous Community combines collective and individual linguistic rights through the joint official status of Euskara and Spanish. The policy of the CAV is distinct from the official status of Euskara in Navarra and the French Basque Country; the legal differences have posed difficulties in the process of revitalization and normalization of Euskara in these other areas (Azurmendi, *et al.*, 2001; Cenoz, 2001).

The Educational Context

As mentioned previously, the Decree of Bilingualism (1983) regulates the development of Bilingual Educational Programs in both official languages,

Spanish and Euskara, and the integration of foreign language learning into the school curricula. There are three models:

- *Model A:* instruction is carried out in Spanish. Euskara has the status of a language subject taught for a stipulated number of hours.
- *Model B:* schooling is carried out in two languages (Euskara/Spanish), and both languages are also taught as specific subjects.
- *Model D:* schooling is carried out in Euskara and Spanish is taught as a specific subject.

By way of illustration, Table 5.1 provides the statistics for the number of three-year olds enrolled in the different linguistic models in the Basque Autonomous Community in the school year 2003–2004.

Model A accounts for only 8.10% of pupils, model B for 30.5% and model D for 61.4%. Although in the 1980s student enrolment in Model A outnumbered that for Models B and D put together, Model A is now in decline. The new generation of parents gives greater value to Euskara, as shown by their choice of linguistic model.

The Basque educational system is also evolving from bilingualism to plurilingualism – the study of more than the traditional two languages of the region; that is, the study of many languages. The imagining of a multilingual society in the Basque Autonomous Community is already in the present, as there are policies and laws in place that promote it. The new Europe needs to find solutions that allow making its own differences to be a source of mutual enrichment. From this perspective one can affirm that monolingualism is finding fewer reasons for being. Thus, the education system attempts, on the one hand, to foster the development of Euskara in its own territory alongside the Spanish or French language and, on the other hand, to foster the development of additional languages. It is the aim of the Basque educational system that, by the end of secondary school or age 16, all pupils should have sufficient bilingual competence in the two official languages to be able to use them both in practical everyday life and to continue their studies. In addition, they are expected to have some level

Table 5.1 Registration of 3 year olds in different linguistic models, 2003–2004

Model	*Medium of instruction*	*%*
A	Spanish (with Euskara as a specific subject)	*8.1*
B	Euskara and Spanish (both also taught as specific subjects)	*30.5*
D	Euskara (with Spanish as a specific subject)	*61.4*

Source: EUSTAT (2004)

of competency in at least one foreign language. In this spirit, since the nineties, schools have been running pilot programs for the introduction of English at an early age.

Language learning attitudes and motivations in bilingual contexts

According to Fishman (1972), Lambert (1980), Gardner (1985) and Siguan (2001), the prestige and use of languages can be associated with the motivations for learning. It has also been found that the sociocultural context is a fundamental aspect of bilingual acquisition (García & Baker, 1995; Hamers & Blanc, 2000). In the Basque context, both aspects have been studied in relation to the importance of attitudes for the promotion of Euskara (Arratibel, 1999; Arzamendi & Genesee, 1997; Espi, 1988).

What are the effects of the contexts of greater integration of the medium as the language of instruction for the acquisition of a second language? In the context of the Basque Country, Euskara has a social base, as it is the language of Basque society. Research has shown that attitudes of parents in relation to their children's learning of Euskara are positive (Torres-Guzmán & Etxeberría, 2005). We consider this an important factor for the motivation of pupils learning Euskara as a second language, since they tend to more positively value the language learnt. Pupils who learn in social contexts with greater opportunities for social interaction are more apt to acquire linguistic competence. Many studies indicate that linguistic skills are reinforced significantly by using the language both in academic contexts and outside the school (Arzamendi & Genesee, 1997; Etxeberría *et al.*, 2002; Hamers, 1992; Lasagabaster, 2001; Siguan & Mackey, 1986).

Scholars studying motivation in second language acquisition also establish two types of attitudes related to individual differences. On one hand, the perception of usefulness can strengthen the knowledge and use of a certain language. This is called *instrumental* motivation. On the other, the desire for integration in the language-speaking group is called *integrative* motivation. In the Basque case, the question arises as to whether these motivations differ according to the model of schooling attended by the students, whether there is any variation in relation to the languages learnt, and how this shows up in the speakers' understanding of norms for behaviour.

When two languages coexist in society, one of the languages has a greater functionality than the other. For the pupil arriving at school speaking the stronger language, the learning of a second language – the weaker of the two – presents no threat and the attitude of the pupil to languages can be positive. Lambert (1974) distinguishes between additive and subtractive bilingualism to explain the differences between school children in relation to their first language. Fishman (1991) expresses his skepticism as to whether bilingual schooling on its own can reverse the process whereby one language is substituted by another, since a minority language requires a solid social base in order to trigger its transmission. At the same time, language is a relevant component of group identification that gives us reason to believe that language behaviour can vary according to the role it plays in different contexts: education, work, friendship, family, leisure, etc. Moreover, according to Krashen (1985), favorable attitudes, positive motivation and low anxiety levels are important for second language acquisition.

Our premise is that the values attributed to languages have a contextual base in the sociocultural order, and that the motivation for language learning is associated to attitude. In this chapter, we will address the reasons given for learning the different languages in order to assess the motivations that guide learning and linguistic behavior, thereby, understanding the attitudes.

The Study

This study of motivations and attitudes with regard to language learning uses a qualitative recursive analysis of the written responses within the questionnaire of a wider research project. This study is fundamentally descriptive and partially associative. The 'dependent variable' is the subjects' perceptions and evaluation of the process of acquiring the different languages studied up to the end of their compulsory education. The associative variables are the linguistic models.

A random sample of 441 pupils (average age 16) in the fourth or final year of compulsory secondary education in the area of Donostia-San Sebastián[5] was selected. This year was chosen because it was the last year of compulsory schooling and, therefore, made it possible to obtain an overview of the perceptions of the first cohort of young people who had such schooling throughout their school life, as these pupils had experienced the first implementation of the Law of Normalization of Euskara in 1983.

In the selection of research subjects, two statistical criteria for a stratified random sample were applied in relation to two variables: *linguistic model* and *type of school*. A representative number of schools of each type was selected and in each centre, if there was more than one linguistic model, a representative number of pupils were selected per linguistic model. Altogether there were 19 schools – 6 Model A, 4 Model B, and 9 Model D – that were representative of the different types of schools:

(1) state schools;
(2) government-funded *ikastolas* (schools where the language of instruction is Euskara;
(3) government-funded religious schools;
(4) schools emphasizing education in a foreign language: English, German or other.

Table 5.2 Linguistic model frequency of the study sample

Models	*Frequency*	%
A	100	22.7
B	223	50.6
D	118	26.8
Total	441	100.0

The language distribution of the study sample is shown in Table 5.2. Students were asked to respond to three open-ended questions:

(1) What are the perceived changes in motivation, attitude or the process of language learning, as well as in knowledge?
(2) What ought to happen in a situation in which a group of friends are speaking to each other in Euskara and another friend comes into the group speaking Spanish? That is, what are the perceived norms associated with linguistic behaviour in groups?
(3) Would you recommend learning Euskara to other students?

Altogether there were 821 written responses to these questions. Each response was coded by model, by language of the response, and by categories that were established in the initial analysis of the data. *NVivo* analytical software was used to facilitate the analysis. In addition, the nature of the arguments about attitudes, motivations, and future learning of Euskara, that is, the reasons for learning Euskara and/or Spanish on the one hand, and a foreign language on the other, were also analyzed.

Data Analysis

Language choice

Our first analysis focused on language choice, as students could choose to respond in any one of the three languages that the instrument was available to them in – Euskara, Spanish, or English. No student chose English. In general, 51% (423) of the students responded in Euskara, and 49% (398) of them responded in Spanish. This apparent linguistic balance dissipates when their linguistic choice is analyzed by model.

In Model A, 99% (143/144) of the responses were written in Spanish whereas in Model D, 99% (346/350) of the responses were in Euskara. In Model B, however, 23% of the responses were in Euskara whereas 77% were in Spanish. There is a polarization in language choice and use, particularly in Models A and D. Figure 5.1 is is a graphic representation of this polarization.

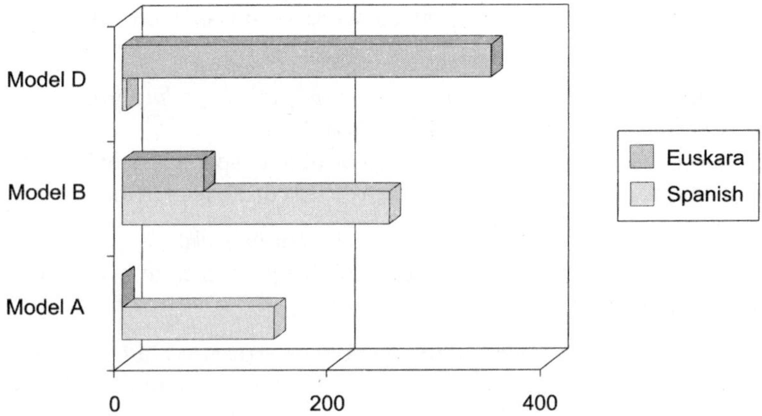

Figure 5.1 Language choice of responses by linguistic model

What this data on language choice suggests is that the school's linguistic cntext is related to the language choice of students' response.

Changes in language attitudes, motivation, and knowledge

One of the questions was related to the perceived changes in language motivation and attitudes toward language learning, as well as knowledge of the language throughout their schooling. More students (169) referred to changes in their motivations toward learning the language, rather than to knowledge of the language itself (63). With respect to motivation, most of the students' comments (85%) indicated that they had experienced positive changes in their dispositions towards the languages learnt, and 87% experienced positive motivational changes while learning the languages. Here is an example of one student's expression of these positive changes.

> *Geroz eta gehiago ikasi ... gehiago ikasten duzu eta gaia errazagoa egiten zaizu. Gustokoa egiten zaizu hizkuntza bat ikastea. Gogo handiagoarekin hartzen duzu.*
> (The more you study ... the more you learn and the subject becomes easier. You experience learning a language as pleasurable. You embrace it with more willingness.)

Language learning is, thus, viewed favorably by these language learners, although there are some differences related to the specific language they are responding about. For example, many respondents speak about experiencing a greater change with regard to English – 51 students made reference to motivational changes towards the English language and 89% of the responses were positive. Here are two such responses:

> *Beste herrialde batzuetara joaten naizenean, ingelesez hitzegin dezaket, eta beste herrialdetako jendearekin hitzegiteko balioko dit.*
> (When I go to other countries, I will be able to speak English, and it will be useful to speak with people from other countries.) (Model B student)

> *Ingelesa hobeto ikasteko jarrera dut interneten ibiltzeko.*
> (I have improved my attitude towards English due to my experiences with the Internet.) (Model D student)

In relation to Spanish, 89% of the responses expressed favorable motivations toward learning it, and Euskara was the language that received most comments, but the fewest students (69%) expressed favorable motivational changes towards Euskara.

To explore how these responses to changes in attitude and motivation were associated with the school's linguistic context, the responses on attitude and motivational changes were analyzed by linguistic model.

There were 11 responses from Model A that addressed the students' views about English. In this model, 91% of the students responded that learning English became more and more positive, and they expressed a very practical rationale. As the following two students state:

> *Sí, que el inglés me interesa cada vez más para tener trabajo.*
> (Yes, I am more and more interested in English as I see it will be good for employment.)

> *Antes no ponía mucho interés en el estudio de lenguas pero desde hace dos años me he dado cuenta que el inglés abre puertas de cara a futuro.*
> (I was not that interested in language learning before but in the last two years I have realized that English opens doors, and a future.)

In Model A, all references to Spanish (10) were positive; for the most part, Spanish is the native language of the enrolled students. With respect to Euskara, there were 11 responses, and of these, only 9% of the students speak about their motivational changes as positive. One of the students' comments embodies the general instrumental attitudes toward language learning of the students enrolled in Model A. The student writes:

> *El alemán y el inglés no me importa estudiarlos porque me parecen útiles para el futuro pero el euskera me parece un idioma inútil.*
> (I do not mind learning German and English because they are useful for my future, but Euskara does not seem very useful.)

The students' motivation for learning English is no different in Models B and D. Some 91% of the students' responses in Model B and 92% in Model D indicate that there is a positive attitude toward learning English, and that changes in motivation have been increasingly favorable towards learning languages. The following are comments from students about languages, including English, in these two models:

> *Antes no pensaba en los idiomas pero ahora me gustan, aprendo euskera porque es importante para vivir aquí y el inglés me está interesando mucho.*
> (Before I did not think much about languages, but now I like them. I learn Euskara because it is important to live here and English in becoming more interesting.) (Model B student)

> *Nire motibazioa, gehienbat euskara eta ingelesarekiko aldatu da, orain gehiago baloratu eta aondorioz interes handiagoz jardun ohi naiz.*
> (My motivation has changed mostly towards Euskara and English; now I value them more and, as a consequence, I pay more attention and interest in learning them.) (Model D student)

In all the linguistic models of schooling, students seem to have a positive disposition toward learning English.

Students in Models B and D, however, are more positively disposed to learning Euskara than those in Model A: 75% of the students' responses in Model B and 89% of those in Model D were about the positive attitudes and motivations toward the learning of Euskara that they had experienced throughout their schooling. One student captured this sentiment in the following comment:

> *Si, me he dado cuenta de que el euskera va a servir para muchas cosas en mi vida y creo que estos años estoy teniendo más interés en aprenderlo.*
> (Yes, I have come to understand that Euskara will be useful in many aspects of my life and over the years I have experienced greater interest in learning it.)

Only a small number of students in Models A (18%) and B (15%) reported that there was no change in their attitudes and/or motivation to language learning throughout their schooling. But as many as 53% of the students in Model D indicated there had been no change. Model D students experienced learning Euskara naturally, either as their first language or in a total-immersion situation. So they do not experience a change in attitude or motivation, as they see the learning of Euskara as natural, as part of their group identity, and as needed for the purposes of revitalization of the language.

Yet, students in Model B and D differ with regard to Spanish. In Model B, 93% of the responses indicated a positive change in attitude toward Spanish, whereas only 73% of responses in Model D showed this.

Students seem to echo the societal belief that English is of greater value because of its world spread and its centrality in the markets, in communication, and in the political life of the country within the larger European sphere, whereas Euskara has limited value beyond the Basque Country. The results also show that students enrolled in the linguistic models that provide greater integration of Euskara in their curricular offerings (Models B and D) express greater motivation for learning Euskara, which suggests that schools can influence personally-held beliefs about languages. Students in Model A do not make significant reference to the learning of Spanish because it is their native and dominant social language and, as such, is not usually socially marked. This is a very different situation from the contentious coexistence of both Spanish and Euskara in the linguistic models B and D within the same community. In the latter models, the learners may perceive a responsibility – be it differentiated or not – towards the learning of both languages. In general, there are differences in patterns of language attitudes and motivations in relation to the different linguistic models.

Language accommodation

The analysis of the student responses on their feelings about what their linguistic behavior might be when a non-Euskara speaker enters a circle of Euskara speakers serves to explore the rationale for the students' perceived governing norms of language accommodation. We caution the reader that we are not reporting actual behavior per se, but the respondents' perception of the norms governing what they claim their behavior might be.

Taken as a whole group, 72% of the responses of students in all Models were in favor of adapting their language behavior to accommodate Spanish speakers. The following are illustrations of accommodation and non-accommodation responses.

Accommodation

> *Bien, porque si el otro no sabe euskera, no va a entender nada.*
> (Fine because if the other one does not know Euskara, s/he will not understand anything.)

Non-accommodation

> *Me parece mal. No se debería imponer ningún idioma a los que están hablando en euskera.*
> (It doesn't seem right. No language should be imposed on Euskara-speakers.')

The students' construction of their responses to accommodate or not were further categorized into three subgroups:

(1) those who had a discourse of tolerance: 48% of responses;
(2) those who had a discourse of loyalty: 41% of responses;
(3) those with a discourse of indifference: 11% of responses.

Below are examples of responses in each of these subcategories:

Tolerance

> *Bien, porque si la persona que llega no sabe euskera, me parece bien que los demás cambien de lengua para poder comunicarse con él.*
> (It seems appropriate to me that if the person who arrives is not Euskara-speaking that the others change the language so that they communicate with the person.)

Loyalty

> *Gaizki, besteak euskeraz hitzegiten ari badira ez du zertan aldatu beharrik.*
> (It's wrong. If the others are speaking Euskara why should they change to Spanish?)

Indifference

> *Si, no me importa en absoluto.*
> (Yes, I do not mind at all.)

When we look at the issue of accommodation/non-accommodation in relation to linguistic model, there is a strong relationship between linguistic model and tendency to accommodate or not, as shown in Figure 5.2.

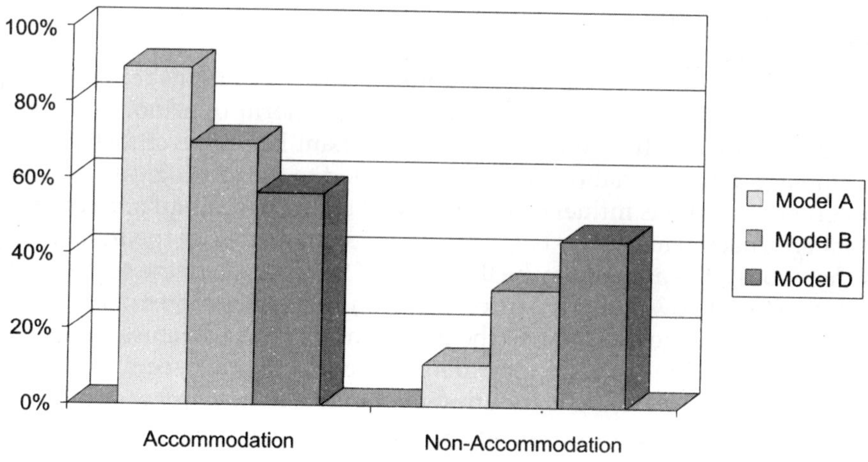

Figure 5.2 Perceptions of norms governing accommodation/non-accommodation behaviors by linguistic model

In Model A, 89% of the responses advocated for linguistic accommodation, whereas only 11% felt that accommodation was not necessary. In Model B, 69% of the responses expressed a need to accommodate, versus 31% for non-accommodation. Finally, in Model D, the difference between the two discrete responses (accommodation/non-accommodation) decreased; 56% wrote about the need to accommodate and 44% felt that accommodation ought not to be the norm for linguistic behavior when a non-Euskara speaker arrived in a Euskara-speaking social group. The differences among the responses of students in the different models may be the result of personal linguistic competency, as this is usually correlated to the linguistic model as well. The data may also be suggesting that the respondents from the model that most strongly promotes the use of Euskara (Model D) have the greatest difficulty in establishing the norms of behavior, as they face a greater tension between the feelings of tolerance towards bilingualism and accommodation of others and their feelings of loyalty toward the minority language.

A different pattern of the underlying beliefs of the norms governing the linguistic behaviors of accommodation emerged when the data were analyzed by linguistic model. As shown in Figure 5.3, the discourse embedded in the responses within Model A were of tolerance to the 'other' speaker (68% of the responses), 14% centered on an argument of loyalty, and 12% expressed indifference. While there is also a strong sense of tolerance in the discourse of students in Model B, their sense of loyalty towards Euskara is significantly higher than that of students in Model A. Students in Model D, however, showed a much stronger sense of loyalty to Euskara, with a significantly lower percentage of responses expressing tolerance.

The results suggest that, while there is a general tendency to feel that the norms governing mixed linguistic groups ought to be linguistic accommodation toward the dominant language, such a norm does not apply for those groups in which Euskara is the dominant language of instruction. Language accommodation is generally related to the ideological stance of tolerance when it is influenced by personal use and/or linguistic contexts that are enactments of the language policies embedded in the models. In other words, the norms may be the result of the position of the speakers in relation to their own language proficiency and/or to the degree of use of the minority language, Euskara, or the dominant language, Spanish, as media of instruction. The results of the different linguistic models seem to suggest that the role of schooling is the stronger variable as many of the students, whether in Model A or D, are speakers of Spanish as their first language. Thus, the proportion of responses in favor of accommodation or non-accommodation is associated with the degree of more or less integration of the minority language in the school curriculum. The norm of accommodation seems to be strongly correlated to the discourse of tolerance, whereas

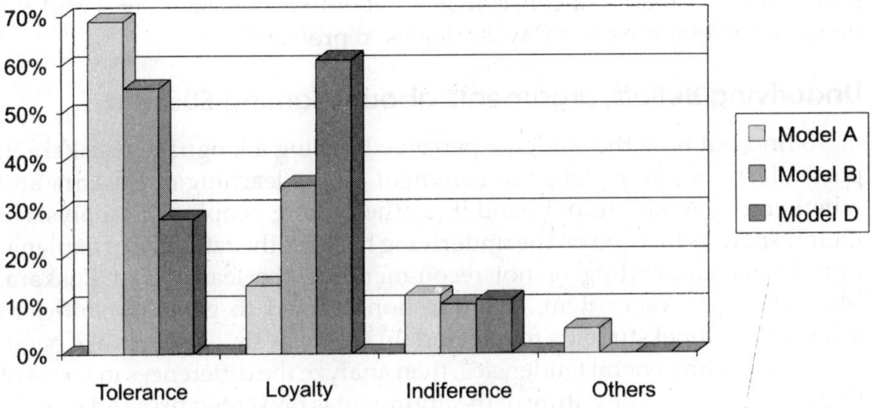

Figure 5.3 Responses indicating motivation changes toward language learning

the discourse of loyalty is most frequently associated with the norm of non-accommodation.

There are various possible explanations. As stated above, for the bilingual student in a strong minority-language environment, the tug between tolerance of the dominant language and the loyalty to the minority language is a strong one. Another possible explanation is that bilingualism, from the minority standpoint, calls on its speaker to develop greater consciousness and strategies of loyalty towards the weaker language. By contrast, those who are less likely to be in an environment that promotes strong forms of bilingualism do not feel the need to take a stance for the minority language and expect the language of communication to be that which is dominant already in most social groups. Another way of stating this is that accommodation is the burden of the bilingual speaker.

Certainly, in Euskara-speaking social groups it is difficult to sustain the use of Euskara because many of the Euskara speakers do not have the skills in the language that are necessary for more sophisticated conversations, making the switch to Spanish more likely when a Spanish-speaker comes into the group. Many Euskara-speakers are dominant in Spanish because it is their first language and many of the native speakers of Euskara have traditionally been bilingual and have spoken Spanish primarily in business transactions. Our findings suggest that the knowledge of a language in society facilitates communication when there is respect for linguistic diversity and when there is a strong linguistic consciousness of languages in contact, and that this is likely to occur when the minority language is strongly integrated in school settings. Schools, in other words, can play a strong role in creating a consciousness about weaker languages and the need for developing everyday strategies to protect them.

Underlying Beliefs/arguments about Learning Euskara

To find out how the students perceive learning a language (Euskara in particular), they were asked to comment on the learning of Euskara and whether they would recommend it to other young people. The analysis of their responses focused on the underlying beliefs – the rationale or explanation for recommending or not recommending the learning of Euskara. More than any other item, this question seemed to generate sufficient interest to compel students to respond. In the analysis, as before, we begin by dealing with general tendencies, then analyze the differences in terms of linguistic models. The nature of the argument is presented first and then an analysis of detailed responses including specific arguments within the categories. A response could be coded more than once if there were more than one category embedded in the argument. Thus the number of times each comment was counted, 926, was more than the number of students' responses (841).

There were seven distinct arguments for learning Euskara constructed in students' responses:

(1) *social arguments*, related to personally lived experiences or related to the social context and its relationship to emotions, uses, and spaces of use;
(2) *practical arguments*, referring to functional communication and its utility in gaining employment;
(3) *pedagogical arguments*, referring to the learning process, cognitive process, or methodological aspects;
(4) *linguistic arguments*, related to the structural aspects of the language or to its aesthetic aspects;
(5) *political arguments*, referring to conflictive power relationships between the languages or to the richness of linguistic diversity and democracy, the process of revitalization and language loss, and the language rights of linguistic groups;
(6) *cultural arguments*, including issues of group and individual identity, as an ethnic, community, or social marker, or as part of the heritage of a people;
(7) *other arguments*, such as personal enrichment.

The arguments for learning Euskara underlying the students' responses in general were, from most to least – social (27%), practical (19%), pedagogical (18%), linguistic (15%), political (12%), cultural (5%), and other (4%).

Social argument

The social argument for learning Euskara had four distinct categories:

(1) emotional;
(2) use;
(3) local;
(4) conflictive.

Below, we provide examples of how students incorporated these four categories in their social arguments for learning Euskara. In each case, we indicate the educational model that the student was following.

Emotional

Sí. Yo creo que es un idioma bonito; y más si vives en Euskal Herria que es necesario.
(Yes. I believe that the language is beautiful and necessary if you live in the Basque Country.) (Model D student)

Use

El aprender euskara te ayuda a entender a la gente que de otra forma no llegarías a conocerla. Y habiendo más gente que aprenda el euskara se irá oyendo más euskara en la calle.
(Learning Euskara helps you to understand people that otherwise you would not have understood. And the more people who learn it, the more often we will hear it spoken on the streets everywhere.) (Model D student)

Gracias a que estoy aprendiendo euskara tengo más amigos. Tengo hasta novia.
(Learning Euskara has meant having more friends. I even have a girl friend.) (Model D student)

Local

Creo que es importante aprender euskàra para la vida laboral y desenvolverte socialmente aquí, en el País Vasco.
(I believe it is important for your work and social life here in the Basque Country.) (Model B student)

Es importante hablar en euskara en Euskadi y para trabajar aquí será importante.
(It is important to speak Euskara in the Basque Country and it is also important for work here.) (Model B student)

Conflictive

Sí, hay que aprender porque es necesario. Lo que no me parece normal y para

nada aceptable, es que estemos obligados a darlo en la escuela. No es justo, lo único que consiguen es incrementar el odio hacia dicha lengua.
(Yes, you need to learn because it is necessary. What is not normal in my mind and not acceptable at all is that we have to learn it in school. It is not fair, the only thing they are accomplishing is that one hates the so called language.) (Model A student)

Sí, hay que aprender porque desgraciadamente es una lengua impuesta y a la vez excluyente para los que no saben.
(Yes, one has to learn it because unfortunately it is an imposed language and at the same time excluding for those people who do not know it.) (Model A student)

Hemen bizi badira beharrezkoa ikusten dudalako euskara jakitea. Ezin dira honera etorri berahien hizkuntza inposatzera.
(If they live here, I think it is necessary for them to know Euskara, otherwise they would be imposing their language.)(Model A student)

Cultural argument

The cultural argument had three distinct aspects:

(1) language as enrichment;
(2) language as identity;
(3) language as nationhood.

These aspects are illustrated in the following examples:

Language as enrichment

Euskara hizkuntza aberatsa eta interesgarria dela iruditzen zait. (Euskara is an interesting and enriching language.) (Model D student)

Sí, porque por saber no pasa nada. Cuanto más sepas mejor.
(Yes, because there is no wrong in knowing it; the more you know the better' (Model A student)

Siempre es válido aprender lenguas y más si es la lengua de tu pueblo.
(It is always valuable to learn languages and more so if it is the language of your people.) (Model B student)

Pienso que es enriquecedor aprender euskara, personalmente me parece un idioma rico con características propias y por otro lado es imprescindible para mantener la cultura del Pueblo Vasco.
(I think it is enriching to know Euskara, personally I feel it is a rich language with its own characteristics and, on the other hand, it is essential to the process of Basque cultural maintenance.) (Model D student)

Language as identity

Euskera ondo hitzegiteak euskalduna sentitzera eraman nau. Aldiz gaztelania hitzegiteak espainarra sentzitzera ez nau eraman. Euskara hitzegiten badut euskalduna sentitzen naiz eta hori oso gustokoa da niretzat. Gure hizkuntza delako.
(To speak Euskara well has made me feel Basque. And, yet, to speak Spanish has never really made me feel Spanish. If I speak Euskera, I feel Basque and I like that because it is our language.) (Model D student)

Porque es una cosa que nos diferencia de los españoles.
(Because this differentiates us from the Spaniards.) (Model D student)

Language as nationhood

Bai, euskara gure herriko hizkuntza delako eta horri garrantzia eman behar zaio.
(Because Euskara is the language of our land and one ought to give that fact importance.) (Model A student)

Pedagogical argument

There were two aspects to the pedagogical argument:

(1) language competency;
(2) methodological aspects of acquisition – the teacher, the materials, the strategies, and so forth.

Here are some examples of students' pedagogical arguments.

Language competency

Bai, hizkuntza gehiago dakizkidala, eta gehiago ulertzen dudala.
(Yes, I know more languages and I understand better.) (Model B student)

Bai, errazago menperatzen dira hizkuntzak eta trebetasun gehiago ematen dizu ikasi eta lan egiteko orduan.
(Yes, you can deal better with the languages and it gives you more freedom when you need to express yourself and when looking for a job.) (Model D student)

El aprender idiomas me ha supuesto aumentar la capacidad para entender muchas cosas y a mucha gente.
(The learning of languages has broadened my capacity to understand many things and many peoples.) (Model B student)

Al ver que domino más el euskera me siento más motivado para el aprendizaje de este idioma y de otros.

(When I see that I am proficient in Euskara, I feel more motivated towards learning this and other languages.) (Model B student)

Nire ustez hizkuntzak ez dira ikasi behar liburu aurrean jarrita, hitzegiten eta praktikatzen baizik.
(In my opinion, a language ought not to be learned out of a book, but by speaking and practicing it.) (Model B student)

Methodological aspects

Me he dado cuenta de que para aprender euskara además de seguir el libro es importante intentar hablar con la gente.
(I have realized that to learn Euskara it is not only important to follow the book; it is important to speak it with people.) (Model B student)

Si soy sincero atendiendo en clase he mejorado en euskara y tengo mejor nota. Y ahora que voy mejor, me gusta más.
(If I pay attention in class, I improve my knowledge of Euskara and have better grades. Now that I am doing better, I like it more.) (Model B student)

Sí, en que sé cómo estudiar una lengua, es decir, que primero hay que saber vocabulario y gramática y luego estudiar el idioma en profundización.
(Yes, in that I know how to learn a language, in other words, first one has to know vocabulary and grammar and then one has to deepen this knowledge.)(Model A student)

Cada vez tengo más interés en aprender las lenguas cuando experimento la fabulosa sensación de poder comunicarme con la gente.
(As time passes I am more interested in learning languages, especially when I experience the fabulous sensation of being able to communicate with people.) (Model B student)

Political arguments

The arguments that were political in nature were subdivided into:

(1) language rights;
(2) language as integrator or differentiator;
(3) inequality of languages;
(4) revitalization of the language.

The following are illustrations of the elaboration of these arguments:

Language rights

Bakoitzak nahi duen hizkuntzatan hitz egin behar du. Bakoitzak nahi duen hizkuntza erabili behar duelako eta ez besteek erabiltzen dutena bakarrik.
(Yes, because each one of us needs to be able to use the language one is

emotionally attached to and not just the language of others.) (Model D student)

Si vivimos en el País Vasco se supone que tenemos que hablar en euskara ya que somos euskaldunes.[6]
(If we live in the Basque County, it is obvious that we should speak Euskara, as we are from the land of speakers of Euskara.) (Model D student)

Language as integrator or differentiator

Porque es una cosa que nos diferencia de los españoles.
(Because this differentiates us from the Spaniards.) (Model D student)

Me parece interesante aprender euskera porque es la lengua del País Vasco por lo tanto es especial, porque sólo lo hablamos nosotros.
(I think it is interesting to learn Euskara because it is the language of the Basque Country, thus, a special thing because we are the only ones that speak it.) (Model D student)

Me parece importante saber y hablar el euskera por ser la lengua de donde uno vive.
(I think it is important to know and speak Euskara because it is the language of the land we live in.) (Model D student)

Inequality of languages

Gaizki iruditzen zait. Ez baita berdina gertatzen gazteleraz hitz egiten ari den talde batean norbait etorri eta euskaraz hitz egiten hasten denean.
(I feel bad that it happens. Because it does not happen in the same way when one is speaking in a Spanish-speaking group.) (Model D student)

Hay más gente que sabe bien el español y menos que se defienda en euskara aun viviendo en el País Vasco.
(There are more people that know Spanish and fewer that know Euskara even though they live in the Basque Country.) (Model A student)

El vasco ahora no está prohibido ¿por qué hablamos más en español? Se debe impulsar el euskara.
(Euskara is no longer forbidden, why do we speak more in Spanish? We should be pushing for Euskara.) (Model D student)

El euskara no me parece un idioma importante para aprenderlo creo que hay otros más importantes que el euskara como español, inglés, frances.
(Euskara is not an important language to learn. I think there are more important languages such as Spanish, English or French.) (Model B student)

Erdera entzunagoa da.
(Spanish is heard more.) (Model D student)

Me da pena porque de alguna manera se aprecia que el castellano tiene más fuerza y a mi me gustaría extender primero la utilización del euskera empezando por mi propio entorno.
(It makes me sad that in whatever way Spanish has more power. I would first like to see the use of Euskara spread, starting from my own surroundings.) (Model D student)

Nos cuesta mucho hablar en euskera porque se habla mucho más en castellano.
(It is hard for me to speak in Euskara because I hear Spanish spoken more often.) (Model D student)

Revitalization of the language

Uste dut euskara ikasi egin behar dela, bestela galduko da eta gu gara bultzatu behar dugunak euskara.
(I believe that we have to study Euskara or else it will die, and we are the ones that need to support the survival of the language.) (Model D student)

Hizkuntza bat ez da galtzen dakitenek hitzegiten badute.
(A language isn't lost, if those who know it, speak it.) (Model D student)

Underlying Beliefs/arguments about Learning Euskara and Linguistic Models

While in all the models the social argument is a strong one, particularly those elaborated around the emotional and use of the language, when the arguments are analyzed by linguistic models (Figure 5.4) we can see some different patterns in the arguments that students construct.

In Model A, the social argument is the most prevalent (33%), closely followed by the practical argument (27%). The pedagogical arguments follows the social and practical arguments in terms of frequency in which they are found in the responses of students within Model A, while the cultural, linguistic and political responses are few.

As in Model A, Model B student responses are more about social aspects of language learning (29%), followed by the practical argument (21%). But 20% of student responses in Model B are pedagogical arguments and 15% are political, compared with only 13% and 7% in Model A, respectively.

The predominant arguments given by students in Model D differ dramatically from those given by students in Models A and B. The cultural argument (specifically the role of language and identity, and language as nationhood) is the one found most frequently in student responses (26%), followed by arguments of a political nature (24%), and of a social nature

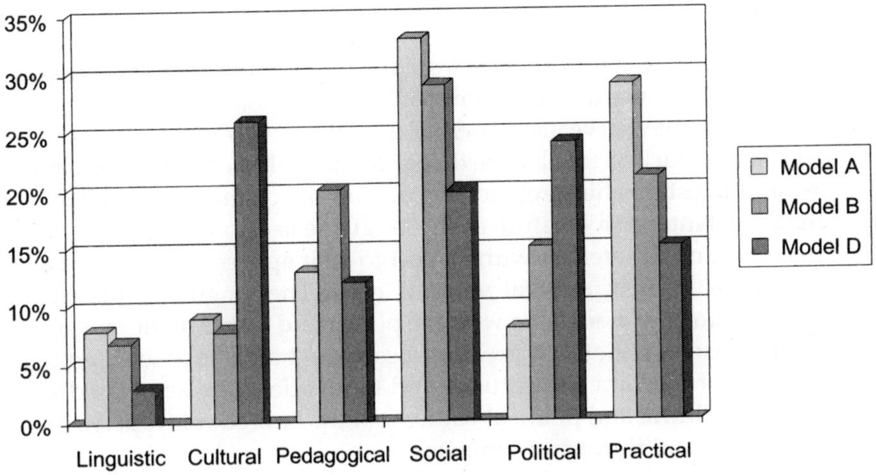

Figure 5.4 Types of arguments underlying students' views about learning Euskara by linguistic model

(20%). Practical (15%) and pedagogical (12%) arguments in the rationale for language learning were less frequently used. The different pattern of discourse in the rationale for learning Euskara in Model D may be associated with a higher degree of consciousness about the social status of the languages in the broader society. Model D seems to elicit the socio-cultural and political dimensions of the arguments more than any other model. Students' responses in Model D were more associated with the image of language as belonging to a collective, as signifying nationhood, and as related to the personal and cultural richness of identity of a group. The social-emotional and communicative aspects of the language were tied to the development of a linguistic consciousness and the responsibility of ownership of the revitalization process for the survival of Euskera.

Model B, on the other hand, is characterized by an argument in favor of learning the local language, where the importance of linguistic knowledge and the social-emotional dimensions are primary. It focuses on the need for social use and contextualization in the development of any language; it promotes bilingualism as enrichment, and multilingualism as desirable.

In Model A, in the construction of student responses reference is made to the social, pedagogical, and practical reasons as well as to the methodological and language competency aspects of learning the language. In the political sphere, what is most prevalent in the argument that languages are in conflict because of the different statuses that society accords them.

Reflections

The analysis in this study generates a portrait of students who have positive dispositions towards the learning of languages. Languages are viewed as valuable, for they serve instrumental as well as integrative motivations – there is value attached to jobs, participation in the life of the region, in the future, and in establishing relationships. And the cognitive as well as the psychological interactive nature of the language is also recognized.

There were no differences with respect to their appreciation of the value of English, as its instrumental value is clear. The languages that show greater variation are associated with the power and status of the languages within the Basque society. Of greatest dissent is the value associated with the learning of Euskara, as attitudes and motivations are associated with lower socio-cultural and political values and the limited role it plays in the wider Spanish and European contexts.

The results, however, show that schools can play a significant role in shaping the linguistic attitudes and motivations of students, particularly toward the least used and most threatened language – Euskara. The differences in language attitudes are associated with the students' lived linguistic experiences within the distinct linguistic models. Whereas for students in Model D (and less so for those in Model B), Euskara has a strong symbolic value related to cultural group identity, for those in Model A Euskara has an instrumental value anchored in its local use.

It would then be worth asking ourselves, as we imagine a future multilingual society – what values do we want our students to develop about language learning in general, and about threatened languages and languages of least use, such as Euskara? How do we ensure that becoming multilingual in the future is not devoid of cultural and affective values associated with the languages we most identify with and call our own? And it would also be important to then ask – what multilingual school models would ensure that future citizens are multilingual? Multilingual, of course, not only in global languages of high prestige such as English, but also in local languages with deep identity links that will continue to hold important values, both instrumental and affective, in the future.

Notes

1. Spain is divided into a number of autonomous communities which, while responding to the central Spanish government in Madrid, have certain autonomy to manage some areas of government through their own local authorities. The *Comunidad Autónoma del País Vasco* (CAPV) or Autonomous Community of the Basque Country is made up of three provinces: Araba, Bizkaia and Gipuzkoa.
2. The Basque language is identified in this chapter as Euskara. Many of the informants refer to the language as Euskera, sometimes with the Spanish spelling, Eusquera.

3. The team members were Iñaki Dendaluze, Iñaki Picabea, Justo Bereciartua, Pilare Mendia, and Iker Laskibar.
4. Given the challenged nationhood of the Basque Country as something separate from the rest of Spain or France, the terms *estado español* (Spanish State) and *estado francés* (French State) are used to indicate the political construction of states which group together different peoples or nations.
5. Donostia in Basque, San Sebastián in Spanish, is the capital of the province of Gipuzkoa located in the Basque Autonomous Community.
6. To understand the force of this statement, it has to be explained that *euskaldun* is the word used to define a Basque person but it defines 'Basque' in relation to the language, literally meaning 'one who has Basque', effectively a 'Basque speaker.'

Summary

This chapter focuses on the language learning attitudes and motivations of the first student cohort to graduate from high school in one of three linguistic models (A, B, and D) under the 1983 Spanish bilingual law within the Basque Autonomous Community. The qualitative analysis of students' written responses to open-ended questions shows that students are positively disposed to language learning, and variations in attitudes are associated with the different languages being learned (Euskara, Spanish, and English) and the linguistic school models the students attended. It is concluded that in imagining multilingual schooling, researchers must account for the role of values associated with language learning and the social contexts.

Artikulu honetan ingurune sozial elebiduneko ikaslek hizkuntzen ikaskuntzarekiko dituzten jarrerak aztertu nahi dira. Lan hau hirigiroko ikastetxetan egin da, Derrigorrezko Bigarren Hezkuntzako ikasleekin. Hizkuntzen alderdi desberdinei dagozkien zenbait galderen erantzunak modu kualitatiboan aztertu dira. Orokorrean hizkuntzen ikaskuntzen aldeko joera baikorra ikusi da baina hizkuntzen baitako ezberdintasunak ere azaldu dira(euskara, gaztelera, ingelera). Argi dago hizkuntzaren sare sozialak eta hizkuntza bakoitzari ematen zaizkion baloreak eraginkorrak direla ikasle hauentzat. (Euskara)

En este artículo se trata de ver la actitud de los estudiantes ante el proceso de aprendizaje de lenguas en un contexto social bilingüe. El trabajo se lleva a cabo con estudiantes de Educación Secundaria escolarizados en diferentes modelos lingüísticos (A, B, D) de una zona urbana de la Comunidad Autónoma del País Vasco. Se ha evidenciado que la actitud hacia el aprendizaje de lenguas es favorable aunque con diferencias respecto a las lenguas específicas (euskara, español, inglés). De ahí la conveniencia a considerar en la investigación de la escolarización multilingüe el contexto social de las lenguas y los valores asignados a ellas en relación con su aprendizaje. (Spanish)

Part 3

Extending Formal Instructional Spaces

Chapter 6

Back to Basics: Marketing the Benefits of Bilingualism to Parents

VIV EDWARDS and LYNDA PRITCHARD NEWCOMBE

Introduction

Contributors to this volume share a vision of what can be achieved in classrooms where all languages are respected and children are encouraged to fulfill their potential using both English and other languages. There are, however, many competing discourses. Students and their parents – the direct and indirect beneficiaries of bilingual education – are bombarded by popular prejudice and media reports that perpetuate long-standing myths about bilingualism. The ultimate success of multilingual classrooms therefore depends on the extent to which advocates of bilingual education are able to communicate their case.

In this contribution to the debate on multilingual classrooms, we look at the changing political fortunes of bilingual education and the impact of shifts in language policy on the decisions which parents make about their children's education. We also examine the central role of parents in language transmission, arguing that it is unrealistic to rely on education alone to halt language shift. Drawing on a highly innovative example of planning in Wales, we consider the potential of treating bilingualism as a product that can be marketed directly to parents, and consider the implications of this course of action for multilingual schools.

Competing Discourses

From early colonial days to modern times, language-in-education policies in both North America and Australia have veered between tolerance and oppression (Edwards, 2004). In one view, linguistic diversity is a fact of life and a valuable resource. Thus in the 19th century, pragmatism dictated that the language of instruction was the language of the community, and the Church played a prominent role in the provision of mother-tongue-medium education (Clyne, 1991; Kloss, 1998). However, tolerance tends to falter as the majority consolidates its power base. With the introduction of non-sectarian education, paid for by taxes, religious schools declined and, as quotas for filling classrooms in public schools were reached, the needs of immigrants were placed lower on the political agenda. From the 1880s, other languages were seen as a potential threat; efforts to curtail them included corporal punishment and legislation.

Linguistic minorities not only in North America and Australia but in many other locations, too, began to reassert their rights only in the 1960s. In the new world order which followed World War II, greater prominence was given to minority rights and issues of social equity, with bilingual education programs emerging to meet the needs of speakers of a wide range of both Indigenous languages and also of 'established' European languages, such as Basque and Welsh (Churchill, 1986; Edwards, 2004). These gains have, however, been contested. The same polarization that marked the debates of the late 19th and early 20th centuries is also evident today. On the one hand, there is near unanimous support for bilingual education from educators and linguists. Writers such as Cummins (2001) have provided the theoretical underpinnings, highlighting the social, cognitive and academic benefits of bilingualism. Large-scale longitudinal studies undertaken in the USA by researchers such as Ramirez *et al.* (1991) and Thomas and Collier (2002) show unambiguously that, the longer children are educated using English *and* the language of the home, the better the results. The findings from research in Canada (and subsequently in many other countries) show consistently that immersion students acquire normal English proficiency as well as a high level in the second language (Baker, 2001).

Many others, however, see linguistic diversity in a very different light. In the UK, language activists have gained growing official recognition for the 'established languages' – Welsh, Gaelic and Irish – but little support for the many 'new minority' language communities established post-World War II (Edwards, 2004; Peate *et al.*, 1998). The 1985 Swann Report, for instance, placed responsibility for mother-tongue maintenance firmly on minority communities, arguing that bilingual programs accentuate divisions within society. In the USA, critics have chosen to ignore the overwhelming evidence that students in English-only classrooms are often unable to access either lesson content or the language of instruction, contending that bilingual programs create a dependency on the first language that slows progress in English (Crawford, 2000; Krashen, 1992). In the Southern Hemisphere, too, there has been a reaction against bilingual education policies. In 1998, the government of the Northern Territory of Australia announced that bilingual programs for Aboriginal students were to be replaced by classes in English as a Second Language (ESL) because of allegedly poor standards in English literacy (Gaglioti, 1999). In a critique of this change in policy, Nicholls (2001) points out that the axing of bilingual education represents a significant cost cutting. She also argues that it is in the interests of non-Aboriginal peoples to extinguish knowledge of Aboriginal languages, since many land claims have failed when there has been insufficient linguistic evidence of ownership.

An examination of coverage of the bilingual debate suggests that the English-only lobby is in the ascendancy. McQuillan and Tse (1996), for instance, show that between 1984 and 1994, 87% of US academic publications had conclusions favourable to bilingual education, compared with only 45% of media reports in the same period. The approval of two initiatives aimed at eliminating bilingual education – Proposition 227 in California in 1998 and Proposition 203 in Arizona in 2000 – would suggest that a large proportion of the American public has been persuaded by the arguments of the media. Legal judgments sometimes have the effect of reinforcing doubts. Samuel C. Kiser, a district court judge in Amarillo Texas warned Martha Laureano in a 1995 custody suit that, if she continued to speak Spanish, her daughter would be condemned to a life as a maid (Baron, 2001). Judge Ronald E. Reagan ordered a Hispanic father in Papillon, Nebraska, in 2003, to speak mainly English to his daughter as a condition of his visitation rights (Ortiz, 2003).

The Role of Parents in Language Transmission

Given the uneven access to the media, on the one hand, of campaigns funded by the personal fortunes of individuals such as the software entrepreneur Ron Unz (see, for instance, Crawford, 2000) and, on the other hand, of alliances of educators and linguists, it is not surprising that parents should feel ambivalent as to whether bilingualism is in the best interest of their children. If, however, parents are to be persuaded of the value of bilingualism, they need to be able to assess the arguments and the evidence for themselves. Because myths about bilingualism are so prevalent, parents are often plagued with doubt (Goodz, 1994). They may mistakenly believe that early exposure to two languages will result in confusion; they may also worry about what will happen when the child arrives in school with little or no knowledge of English. When the minority language is in competition with an international language such as English, the decision to use another language in the home is particularly difficult. Minority languages can seem old-fashioned and unglamorous when they are in competition with the language of Bill Gates and Coca Cola. When imagining multilingual classrooms, it is clearly essential to understand the conflicting messages to which parents are exposed.

Three very different examples can be used to illustrate the centrality of parents to bilingual education – Hispanics in the USA, monolingual speakers of African languages in South Africa and Welsh/English and English speakers in Wales.

In the United States, although the numbers of people speaking a language other than English in the home increased in the 10 years between the 1990 and the 2000 US censuses (Crawford, 2002), the proportion of the population speaking English 'well' or 'very well' increased even more rapidly. The shift from the home language to English would seem to be more rapid now than at any point in the past. Most Hispanics today, for instance, speak English as their dominant language by the second generation, and as their only language by the third (Nicolau & Valdivieso, 1992). As long as parents feel pressure to shift rapidly to English, however, there will continue to be shortages of bilinguals who are able to make valuable contributions to US economic competitiveness, to public services, and to national defense (Edwards, 2004).

In South Africa, as indeed in other African countries, English is a minority language. Nonetheless, its use as the medium of instruction is defended not only by the small proportion of the population who speak it fluently, but also by the majority who continue to use only local and regional languages in their everyday lives. Fluency in an international lingua franca is associated with 'being educated', a pre-requisite for upward social mobility; European languages therefore serve 'as models for the aspiring masses' (Myers-Scotton, 1993). The official policy of multilingualism (in 11 languages) adopted by the South African government represents a serious attempt to challenge the hegemony of European languages. There are, however, problems not only in terms of training and resources, but also in persuading parents of the advantages of bilingual education for their children, particularly given the history of Bantu education under the apartheid regime (Rassool *et al.*, in press). As was the case for bilingual education in the USA, there is a palpable tension between the perception of parents that the surest route to upward mobility is through English-medium education and the firm belief of activists that a strong foundation in the children's mother tongue will lead to better and more equitable outcomes.

The Welsh situation offers different challenges. The 2001 Census indicates that the rapid decline in the number of Welsh speakers that began in the mid-19th century has finally been halted. The most significant developments have been in education, where one in five primary school children in Wales is currently taught in classes where Welsh is used either as the main medium of education or for teaching part of the curriculum (NAW, 2003a). There is, however, no room for complacency: Welsh-speaking teenagers use the language less frequently as they get older (Baker, 2003b: 100), and many of the students who have acquired Welsh in school do not later transmit the language to their children (Aitchison & Carter, 1988; Gruffudd, 2000). As Fishman (1991) points out, over-reliance on education leads to a frustrating struggle against the tide, with each new generation starting at the same point as the previous one. Educational interventions are simply not sufficient in themselves to reverse language shift. Yet most parents require persuasion to take responsibility for bringing up their children in two languages, for reasons already outlined.

The linguistic issues in the USA, South Africa and Wales are very different. The centrality of parents to any attempt to imagine multilingual solutions, however, is a constant in all three settings. We turn now to a description of a Welsh initiative for addressing the concerns of parents, which has the potential to be adapted to a much wider range of situations.

Marketing Bilingualism to Parents

The application of marketing principles to language is a very recent development, but one that has considerable potential for challenging myths about bilingualism. For those wishing to halt or reverse language shift, the main targets are the parents and prospective parents who are making decisions both about transmission within the family and about the education of their children. The Welsh Language Board (WLB), a statutory body established by the 1993 Welsh Language Act 'to promote and facilitate the language,' is responsible for a highly innovative project designed to raise awareness of the benefits of bilingualism. *Twf* ('Growth') was launched in 2002 with funding from the National Assembly for Wales. The present authors were responsible for an independent evaluation of this project (Edwards & Pritchard Newcombe, 2003).

By working strategically with two groups of health professionals – midwives and health visitors – a small team of project officers is now able to reach every parent of pre-school children in Wales. Midwives play a crucial role in antenatal care and childbirth in the UK and are held in high regard by mothers, who depend on them for advice and support. In strongly Welsh-speaking areas, the Record of Pregnancy (a document that women take with them to antenatal clinics), now includes two key questions: *Which language/s do you intend introducing to your baby?* and *Have you received information about bilingualism from your midwife?* In predominantly English-speaking areas, parents are simply informed: *Speaking two languages can help your child: For an information pack contact the above.* In both cases, these questions serve as a reminder to midwives to discuss language choice at an early stage.

Twf project workers are also often invited to contribute to childbirth preparation classes. Health visitors take over from midwives soon after birth. Language issues are routinely raised at the eight-month assessment and at other points as the opportunity arises. The importance of collaboration with midwives and health visitors is that these professionals have access to families at the time they are making decisions about language. The project also works with other partners, distributing information through signposting organizations such as children's information bureaux and libraries, giving presentations to pre-school groups, and working with other Welsh-language organizations to stage events to promote the language. This collaboration has the effect of reinforcing the information offered by health workers.

The management and full range of activities of the project are discussed elsewhere (Edwards & Pritchard Newcombe, 2005a, 2005b). The present focus, however, is on the effectiveness of the *Twf* marketing strategy. Most discussions of marketing stress the importance of achieving the best possible mix, and refer to four major elements – product, price, promotion and place. These '4Ps' serve as a useful framework for the discussion of the marketing of Welsh to parents.

Product

Kotler *et al.* (1999) define *product* as 'anything that can be offered to a market for attention, acquisition, use or consumption that might satisfy a want or need'. In the case of the *Twf*, the product is bilingual children. The test therefore is both to challenge myths associated with bilingualism and to replace the widespread image of the Welsh language as old-fashioned, as something to be conserved rather than used, by making it 'attractive, relevant and enjoyable' (R. Williams 2004: 16).

Elinor Williams, director of Marketing and Communications at WLB, makes the case for treating Welsh not only as a product but as a particular brand that people want to identify with:

> For the Welsh language to become a recognized brand, a seal of approval that creates trust and involvement and increases the use of the Welsh language, it needs to connect with people. It needs to strike a balance between aspiration – 'I want to be part of that club' – and identification – 'this is for me, for my life'. The important thing is to increase [the] consumer's connection to the brand so that it has more meaning for real people. (Williams, 2004: 50–1)

A central part of the success of the *Twf* project has been the development

Figure 6.1 The *Twf* logo and strap line

Figure 6.2 *Twf* cartoon characters

of a strong brand image. The logo is instantly recognizable: two superimposed hands, one adult, one child, in shades of purple against a contrasting yellow background; '*Twf*' written in a playful purple font reminiscent of a child's handwriting; and the bilingual strap line – *Magu plant yn dwyeithog/ Raising children bilingually* (Figure 6.1).

The use of child cartoon characters (Dil, Dan, Tomos and Teleri) also reinforces the brand image (Figure 6.2).

Price

Price, the second P in the marketing mix, has been defined as 'the sum of the values that consumers exchange for the benefits of having or using the product or service' (Kotler *et al.*, 1999). The main investment for consumers of the *Twf* product is time and personal commitment. Even when parents are persuaded, in principle, of the value of bilingualism, they may harbour doubts as to their ability to bring up children bilingually. The challenge for the project has therefore been to translate an abstract notion – bilingualism – into something concrete that parents can relate to their everyday lives, to reassure them that bringing up children in two languages is both feasible and achievable, and to remind them that their efforts will yield dividends.

The *Twf* newsletter is playing an important role in this process. Circulation has increased from 20,000 to 40,000, with two new issues each year. The newsletter features stories of families who have successfully brought up their children to be bilingual and makes extensive use of celebrity endorsement. The first issue, for instance, featured the family of Huw Edwards, a BBC newsreader and television presenter. The aim is to provide role models who can offer practical advice and reassurance that it is possible to transmit the language, even in situations that are far from ideal. *Twf* also produces a range of free materials featuring the *Twf* cartoon children, aimed to help parents to use Welsh with their children. A CD of Welsh songs for parents to sing with their children has proved extremely popular, as has a bilingual colouring and activity book. Activities for children that teach Welsh vocabulary have been included in a special *Twf* supplement of a South Wales newspaper; and interactive games are an important feature of the newly-launched *Twf* website (www.twfwales.com). A *Twf* storybook is also in production.

By making the materials and information available free of charge, the project is seeking to provide parents with the reassurance that their investment in terms of time and personal commitment is worthwhile. The Welsh Assembly Government, for its part, has demonstrated the political commitment to intergenerational transmission by providing the necessary funding. The commissioning of three project evaluations between 2002 and 2005, however, is indicative of an understandable concern to demonstrate the effectiveness of *Twf*.

Promotion

Efforts to promote bilingualism in Wales have traditionally appealed mainly to middle-class parents. The video produced by the Welsh Language Board and used widely in the early stages of the *Twf* project, for instance, featured only middle class, two-parent families. A parent pamphlet on *Raising Bilingual Children* (WLB, n.d.) is highly informative, but has dense text and few illustrations, and may well be off-putting for less confident parents. *Twf*, in contrast, has made a deliberate effort to be socially inclusive, developing a range of marketing materials likely to appeal to the widest possible audience.

The centrepiece of *Twf* marketing is a small brightly-coloured booklet, with a distinctive square shape and minimal text. Dil, Dan, Tomos and Teleri are used to illustrate *6 good reasons for making sure your children can speak Welsh* (see Figure 6.3). This booklet was developed in response to questions that parents frequently asked about bilingualism. An earlier version featuring ten questions was rewritten with a sharper focus to ensure that the message came across more clearly.

The six good reasons set out in the booklet also appear as animations at the head of the *Twf* home page (www.twfwales.com) and are available in poster form. The appearance of the poster on the wall of a waiting room in the TV Welsh language soap, *Pobol y Cwm*, leaves little doubt as to the extent of market penetration! One of the strengths of *6 good reasons* is the conciseness of the message. Another is its power to connect with issues of importance for parents – giving children a head start in school and in the wider world, having the chance to revel in their achievements, being proud of their heritage. These issues, of course, have resonance with parents everywhere. As a follow up to the *6 good reasons* booklet, the *6 good questions* leaflet was designed for parents and others requesting further information. Its particular strength is that it recognises the different needs of Welsh- and English-speaking parents: the English version addresses anxieties of

Yn yr ysgol

Mae plant sy'n dysgu dwy iaith ar y blaen wrth ddarllen a chyfri. Maen nhw'n aml yn gwneud yn well mewn arholiadau yn nes ymlaen.

At school

Children who learn two languages have a head start when reading and counting. They often do better in exams later on.

Yn y teulu

Mae dysgu dwy iaith yn haws i blant bach. O fewn dim, byddan nhw'n symud yn hwylus o un i'r llall. Fe fydd yr holl deulu wrth eu bodd.

In the family

Learning two languages is easier for young children. In no time at all they'll be switching easily from one to the other. The whole family will be proud.

Yn y gwaith

Mae dwy iaith yn rhoi gwell dewis ym myd gwaith. Mae llawer o swyddi yng Nghymru angen sgiliau Cymraeg a Saesneg.

At work

Two languages offer a better choice of work. Many employers in Wales ask for Welsh and English skills.

Figure 6.3 6 good reasons for making sure your children can speak Welsh

Yn y gymdeithas

Mae'n deimlad braf gallu symud yn hawdd o un iaith i'r llall. Fe fydd siarad y ddwy iaith yn agor y drws i wneud ffrindiau newydd.

In the community

It gives you a buzz to be able to switch easily from one language to another. Speaking both languages opens doors to make new friends.

Yn y byd

Mae'r rhan fwya o bobl y byd yn gallu siarad mwy nag un iaith. Ar ôl dysgu'r ail, mae'n haws dysgu rhagor wedyn. Mae Cymraeg yn rhoi dechrau da.

Around the world

Most people throughout the world can speak more than one language. After learning two, it's much easier to learn more. Welsh gives you a good start.

Mewn bywyd

Mae Saesneg a Chymraeg yn gyfoethog iawn, yn llawn straeon a chaneuon, hanes a hwyl. Fe fydd eich plentyn yn cael y gorau o'r ddau fyd.

In life

Both English and Welsh are like treasure troves, full of stories and songs, history and fun. Your child will have the best of both worlds.

Figure 6.3 *continued*

English-speaking parents; the Welsh version, the concerns of Welsh-speaking parents.

Place

The fourth P – place – focuses on where a service is delivered. Advertising materials are distributed at events, through libraries and children's information bureaux, via hospitals and health centres and in response to inquiries received by the project team. The *6 good reasons* leaflet has particularly wide distribution: it is placed as an insert in each woman's record of pregnancy and is also included in the 'bounty packs' of free samples and advertising literature distributed to new mothers who give birth in hospital. As already mentioned, midwives and health visitors are asked to discuss the question of language choice during pregnancy and at the eight-month developmental screening. *Twf* project workers often make presentations to parents at childbirth preparation classes and at meetings of a range of early years organizations. They also offer a range of promotional activities that help to communicate the message that learning Welsh is both enjoyable and achievable. These include: 'taster' language classes for mothers with their children attending toddler groups; fun evenings for the family, where parents are given the opportunity to learn some Welsh; colouring competitions for children sponsored by local branches of MacDonalds; and a *Twf* presence at local and national shows and other events. The website is, of course, available for access by parents and children in their homes at any time convenient to them. The emphasis, then, is on bringing the *Twf* message to places where parents regularly spend time.

The marketing efforts of *Twf* need, of course, to be seen within the context of the wider strategy of the Welsh Language Board (WLB). There has been a marked change in emphasis in recent years. When the Welsh Language Act established WLB in 1993, its mission was 'to promote and facilitate' the use of the Welsh language. Ten years later in the national action plan for a bilingual Wales (NAW, 2003b), the WLB were charged 'to *market* and promote the language in all aspects of Welsh life'. Rhodri Williams (2004: 16), the current chair of WLB, underlines the importance of this new approach: 'We cannot expect to succeed in selling the benefits of the language without promoting it professionally'.

Lessons to be Learned

The clear message of this volume is that schools have the potential to preserve, recover, and expand the world's linguistic diversity. In many situations, however, it is unrealistic to place this responsibility on schools alone. The active involvement of the family is essential to avoid a frustrating struggle against the tide, with each new generation starting at the same point as the previous one (see, in particular, Fishman, 1991). As we imagine multilingual schools, we ignore parents at our peril.

The *Twf* project is, without a doubt, a highly innovative example of the use of modern marketing methods to challenge widespread myths about bilingualism. It is important, however, to address two central issues: the effectiveness of the project in influencing language choice within the family in Wales; and the extent to which methods developed in Wales can be applied in other contexts.

Twf has been in operation only since 2002; it is therefore too soon to assess the impact of its marketing strategy with any degree of confidence. The most persuasive evidence for its effectiveness would be an increase in the number of families deciding to use Welsh as the language of the home, but the next opportunity to evaluate intergenerational transmission will not be until the 2011 UK Census. Increased enrolment for bilingual education will be another indicator. But since the target audience for *Twf* is pregnant women and the parents of very young children, it may take some time before its influence is apparent. Equally problematic, it is difficult to see how it would be possible to separate the effects of *Twf* marketing initiatives from the many other factors that determine language choice. Other examples include the appointment of marketing officers to work with young people and young people's organizations, a poster campaign promoting Welsh in work, play and everyday life on billboards and buses across the country, and a TV advertising campaign (www.workplaylive.org).

The second issue concerns the extent to which marketing methods developed in Wales can be applied in other contexts. The current status of Welsh is the result of both bottom-up and top-down activity (Edwards & Newcombe, 2005a, 2005b). Decades of grassroots pressure have yielded major political concessions for the language in the areas of education and public life; and the devolution of limited powers from central government in Westminster to a National Assembly for Wales has translated into a larger budget for marking initiatives, of which *Twf* forms just one part. It can therefore be argued that Welsh now has a much stronger power base than many other minority languages.

Nonetheless, the central marketing messages of *Twf* – that bilingualism is something that parents should aspire to for their children, that the ability to speak another language increases children's life chances and makes the family proud – are ones that are likely to resonate with parents not only in Wales but in a wide range of other settings. Informal indications suggest that *Twf* has arrived at a good marketing mix, and that there is considerable potential for adapting strategies already implemented in Wales to other minority language settings. One such indication is what might be described as the 'Aahh factor'. The *Twf* marketing materials – and particularly the *6 good reasons* booklet – that we have shared with various international audiences, have consistently produced enthusiastic and excited responses. Interest has already been expressed in adapting the *Twf* materials for use in South Africa, Hispanic communities in the US, an Indigenous North American language community, and with new minority languages in Canada. Belatedly, it seems, educators and linguists are beginning to understand that the medium may well be the message.

Summary

This chapter examines the central role of parents in language transmission and argues that the ultimate success of any attempt to imagine multilingual schools depends on the extent to which advocates of bilingual education are able to communicate their case to families. Using the example of *Twf*, a highly innovative project that promotes the benefits of bilingualism to parents and prospective parents in Wales, the chapter explores the ways in which modern marketing strategies can be used to challenge myths about bilingualism. While recognizing that the linguistic issues vary from one setting to another, it proposes that the central marketing messages of *Twf* – that bilingualism is something that parents should aspire to for their children, that the ability to speak another language increases children's life chances and makes the family proud – are ones that are likely to resonate not only in Wales but in a wide range of other settings.

Mae'r papur hwn yn archwilio swyddogaeth rhieni wrth drosglwyddo iaith ac yn dadlau bod llwyddiant unrhyw ymgais i ddychmygu ysgolion amlieithog yn dibynnu yn y pendraw ar faint mae hyrwyddwyr addysg ddwyieithog yn gallu cyflwyno'u hachos i deuluoedd. Gan ddefnyddio enghraifft Twf, prosiect dyfeisgar iawn, sy'n hybu manteision dwyieithrwydd i rieni a darpar rieni yng Nghymru, mae'n archwilio sut y gall strategaethau marchnata cyfoes gael eu defnyddio i herio syniadau anghywir am ddwyieithrwydd. Er bod y papur yn cydnabod bod pynciau llosg ieithyddol yn amrywio o un sefyllfa i'r llall, mae'n awgrymu bod negeseuon marchnata allweddol Twf – sef bod dwyieithrwydd yn rhywbeth y dylai rhieni ei ddymuno ar gyfer eu plant, a bod y gallu i siarad iaith arall yn cynyddu cyfleoedd ym mywydau plant ac yn gwneud y teulu yn falch – yn debygol o gyseinio nid yn unig yng Nghymru ond mewn amrediad eang o sefyllfaoedd eraill. (Welsh)

Chapter 7

Popular Education and Language Rights in Indigenous Mayan Communities: Emergence of New Social Actors and Gendered Voices

KAREN OGULNICK

The indigenous struggle in Mexico is a dream which not only dreams the tomorrow which includes the color of the earth, it is, also and above all, a dream which fights to hasten the awakening of that tomorrow.
Subcommandante Marcos. Speech delivered at *Paths of Dignity: Indigenous Rights, Memory and Cultural Heritage*, March 12, 2001

Chiapas: Sociolinguistic and Sociopolitical Context

Through the persistence of racism and discrimination against indigenous people in Mexico, public education has served to reproduce a cultural ideology that situates indigenous people in submissive and subordinated positions. One of the ways this is played out is through language policies and the reality of 'bilingual education' in indigenous communities. Official recognition of the multicultural and multilingual composition of the more than 10 million indigenous people in Mexico has come about in recent years, most notably in the amendments made in 1991 to Article 4 of the Mexican Constitution, which states that:

> *La Nación mexicana tiene una composición pluricultural sustentada originalmente en sus pueblos indígenas. La ley protegerá y promoverá el desarrollo de sus lenguas, culturas, usos, costumbres, recursos y formas específicas de organización social, y garantizará a sus integrantes el efectivo acceso a la jurisdicción del Estado.* (Nahmad, 1998)
> (The Mexican nation has a multicultural composition sustained originally in its indigenous peoples. The law will protect and promote the development of their languages, cultures, practices, customs, resources, and specific forms of social organization, and it will guarantee effective access to the State's jurisdiction to its members.)

In Chiapas, a state in south-eastern Mexico with a population of more than three million, one-third of the people are indigenous. In addition to Spanish, 11 distinct Mayan languages and one language (Zoque) that stems from the Olmec tree are spoken. Seven of these languages (Chuj, Canjobal, Catchikel, Mochó, Jacalteco, Lacandón, and Mam) have fewer than 100,000 speakers and are in danger of extinction. The other five languages more widely spoken in Chiapas are: Tzeltal (547,000 speakers), Tzotzil (514,000 speakers), Chol (274,000 speakers), Zoque (88,000 speakers) and Tojolabal (74,000 speakers) (Cornejo & Enríquez, 2002). Speakers of each of these languages live in distinct communities where they have retained their own customs, practice different religious beliefs, are governed by their own political parties, exercise their own forms of justice, and wear their unique traditional clothing which identifies their communities and language groups.

A great challenge that exists today for indigenous people in Chiapas is educating the next generation to be part of the larger society while not losing their traditional languages and cultures. Formal public education for indigenous children consists primarily of passive learning from authoritarian teachers who transmit linguistic and cultural values that are markedly distinct from those of the communities in which they are teaching. Within this system, children are taught to reproduce the cultural capital (Bourdieu, 1977) of the dominant class, thus complying with their own subjugation. The Secretary of Public Education's (SEP) recent proposal to omit Pre-Hispanic studies from its primary school curriculum has generated further conflict and tension between the government and indigenous people. At present, fourth graders are introduced, albeit only briefly, to the history of the Mesoamerican people, the diversity of Prehispanic cultures, and the *Popol Vuh,* which is celebrated by descendants of the Mayans as the most important text depicting their creation, traditions, and history of the first people on the continent. SEP's plan to delete these pages from the primary school history texts contributes to the exclusion of more than 10 million inhabitants of Mesoamerican heritage. Such paternalistic attitudes and attempts to institutionalize the invisibility and assimilation of the indigenous people have led to ongoing demands for cultural and political autonomy.

A study conducted by the Center of National Evaluation (CENEVAL) in 2004 on the quality of public education in Mexico found Chiapas to rate the lowest in the country in terms of literacy and general knowledge. Given the dire conditions of the public school system for indigenous children in Chiapas, alternative educational programs have been developed to counteract the enforced acculturation process that maintains the hegemonic stronghold of the dominant Spanish-speaking culture.

One of the most visionary movements to have helped pave the way for linguistic and cultural human rights for indigenous people all over Mexico was the ratification of the San Andrés Accords on Indigenous Rights and

Culture. This document was signed in 1996 in the state of Chiapas by the Mexican federal government and the Zapatista National Liberation Army (EZLN) in order to rectify the extreme racism, marginalization, and exclusion of indigenous people all over Mexico. Similar to the situation for Native Americans in the US and other native people throughout the world, in Mexico there is a long and brutal history of oppression and cultural genocide of indigenous people. The 10 million or so indigenous people of Mexico live in conditions that are among the poorest in the continent. The Mayan people in Chiapas remain overwhelmingly illiterate; they live in homes with no running water, disease is rampant and their life expectancy is lower than in any other part of Mexico (González, 2002). These are the conditions that led to the Zapatista uprising on January 1st, 1994, when some 3000 Zapatista rebels (whose name derives from the revolutionary leader of peasant farmers, Emiliano Zapata), took up arms to reclaim the land, rights, dignity – and education – that had been stolen from them by the Mexican government.

The masks that the Zapatistas don, as well as protecting their identities, also deliver a message. They draw attention to the centuries of silence and invisibility the indigenous people have had to endure. According to the charismatic Zapatista leader, Marcos, more affectionately referred to as 'El Sup' (subcommandante), 'the truth is that masks also reveal and silences speak' (Marcos, 1998). The masked faces of the EZLN have become symbols of a worldwide solidarity movement, a global movement to create, as they say, 'a world where all worlds will fit.'

Five hundred years of oppression have given the indigenous people of Chiapas a strong history of resistance and survival. The force of their perseverance is clearly conveyed through the power of their words:

> Brothers and sisters: Through my voice speaks the voice of the Zapatista Army of National Liberation. Indigenous Brothers and Sisters of the People of Mexico, we, the indigenous, wish to speak to you of our right to be Mexicans. We do not need to change our culture, our clothing, our language, our way of prayer, our way of working and respecting the land, we cannot stop being indigenous in order to be recognized as Mexicans. They cannot take what we are way from us. Yes, we are dark-skinned. They cannot turn us into whites. Because our grandparents resisted more than 500 years of contempt, humiliation and exploitation, we continue to resist. They will never be able to humiliate us or do away with us. (EZLN, 2003)

The San Andrés Accords have also been a driving force behind imagining the promise and justice of multilingual education. Indeed, education is one of the most prominant demands published within this lengthy document. In particular, there are many sections that reflect a commitment to providing bilingual, intercultural, high quality, free public education that respects and promotes the development of indigenous languages, cultures and ways of life. The following.is an example of one of the agreements regarding indigenous education:

> The federal government is obligated to the promotion, development, preservation and practice of the education of the indigenous languages and it will promote the teaching of literacy in the native languages; it will adopt measures that assure the indigenous people of the opportunity to acquire Spanish. The knowledge of the indigenous cultures is a national treasure and a necessary step to eliminate misunderstandings and discrimination against the indigenous. (*Acuerdos de San Andrés*, 2003: 60)

Although both the federal government and the EZLN signed this agreement after lengthy negotiations, the implementation of these accords remains extraordinarily conflictive today. In 2003, the document was translated from Spanish into ten indigenous languages in the state of Chiapas. For the first time since the accords were written, the indigenous people could conceptualize – and name – in their own languages the terms used to describe their constitutional rights. A translator of the language Mam, Jorge Pérez Hernández, expressed his excitement of the project as follows:

> We have begun to fight through words. We are learning new ways to raise consciousness among our people. The people are dominated. They have bandages on their eyes ... the accords of San Andrés are waking up the people. (Bellinghausen, 2003)

Bilingual Education in Chiapas

In spite of the innovative educational framework outlined in the San Andrés Accords, as well as the changes to Article 4 of the Mexican Constitution, the public educational system has not adequately addressed the educational needs of the culturally and linguistically diverse sector of the population (for more on this in other Latin American countries, see López, Chapter 12). Indeed, the reality of public education for indigenous children in rural areas is far from the promises made in the San Andrés Accords.

In many rural areas in Chiapas, schools hardly existed 50 years ago and even today there isn't an adequate educational system. Many children, particularly girls, continue to be schooled only up to the third grade. Although many schools in indigenous towns are called 'bilingual,' when asked if the schools are bilingual, many indigenous parents respond by saying, '*supuestamente*' (supposedly). The comments of Juan de la Torres, a Tzotzil writer, speak clearly to the indigenous parents' widespread distrust of bilingual education programs:

> They say that education is bilingual and bicultural, but it really isn't. Only a little. Most teachers don't speak the languages of the students, so they teach in Spanish. They don't teach the native languages. (personal communication, July 2004)

Although the Secretary of Public Education (SEP) claims to offer 'bilingual and bicultural education,' in reality bilingual education in Chiapas is barely functional. In addition to lack of adequate materials and training necessary to successfully implement bilingual education, a main obstacle is the fact that teachers are often assigned to schools in communities where other languages and dialects are spoken. This is due to the practice of assigning teachers according to a seniority system. Teachers who have been teaching longer often choose schools that are closer to the cities. Therefore, regardless of the languages they speak, new teachers with the least experience are placed in rural communities where indigenous languages are spoken.

Because of the existence of many dialects and the lack of effort to standardize the languages, even teachers who speak the same language may speak a different 'dialect' if they come from another community. Although dialects are mutually intelligible, there are differences in spelling, pronunciation, grammar, and vocabulary. The lack of a standard dialect makes it difficult to create important resources in the native languages, such as dictionaries, grammar books, and literature books. Although neither a dictionary nor a comprehensive grammar book written entirely in indigenous languages exists, there is a Tzotzil/English dictionary (Laughlin, 1975) and a Tzotzil/English (which has also been translated into Spanish) grammar book (Haviland, 1981) written by American linguistic anthropologists for non-indigenous people learning Tsotzil. Both of these books were researched in the town of Zinacantán, which has its own particular dialect of Tzotzil, which differs markedly from the Tzotzil of the town of San Pedro Chenalhó, for example. Just as people believe that the center of the world is their own town, they also believe that the dialect they speak is the superior one. While this is a healthy and justifiable belief, it does lend itself to practical problems when it comes to standardizing the languages. The Mexican government has made some pretense of providing schools with books written in Tzotzil and Tzeltal but, because of dialectal differences, not all the communities could make use of them. Children have the capacity to learn many varieties of their languages, as well as other languages. However, when they are not taught to read and write in the language varieties that they know from their homes and communities, they not only encounter greater difficulties acquiring literacy, but they also learn in insidious ways to devalue their native languages, cultures, and identities. One possible solution, which is currently being considered by writers and academics, is to create an academic variety of each language by combining different aspects of each of its dialects. At the same time, the diversity of dialects, which contain regional expressions related to the particular customs and history of each community, would be maintained through literary works.

Perhaps the most insidious obstacle to bilingual education is the situation of indigenous teachers who speak the same languages as their students, but prefer to use Spanish because of ideological beliefs that the children will be left behind in Mexican society if they learn in their native languages. Trujillo (1999: 85) discussed this phenomena in his study of bilingual education in Chiapas when he wrote that the indigenous: '*piensan y se autodefinen como un ser "no civilizado" por no ser portador de la escritura y porque no hablan correctamente el español*' ('think and define themselves as "uncivilized" for not being writers and for not speaking Spanish correctly'). Such misconceptions fly in the face of studies that show proficiency in more than one language improves indigenous peoples' economic opportunities and reduces the probability of poverty (King, 1998; Modiano, 1973; Patrinos & Panagides, 1994).

Indigenous people who speak only Spanish also suffer from discrimination when they lack proficiency in their native languages. Educated indigenous adults are sometimes expected to know how to read and write in their native languages, even when they were not given the proper educational tools that would have enabled them to develop these abilities. For example, one indigenous woman interviewed reported that, after years of struggling to further her education at her own expense, she attempted to obtain a position as a bilingual teacher. However, she could not realize this goal because she failed an exam that required her to write in her native language, Tzeltal, even though her entire public school education had been in Spanish.

Another Tzotzil-speaking woman described her experiences in public schools as a '*pesadilla*' (nightmare). She said that as a child she could not understand anything the teachers said because, 'although the teachers were indigenous, they did not speak the same language as the students in the community.' It wasn't until about the 3rd grade that she began to learn Spanish. She worked hard at succeeding in school, and her parents, unlike many other parents of indigenous girls, allowed her to continue her education until the 9th grade. Her public education did not include instruction on how to read or write in her native language. It wasn't until after she left school that she began to participate in native-language literacy workshops where she learned to read and write Tzotzil. Through popular education programs such as those described below, she also became trained as a photographer. Combining her photography and bilingual literacy skills, she has now published books of her photos with trilingual descriptions written in Tzotzil, Spanish and English.

Indigenous teachers who are educated within a hegemonic system to reject their traditional cultures and languages may recognize the contradictions that exist between the learners' needs and the public school curriculum; however, they often lack the tools and institutional resources necessary to provide alternatives. Assimilationist approaches to teaching stem from teacher education programs that neither provide training in pedagogical models that reflect indigenous perspectives nor promote the value of building on learners' prior knowledge and experiences. As one Tzotzil parent explained:

> Many teachers, though they are indigenous, no longer know our customs because they were only with their parents for six years before they went to boarding schools and then to live in the city of San Cristóbal. They no longer saw how their parents lived, nor could they receive their parents' teachings. They cannot orient our children then because they do not know our way of life, how our thinking develops, how we speak in the community. (González & Pérez, 1998: 42)

Other obstacles preventing the implementation of the educational ideals outlined in the San Andrés Accords include administrative disorganization of the government, lack of effort or capability in standardizing the indigenous languages, ignorance, or as many believe, a conspiracy by the dominant Spanish-speaking culture to keep indigenous people subjugated and oppressed. Institutional racism and discrimination against indigenous students remains extremely widespread in Chiapas and has created an atmosphere of severe distrust and cynicism toward governmental programs designed to 'help' and provide 'opportunities' to the indigenous people. In the summer of 2004, approximately 120 indigenous students from Chol, Tzeltal, Tzotzil, Zoque, Mam, Kachikel, Mocho, Chuj, and Tojolobal speaking communities camped out in front of the Municipal President's building in San Cristóbal de las Casas for several months, beginning June 7, 2004. They were protesting the government's plan to close all indigenous intercultural–bilingual Normal schools in Mexico, schools where indigenous students prepare to become bilingual teachers. As the literature that the students distributed explained:

> Intercultural bilingual indigenous education is not a gift of the government or a new idea, it has been a demand for centuries and has been enforced through the indigenous struggle, above all by the armed uprising of the EZLN who demands that education for the indigenous people be based on our needs and the context in which we live. This is upheld in article 2 of the Indigenous Rights and Culture Act, which remains unrecognized only by the government. (Gonzàlez & Pérez, 1998: 42)

Many of the students who participated in the strike have lost their grants and have been expelled from their school. Some have attempted to go on a hunger strike. The government's plan to replace these public, low-cost Normal schools with private monolingual institutions will make it much harder for indigenous students, many of whom come from impoverished remote areas, to become teachers. This will greatly reduce the number of future bilingual teachers.

Alternatives to Public Schools: Autonomous and Popular Education Programs

Autonomous schools

In spite of all the obstacles facing indigenous people in realizing a free, public education that respects and promotes their rich linguistic diversity and cultural heritages, the perseverance and deeply held belief in the right to learn and maintain ones' own language is keeping this dream alive, and indeed making it a reality for many children and adults. There have been two main models through which the indigenous people of Chiapas have organized their resistance to the public educational system. One of these models is the *autonomous school movement* created by the Zapatistas. Another one, which I will address in the next section, is the popular education programs.

Although the Mexican government and media ignore the amazing educational initiatives of the Zapatistas, visitors to these autonomous schools located in rural communities in Chiapas would be astounded to see the sophisticated, academic curriculum the Zapatistas have created, coupled with a profoundly humanistic teacher training program that is facilitated by Mexican and international volunteers, or '*asesores*' (mentors). The Zapatistas refuse all government support and receive all monetary, technical, and professional assistance from both Mexican and international individuals and non-governmental organizations in solidarity with their cause. Through an interchange of ideas from educators from all over the world, the Zapatistas have created a new concept of education for Indian communities based on the theories of liberatory and progressive educational theorists, such as Paolo Freire, Célestin Freinet, John Dewey, and bell hooks. Their goal is to attain the same high level of education as in more highly developed countries, while maintaining their own values and the practices of their ancestors by developing expertise in areas such as medicinal herbs, agriculture, and by creating a sustainable society. At the same time, their education is highly politicized, and strongly reinforces concepts such as resistance and autonomy, dignity and responsibility for defending the Indian cultures, languages, and people.

Following the uprising in 1994, government teachers were asked to leave autonomous territories that had been taken over by the Zapatistas. They were replaced with members of the communities (many of whom had completed their education only up to the 6th grade) who serve as educational *promotores* (promoters) and perform the role of facilitators or mentors.

The Zapatistas' philosophy toward governance, *mandar obedeciendo* ('to lead by obeying'), turns the traditional authoritarian approach to governing on its head. This concept reflects a rejection of the traditional authoritarian role of 'teacher,' an identity many indigenous people have associated with oppression and fear. In the words of one of the *promotores* interviewed on a Zapatista documentary on autonomous schools, entitled, *Educación en Resistencia*:

> *Hay una gran diferencia entre nuestros maestros y los maestros del gobierno porque ellos nos maltrataban. Nos reprendían y nos ridiculizaban. Porque somos pobres y ellos tienen dinero, el gobierno no nos respecta, pero nosotros nos respetamos. A ellos no les importa si estamos aprendiendo o no, pero sabemos si estamos aprendiendo y nos importa.*
> (There's a big difference between our teachers and the government teachers because they mistreated us, they scolded and ridiculed us. Because we are poor and they have money, the government doesn't respect us, but we respect ourselves. They don't care if we are learning or not, but we know if we are not learning, and we care.)

Although some autonomous communities still lack functioning schools, or even buildings and classrooms, the power of their imagination is enabling them to overcome their limited resources. In fact, since the Zapatista uprising in 1994, they have realized their dream of opening autonomous primary and secondary schools in all of the five main Zapatista municipalities (or '*Caracoles*,' as the Zapatistas refer to the governed regions within Zapatista territories), where they are teaching and creating their own materials in Tzotzil, Tzeltal, Chol, Tojolobal, and Mam languages, as well as in Spanish. Their curriculum, which they refer to as *la educación verdadera* ('true education') is designed to instill pride in their cultural heritage and develop the skills and knowledge necessary to be active, productive members of their own communities, as well as critical observers and actors in the wider society. In contrast to the 'bad education' they received at the hands of the government, they have created what they call 'true education.' As a coordinator of autonomous education in one community explains:

> *La educación verdadera es donde todos tienen voluntad propia para el rescate de la cultura. La enseñanza colectiva rompe los esquemas de lo que sucede en la educación oficial en una formación integral que fortalezca a nuestros pueblos. Los cuatro ejes de esta enseñanza son matemáticas, vida y medio ambiente,*

write is not divorced from the social, economic, and political contexts in which meanings and realities are interpreted, defined and valued.

Working within the same philosophical framework, Augusto Boal (1979), developed a method of liberatory education entitled, 'Theater of the Oppressed,' in which participants role play real-life incidents in which people have been positioned as voiceless and powerless. This method applies Freire's ideas of educational *praxis* – action and reflection – described in his book, *Education of the Oppressed* (Freire, 1973b). By taking on the role of 'actor,' and recreating a situation in which individuals and groups have been oppressed, participants have the opportunity to reflect on and reverse their subjugated positions in society.

Also working within a Freirean milieu, Miguel Escobar (1985, 1998) has promoted the idea of a liberatory informal education for adults in Mexico that challenges the hierarchical and authoritarian structure of Mexican public schools. In such alternative frameworks, learners are more empowered to engage in dialogue and problem posing (*'pedagogía de la pregunta'*) through literacy education. Although there is still much work to be done in this area, these theorists, among others, have helped to critique the idea of neutrality in education and re-envision education as a transcendental process of resisting cultural domination.

The basic characteristics of popular education, according to García Huidobro (1985) include:

- being based in the linguistic and cultural reality and perspectives of the poor and marginal people;
- seeking to transform and empower the poor by helping them to improve the conditions in their lives;
- having teachers act as facilitators, not authorities; with student relationships that are dialogue-based;
- basing the educational process on the participation of the people.

Some researchers have distinguished between community education and popular education program in Mexico (Gochicoa, 1996; Street, 1990). The former, which are supported by government organizations, consist of programs aimed to develop vocational, domestic, and technical skills of marginalized groups in society, with the general aim of contributing to the productivity of the state economy. In contrast, popular educational programs are concerned with the interests, needs, and empowerment of poor, marginalized people in a community, rather than how they can be more productive members in society (Gochicoa, 1996). While both programs offer non-formal education in a variety of areas that contribute to the development of communities, popular education is more concerned with questioning the status quo, while community education tends to reproduce it by

> *historia y lengua. Todos relacionados con nuestras demandas.* (Bellingha
> 2004)
> (True education is where everybody has free will to rescue the cu
> The collective teaching breaks the patterns of public education in
> integral formation capable of empowering our people. The four a
> our teaching are mathematics, life and earth science, history,
> language. They are all related to our demands.)

The US-based non-governmental organization, *Schools for Chiapas,* g
the following report from their recent visit to autonomous schools in
highlands of Chiapas:

> On Monday, September 6, 2004, 83 new primary schools will open th
> doors to Tzotzil boys and girls from Indian communities through
> this chilly, mountainous region. Most of the education promot
> offering instruction in these schools will be graduates of the First
> January Secondary School. The decision to open autonomous prima
> schools in the highlands was just taken last November 2003 on the ter
> anniversary of the Zapatista uprising, however everyone here seen
> surprised at the speed with which the autonomous communities hav
> moved to open autonomous schools. Since these Zapatista schoo
> operate without any government teachers, books, or other forms o
> funding it requires a great deal of sacrifice for the desperately po
> Indian communities of Chiapas to open an autonomous scho
> (*Schools for Chiapas Update*, September, 2004)

Popular education in Mayan communities

A less radical, but perhaps even more subversive approach to resist
the public educational system is the development of popular educa
programs by Mayan cultural organizations in Chiapas. Paolo Freire (19
1973b) created the term 'popular education' to refer to grassroots progr
designed to help poor, illiterate peasants in Brazil, by providing the t
they needed to confront oppression while empowering themselves
their communities. Strategies of resistance and consciousness-ra
include learning how to critically interpret signs of domination thr
native language literacy training; in Freirean terms, learning how to
the word and the world.' For example, the material used to teach lit
deals with real problems in the learners' lives, such as socio-econom
work-related issues. Popular education programs emerged in deve
countries in Latin America as a response to the poor socio-econom
public educational system that has served to empower the rich, while
ducing the marginal and subjugated positions of the poor and w
classes. Within the popular educational framework, learning to re

offering compensatory, vocational programs that do not attempt to seek radical solutions to social and economic problems (Street, 1990).

This distinction is particularly relevant in the case of educational programs directed toward women. Community programs offered to women rarely help them to reflect on their limited roles, discrimination, and economic exploitation. Popular education programs, on the other hand, aim to problematize the processes involved in reproducing gender oppression and help women develop consciousness of the need to develop skills that can help them to become more independent, save money, and organize themselves to be trained in areas that have traditionally been dominated by men, such as politics, business, technology, and agriculture.

Education for Language and Cultural Survival in Chiapas

A beginning

In 1951, the National Indigenous Institute (INI), a governmental organization, began to establish educational programs in Chiapas with the mission to 'civilize' and 'assimilate' the Indian (Alvarez, 2002). Although these programs were initially only in the areas of health and agriculture, they began a process of greater entitlement. Prior to this, indigenous people were violently persecuted and their movements were greatly controlled. They were restricted from entering the city at certain times and were prohibited from walking on the sidewalks (they had to walk in the street).

Although outsiders studied indigenous languages and customs and wrote about them for international audiences, there were no educational programs for indigenous to learn to read and write in their own languages or study their histories and cultures. As a way to of reclaiming cultural control, some indigenous people began to consider that they needed to tell their stories from their own voices for the benefit of their own communities (Laughlin, 2002).

The present

There are two internationally-known Mayan non-governmental organizations in Chiapas that are working toward indigenous cultural survival through popular educational programs. These are: *Sna Jtz'ibajom* (The House of the Writer) and *Fortaleza de la Mujer Maya (FOMMA)* (Empowering Mayan Women). Both organizations are well established in many of the thousands of Tzotzil and Tzeltal communities that surround the colonial city of San Cristóbal de las Casas. The two collectives share similar goals: developing native language literacy, and promoting Mayan language and culture through theater and writing on topics affecting their communities. However, the focus of the two groups is distinct.

Sna Jtz'ibajom, a mixed-gender group, deals more with the revival of ancient Mayan folktales and customs, as well as with current problems affecting indigenous communities, such as alcoholism, ecology, bilingual education, and immigration. *FOMMA* is an all-female organization whose work is based on the problems and issues of indigenous Mayan women.

Sna Jtz'ibajom

The stated objectives of Sna Jtz'ibajom are:

(1) to reinforce the mother tongue, as much in oral as written form and the creation of written materials from the Tzeltal and Tzotzil cultures;
(2) to promote bilingual education, giving preference to the mother tongue, with appropriate educational materials;
(3) to educate Spanish-speaking Mexicans about the essential aspects of autonomous cultures to build up appreciation for them and stop discrimination against them;
(4) to support the creation of indigenous literary works, dramas, and audiovisual materials through literacy workshops. (Sna Jtz'ibajom, 2004)

Common themes in the group's stories and plays include: Mayan culture, customs, traditional ceremonies and celebrations, religious beliefs and spirituality, history, human rights, education for indigenous children, cosmovision, environment, food, problems in contemporary society, work, justice, land and territory.

While Sna Jtz'ibajom began as a writer's collective in 1985, the organization began to use theater and puppetry as a vehicle to educate people in the rural communities. They named the group *Lo'il maxil*, which translates into English as 'Monkey Business Theater' and took their work on the road, traveling and performing in various indigenous communities in the Chiapas highlands (Sna Jtz'ibajom, 1996). Sna Jtz'ibajom tours Mexico annually and performs in rural indigenous communities in Chiapas twice a month. They have also performed in several countries in Central America, Canada, and up until September 11, 2001, they performed annually in the US.

The title of their traveling theater company reflects strong cultural traits and values such as humor, revealing lies, teasing, and also as the symbolic role of animals in Mayan folktales. Collectively, they have created 14 plays with themes ranging from dramatic representations of ancient Mayan customs that date back to the 16th century, to problems and issues facing indigenous people in contemporary Mayan society today. According to the actors, their theater has helped to revive many of the Mayan traditions that have almost been forgotten and are at risk of being lost. While they are sometimes invited to perform their plays to schoolchildren in rural communities, more often, their 'classrooms' are open-air arenas, such as basketball courts, where through bilingual performances to audiences comprising of people of all ages, they seek to stimulate people to reflect on the problems affecting their communities, while counteracting the hegemonic effects of the dominant culture by instilling pride in the native languages and cultures.

The topics of their plays vary. *Trabajadores en el Otro Mundo* (Workers in Another World) tells of the hardships that Mexican immigrants face when they travel north to the US to seek employment. This is a situation that is highly relevant to Mayans, as about one million are currently working under such poor conditions in the US. *De Todos Para Todos* (From All for All) addresses the recent violent conflicts in communities over territory and natural resources, such as the water supply. *La Historia del Maíz* (The Story of Corn) tells the story of the Mayan Gods' creation of their sacred food.

In traditional Mayan communities, there is a long history of gender discrimination. Up until recently, women did not vote and girls were not sent to school. With the Zapatista uprising in 1994, women became somewhat more organized and political. Women actors in the theater company have to deal with patriarchal customs that require them to get their husbands' permission before traveling and working with men who are not their husbands. Since actors perform in open-air theaters with no microphones, women especially have to learn to project their voices strongly. Through rehearsals and exercises they have learned from guest directors, they become more aware of their body language and are able to use their voices and bodies in ways that once caused them great embarrassment. Although gender discrimination is not a main focus of the collective's work, some of the female members of the collective are writing and publishing stories that deal with this discrimination. Socorro Gómez Hernández, a very talented young writer and actress at Sna Jtz'ibajom has also become involved in a radio program in which she reads educational plays in Tzotzil that deal with problems that indigenous girls and young women face, such as domestic violence, and lack of educational and employment opportunities. Listeners are encouraged to consider the issues presented in the play by responding to reflective questions following the reading.

Since 1987, Sna Jtz'ibajom's Native Language Literacy program, also known as, *Chanob vun ta batz'ikop*, has awarded about 7000 diplomas to children and adults, ranging in age from 10 to 60, who learned to read and write in Tzotzil and Tzeltal (De la Torre López, 1998; Laughlin, 2004). The workshops last about six months and take place at weekends in schools or in rooms in teachers' homes. The members of Sna Jtz'ibajom provide biliteracy training to 15 teachers, five in each of the three neighboring towns: Chamula (Tzotzil), Zinacantan (Tzotzil) and Tenejapa (Tzeltal), and supervise their teaching in the communities. Many of the instructors are university students who have received a Mayan Foundation grant. They learn how to use the Sna Jtz'ibajom literacy manuals, as well as supplementary materials, such as audiovisuals and stories to teach reading and writing in the native languages. When the program first began, most of the participants were men; however, now most of the participants are women and children (Laughlin, 2004). Sna Jtz'ibajom (2003) published a trilingual (Tzotzil, Tzeltal, and Spanish) collection of short stories written by the children attending the workshop, entitled, *Sts'unbal jts'ibtik:Nuestras semillas literarias, Cuentos infantiles* (Our Literary Seeds, Children's Stories).

The Centro Estatal de Lenguas, Arte y Literatura Indígenas (CELALI), is a governmental organization in Chiapas which also provides native language literacy workshops and language and literature classes in Tzotzil, Tzeltal, Chol, Tojolobal, and Mam. CELALI organizes an annual competition in which writers of all age categories, from early primary school grades to the elderly, are given opportunities to win monetary awards for their short stories and poems. Thus, while these types of incentives and funding have not yet reached the public schools, Sna Jtz'ibajom's work, as well as FOMMA's (described in the next section) has helped to inspire government support of native language literacy instruction, which has been an important step toward achieving greater official recognition. In fact, Sna Jtz'ibajom was last year's recipient of the National Prize for Arts and Sciences, which they won for the category of 'Popular Arts and Traditions.' This is the highest honor that the Mexican government grants in recognition of significant contributions in the arts and sciences, and includes a diploma, medal and $40,000 award, which was presented to Sna Jtz'ibajom by President Fox on December 1, 2004 (Jiménez, 2004). Sna Jtz'ibajom is using part of the money to create an Academia de Ciencias y Artes Maya-Zoque. What has been a dream for many years for these ten Mayan writers is becoming a reality. Indeed, the power of the imagination cannot be underestimated.

FOMMA: Fortaleza de la Mujer Maya

FOMMA is a civil organization that serves both indigenous and mestiza women who come from various communities in the highlands of Chiapas. The organization was formed in 1994 for the purpose of helping women to become more autonomous and empowered. Both female founders of the group began their acting careers as members of Sna Jtz'ibajom. The theater group was called *Fortaleza de la Mujer Maya* (Empowering Mayan Women).

It's no coincidence that the organization developed the same year that the Zapatista uprising took place. As I said earlier, the Zapatistas brought a new consciousness to women and encouraged them to be more political and organize themselves. Thousands of Indians who were forcibly expelled from their communities took refuge in the city. Women needed to learn how to survive in a different linguistic and cultural environment. They also needed to learn how to support themselves. These urgent needs and the reality of the times shifted the group's focus from that of an artistic endeavor to one with a more educational and pragmatic purpose.

While FOMMA is also involved in literacy education in indigenous communities, FOMMA's work focuses on issues related to the empowerment of women, such as domestic violence, women's health, and children's rights. In addition to these activities, the group provides training to women in a variety of areas, such as native language literacy, how to use computers, radio broadcasting, and sewing. Collectively, the members of FOMMA have developed the following seven objectives:

(1) the empowerment of indigenous women and respect of their rights;
(2) the empowerment of Mayan culture, whilst severely challenging all cultural aspects that affect the dignity and integrity of women;
(3) the promotion of indigenous theater and literature that contributes to raising consciousness and allows indigenous women to express their problems;
(4) the construction of collective spaces in order to reflect about the problem of ethnicity and gender, while creating conditions that free the time and workload of women, through nurseries and children's workshops;
(5) the development of activities to enable indigenous women to acquire new skills, such as literacy and technical training, in order to improve their employment opportunities and urban lives in San Cristóbal de las Casas;
(6) the development of jobs for indigenous women;
(7) the creation of economic activities to generate earnings that could sustain the organization (FOMMA, 2004).

The women who take classes at the center teach what they learn to others in their communities. Children and adults are learning to write their stories in their native languages. This is especially valuable to indigenous children who move to the city of San Cristóbal and experience great pressure to assimilate into the dominant culture. The workshops the organization offers to children teach them about their rights and increase their self-esteem through activities that increase body awareness, movement, self-expression, storytelling, as well as workshops on computers, sewing, baking, and literacy.

The plays they perform in communities have strong social and political messages about the role of women in society. 'Confined Souls,' is one example of an alarming tale about a family who sell their daughter to a man for some bottles of liquor. 'The Migration' addresses the changes women and families go through when they leave their communities in search for new opportunities in the city. 'The Desperate Woman' is a play that deals with the disastrous affects of machismo and jealousy. At an international anti-militarization conference held in San Cristóbal de las Casas in 2003 the group performed a play about the manipulation of the vote, and how politicians often trick women into exchanging their voter's identification for a few chickens or bottles of soda. The play sends the strong message to women that they need to be more aware of the different interests of each political candidate and the importance of participating conscientiously in the voting process.

In the summer of 2004, they staged the play *Solidaridad y Esperanza,* with the help of guest director, Doris DiFarnecio. This poignant autobiographical story of the life of one of the women was performed for the first time in a rural Tzotzil community called Huixtan. Two actresses performed all six or seven roles in the play. Although most of the play was in Spanish, parts were in Tzotzil.

Building a Mayan Future

With the support of the Mayan Educational Foundation, Sna Jtz'ibajom, and FOMMA, about 20 indigenous youth from various communities are receiving grants that partially fund their university education. All these students are graduates of Sna Jtz'ibajom's and FOMMA's literacy programs and have learned to read and write in their native languages. They are the first generation in their families to study at university. Many are from rural communities and have not had much, if any, experience in the city – much less so studying with *Ladino* (non-indigenous) students. They are all focused on studies that will help to enrich or provide necessary services to their communities. For example, one woman is conducting an anthropological study of beliefs in witchcraft among elders in a Tzeltal community for the purpose of reviving and documenting Tzeltal stories and practices. One young Tzotzil-speaking man is studying medicine in order to improve the quality of healthcare in his community, where currently there are only Spanish-speaking doctors who cannot adequately communicate with non-Spanish speaking patients. A sociology student who herself has been the victim of male violence is highly motivated to work toward helping women in her community of Zinacantán, where counseling services are currently unavailable.

Within the context of the dominant Spanish-speaking culture, many find it challenging to maintain their cultural dignity and pride, let alone their languages and cultures. One woman described her physical changes as she peels off her traditional Mayan *huipile* and long woven skirt and replaces them with jeans and a T-shirt as soon as she arrives at her college. Another student disclosed how once, on the first day of class when every student was asked to introduce him/herself, rather than telling people the name of his small rural indigenous village, he told his classmates that he was from the city of San Cristóbal. All of them described the subtle and not-so-subtle ways in which they felt discriminated against, from being excluded to what they perceived as inappropriate attention to their 'otherness.' One student seemed to express the sentiment of the group when he said:

> *La única cosa que ellos (los Ladinos) tienen y que nos falta son las oportunidades para mostrarles de que somos capaces de cumplir nuestras metas.*
> (The only thing they (the Ladinos) have that we lack are the opportunities to show them that we are capable of accomplishing our goals.)

In a strong voice, a young woman emphatically implored the group to resist: '*No podemos dejarles discrimar en contra nuestra. No los dejen!*' ('We cannot let them discriminate against us. Don't let them!') These voices speak clearly to the strength and resilience of the Mayan culture: a culture with an amazing history and, to be sure, a vital and enduring future.

Acknowledgement

The author gratefully acknowledges Sna Jtz'ibajom's generosity, patience and friendship. A special thank you to Juan de la Torres Teratoh for the Tsotsil summary, and also to Long Island University's Faculty Research Committee and the Mexico-North Rsearch Network for their support.

Summary

Formal public education for indigenous children consists primarily of passive learning from authoritarian teachers who transmit cultural and linguistic values that are markedly distinct from those of the communities in which they are teaching. Within this system, children are taught to reproduce the cultural capital of the dominant class, thus complying with their own subjugation. Many obstacles face indigenous people in realizing a free, public education that respects and promotes their rich linguistic diversity and cultural heritages. Nonetheless, the perseverance and deeply-held belief in the right to learn and maintain one's native language, or *batsi'kop* (literally, 'true language' in Tsotsil) is keeping the dream of multilingual education alive, and indeed making it a reality for many children and adults in Chiapas, Mexico, where one-third of the population is indigenous and 11 indigenous languages are spoken, many of which are endangered.

Beginning with the historical and sociopolitical context of indigenous native language rights and bilingual education in Mexico, this chapter describes two main models through which the indigenous people of Chiapas have organized their resistance to the enforced acculturation process in public schools for indigenous peoples. One of these models is the autonomous school movement created by the *Zapatistas*. Another one is the popular education programs of two Chiapas-based Mayan non-governmental organizations – *Sna Jtz'ibajom* (House of the Writer) and *Fortaleza de la Mujer Maya* (Empowering Mayan Women). This chapter demonstrates how these grassroots organizations are succeeding in reviving and promoting the native languages for the indigenous people in Chiapas. In addition, with the support of national and international organizations, the work of these grassroots organizations is influencing national language policies in Mexico, and inspiring people across the Mexican borders to promote similar movements for social justice and linguistic human rights in their own communities.

Comenzando con el contexto histórico y sociopolítico de los derechos a los idiomas nativos indígenas y la educación bilingüe en México, este artículo describe dos modelos principales a través de los cuales los indígenas de Chiapas han organizado su resistencia hacia el proceso de aculturación forzada en las escuelas públicas para los pueblos indígenas. Uno de estos modelos es el movimiento de autonomía escolar creado por los zapatistas. Otro es los programas de educación popular de dos organizaciones no gubernamentales mayas radicadas en Chiapas: Sna Jtz'ibajom (La casa del Escritor) y Fortaleza de la Mujer Maya (FOMMA). Este trabajo demuestra cómo estas organizaciones de nivel local no sólo están teniendo éxito al revitalizar y promover los idiomas nativos no sólo para los pueblos indígenas en Chiapas, sino que con el apoyo de organizaciones nacionales e internationales, sus labores están influyendo en las políticas nacionales sobre los idiomas de México, e inspirando a otros pueblos a través de la fronteras mexicanas para promover movimientos similares en busca de justicia social y derechos humanos lingüísticos en sus propias comunidades. (Spanish)

Ja' ta jlikesbetik sk'oplal slo'ilal xchi'uk ti k'u x'elan stsoboj sbaik ta sa'beik smelol ti k'usi lekik xk'ot ta pasel skuenta slumalik, ti oyuk yich'el ta muk' ti sbats'i k'op stukik li bats'i jnaklejetike, xchi'uk xcha'tosol k'op oy ta Mejikoe, li jpok vun meltsajem li'e ta xal ka'itik cha'tos lo'il, ja' ta xalbe smelol skuenta li bats'i jnaklejetik ta Chyapae, yu'un tey to ta sjol ta yo'onik mu to bu batemik ta stojol ti yan o talel kuxlejale, ti yan o talel kuxlejale yu'un ja' tey ta staik sujel ta snail chanobvunetik skuenta li bats'i jnaklejetike. Ali jtos k'usi ta xkalbetik smelole ja' li k'uxi likem tal sk'oplal yu'unik xchanobvun stukik li jsapatistaetike. Li jtose ja' li xchanobvun likem ta stojol stukik ti buch'utik stsobanoj sbaik ta abtel ta chayapae, ti ma'uk ta skuenta jyue'ele: Ja' li sna Jtz'ibajom xchi'uk stalel yip antsetik. Li' chal ka'itik li vun li'e, ja' ti juchop j'abtel stsobanoj sbaik tey ta yut yosilalike, yu'un stsakoj xa yipik ta xcha'kuxesel ti sbats'i k'opik ta Jujun slumalike, mu ja'uk nox ti buy nakalik ti bats'i jnaklejetike, yu'un ta skolta sbaik xchi'uk yantik o nasyonetik noxtok, ti yabtelike yu'un pukijem xa ech'el ta sjunul mejiko skuenta ti bats'i k'opetik ta yosilal Mejikoe, ja' nox yech tey xa yatel yo'onik ta sjam ech'el sbeik ta yan o jteklumetik k'alal buy sts'ak ti mejikoe, skuenta ta xak'beik yipal k'u cha'al yolel ta xkaltike, yu'un ta sa'ik ti oyuk xchapaj lek sk'op ti jchi'iltaktike xchi'uk oyuk yich'el ta muk' skotol jchi'iltaktik xchi'uk ti sbats'i k'opik te yo' buy nakajtik ta sparajelike. (Tsotsil, a Mayan language. Translated by Juan de la Torres Teratol)

Part 4

Tensions between Multiple Realities

Chapter 8

Imagined Multilingual Schools: How Come We Don't Deliver?

ELANA SHOHAMY

Introduction

This chapter begins with a description of my own fantasies, 'the imagined' with regard to the role of languages in schools. It then portrays 'the reality' of how languages are in fact used in most schools today. The main argument will be that major obstacles exist that prevent and hinder the fantasies from becoming a reality. The chapter concludes with some suggestions as to steps that can be taken to change the situation and bring us closer to 'the imagined'.

Imagining

A number of elements and components can be included in a list of 'the imagined' features of multilingual schools. The most obvious one is that of maintaining and developing multilingual competence. This refers first to the students who arrive in schools equipped with multilingual competence. These students should have the right and legitimacy to use, maintain, and preserve these multilingual competencies in all school contexts. But these multilingual students should also have the opportunity to further develop their multilingual competence and reach higher levels. This development can be through using multiple languages as medium of instruction, having access to sources in these languages, and being assessed in these languages. It is clear that not making use of these competencies results in their attrition, elimination, and suppression, as well as creating feelings of marginalization and exclusion. It also implies that students who arrive in schools as monolinguals (in terms of old notions of languages having distinct boundaries, a point I will return to later) should have the opportunities to learn and acquire additional languages, whether from their peers or from the curriculum and instruction of the school.

Multilingual competence is needed and should be an important aspiration, given the realities of most societies and nations nowadays where multi-languages are a reality, at both the local and national levels and in the global world. In other words, our reality supports a multilingual ideology. It is clear that, while nation states in the past were as multilingual as they are today, the nation-state ideology was so dominant that it denied and delegitimized the reality and refused to face it head on. The traditional nation state was more about aspirations, myths and imagination of 'sameness' than about the ecological reality, as languages served as a symbolic goal. But even then, it was clear that most nation states consisted of users of multiple languages in different realities – local, regional, global, as well as any imagined combinations of languages and dialects, often used by immigrants from one generation to the next, as well as within communities.

Immigrants and other groups continue to construct meanings in the most creative ways, holding multiple identities and using multiple varieties of languages, especially in the current era of a trans-national world. This reality must be recognized by educational systems where languages and their varieties need to be acquired, used, and developed harmoniously, if only to reflect the 'real world', as schools are meant to prepare students for the 'real world.'

Further, multilingual competence does not refer only to a 'number of languages,' but also to a variety of competencies that result from a mixture and hybrids of different languages. Thus, fantasizing about multilingualism in school implies not only legitimacy for a number of languages in classes and schools, but also to mixing of languages and the creation of language hybrids and fusions whereby different codes are used for the purpose of communication and expression. Specifically, this means that languages do not need to have distinct boundaries as linguists have led us to believe, as there is recognition nowadays of the existence of these different combinations of languages.

The legitimacy of language hybrids further recognizes the use of multicodes *within* one language, that is, languages are also known to consist of elements such as visuals, pictures, images, music, art, graphs and a variety of symbols with no language boundaries and varied ways of '*languaging*' (Kress & Leeuwen, 1996; New London Group, 1996; Shohamy, 2006).

Multilingual competence implies also the acceptance of languages as flexible units beyond the artificial boundaries that were assigned to them. Thus, language 'correctness' and language 'purity', within first language (whatever this 'thing' is) may be imagined, and prescribed notions often have no place in reality as well. In the imagined schools there is legitimacy for different ways of creating language, even if they do not follow prescribed rules. There is room, therefore, for oral, as well as written varieties, and any possible combination and interaction among them. It also means that there is a need to challenge and reject the notion of the single, homogenous, standard criterion of the language of 'the native speaker' being 'the truth' and the ultimate model of 'correctness', whoever the 'native speaker' is. This criterion is not useful as it represents some kind of norm that includes some and excludes others, based on their language manifestations, and rejects variations. Thus, in the imagined schools, the emphasis and focus is more on *what* people say, and less on *how* they say it, so languages become mostly means of communication, expression, social interaction, and tools for meaningful learning.

In summary, in the 'imagined schools', students obtain legitimacy for multilingual competence or strive to acquire it as a reflection of multilingual realities, since monolingualism is a myth detached from reality that must be recognized as such by educational systems. Monolingual competence has been an ideological aspiration rather than a reality, and educational institutions have been asked to play a role in carrying out this ideology. There is no need for education to play the role of serving political ideologies of the traditional nation states that strive to make people homogenous and similar to one another in aspects which have no ground in reality. There is a need, therefore, to deconstruct the myth of the native speaker as the language norm and the one that people should strive for. This results only in the exclusion of other groups based on language criteria.

These views represent beliefs that languages serve as codes that should be followed in civil and democratic societies whereby there is a need for inclusion, and not of exclusion. They also support people's right to use languages in ways they feel most useful for them and for those with whom they communicate. In civil societies there is a need for accepting differences, for striving for inclusion, and for the co-existence of a wide variety of groups. These fantasies also oppose a view of schools as servants of the nation state where some groups obtain benefits, while others – those who do not master the non-dominant language – become the victims of the system, their languages viewed as 'wrong', 'incorrect', 'polluted', 'low' and inferior.

The Reality

The reality is very different. In most educational contexts in the world, a specific national language, spoken by the powerful groups in the society, is the only legitimate language in schools. In many countries nowadays, English obtains legitimacy as well, being the global language believed to serve national ideologies of globalization, commerce, world status, and economic purposes. Even countries such as France are beginning to accept the need for English as a powerful language that is highly popular among parents and students (see Hélot, Chapter 3). At the same time, other languages, especially those used by immigrants and indigenous groups, are viewed as having low value and status with no legitimate place in schools. Thus, in most schools, a subtractive ideology is pursued and promoted whereby students are encouraged to lose the other languages they possess in favour of 'the national languages' and English. This means that students who are proficient in one or a number of these 'other' languages are not encouraged to maintain these home languages, and this leads to their suppression, and contributes eventually to their loss.

Additive multilingual approaches are still rare in most schools. National languages are still viewed in ideological terms as part of a national identity embedded with notions that language is an indicator of loyalty, patriotism, belonging, inclusion and membership. The national languages are viewed as hegemonic, and speakers of other languages un-do these languages while embarking on the route to monolingualism striving to be like 'the native speaker' (who has used the language from birth). This is perpetuated by using terms such as 'accurate', 'correct' and 'standards' in terms of grammar, lexicon, and accent that are expected to be reached by all, while no other languages have any formal legitimacy. It is still the written variety of the national language that has power, while other varieties (e.g. text messages, emails, oral languages, chats) have no legitimacy in formal learning. Schools encourage students to use what they consider to be correct, accurate, and pure language. There is still no legitimacy for multi-modalities, for mixing of languages, for hybrids, or for non-verbal varieties of expression. All this is perpetuated by national tests that assess standards of the language for all students.

Comparing the 'imagined' versus the 'reality' makes us realize the wide gap between the two. The issues that will be considered next are descriptions of the very devices that prevent the imagined from becoming a reality. It is the main argument of this chapter that it is these very mechanisms, used by political authorities and ideologues in implicit ways, that become the major hindrances to the realization of 'the imagined'. These very mechanisms serve as devices that prevent the introduction of more open views of language. The mechanisms undermine 'the imagined' in ways that continue to perpetuate monolingual hegemonic ideologies, while viewing

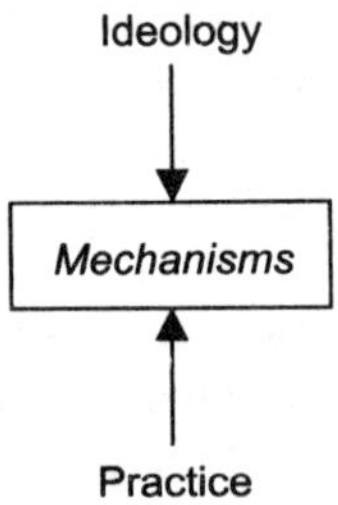

Figure 8.1 Language policy: the place of mechanisms between ideology and practice

multilingualism as a threat. In other words, these mechanisms are instrumental in turning ideologies into practice. The place of the mechanisms within ideology and practice is illustrated in Figure 8.1. The ideology represents the aspirations of those who introduce language policies, while the practice is the reality; the mechanisms serve as the tools between the two. The rest of the chapter will focus on these very mechanisms to illustrate their power and influence in affecting *de facto* languages policies.

The Mechanisms

It is argued here that various mechanisms are used, often in covert ways, to affect, create, and perpetuate *de facto* monolingual policies. These mechanisms lie between ideologies and practice. They serve the existing ideologies, as they are used by those in authority who represent powerful institutions that can exercise control and influence and create *de facto* policies. Figure 8.2 depicts five such mechanisms: (1) declared policies, (2) language education policies, (3) language tests, (4) language in public space, and (5) ideology, myths, propaganda and coercion. Although the list is clearly not exhaustive, only the first three will be discussed in this chapter. These mechanisms are discussed more elaborately in my book, *Language Policy: Hidden agendas and new approaches* (Shohamy, 2006).

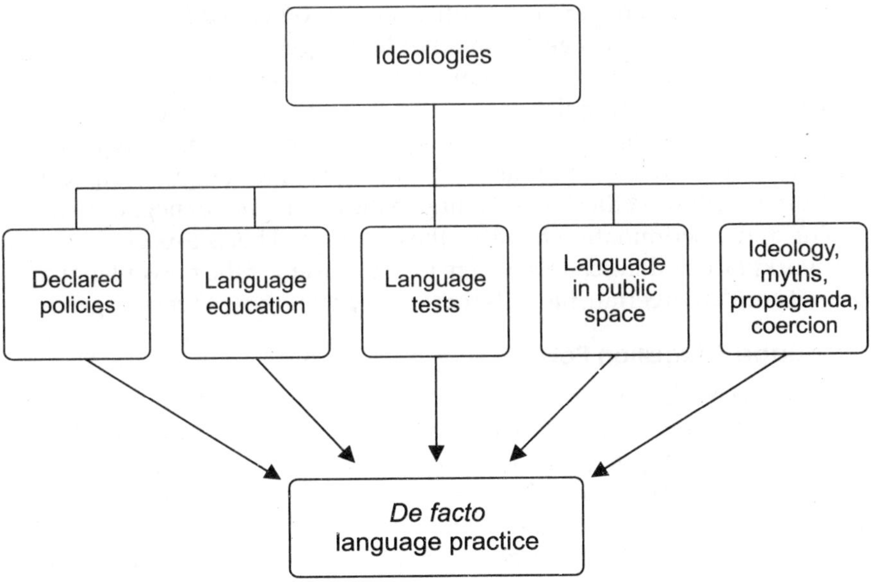

Figure 8.2 Mechanisms that influence language policies

Declared policies, standards and regulations

This mechanism refers to specific ways by which society chooses to legitimize one language or a number of languages, and to exclude others. By declaring a certain language or languages as standard or official, the message that is delivered is that only that language is legitimate, while other languages used in the society are 'illegitimate'. Further devices include making the written languages the norm of correctness and purity, and deciding on strict and specific criteria for determining what is 'acceptable' and 'pure' language and what is not (Spolsky, 2004). In most situations, it is the language of the 'native' speakers, its grammar, lexicon and pronunciation (i.e. accent) that is considered to be the 'good and high quality language'.

Additional declared policies include announcing certain languages as 'official,' as in the case of English, legislated as official by a large number of states in the US while other languages are not, thereby granting the official languages specific priorities in society through language laws. Language academies, which exist in most countries, serve as another mechanism for control as they guard and police 'deviations' from what they consider to be 'the' standards and the norm. Declaring certain languages as official implies granting legitimacy to certain languages and de-legitimizing others. Similarly, language laws grant special privileges to specific languages to be used in given situations, as in official documents, government institutions, educational entities, and in other public spaces, while taking away such privileges from other languages.

The consequences of the implementation of declared policy documents, standards, and other regulations are direct marginalization, exclusion, and stigma to those people who do not speak the 'official' and 'legitimized' languages. It also categorizes users of non-legitimized languages as 'different', often excluding them and leading to the emergence of negative stereotyping and discrimination towards these groups. This is especially true in the workplace and in schools, where the non-users of the power languages are not entitled to certain benefits that society offers only to certain groups.

Language Education Policies

This mechanism refers to educational decisions that impose specific language behaviors in school settings. Language Education Policies impose *de facto* language behaviors on all public educational institutions. They are manifested especially in political entities (countries, regions, and districts) where centralized educational systems exist and where provisional governments, or other groups in power, are capable of determining the specific languages that should be used, learned, and taught in schools. Specifically, Language Education Policies determine which languages should be taught and learned, when to begin, for how long, by whom, the type of language students should acquire, for what purposes, by which methods, textbooks, tests, the number of hours, etc.

Language Education Policies are powerful devices, as they are generally imposed by political entities in a top-down manner with no involvement of those who are to carry out the policies such as teachers and parents. Thus, these policies serve as weapons, representations, and manifestations of national ideologies. Yet, it is very difficult to resist these impositions, as education and curricula are compulsory in most nations and are enforced in a top-down manner so that students and teachers have no opportunity to resist and must comply. Language Education Policies are further enforced by teacher training institutions, teaching materials, curricula and especially tests, as will be shown below.

A number of problems associated with Language Education Policies are explicitly described in Shohamy (2003). Yet, one problem is that they are almost always ideological, and represent mostly wishful thinking of those in power, often totally detached from reality. For example, the statement in a number of Language Education Policies that students should acquire national languages in a given length of time is not substantiated by research. Specifically, research demonstrates that mastering national languages, which are different from home languages, is a long venture, as will be shown in the data presented below.

There are various consequences of Language Education Policies as manifested in schools. They often result in the marginalization and exclusion of students who are not proficient in the dominant language, and they create a 'second class' group of students who are marked for life because they rarely achieve levels of language proficiency or academic knowledge that are equal to those born into the language. Yet, all achievement measures are compared with those native speakers, and no credit is given to the knowledge and languages previously acquired in the home countries or in other contexts of family and home.

The consequences of Language Education Policies can best be demonstrated through research which shows that it takes a long time to achieve levels that are similar to those born into the language. The data in Figures 8.3 and 8.4 are based on a large-scale study conducted by Levin *et al.* (2003) that depicts the number of years it takes immigrants from the Former Soviet Union (FSU) and from Ethiopia to reach levels of proficiency in Hebrew and in mathematics that are equivalent to those who were born into the language. It should be noted that the group from the FSU have very high levels of education, and are enriched and cultivated in terms of literacy because of the high value that society grants to language and mathematics. Nevertheless, it takes those immigrants a long time to reach similar levels of proficiency to other Israelis, even in the area of mathematics. Figure 8.3

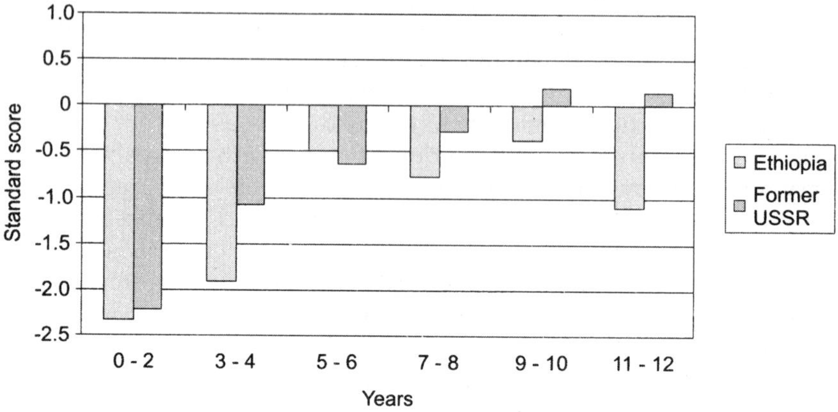

Figure 8.3 9th grade Hebrew standard scores according to years of residence
Source Levin *et al.* (2003)

gives the results for 9th graders in Hebrew, and Figure 8.4 gives the results for 11th graders in mathematics. The lower scores in mathematics than in Hebrew indicates that success in mathematics is even more complex since it requires knowledge both of Hebrew and of Mathematics.

It is also interesting to note the difference in achievement between groups of immigrants according to their country of origin (Figures 8.3 and 8.4). Students coming from the former Soviet Union perform better than students coming from Ethiopia, who in fact never reach the same levels as native speakers. These two groups, it should be noted, differ in their back-

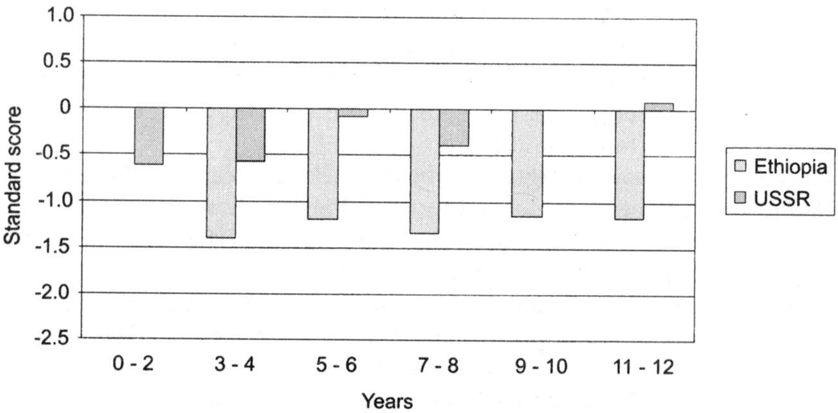

Figure 8.4 11th grade mathematics standard scores according to years of residence
Source Levin *et al.* (2003)

ground, socio-economic status, parental support, financial situation and the value they give to education.

The significant role that language plays in reaching high levels of academic achievement can also be deduced from data on test accommodations (Abedi, 2004). In our study, 11th grade students whose tests were presented in a bilingual version had much better results than those who received the test in a monolingual version, that is, in Hebrew only. As Figure 8.5 shows, when immigrant students received such accommodations as a bilingual version of the test whereby the mathematics questions were presented in two languages (Russian and Hebrew), they performed significantly better than a control group that received the questions in Hebrew only. This advantage holds for up to eight years of residence in the new country.

The finding that bilingual accommodations enhance achievement implies that not obtaining these accommodations actually prevents the immigrants from demonstrating their full knowledge in mathematics. Similar findings were found when the test texts were based on material that was familiar to the students, as well as on texts that used simplified language; in both cases students reached significantly higher scores.

Another important result of this study for Ethiopian students is that an important predictor of academic success in school was use of their L1 at home. After SES (socio-economic status), use of L1 at home is the most important predictor of achievement for Ethiopian students. Further evidence of the contribution of L1 is shown through the high correlations obtained in this study between scores in mathematics and those in Hebrew.

Imposing the national language as the only medium of instruction and as the main criterion for success is bound to hurt students academically,

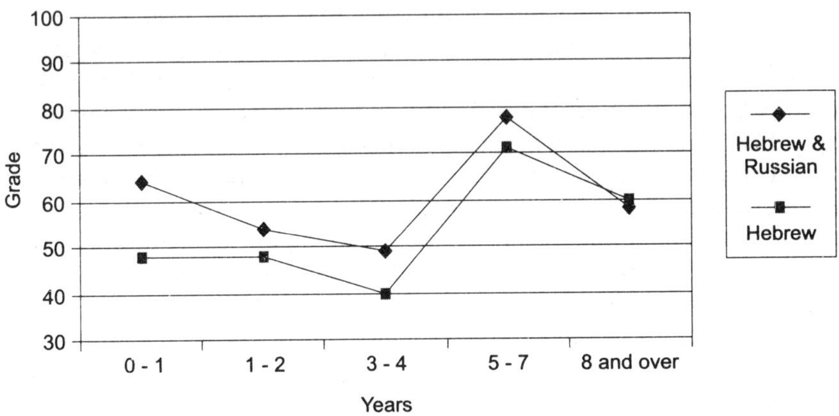

Figure 8.5 Bilingual test accommodations as enhancing achievement

eventually leading to discrimination and marginalization and over time to even lower achievements.

Language tests

Although data about language tests were presented in the previous section, the emphasis here will be on the uses of tests as a mechanism that creates *de facto* situations whereby national languages are imposed in very powerful ways – often even in contradiction to school or state policies that declare multilingualism or that honor L1 users. Language tests, especially those mandated by the state, are powerful mechanisms that are generally imposed in a top-down manner (Byrnes, 2005; Cheng *et al.*, 2004; McNamara 1997; Shohamy, 2001, 2004). Tests are used as disciplinary tools – they lead to high-stake decisions for individuals and societies, they affect success, failure, rejection and acceptance. Thus, when it comes to tests, especially those inscribed by law such as the *No Child Left Behind Act* in the USA (see Escamilla and Hornberger, this volume), individual test takers often have no choice but to comply with the demands of the tests, change their behaviors accordingly, and accept different language knowledge that fits the requirements of the tests.

Given their power, tests can determine the language hierarchy, as the languages that are being tested are those considered to be of greater significance than other languages that are not being tested. Thus, the tests affect *de facto* language practices; they define knowledge, and also stipulate criteria for correctness. Most language tests use 'the native speaker variety' as the criterion for correctness, and thus perpetuate 'pure' language that follows strict criteria of correctness, detached from how languages are actually used.

The consequence of the uses of tests in schools is that they deliver a message about language priorities and are capable of suppressing, eliminating, and marginalizing those languages that are not tested. Thus, in most cases, tests become tools capable of perpetuating national languages. In the case of *No Child Left Behind Act*, tests that are administered in English in the USA deliver a clear message as to which language really counts in society. Language tests are, at times, administered in contradiction to the declared language education policy that may underline the importance of multilingualism. Tests, however, often deliver a monolingual message. There are numerous situations when the declared policies are multilingual, yet the tests are given in one language only, thus creating a *de facto* situation where only the tested language counts. Test-takers are quick to interpret the 'testing message' of which languages really count. The administration of tests in certain languages can thus contribute to the loss of languages and diminish 'other' languages, as they act as gatekeepers and mechanisms of exclusion of people of 'other languages' from education and from the workplace.

In a large number of countries nowadays, especially in Europe and in the US, immigrants are required to pass language tests in order to obtain citizenship and to gain legitimacy in their country of residence. This may be viewed as a violation of democratic principles of inclusion and freedom of speech, as having a language test stipulates that proficiency in the national language is needed as a condition for residing in a country. These tests serve a nationalist ideology of exclusion of unwanted groups. Tests, then, serve as major tools for affecting practice that are exercised by those in authority. Given their power, it is likely that tests contribute greatly to perpetuating monolingual ideologies.

Other mechanisms

The mechanisms described so far represent only a small number of those used in most societies to ensure that national languages, tied to national ideologies, are perpetuated. Another such mechanism included in Shohamy (2006) is 'language in the public space', referring to the *de facto* policies which are created by displays of language in the landscape manifested through government signs, labels on products and instructions, the media, the Internet, graffiti, language of the cell phone, etc. The public space is an arena where language realities are created and where certain languages are legitimized or not.

Other mechanisms include myths, ideology, coercion and propaganda about languages that are spread and are very influential in creating *de facto* policies. Some of these myths refer to the ideas that knowledge of language is equal to being a member 'of the nation' and that it symbolizes loyalty and patriotism, i.e. those who do not know the language are excluded. It refers to the myth of subtractive language knowledge whereby people are not capable of having more than one language and also to propaganda that those who have not mastered the language are considered 'the others'. It also refers to the notion of language correctness and accuracy (i.e. purism) as being the only way to use languages, and of the use of words from other languages as language pollution.

Those who abide by any of these mechanisms are often unaware of the political and ideological agendas. They are also not aware of how these mechanisms promote monolingualism and reject multilingualism, especially in schools. It is these mechanisms that prevent us from changing our approaches about languages. These mechanisms are very powerful since those who use them often have better access to power through educational systems, laws, sanctions, and penalties, and therefore manipulate them easily. *No Child Left Behind*, scripted as law, is a case in point.

Actions

Given all of the above, how can things change? How can these mechanisms be used to undo the reality and work towards the acceptance of the fantasies? A number of steps are proposed here:

Language awareness refers to the need to become aware of different notions with regards to language. It first implies the need to understand the ways in which languages are used undemocratically to exclude and discriminate. This implies also that the public must learn how such perceptions of language lead to its use for discriminatory and exclusive purposes, and how it can be used for democracy of inclusion and for the protection of the personal rights of individuals. Language awareness needs to lead to language activism whereby educationalists and applied linguists are involved in framing the language argument in different ways. Specifically, there is a need to break the myths that additive bilingualism is harmful and subtractive bilingualism is advantageous. Research such as that conducted by Bialystok (2001) is essential, for it empirically shows the advantages of multilingualism. This can lead to a call for legitimizing the multilingual reality whereby tests and textbooks can be multilingual and classrooms can include a variety of languages without the need to restrict their boundaries.

Language activism refers to actions that are needed in order to make the public aware of those mechanisms that are used for preventing more open approaches to languages. It also calls for the need to expose the hidden agendas behind them, such as the fight against tests that are used for ideological purposes. For the public in general, and for educators and applied linguists in particular, it demands participation, inclusion, representation and resistance, as needed.

Conclusion

This chapter has tried to explain some of the difficulties of turning the imagined to reality. It has tried to answer its main question – Why don't we deliver? It is hoped that by understanding the mechanisms that operate behind *de facto* language policies, by revealing the way in which systems work and the mechanisms that they employ, better understanding of this phenomenon will be reached. This in turn can lead to materializing the multilingual agenda.

Summary

The chapter begins by portraying the 'imagined multilingual schools' where it is legitimate to use and develop multilingual languages, fusions and hybrids, even beyond languages and towards multimodalities, and where languages are used in free and creative ways beyond monolingual boundaries, purity and correctness. By identifying specific mechanisms that prevent the fantasies from becoming realities, the chapter then proceeds to describe reasons why such goals remain fantasies. Specifically, it claims that it is through a number of powerful mechanisms, used to promote ideologies of nation states, that monolingualism and standards for language correctness continue to be perpetuated. Presenting empirical data on academic achievements of immigrants in schools, as well as appropriate test modifications, the chapter argues that different language policies, language educational policies and especially high-stake language testing policies (e.g. the *No Child Left Behind* Act in the US) mean that the messages that are delivered and perpetuated are those of de-legitimacy and suppression of other languages, and promotion and perpetuation of criteria based on 'native' varieties and language correctness. The chapter also identifies other mechanisms, such as language in the public space, language myths and propaganda. It is by examining the mechanisms that operate behind *de facto* language policies that we can reach some understanding of why 'we don't deliver'. The author calls for increasing understanding of these issues through language awareness and activism.

המאמר מתחיל בתיאור אידיאלי של בתי ספר רב לשוניים. בבתי ספר כאלה קיימת לגיטימציה לשימוש במספר רב של שפות, לעירוב ושילוב של שפות ואף לשימוש במיומנויות חוץ לשוניות כאשר השימוש בשפות הוא חופשי , יצירתי, פתוח וללא גבולות של חד לשוניות , טוהר ונכונות דקדוקית של ה'דובר הילידי', במיוחד בהתייחס למגוון הרחב של התלמידים . המאמר עובר לתאר ולהסביר מדוע מטרות כאלה אינן ברות ביצוע ואינן ישימות בהקשרים הנוכחיים. באופן ספציפי דן המאמר בשורה של אמצעים (mechanisms) כוחניים המונעים את יישומן של מטרות אלה במציאות. הטענה היא שדרך אמצעים אלה ממשיכה מדינת הלאום להשריש ולהשליט אידיולוגיות לאומיות של חד לשוניות וסטנדרטים אחידים של שימושים לשוניים, בעיקר בתחום של נכונות לשונית. המאמר מציג ממצאים מחקריים המצביעים על הפער הגדול הקיים בהישגים לימודיים של תלמידים מהגרים כאשר שפת הלאום היא האמצעי העיקרי למדידת הישגים ויחד עם זאת את השיפור בהישגים כאשר ידע לימודי נמדד בדרכים שונות. מועלית הטענה ש דרך אמצעים של מדיניות לשונית כללית וחינוכית וכן דרך מדיניות מבחנית כגון

***No Child Left Behind*, המסר המועבר הוא של דה-לגיטימציה**

של שפות אחרות, בעיקר של שפות מהגרים, והשלטת הקריטריון של 'הדובר הילידי' כמדד העיקרי של שפה 'נכונה'. דרך בחינה של אמצעים אלה, כולל גם שפה במרחב הציבורי, תעמולה ומיתוסים לשוניים, אפשר ללמוד מה היא מדיניות הלשונית האמיתית, זו המונעת תפיסות לשוניות פתוחות ומגוונות יותר. לפיכך, על מנת להבין מדוע אין מצליחים ליישם מדיניות לשונית חינוכית רב לשונית יש ללמוד ולהבין את האמצעים הספציפיים המונעים ממנה להתקיים.המאמר מסתיים בקריאה להבנה רבה יותר של התהליכים החינוכיים והפוליטיים וכן למודעות ואקטיביזם.

(Hebrew)

Chapter 9

Monolingual Assessment and Emerging Bilinguals: A Case Study in the US

KATHY ESCAMILLA

> *When a bilingual individual confronts a monolingual test ... both the test taker and the test are asked to do something they cannot. The bilingual test taker cannot perform like a monolingual. The monolingual test cannot 'measure' in the other language.*
>
> Valdés & Figueroa, 1994: 87

Introduction

The number of persons in the United States who are labeled as language minority people is large and growing. The term 'language minority' is commonly defined as people for whom English is a second language. However, included in this definition are people who are bilingual, or whose heritage language is not English. In 2003, the number of language minority people in the US was estimated to be 7.5 million (Ovando *et al.*, 2003). The US Department of Education requires that all schools in the US determine the extent to which students who are language-minority students are also limited in English proficiency. At one time in the US limited English proficient children were labeled LEP, but they are now more commonly referred to by federal, state and local school districts as ELL – English Language Learners (Ovando *et al.*, 2003). The US Department of Education (2003) estimates the total number of ELLs in US public schools to be about 5 million, and further estimates there are about 350 different language groups included in the population of language minority students and ELL students. Many federal and state documents tout the existence of enormous linguistic diversity in US schools. The state of Colorado, for example, has documented more than 102 language groups represented in its public schools (Escamilla *et al.*, 2003b). However, on closer inspection, this statistic is somewhat deceptive for in reality the vast majority (about 70%) of ELLs in the US speak one common language – Spanish.

The study reported in this chapter focuses on Colorado, a state whose demographic situation parallels the national one. In 2003, about 70,000 public school students in Colorado were identified as ELLs. This constituted about 10% of the entire school population. Further, although there were 102 documented language groups in Colorado schools, the vast majority (56,000 students or 80%) spoke Spanish as a first language (Escamilla *et al.*, 2003b).

In spite of national and state data showing that the overwhelming majority of language minority and English Language Learners speak a common language (Spanish), language diversity is frequently used as a reason to promote monolingual English assessment policies, and in many places to require that assessments be conducted only in English. In the case of Colorado, Colorado Department of Education officials frequently argue for assessment and testing to be conducted only in English because, in their view, it would be 'too expensive' and 'not feasible' to develop assessments in 102 languages (Lenhart, 2003). It is important to note that the creation of assessments in Spanish would account for 80% of the linguistic diversity and possibly create a more equitable and accurate assessment system for ELLs, a point that will be expanded on later in this chapter.

Ruiz (1988) proposed that there are three basic language orientations utilized by nations, communities and schools as they engage in the creation of language policies and planning: language as a problem, language as a right and language as a resource. Ruiz posited that ELLs in the United States, particularly those ELLs whose first language is Spanish, have historically been viewed as 'problems' in US schools. Since students' limited ability in English is viewed as a 'problem,' US schools have been charged to create policies and practices to 'fix the language problem' of Spanish-speaking students. Recent educational reform movements such as standards-based education and high-stakes testing have served to exacerbate the notion that speaking a language other than English in the US is a problem that must be remediated by the schools.

Standards-based education in the US began in the early 1990s and was designed to improve academic achievement for all students (McLaughlin & Shepard, 1995). By the year 2000, 49 states had implemented some form of standards-based educational reform (Cunningham, 2000). The standards-based reform movement has two basic components – content and assessment. *Content standards* include the knowledge, skills, and other understandings that schools should teach in order for students to attain high levels of competency in challenging subject matter (McLaughlin & Shepard, 1995). *Assessment standards* (sometimes referred to as performance standards) describe how students should be able to demonstrate that they have acquired the requisite content and/or skills. While assessments can be conducted in many different formats, the predominant assessment format is a standardized test.

The implementation of wide-scale assessments for all students to meet the requirements of standards-based education reforms has been reinforced and expanded by the passage of the *No Child Left Behind* Act (NCLB, 2002). *No Child Left Behind* is a federal mandate that now requires all states to carry out annual assessments of student progress in reading, writing and various content areas (for more on the consequences of NCLB see Hornberger, Chapter 11 and Shohamy, Chapter 8). Results of this annual testing are now used as measures of school accountability and effectiveness. Test results are used to determine the schools' effectiveness and monitor the children's progress. The use of wide-scale testing is now the predominant means by which schools and school districts demonstrate that they are meeting the mandates of *No Child Left Behind* and the standards-based movement. Wide-scale testing, for this reason, has come to be known as 'high-stakes testing.' Wide-scale testing involves giving the same standardized test to a large population of students (Amrein & Berliner, 2002). Wide-scale tests become 'high-stakes' tests when consequences (either sanctions or rewards), are applied to their results. Amrein and Berliner (2002) document the consequences that have been attached to schools and school districts with the onslaught of wide-scale, high-stakes testing programs. For example, currently, 45 states use the results of wide-scale tests to rank and rate schools – from best to worst (Amrein & Berliner, 2002). Further, punishments are attached to testing outcomes twice as often as rewards are. Schools that receive unsatisfactory ratings over the course of several years are threatened with closure, firing of teachers and administrators, and/or conversion from public schools to private schools. In many cities in the US, conversion from public school to private or charter school status means that the public school has failed. In short, there is enormous pressure on public school teachers and students to do well on high-stakes tests.

Since the inception of the standards-based education movement questions and concerns have been raised about the application of these policies to students who are learning English as a second language (ELLs). Little or no controversy has surfaced with regard to content standards. Indeed, there is widespread agreement that ELLs can, and should, meet challenging content standards. However, significant issues have been raised with regard to assessment standards for ELLs. August and Hakuta (1997) list some of these issues:

- Standardized tests that most states currently employ to meet state and federal mandates were developed for the assessment of native English speakers, not for ELLs.
- For second language learners, paper/pencil content assessments in English often measure students' lack of proficiency in English and NOT their knowledge of the content.

- ELLs are often placed in short-term educational programs with inadequate materials and poorly prepared staff, which limits their opportunities to learn.
- Many state assessment programs are available only in English. They do not provide opportunities for students to demonstrate their knowledge of content in a non-English language.

For the purposes of this chapter, it is important to note that most wide-scale high-stakes tests utilized in the US use native English speakers as the norm (Abedi, 2001; Menken, 2000). Many have argued that it is is invalid to use high-stakes monolingual English tests to assess ELLs (Gottlieb, 2001; Abedi, 2001; Menken, 2000). Nonetheless such tests continue to be used to evaluate the academic achievement of ELLs and other students, and to rate and rank the efficacy of their school programs and the competency of their teachers and administrators. In school districts and schools where there are large numbers of ELL students, the English-only assessment policies are particularly problematic, for it is unlikely that students just beginning to learn English will do as well on these assessments as their monolingual English counterparts. While the debate on the equity and validity of high-stakes testing in general continues, as does the debate on including ELL students in wide-scale high-stakes testing programs, federal and state mandates are dictating that all students, including ELL students, be included in such testing programs.

It is important to note that 20 states, as well as the federal government, have created special testing policies with regard to ELL students with the hope of being more equitable to these students (Rivera & Stansfield, 2000). Special policies include the following:

(1) exemption for ELLs from testing in English for three years;
(2) special testing accommodations such as allowing ELL students more time to take the test, allowing ELLs to use bilingual dictionaries, allowing students to respond to test questions in their native language with bilingual personnel;
(3) taking the assessment in the student's native language.

Each state varies with regard to its special testing policies. However, most states utilize exemptions and accommodations, and very few provide high-stakes tests in students' native languages (Rivera & Stansfield, 2000).

The state of Colorado utilizes all three special testing policies – exemption, accommodation, and limited opportunity for native language assessment. Colorado allows students to be exempted from English CSAP (Colorado Student Assessment Program) testing for 3 years; it provides limited accommodations and allows students to take assessments in reading and writing in Spanish at the 3rd and 4th grade levels only.

This chapter presents results of a case study involving Spanish-speaking ELLs and high-stakes tests in the state of Colorado. First, it examines the way in which high-stakes assessment programs have served to perpetuate the 'language as a problem' paradigm in US schools with large numbers of ELLs. Second, it examines the results of Spanish-speaking ELL students who were allowed to take the assessment in Spanish and compares these results to those who took these assessments in English. Finally, the chapter discusses the privileging of English testing data over test data in other languages (e.g. Spanish) and how the privileging of English outcomes mitigates against the development and implementation of more effective school programs for emerging bilingual children.

High-stakes Testing and Spanish-speaking Children in Colorado

The high-stakes test in the state of Colorado is the Colorado Student Assessment Program (CSAP). This test has been given since 1997 and the number and types of CSAP tests have increased over the years. As with other states, CSAP results are used to rate and rank all Colorado schools and school districts (Colorado SB 186, 2000). Results on the CSAP are used to assign one of five labels to Colorado schools: excellent, high, average, low, and unsatisfactory. As with many other states, Colorado has sanctions for schools that are consistently ranked as unsatisfactory. Sanctions include firing teachers and administrators, and state-mandated conversion to charter schools if unsatisfactory ratings persist for three years (SB 186, 2000). Further, several school districts in Colorado have begun to require that teacher raises and salaries be tied to outcomes on the CSAP test.

With regard to English Language Learners, Colorado provides two basic accommodations. ELLs in Colorado can be exempted from the CSAP for three school years while they are learning English. This exemption was intended to avoid unfair and punitive sanctions for schools with large numbers of ELLs. The three-year exemption accommodation is widely used across the US, and is also allowable in *No Child Left Behind* (Rivera & Stansfield, 2000). Colorado also allows for a less common accommodation for Spanish-speaking ELLs – the opportunity to take the CSAP test in reading and writing in Spanish in the 3rd and 4th grades. This accommodation is designed to give schools that are providing some type of bilingual instruction an opportunity to assess children in a manner that matches the schools' instructional practice.

The CSAP results in Spanish and English for the year 2002–2003 provide the data for this chapter. These data illustrate the pervasive view that ELLs, in this case Spanish speaking ELLs, present language problems that schools need to remediate. The data further reveal how high-stakes testing has been used to reinforce the 'language as a problem' paradigm even in the presence of powerful evidence to the contrary. The data presented below are a part of a larger five-year study that examines the impact of the CSAP on ELLs in Colorado (Escamilla *et al.*, 2000, 2001, 2002, 2003a, 2003b). Findings across the five-year span of this study have yielded similar results.

In July 2003, the Colorado Department of Education released the annual results of the CSAP assessment to the public. Results are placed on the CDE website and are released and reported by the popular media in Colorado. Data in Table 9.1 represent 10 schools in Denver. Scores are reported by the state and individual schools in terms of the percentages of students whose results earned them one of four labels (unsatisfactory, partially proficient, proficient or advanced). The table reports percentages of students in Spanish and English who scored at proficient or advanced. These two categories are considered to be indications that students are performing at grade level. Of the 10 schools, 8 were ranked as low, 1 was ranked as average and 1 was ranked as unsatisfactory. The state called the CSAP results 'alarming' for Denver public schools. The popular media reported that the results demonstrated a 'gap in achievement' between Denver and other schools districts, and district officials and teachers were asked to account for why the rankings at these schools were low.

Among the responses given for the low rankings in press releases and interviews with district officials were the following: (1) poverty, (2) large numbers of Spanish-speaking students, (3) large numbers of students who are ethnically Latino and (4) bilingual education programs. All sample schools are implementing a form of early-exit bilingual program, labeled ELA by the Denver Public Schools. The press, the Colorado Department of Education, school district administrators, and teachers cited common reasons for the perceived under-performance of these schools. The schools and the community attributed perceived low performance to language, ethnicity, poverty, and to the bilingual education program. Data presented on Table 9.1 seem to confirm these perceptions. For example, 8 out of 10 schools have a student population that is over 90% Latino. Six of the schools have a population where over 50% of the students are ELLs and speak Spanish as a first language. The other four schools have a Spanish-speaking ELL population that accounts for one-third of the student body. Finally, in 8 out of the 10 schools 90% of the students live in poverty.

Each of these schools provides a short-term bilingual program to students who enter school speaking Spanish and as ELLs. In these programs, students learn literacy and content area subjects in Spanish first and receive daily instruction in English as a Second Language. At each of these schools, students who were in the early exit bilingual program, who were in 3rd or 4th grades at the time of the study, and who were learning to read and write in Spanish were given the CSAP assessments in Spanish. At

Table 9.1 Denver Public Schools: Demographics, school rankings, and comparison of 3rd grade Spanish and English reading and writing outcomes (Spring 2003)

School	*State-rating 2001–2002*	*School population*	*% Latino*	*% ELL Spanish*	*% Poverty*	*Spanish CSAP reading% proficient/ advanced*	*School wide English reading CSAP % proficient/ advanced**	*Spanish CSAP writing % proficient/ advanced*	*School wide English writing CSAP % proficient/ advanced**
Beach Court	low	454	91	37	84	79	35	74	42
Bryant Webster	average	460	97	51	92	91	67	96	60
Cheltenham	low	601	92	43	97	67	42	74	21
Cowell	low	625	92	55	95	82	44	72	27
Eagleton	low	556	94	50	90	70	27	79	19
Fairmont	low	475	89	47	97	76	45	71	15
Gilpin	low	440	63	33	85	75	33	63	16
Knapp	low	661	91	55	91	56	52	42	19
Munroe	low	608	93	54	95	67	39	63	42
Smedley	unsat.	545	95	52	96	59	29	68	21

* For Spring 2003, 51% of the 3rd grade students across Denver Public Schools who took English CSAP in reading earned a rating of proficient or advanced, and 35% of those who took English CSAP in writing earned a rating of proficient or advanced.

each of these schools there are grade levels and strands of students who are not in the early-exit bilingual program. They are in English-only instructional programs. The students in the English-only instructional programs learn to read and write in English and were given the CSAP in English. The data in Table 9.1 also present the reading and writing outcomes for these schools and compares Spanish and English results. From these data, a different pattern emerges.

The CSAP reading and writing data are reported by school and by grade according to the number and percentage of students who fall into one of four categories (advanced, proficient, partially proficient, and unsatisfactory). Numbers presented in Table 9.1 indicate the percentage of children at each school who scored in the proficient and advanced ranges. Proficient and advanced ranges equate to grade level proficiency.

To illustrate these results further, consider the example of Beach Court School. At this school 79% of the children who took the CSAP reading assessment in Spanish scored in the proficient/advanced range, while 35% of the children who took the CSAP in English scored in the proficient or advanced range. The district average for students scoring in the proficient or advanced range is 51%, meaning that the students who took CSAP in Spanish outpaced the district average in English and outpaced the students at their own school who took the test in English. Students at Beach Court who took the test in English performed lower than the district average. Results for each of these 10 schools illustrate that the achievement for students taking CSAP reading in Spanish is higher than that for students taking the CSAP in English. Further, Spanish results in each of these schools are higher than the district-wide average in English. These data raise serious questions with regard to the assumption that the school's overall ranking was a result of having too many poor Spanish-speaking students who were participating in bilingual programs. The 10 schools represented in Table 9.1 reflect 10 elementary schools in Colorado that are the very heavily impacted by Spanish-speaking immigrant students and thus have very high numbers and percentages of ELL students.

Table 9.1 also presents the results on the writing portion of the 3rd grade CSAP and compares results on the Spanish CSAP and English CSAP on the writing portion of the exam. These results mirror the reading portion of the exam and once again illustrate that the achievement levels in Spanish are higher than the achievement levels in English. Again to illustrate the findings, let's take the case of Cheltenham School. At Cheltenham, 74% of the students who took the CSAP Spanish writing exam scored proficient or above, while only 21% of the students who took the CSAP writing exam in English scored proficient or advanced. Students taking the CSAP in Spanish were above the district-wide average of 35% and students who took the test in English were below. Again, students taking the writing test in Spanish at all 10 schools had better outcomes than those students taking the assessment in English at these same schools and better outcomes than the entire district.

It is important to note that the intent of the standards-based education movement in Colorado and the US is to improve student achievement vis-à-vis content standards. In the data reported above, the content standards relate to reading and writing. The law did not specify that students must demonstrate their emergent knowledge of reading and writing in English, it simply mandates demonstration that students are becoming literate. In this case, it seems that Spanish-speaking students are becoming literate in Spanish at higher levels than peers learning only in English.

The data comparing outcomes between students taking the CSAP in Spanish and those taking the CSAP in English are remarkable for several reasons. First, the results question the conventional wisdom reported by the Colorado Department of Education, the popular press, teachers, and administrators that poverty, speaking Spanish and being Latino are explanations for low school ratings and academic under-achievement. In fact, the converse seems to be the case. It is interesting and noteworthy that the state does not display Spanish results and English results for schools in Colorado side by side. Spanish results and English results are reported on separate areas in the state website, even for students who attend the same schools.

Further, in the 8 years since the CSAP results have been reported by the Department of Education to the popular media in Colorado, outcomes of the Spanish CSAP have been inconsistently and infrequently reported to the public. For example, all of the English CSAP results for the English CSAP are available from the Colorado Department of Education website (http://www.cde.state.co.us). Though the Spanish data are also public domain information, accessing the Spanish data is more of a challenge. For example, to access the Spring 1999 data, researchers had to wade through boxes at the Colorado Department of Education that were still as they had been turned in by school districts. In the year 1999, the data were neither summarized by the Department, nor reported in any official documents or other outlets. There are no data for 1999 on the CDE CSAP website. For the Spring 2000 data, the Spanish data were summarized by CDE and placed in notebooks, but were still not placed on the CDE website or available to other outlets. After much pressure, in Spring 2001, data, for the first time, were summarized, and placed on the CDE website. However, data were catalogued in separate areas on the CDE web-site and it was difficult to locate the Spanish results. For example, English results could be located under 3rd grade English reading (http://www.cde.state.co.us/cdeassess/csap), while Spanish results were located under *'lectura'* (http://www.cde.state.co.us/cdeassess/csap). In order to find the Spanish results and compare them to English, one had to know that '*lectura*' meant 'reading' in Spanish. The same is true for the writing results that were categorized under 'writing' in English and '*escritura*' in Spanish. Since data for English and Spanish are not reported nor presented side by side, it is difficult to question the pervasive assumptions that Spanish speakers are responsible for low and unsatisfactory school ratings.

There are several other reasons why the Spanish reading and writing outcomes are rather remarkable in the Denver school district. The CSAP testing company annually releases 25% of the test items on all CSAP tests so that teachers can use these items to help children practice for the test (CSAP: 1998). Test items, however, are released only in English, not in Spanish. Reasons for releasing items only for the English version of the test vary. One explanation from the Colorado Department of Education is that it's too expensive to release items in Spanish. Another from CDE claims that too few children take the test in Spanish to justify this exercise. Yet, another claims that the test in Spanish is 'easier' because Spanish is an easier language to learn to read and write and, therefore, no practice is necessary. Whatever the rationale for not allowing the Spanish-speaking children to practice for the CSAP, the fact is that the preparation to take the test is not the same for Spanish and English test takers. English speakers get to practice for the exam and Spanish speakers do not. Still, Spanish speakers over the past five years have consistently outperformed comparable English-speaking peers on the CSAP test (Escamilla *et al.*, 2003b).

The test results are similarly remarkable in that despite claims by the testing company that the CSAP is free of cultural, economic and linguistic bias (CSAP, 1998), there is evidence to the contrary. For example, the third grade writing prompt for the 2004 CSAP asked the children to write about their favorite camping trip. Taking vacations to the mountains and camping are arguably experiences that few poor immigrant children have had, thereby placing them at a disadvantage when having to write a narrative about this kind of experience. Again, in spite of this apparent disadvantage, children taking the CSAP in Spanish did well.

Finally, there is a general tendency to undervalue the results on the Spanish CSAP. As stated above, Spanish results are not regularly reported to the press, and the public has paid scant attention to them over the past 8 years. Further, the state legislators and policy-makers have been ambivalent about the Spanish CSAP since its inception. For example, during one school year (2000–2001), the Colorado Department of Education issued three different policy directives about how the Spanish CSAP would be used and factored into school ratings. One directive stated that children could take the CSAP in Spanish but that it would count negatively toward a school's overall ratings. In this directive, schools were informed that each child taking the test in Spanish would receive a score of minus 0.5 toward the overall school ratings. In other words, testing in Spanish would result in a negative (below zero) score for a school. Having many children take the test in Spanish would have resulted in the lowering of an overall school ranking. Threats of litigation and accusations that the Colorado State Department of Education had overstepped its legislative authority prompted a second policy directive stating that if students took the CSAP in Spanish, it would not count negatively toward the school ranking, but it would also not count positively. In other words, it would have zero impact. This directive amounted to making the Spanish test results, while not negative, invisible and irrelevant. Further, this directive meant that only English CSAP outcomes would count toward a school's rating. The threat of punitive measures if children took the test in Spanish followed by the threat to discount (zero count) test results in Spanish caused many schools to question whether or not they should be teaching children to read and write in Spanish, given the potential negative consequences associated with teaching and testing in Spanish. It finally took a legislative act (SB 98, 2001) to establish that outcomes on the Spanish CSAP tests would be given equal weight to the outcomes on English CSAP assessments.

It is fortunate for children in Colorado that currently Spanish and English CSAP outcomes must be given equal weight in the calculation of school ratings. Unfortunately, SB 98 was passed in April 2001, one month after children had taken the CSAP tests for the year 2000–2001. Fearful of being punished for teaching in Spanish, many schools decided that it was not worth the risk to teach and assess children in Spanish and switched children from Spanish to English instruction. The schools that decided to stay the course and continued to teach and test in Spanish did so in a negative, even hostile climate. Again, given the environment, the consistent and positive testing outcomes in Spanish are remarkable.

Implications

The data presented above have significant implications for monolingual high-stakes assessment systems. Ironically, even in a state like Colorado where children are allowed to take high-stakes tests in a limited way in their native language (in this case Spanish), the high-stakes testing environment seems to have reinforced the notion that 'language is a problem' in spite of overwhelming evidence to the contrary. In fact, the documentation and presentation of counter-evidence to the mentality that 'language is a problem and causes low CSAP scores' has resulted in political activity designed to limit the number of children who are eligible to take the assessment in Spanish. Using the federal mandates under *No Child Left Behind*, the state has instituted very strict policies requiring that all children be tested in English after 3 years, no matter what the child's level of English proficiency.

This policy does not prevent a school or school district from testing a child in both English and Spanish. Indeed, from a research perspective this may be the most interesting and appropriate means to assess the academic achievements of Spanish-speaking ELL students. However, given the expense associated with the CSAP assessment program and the time the assessments take, there are currently no schools or school districts in Colorado that have the resources or time to carry out double assessments. Thus, for a limit of three years, children are allowed to take assessments in Spanish, but under no circumstances are emerging bilingual children assessed in both of their languages.

An additional layer of complexity was added to the assessment picture in Colorado in 2004–2005. A CSAP assessment test in mathematics was developed for 3rd and 4th grade students and was administered for the first time in Spring 2005. These two math tests were developed in English only. Therefore, teachers who had taught children in Spanish because children could take assessments in Spanish are now faced with a situation where children can take reading and writing tests in Spanish in 3rd and 4th grade, but these same children must take mathematics assessments in English. The emphasis on testing outcomes in English and the development of new assessments in English only are placing increasing pressure on schools and teachers to abandon teaching in Spanish in spite of positive test results.

A significant implication of this study is that conventional wisdom is hard to change. The notions that being poor, and speaking Spanish are explanations for low achievement are so prevalent that they go unquestioned. When counter evidence is presented, this evidence is often ignored. Most alarming, however, is the great potential that exists for educators and policy-makers to prescribe inappropriate educational solutions to ELL students because they have misdiagnosed and misunderstood the nature of perceived underachievement.

Evidence is beginning to emerge in Colorado of ill-advised solutions being applied to misidentified problems. There are new policy initiatives that are designed to curtail the ability of teachers and schools to teach and test in Spanish. For example, the new English-only math test and the 3-year mandate to test in English, together with policies that do not test children in two languages, are reducing the number of children who are being taught and tested in Spanish, and are limiting the time that children may learn in Spanish. If children are not being taught and tested in Spanish, it is not possible for them to demonstrate what they know in Spanish. If sufficient pressure is placed on schools and teachers to teach and test only in English, then there will be no Spanish outcomes to be reported, and therefore, no opportunity to document the potential of emerging bilingual children when assessed in their native language. There will also be no evidence to document the efficacy of bilingual education programs. No native language teaching and assessment means no opportunity to collect evidence to challenge conventional wisdom, thereby protecting the status quo 'language is a problem' paradigm.

In spite of evidence of the success of teaching and testing ELL children in Spanish, school districts in Colorado continue to propose to solve the 'problem of educating Spanish-speaking students' with programs that devalue Spanish and emphasize English. Many school districts in Colorado are proposing instructional programs that use more English and less Spanish. They are suggesting that more English as a Second Language classes be implemented to take the place of physical education, music and art. They are also proposing more homework in English and more skills-based learning (in English). English classes for parents are also being recommended, so that parents can help their children in English. Finally, they are advising more practice for high-stakes tests in English for all ELL populations, particularly Spanish speakers.

This type of curriculum has been labeled the intensification curriculum by Berliner and Biddle (1995). In this case, since educators and policy makers view the problem of underachievement to be one of too much Spanish and too little English, they propose to reduce teaching and testing in Spanish and to intensify teaching and testing in English. Berliner and Biddle suggest that intensification strategies designed to 'improve English' may not produce the desired academic achievement. More English may not be better.

If high-stakes testing in Spanish is further limited or eliminated altogether in Colorado, the consequences are likely to be negative for Spanish-speaking children. Shohamy (2004a) has stated that a language test is a dangerous weapon, potentially lethal to all children (for more on this, see Shohamy, Chapter 8). Language tests in the form of high-stakes tests are potentially lethal weapons if they are given in English only to children who are learning English as a Second Language. Used in this manner, such tests serve only to legitimize the notion that there is a 'gap' in achievement, that ELLs are underachievers, and that speaking a non-English language causes problems in learning (Black & Valenzuela, 2004). However, the use of high-stakes tests in languages such as Spanish, even in a limited way such as in Colorado schools, provides the opportunity for children to be tested in their native language, thus illuminating a different set of outcomes and realities.

In this study, the outcome of the Spanish CSAP documented that poor Spanish-speaking immigrant children can learn to read and write well, can meet state content standards, and can meet the demands of high-stakes testing when allowed to demonstrate in their native language what they know. The use of high-stakes tests in Spanish in Colorado has allowed us to document a different outcome – a profile of an emergent bilingual who outperforms comparable monolingual English peers in their schools.

Rather than an under-performing English Language Learner, we now have a profile of students who are helping schools be better than they would be if only monolingual students were in attendance. Sadly, such positive results have largely gone unnoticed and unreported in Colorado; and no doubt much more documentation and dissemination of results will need to occur for such positive results to begin to change the current conventional wisdom. Moreover, results such as those presented in this chapter threaten the status quo. Current trends in Colorado evidence greater efforts to maintain and protect the status quo through more intense English programs and fewer opportunities to teach and learn in Spanish.

I end this chapter where I began, and with a note of hope mixed with frustration. As Valdés and Figueroa (1994) have stated, we will never adequately assess the bilingual mind through the use of monolingual tests. In a perfect world, our emerging bilingual students would be assessed in both English and Spanish to document and support their bilingualism. In Colorado, we have an assessment system that enables us to begin to understand how high-stakes tests, rather than being lethal weapons, might be tools to document the linguistic strengths of Spanish-speaking students. Such assessments might be used to counteract arguments that language is a problem and a cause of underachievement. Further, outcomes of these assessments might become tools to argue for the expansion of dual language and other bilingual programs designed to fully develop bilingualism and biliteracy in children who currently carry negative labels such as ELLs.

It is conceivable that these high-stakes tests could be given in both English and Spanish to emerging bilinguals to also document and affirm the value of bilingualism and give added weight to knowledge that can be demonstrated in each language. In such a system, the outcomes in two languages of emerging bilingual children could be used as a positive weight in a school's ranking. In other words, there might be an incentive for students to learn and take assessments in two languages. Optimistically, these potentially lethal tools could be used to validate that two is indeed greater than one. In reality, however, in Colorado, as in other states, high-stakes tests in languages other than English are devalued, results in Spanish are ignored, and policies are based on conventional wisdom rather than on a thorough understanding of the data. To imagine, invent, implement and evaluate multilingual schools will require utilizing a range of assessments and tools to allow children to demonstrate what they know and are learning in all of their languages. The current US policies that emphasize monolingual-English-only assessment mitigate against the potential of multilingual schools.

Summary

This chapter presents a case study examining the implementation of large-scale programs for testing emerging bilingual students. US schools have become increasingly diverse linguistically. However, assessment systems to determine student academic achievement have become more monolingual in their focus. Second language learners are frequently blamed for any perceived under-performance on these exams. In a few states, including Colorado, Spanish/English emerging bilinguals are allowed to take assessments in Spanish. Data collected in this case study compared academic achievement in reading and writing between students who took the Colorado CSAP test in Spanish and English. Findings indicated that students taking the assessments in Spanish outperformed students taking the CSAP in English, and in the schools studied, Spanish outcomes exceeded district-wide English averages. Findings support the need to assess emerging bilinguals in both their languages.

Este capítulo demuestra cómo las pruebas de serias consecuencias afectan a los estudiantes que se están desarrollando como bilingües. Las escuelas estadounidenses cada año tienen más diversidad lingüística. Sin embargo, el sistema de asesoramiento que determina los logros de los estudiantes cada día se enfoca más en el inglés. La culpa de no tener éxito en estos exámenes se le achaca a los estudiantes que están aprendiendo inglés como segundo idioma. En algunos estados como Colorado, los estudiantes que van a ser bilingües tienen la oportunidad de ser asesorados en español. En este estudio comparamos los logros en lectura y escritura de los estudiantes que tomaron el examen CSAP en Colorado en español y en inglés. Los resultados indican que los estudiantes que tomaron la prueba en español tuvieron más alto rendimiento que aquellos que la tomaron en inglés, y que en las escuelas que hemos estudiado, los resultados en español son mucho más altos que los del distrito en inglés. Los resultados apoyan la necesidad de que se le dé los exámenes a estos estudiantes en los dos idiomas. (Spanish)

本文欲呈現單一個案研究：此一個案乃全面性察驗具有雙語能力的學生，將如何面臨未來美國的考試制度。當代美國的校園環境已漸漸呈現多元語言風貌，但是，在考試制度方面卻仍然偏向使用單一語言來測試學生在學科上的表現並藉此判定其學業成就。在面臨考試時，英語為其第二語言的學生多半被視為學業成績低落者。目前在美國境內有幾個州，包括科羅拉多州，已開始實施以下應考政策：具有西班牙語和英語雙語能力的學生，將可選用自己的母語--西班牙語文來應考。此一個案的研究資料，即是搜集學生以西班牙語和英語來應考科羅拉多州的州立考試的資料並加以比較其應試結果。研究結果顯示，以學生本身而言，選擇使用本身西班牙母語來應考的學生，其應試成績乃遠勝於那些不用母語而使用英語去應考的學生之應考成績。同時，研究成果並指出，以學校整體而言，那些選擇採用西班牙語來讓學生應考科州州考的學校學生應試成績，亦高於只選用英語來進行該州州考的學校之學生成績。此個案研究結果，將進一步支持未來以兩種語言來測試具有雙語能力學生之考試需求。

(Chinese)

Chapter 10

The Long Road to Multilingual Schools in Botswana

LYDIA NYATI-RAMAHOBO

Multilingualism in Botswana

Like most countries, Botswana is a multilingual and multicultural society. Cook (2003) identified 26 minority languages spoken in Botswana. Table 10.1 indicates these languages of which 11 are Khoesan.

Table 10.1 Minority languages in Botswana*

1.	Afrikaans	14.	Naro **
2.	Chikuhane	15.	Otjiherero
3.	| |Gana **	16.	Rugciriku
4.	|Gwi **	17.	Sebirwa
5.	≠Hua **	18.	Setswapong
6.	Ikalanga	19.	Shekgalahari
7.	Isindebele	20.	Shiyeyi
8.	Ju|'hoan **	21.	Shua/Tshwa **
9.	Khwedam **	22.	Silozi
10.	Kua **	23.	Thimbukushu
11.	≠Kx'au| |ein **	24.	Tsowa **
12.	Nama	25.	!Xóõ **
13.	Nambya	26.	Zezuru

* Some linguists classify Kwangali as a broad category that includes Rugciriku and Thimbukushu, and this may be the reason why it is not reflected in the table. Talaonde is also not included because it is a dialect of Ikalanga that has become exinct.
**Khoesan languages
Source: Cook (2003: 1)

Walter and Ringenberg (1994) have also identified 26 minority languages in Botswana and claimed that 99% of the population speaks a minority language. The Botswana Language Use Project (1998) also identified 26 minority languages, while the Department of African languages at the University of Botswana identified 23 (Batibo & Smieja, 2000). It therefore seems accurate to say that with the addition of the two official languages (English and Setswana) there are at least 28 languages spoken in Botswana.

Figure 10.1 Map of Botswana

Source: Nyati-Ramahobo (2001: 132)

Other scholars have likewise confirmed the multilingual nature of the country. Hasselbring (2000) and Hasselbring *et al.* (2001) conducted surveys in the Boteti Sub-district and the Ngamiland district of Botswana (Figure 10.1). The study indicated that respondents spoke more than two local languages. Those who were educated spoke English, Setswana, and their own language. Lukusa (2000) carried out a similar survey in the Kgalagadi district, where most respondents reported to speak an average of four languages. These studies further indicated that multilingualism was mainly in the home, while the public and formal sphere is reserved for the official language, English, and the national language, Setswana.

For the first time since 1946, the 2001 population and Housing Census included one language question. It was included as a result of pressure from non-governmental organisations and external agencies that had long campaigned for, and demonstrated the importance of, having linguistic data. The question solicited the language spoken often in the home. The respondent had three options: Setswana, English and 'other' – to be specified in the space provided. Though the question posed a number of problems related to data coding, analysis, and interpretation (Chebanne & Nyati-Ramahobo, 2003), it provided basic information on languages currently spoken in Botswana. The study indicated a total of 18 local languages, of which 10 were Khoesan. It also indicated cross-border languages such as Ndebele, Afrikaans, Zezuru, and Shona, which are vibrant in South Africa and Zimbabwe, but have fewer speakers in Botswana.

Data from the census also indicated that 78% of the population speak Setswana[1] in their homes. This figure is understood to include both first and second language speakers. The non-Tswana-speaking[2] areas of Ghanzi, Kgalagadi and Ngamiland (see map, Figure 10.1) also reported low figures for the use of Setswana in the home – 20%, 53%, and 59% respectively. This meant that 80% of the children in Gantsi, 47% of those in Kgalagadi, and 41% of those in the Ngamiland district, speak languages other than Setswana at home. As shall be seen below, these areas have also been characterised by low academic achievement (Nyati-Ramahobo, 2001).

The census data did not reflect the existence of Nambya, Ruqciriku, Talaonde, and Kwangali. This could mean that, although the ethnicities are presented in the country, the languages may have disappeared. This is the case for Talaone (Chebanne, 2002). Kwangali may have not been reflected in the census data because it is a broad category, which includes Thimbukushu and Rugciriku, and its speakers identify themselves as Hambukushu. The other explanation could be that the respondents felt that the expected and official response could only be Setswana and English and, therefore, their unrecognised languages would not be accepted. This is most likely to be the case with Nambya and Ruqciriku, which Hasselbring

(2000) and Hasselbring *et al.* (2001) found to be spoken in the Boteti and Okavango areas respectively.

In comparison with other Southern African Countries, Botswana has fewer languages than South Africa (31), Zambia (73), Angola (42), and Mozambique (39). It is more comparable to Zimbabwe (20), Malawi (16), and Namibia (29). Lesotho and Swaziland have less than 5 languages each (Summer Institute of Linguistics, 2005). Other parts of Africa have more languages, for instance, Nigeria has over 500 spoken languages. Thus the linguistic situation in Botswana can be described as moderately complex.

Language-in-Education Policy in Africa: Introduction

While most African countries are multilingual, language-in-education policies differ from one country to another. Further, some countries have more than one official language including local languages. This is the case in South Africa with 11 official languages, Zambia with 7, and Nigeria with 8 official languages.

Most countries in Southern Africa have introduced bilingual education in the early years of schooling, which includes the use of the local languages; these countries include Zambia, Zimbabwe, Namibia, and South Africa. In South Africa, communities decide on the language of instruction for their children (Heugh, 2000). While the implementation of this policy may be problematic because of competition with English and Afrikaans (Vesely, 2000), progress is being made because of the enabling environment from the policy perspective.

On the other hand, countries such as Malawi and Botswana permit only the use of the national language in education (Chilora, 2000). The language in education policy in Mozambique permits the use of Portuguese only. However there are current efforts experimenting with bilingual education (Benson, 2000) with the goal of moving onto implementation. There are therefore three scenarios in Africa with regard to multilingual education:

(1) the extreme case of monolingual schools in a former colonial language;
(2) the middle ground of using the national language along with the colonial language;
(3) the liberal process of using as many local languages a possible in the school system in addition to foreign languages.

The first two models are characterised by highly-centralised curriculum systems while the latter works in decentralised systems.

Language-in-Education Policy in Botswana

At independence in 1966, the Botswana government banned the use of languages other than Setswana and English in education, the media, and all other social domains. English was declared the official language, and Setswana was adopted as the national language. Setswana is the mother tongue of eight tribes who mainly reside in the southern part of the country. Between 1966 and 1976 English was the medium of instruction in schools, and Setswana was a subject whose grade was not part of the aggregate mark (Nyati-Ramahobo, 1997). In 1977 Setswana became the medium of instruction for the first four years. However, in 2000 the use of Setswana as medium of instruction was limited to the first two years, while English was declared the medium of instruction for the rest of schooling. Children from non-Tswana-speaking ethnic groups learn Setswana in school for the first two years, after which they switch to English. In 2000, French was piloted in 20 schools as a subject. The policy, therefore, seems to indicate a move towards monolingual schools in English with French as a subject.

In addition to the language-in-education policy, there are other laws and policies that foster assimilation into Tswana culture within the broader social context in which the schools operate. Mechanisms were set and remain in place to spread Setswana across the country. For instance, Setswana-speaking chiefs, teachers, nurses, police officers, agricultural extension workers, and so on, were posted in non-Tswana speaking areas (Reimer, 1996). As government employees, they insisted on the use of the national language in all these domains. In most cases, they tended to despise the non-Tswana cultural traditions and practices and did not learn the local languages. This resulted in an inferiority complex on the part of the non-Tswana and they strived to learn and use Setswana as they sought services from the public officers. Further, non-Tswana-speaking areas have fewer schools. Children from these areas have to go to Tswana-speaking villages for further education, where they would be immersed into Setswana for the first two years and later into English. The goal was not only to spread Setswana, but also to assimilate all other ethnic groups into Tswana language and culture and eventually into English.

The curriculum reflected Tswana history, language, and culture at the exclusion of others represented in the country. Pictures in English school textbooks reflected English values at the exclusion of local values (Milon, 1989) and all other textbooks exclude the values and cultures of the non-Tswana-speaking tribes (Nyati-Ramahobo, 1997). Thus the Tswana have come to represent the State power (Solway & Nyati-Ramahobo, 2004) and are viewed as the majority, and non-Tswana are powerless and are referred to as minorities.

The Tswana children learn in Setswana and about Tswana history and culture. The non-Tswana children learn in Setswana and about Tswana cultures and traditions. The non-Tswana children, therefore, learn to look down on their own histories, languages and customs as not applicable to education or to life. They develop low self-esteem and consequently underachieve. Studies covering the period 1994 to 2000 indicate that the areas of Ghanzi, Ngamiland, and Kgalagadi (see Figure 10.1), which are predominantly minority areas, have had the highest failure rate at Primary School Leaving Examinations, the highest drop-out rates, and the highest number of unqualified teachers (Nyati-Ramahobo, 2001; Malete, 2003). These are the areas in which the use of Setswana in the home is not very high, as indicated above.

Of great relevance to education is to understand that for many language minorities there is no choice in the use of their languages even when they desire to do so. For example, it has been found that most non-Tswana speakers desire to learn to read and write in their own languages (Hasselbring, 2000), especially to read school and religious materials. Embedded in this positive attitude is their desire to have their children learn in their own languages, hence creating an opportunity for multilingual schools.

Cook's (2003) study among the Kua (Cua) and Tshwa (San) people revealed the importance of asking the right question in order to obtain reliable data on language preferences. He found out that the answer would differ depending on how the question was phrased. When viewed as an 'either/or' possibility, they chose Setswana. When viewed as a 'both/and', they gave the priority to their mother tongue. In an ('either/or') option, respondents are restrained by state policy that Setswana is expected to be espoused by every one in the country in order to show patriotism. On the other hand, when the question is phrased in a way that would not result in the rejection of Setswana (the 'both/and' option), the respondents feel free to express their preference for their own language.

Language Endangerment in Botswana and Efforts for Revival

A barrier to the development of multilingual schools is the endangerment of many of the languages of Botswana. If as UNESCO (2001) has said, language loss results in the loss of an irreplaceable cultural heritage, Botswana is faced with a great loss – that of the knowledge embedded in the many languages that are dying as a result of state efforts to create monolingual schools in a multilingual context.

Minority languages in Botswana are either potentially endangered, endangered or seriously endangered, depending on the geographical area. For instance, Shiyeyi, Sebirwa, Setswapong, and Nambya are no longer being passed on to children. In some areas, the youngest speakers of these languages are young adults, while children may or not be able to speak these languages, although they may understand them. In some areas, the youngest speakers are middle aged and beyond, in which case the language is seriously endangered.

On the other hand, most Khoesan languages (see Table 10.1) and Chikuhane, Ikalanga, Otjiherero, Nama, Shekgalahari, Thimbukushu, Zezuru, and Rugciriku are being passed on from generation to generation. However, faced with the support toward Setswana and English, they, too, are potentially endangered. All minority languages are in danger of disappearing because they are politically powerless and culturally non-aggressive. Most of the languages in Botswana are at stage 6 of Fishman's (1991) model of language endangerment or stage 3 according to Schmidt's (1990) model.

Some of the Khoesan languages, for instance, Hua and !Xoo can be described as moribund, since they are spoken only by a few old people. In the case of !Xoo, there are about 800 speakers in Zutshwa and Ukwi in the Kgalagadi district (Central Statistics Office, 2001). Hua has only a handful of old speakers in the Central Kgalagadi game reserve (Visser, 2000). However, efforts are under way to arrest this situation, as described below. A significant number of Khoesan languages are reported to have disappeared, including Haba, Ts'ao, Xam, and Xegwi (Visser, 2000).

Speakers of minority languages in Botswana have begun private efforts to revive them by supporting efforts for linguistic and cultural revival, as well as developing literacy classes in local languages. Some initiatives are focused on cultural rights such as land.

Movements for linguistic and cultural revival

One of the languages that were banned at independence from use in education was Ikalanga. Ikalanga was taught in the Northeastern part of the country and in Zimbabwe. The writing system for the language was developed in Zimbabwe and was adopted for use in Botswana. The Bakalanga people were not happy about the ban on the use of Ikalanga, and in 1981 they formed an Association called *The Society for the Promotion of Ikalanga Language*, popularly known as SPIL. SPIL was aimed at developing the Ikalanga language and culture. Currently, Ikalanga has a published orthography, a Bible, a hymnbook and numerous reading texts (Nyati-Ramahobo & Chebanne, 2005).

The Bakalanga were a lone voice for marginalized groups until 1995, when the Wayeyi formed the *Kamanakao Association* to promote the Shiyeyi language and culture (Nyati-Ramahobo, 2002). Currently Shiyeyi has a published orthography, a grammar book, a hymnbook, and some reading texts.

The Batswapong formed the *Lentswe la Batswapong* in 1997. They published a newspaper in Setswapong language that dealt with Batswapong history and culture. Though the paper has been irregular because of funding problems, it has raised awareness on language issues and promoted the use of Setswapong language.

The *First People of the Kgalahari (FPK)* was formed in (1992) to promote the Gana and Gwi culture, but also to advocate for land rights in the Central Kgalahari Game Reserve (CKGR). FPK also promoted song and dance and advocated for use of local languages in schools.

Currently, there are six registered organisations dealing with language development, and seven non-registered ones. All these organisations came together in 2002 and formed a coalition called RETENG: The Multicultural Coalition of Botswana (Solway & Nyati-Ramahobo, 2004). This organisation initiated orthography development for four of the non-written languages – Sebirwa, Chikuhane, Shekgalahari, and one of the Shua dialects (Cirecire). Each of these now has an initial writing system. Work to continue to develop these writing systems to an acceptable stage is on going. RETENG has also taken the matter on non-recognition of the non-Tswana-speaking groups to the United Nations' Committee on the Elimination of Racial Discrimination (CERD) (2002) which has recommended that all laws that discriminate should be reviewed.

The Lutheran Bible Translators (LBT) from the United States have played a significant role in the development of languages in Botswana. They have assisted the *Kamanakao Association* to develop Shiyeyi and SPIL to develop Ikalanga by funding writers' workshops and printing materials. UNESCO also funded a project, through the Department of Adult Education at the University of Botswana, to produce materials in Ikalanga and Shiyeyi (Nyati-Ramahobo & Chebanne, 2005).

The surveys carried out by Cook and Hasselbring were also funded by the Lutheran Bible Translators (LBT). These surveys have proven invaluable in assessing the status of languages in Botswana. LBT has also initiated work on !Xoo in Zutshwa and an orthography is being developed. LBT is also assessing if work could be started in Tsowa and Kua in the Sand Veld areas, for these Khoesan languages.

The Department of African Languages and Literature at the University of Botswana has developed a course in which students can choose to learn any of the local languages, as long as there is a lecturer available in any given academic year. The Department of Languages and Social Sciences Education offers language teachers a core course on multicultural education. These initiatives are aimed at preserving as many languages of Botswana as possible with the ultimate goal of using them in schools in the future, especially at lower grades. They are also meant to raise public awareness on the importance of using local languages in education and its impact on development.

Literacy efforts for linguistic and cultural revival

The national literacy program of the Department of Non Formal Education at the Ministry of Education provides literacy skills in Setswana across the country. Critics have attributed its current failure to the exclusion of other languages and cultures, and some adults have stated that, if their languages are not used, they would prefer to learn in English (Kazombungo, 2000).

The Botswana Christian Council established literacy classes for children in Thimbukushu, at Etsha 6, in the Ngamiland district. Reimer (1996) attributes the eventual collapse of these classes to a number of factors, including high levels of illiteracy among the parents, top-down decisions, lack of books to take home, methodological issues, lack of training for teachers, lack of government support, and non-sustainable funding. Other efforts were also initiated in Otjiherero, which suffered the same fate for similar reasons.

One of the most successful efforts for literacy in minority languages is the Naro Language Project at Dakar, in the Ghanzi district. It is funded by the Christian Reformed Church in the Netherlands, and runs a pre-school for Khoesan children of Naro descent. Naro is a Khoesan language with low status and spoken by the most despised and neglected ethnic groups in Botswana, the Basarwa. A language that was nearly extinct has now been revitalised and is used on a daily basis by Naro people of Dakar. They are now proud to identify as Naro and grateful to see their language in writing. Evaluations of the program have been positive (Biesele & Hitchcock, 2000; Visser, 2000).

A project proposal to fund a model primary school for Naro in Dakar has been submitted to the World Bank and De Beers (Botswana). The success of the project is attributed to the full-time commitment of the Visser family to the project. There was also sustained funding from the Church in the Netherlands. The fact that the Vissers were trained linguists provided the professional guidance to the project. There was also a program to train Naro-speaking teachers. The consultative process and involvement of the parents in the program proved to be vital. Culturally relevant materials were developed for Naro children and there was on-going research on the program to inform teacher training, material development, and teaching approaches. The inclusion of English and Setswana served to provide the bi- and multilingual perspective, which is necessary for the success of a language program (Biesele & Hitchcock, 2000) and a positive step towards multilingual schools.

Problems encountered in language development and revival

The development of local languages has met with problems, some of which are similar to those in other parts of the world, while some may be unique to Botswana. One of the major factors that have hampered the use of local languages in the education system, as stated earlier, is policy. The government of Botswana, more than any other in the Southern African region, has taken a hard stance on the use of local languages. In 1973, the *National Commission on Education* recommended the use of local languages at pre-school level, but Parliament rejected the recommendation on the basis of lack of resources. This attitude continued even after the publication of the *Vision 2016* document (Republic of Botswana, 1997), which called for the development and use of local languages in education.

Supporters of multilingual education find radio to be an important tool for language spread and maintenance, and for education as well. Over time, they have advocated for the establishment of community radio stations as a way to revive the various languages. But as of today, licensing for community radio stations lies with the Office of the President (OP) and not with the Botswana Telecommunications Authority. The OP has thus far issued only two licenses for private radio stations on condition that they broadcast in Setswana and English only and are confined to the capital city. The application by Mr Gumbo, a citizen who wanted to broadcast in Ikalanga, has been pending since 1994. The government, therefore, is not only against the use of these languages in official institutions but seems to discourage even private efforts.

In 1985 and 1988, the government would not accept funding for bilingual education from the German Foundation for International Development (GTZ) (Komarek & Keatimilwe, 1988) and this weakened the argument of lack of resources as the reason for not using local languages in education. One of the reasons the Thimbukushu classes collapsed was lack of funding, as the donor was discouraged by government agencies from continuing with the project. and had to leave the country.

The main hindrance for the creation of multilingual schools in Botswana is the power relations between the Tswana and the non-Tswana-speaking groups. Most of the minority tribes were subjects of the Tswana tribes during the colonial period. The Tswana are currently in power, and they decide who should be literate in what language. Botswana is a rich country with a small population. The issue of resources, lack of materials, and lack of trained teachers could be easily overcome if there was political will to use some of the local languages in education.

The approach that has been adopted up to now for provision of literacy to minority children in schools is the functional approach, which focuses on the acquisition of reading and writing skills (Ferdman, 1999). In this approach, the sociocultural context is not considered important in the acquisition of literacy. The centralised curriculum does not take cognisance of differences between school and the home either as possible barriers or as facilitating tools if incorporated into the learning process. In other words, the sociocultural approach to literacy is not valued by the school system in Botswana, and this poses a barrier even for private efforts which have to conform to the centralised system.

An inclusive sociocultural approach in the teaching of literacy would facilitate its acquisition by the minorities. This approach would eliminate oppressive and discriminatory practices. It would generate awareness of and respect for human rights and cultural diversity. The education system in Botswana needs to go through a systematic organisational change in order to provide literacy to minority children from a multilingual and multicultural perspective.

Prospects for Revival of Local Languages and the Creation of Multilingual Schools

Can local languages be revived and eventually find their way into schools? Around the world, the use of languages in education, whether formal, informal, state funded or not, has played a major role in the revitalisation of threatened languages. Successful educational programs need to link language and culture, and they need written materials, community support, and parental involvement (Anonby, 1999; Stiles, 1997).

The opposition parties in Botswana took ethnic inequality and the use of local languages in education as a campaign issue during the 2004 general elections. Thus the ruling party had to take some positive steps on use of local languages, at least for election purposes. Although the ruling party incorporated the document *Vision 2016* (which includes the use of local languages in education) no effort was made to implement it. Nevertheless, the slogan 'Vision 2016 is mine' was translated into five local languages, in addition to Setswana. Further, the election message from the Independent Electoral Commission to encourage people to vote was televised in five local languages – Shiyeyi, Ikalanga, Chikuhane, Naro, and Shekgalahari – for the first time since independence. This was also the first time the international community observed the general elections. There was a drastic decrease in the popular vote for the ruling party from 60% in 1999 to 51.7% in 2004. The opposition increased their popular vote from 30% in 1999 to 48.3% in 2004, thus putting more pressure on the government.

The official discourse on language issues has changed over time. While in the past, Ministers and other Government officials would describe Botswana as a monolingual country, current speeches acknowledge the multilingual and multicultural nature of the country. A recent speech by the Minister of Home Affairs emphasized the need for a national language, but also expressed the importance of the development of other languages. The minister stated that the issue was no longer political will, but lack of resources, which is a weak argument. However, this was a positive policy statement in that it opened the gate for the development of local languages as long as resources could be secured, even through private efforts.

On December 15, 2003, President Mogae stated in a televised interview that local languages would be taught in schools. This was yet another important policy statement that gave hope for the use of local languages. However, after elections, one of the newly-appointed ministers told Parliament that the government was not ready to introduce local languages in schools. This implies that policy statements may be only a campaign strategy that are not meant to be implemented.

The Battlefield: The School

Education in general is one of the most important instruments for language spread and language revival. It is the language-in-education policy that has successfully promoted the use of Setswana to the current level of 78% of the population. The school is therefore the battlefield for opposing forces, and it is what happens in the school that may eventually determine the direction for social change.

Estha 6 Primary School: Sociocultural background

This section describes the *Estha 6 Primary School* as an example of the battlefield for and against monolingualism and the tensions that affect learning. The war in Angola caused an influx of the Hambukushu people into Botswana in 1969. The Government of Botswana received and resettled them in 13 villages in the Ngamiland district, specifically the Okavango subdistrict, in an area known to the local people as Gqchawancwa, between Gumare and Sepopa (see Figure 10.1 above). This was essentially grazing land for the Wayeyi people who lived in Gumare, Sepopa, and the Okavango delta. The government had to negotiate with the Batawana chief, who informed the village headmen in Gumare, Ikoga, and Sepopa to resettle the Hambukushu population of about 20,000 in 13 settlements, named Etsha 1 to 13. A cooperative store was built in 1970 at Etsha 6 and the village currently has a primary school, a community junior secondary school, and a petrol station, making it a centre of attraction. It also has a clinic and an Ecumenical Centre, where the Thimbukushu literacy project described above was located.

In an effort to diversify the economy, the government developed a strategy to deny communities in tourist areas some social amenities as a way to force them out of those areas. Consequently, for years the government had refused to give village status to the Zhao settlement in the Okavango delta, which is predominantly Yeyi-speaking. This meant that this settlement of over 5000 people, had, and still has no school, telephone, piped water or a shop. There is a clinic that rarely has a nurse or medication. As a result, most of the Wayeyi moved into Etsha 6 after 1972 and resettled there or lived a dual life between the two places.

The current population of Zhao Island fluctuates between 300 and 500 because of seasonal factors and the need to access social services. Other ethnic groups have also moved into Etsha 6, especially the Herero, but in smaller numbers. Currently, Etsha 6 is a Hambukushu- and a Wayeyi-dominated area, with a population of 2629 and the Hambukushu in the majority. Both the Hambukushu and Wayeyi are bilingual in Setswana. However, the Hambukushu use their language in their daily lives more than the Wayeyi, who seem to use Setswana more. Wayeyi parents speak Shiyeyi among themselves and Setswana to their children.

Etsha 6 is one of the 23 primary schools in the Okavango subdistrict. In 2001, it had an enrolment of 1263 students (635 boys and 628 girls). There were 32 teachers from nine ethnic groups as follows: Wayeyi (12), Kalanga (7) Hambukushu (3), Herero(3), Batswapong (2) and Tswana speakers (10). Twelve of the 32 teachers (37.5%) were untrained. All teachers speak Setswana, either as a first language (for the Tswana groups) or as a second language (for the other groups). They also speak English and are expected to teach in English from grade 3 onwards. While some of the Wayeyi may be bilingual, they speak Setswana most of the time. Other non-Tswana teachers speak their own languages outside the classroom to their own people.

With regard to students, there are more Hambukushu children than any other ethnic group, followed by the Wayeyi and a few Gciriku. The Hambukushu children speak their language in the school compound and at home. Their parents speak Thimbukushu to them most of the time. The Wayeyi children speak Shiyeyi only on rare occasions. They speak Setswana in the school compound and at home. However, the majority of the Wayeyi children at Etsha 6 comprehend and respond when spoken to in Shiyeyi. They have a passive knowledge of Shiyeyi. The Wayeyi established a popular traditional dance group in the school in 1999. The school headteacher was a Muyeyi with an active knowledge of the language, and she taught the children to sing in Shiyeyi. The group has since become popular among tourists and in 2004 they were invited to perform at the Independence Day celebrations in the capital city, Gaborone. They also perform at functions when government officials visit Etsha 6. It seems, therefore, that while Thimbukushu language is visible in Etsha 6, Shiyeyi cultural song and dance is also visible.

Language in Estha 6

In 2002–2003 I conducted classroom observations and interviews in the school. A total of 30 lessons in social studies, English, Setswana and science were observed and audio-taped. Interviews were conducted with 15 of the 32 teachers on what they observed as factors affecting learning in the school, and specifically whether they thought language was one of them. The findings of the study were that:

(1) Children have problems participating effectively in discussions during lessons that are conducted in English. In response to the teachers' questions, they supply words, and short sentences. For example (Standard 3 social studies lesson, June 6, 2002):

Teacher: Why is 'boat' the correct answer?
Student: Water.
Teacher: Now, who can tell me three ways we transport goods?
Student: Air, water and road.

(2) Group discussions are conducted in Setswana especially when the teacher is not watching, and they are discouraged from doing so if they are in grades 3 and above since the expected language is English. For example (Grade 4 science class, July 9, 2002):

Teacher: *Ke le boleletse gore le bue Sekgoa, ga kere*? Didn't I say that we should use English?
(I told you to use English, didn't I? Didn't I?)

(3) When the majority of the children in a group are Hambukushu, they talk in Thimbukushu, especially when the teacher is at a distance. If they are heard, they are discouraged

Teacher: *Le bua sekae*?
(What language are you using?)
This would happen at all grades, since Thimbukushu is not one of the two school languages.

(4) Most of the teaching is done in Setswana in grades 1 to 5 and in English from grade 6 to 7. The model is therefore neither monolingual Setswana in grade 1 or 2 nor monolingual in English from grade 3 to 7 as stipulated by the language in education policy.

(5) Students and teachers use both Setswana and their local languages outside the classroom, depending on their interlocutor.

(6) Children have problems understanding Setswana as spoken by teachers who are native speakers of Setswana, living outside the Ngamiland district. There are words that have different meanings in standard Setswana and the Setawana variety (of Setswana) spoken in the Ngamiland district. Words such as those in Table 10.2 (and many others) pose comprehension problems for children and are sometimes a source of ridicule from teachers.

(7) Interviews with students indicated that they understand teachers from the Ngamiland district better, both when speaking Setswana and English. They further stated that Hambukushu teachers occasionally

Table 10.2 Differences between standard Setswana and Setawana variety

Word	*Setawana variety*	*Standard Setswana*
go soba	to urinate	to move on one's buttocks (if one is disabled)
go lesela	to leave something or someone alone	*go tlogela*
go taboga	to have a running stomach	to run (especially very fast)

use Thimbukushu in class. For example (after a Grade 4 social studies lesson, August 7, 2003):

Researcher: *A Teacher X, o atle a rute ka Sembukushu?*
(Does teacher X [one of the Hambukushu teachers] use Thimbukushu in class?)
Student: *Ee, mme eseng thata.*
(Yes, but not much.)

(8) The Wayeyi teachers, though they are the majority, were reported not to use Shiyeyi in the classroom. On the other hand, they liked drawing on Shiyeyi cultural themes to illustrate certain topics in social studies. For example (interview with a Standard 5 student after a science class, July 11, 2002):

Researcher: Does your teacher teach about Shiyeyi culture?
Student: *Ee,* Teacher X *one a re bolela ka kalafi ya phogana ka Shiyeyi.*
(Yes, Teacher X was telling us how to cure children's disease in the Shiyeyi culture.)
Researcher: *A o dira jalo gantsi?*
(Does she do that often?)
Student: *Ee.* (Yes.)
Researcher: *A o atle a bue maina a ditlhare, dinonyane jalo jalo ka Shiyeyi?*
(Does she give names of trees, birds and so on in Shiyeyi?)
Student: *Nyaa.* (No.)

It therefore seems that, while the official policy encourages the use of Setswana in grades 1 and 2 and English in the rest of the classes, other languages and cultures do find their way into the classroom and the school compound. The school is, therefore, multilingual and multicultural. However, the state policy as enforced by teachers creates a seemingly monolingual school at the detriment of the learning process. The 'creeping in' of other languages and cultures is testimony to the existence of multilingualism in the school, and the inherent need for mother-tongue education to facilitate active student-centered learning.

The current national debate on constitutional amendments and the renewed ethnic identities and political forces that continue to resist monolingualism in society and in the school result in the 'creeping in' process. All these forces seem to suggest that not only is government under pressure to create an enabling environment for multilingual schools, but communities are also asserting themselves in several ways. For instance, in previous years the community of Etsha 6 voted for the ruling party, but the last elections saw a shift to the opposition when the issue of marginalisation of local languages and recognition of non-Tswana-speaking groups became an election issue. Since the major impediment for the actualisation of multilingual schools is political will, it needs a political solution. There are already indications that this may lead to policy change and the shift of some resources towards the implementation of some of the current progressive policies contained in *Vision 2016* (Republic of Botswana, 1997). Should this happen, Etsha 6 would be a true multilingual and multicultural school.

Estha 6 represents the battlefield between reality and political considerations, and power relations between teachers as the state representatives for monolingualism and students and parents as representatives for multilingualism.

Performance in Estha 6

Over the years, like most schools in this district, Estha 6's school performance has been low. In 2000, the school had the lowest pass rate in the district (44%) and the lowest pass rate in Setswana language (51%). Table 10.3 indicates the school performance over a three-year period.

Over the three years, the total number of those obtaining grades A and B is

Table 10.3 Primary school leaving results for Etsha 6

	2002		*2000*		*1999*	
Grade	#	%	#	%	#	%
A	2	2	6	5	6	6
B	39	33	27	25	29	30
C	53	45	48	44	40	42
D	23	19	29	26	19	20
F	2	2	0	0	2	2
Totals	*119*	*100*	*110*	*100*	*96*	*100*

less than 40%, and more than 60% obtain grades C and D. In 2002 five and in 2000 seven students had absconded after registering for the examinations.

Interviews with teachers who are native speakers of Setswana indicated that children seem to do better in English than in Setswana. While they think that the Setawana dialect they spoke as a second language is the standard Setswana, this is not the case. This dialect has a lot of Shiyeyi vocabulary (Nyati-Ramahobo, 2001) with an underlying Setswana sentence structure. As such, children often think that they understand the content and questions, when in fact they do not. This results in under-performance. Teachers also felt that other factors contributed to low performance, such as teacher training, teacher morale, lack of facilities, and lack of books. The school language is different from the home language, resulting in low performance. Most teachers were from other cultures, creating cross-cultural communication problems, which also affects learning.

Social integration at Etsha 6

Most teachers reported that students social groups are formed along ethnic lines and within ethnic groups, related area of origin. For instance, within the Wayeyi groups, there were subgroups of those children from Zhao, Guda, and so on. Hambukushu children tended to prefer to form their own social groups since they use their language more often. Interviews with students about their knowledge of the culture of the other groups of children revealed that the Hambukushu seemed to know more about the Wayeyi culture than the other way round. For instance:

Researcher: *O rata eng ka ngwao ya Wayeyi?*
(What do you like about the Wayeyi culture?)

Hambukushu child: *Modokoto.*
[This is a name of one of the Wayeyi traditional dances.]

Researcher: *Ko ntle ga mmino o itse eng gape?*
(What else do you know about the Wayeyi besides dancing?)

Hambukushu child: *Ba rata tswii le ditlhapi*
(They like water lily roots and fish)

This child knows about the Wayeyi dance and food:

Researcher: *O rata eng ka ngwao ya Hambukushu?*
(What do you like about the Hambukushu culture?'

Muyeyi child: *Ga ke itse.*
(I do not know)

Researcher: *Ga o itse mmino wa bone, kana ga o o rate.*
(You mean you do not know their dance or you just do not like it?)

Muyeyi child:	*Ba bina ka maheta.* *(They use their shoulders a lot when they dance'.*
Researcher:	*O bidiwa eng one mmino oo.* *(What do you call that type of dance?)*
Muyeyi child:	*Gake itse* (I do not know.)

Within the community, the parents had substantive knowledge about each other's language and culture. However, the Wayeyi seemed not to like the Hambukushu food and their conservation strategies. The Wayeyi complained that Hambukushu cut trees when gathering fruits, and that they cut the reeds used for making baskets in such a way that they will not grow again. They also complained that Hambukushu eat worms and monkeys, and they mix pumpkin seeds with meat. When asked whether these foodstuff were not nice, the majority of respondents said they have not tasted it, while a few said it is not. It was clear that while the Hambukushu eat Wayeyi food such as water lily roots and fish, the Wayeyi do not eat the Hambukushu food such as the kraal worm and monkeys. On the other hand, the Wayeyi respect Hambukushu for their traditional medicine and rain-making skills.

The Village Senior chief's representative was a Hambukushu. He did not have a good relationship with the Wayeyi headmen. But ordinary citizens did not seem to harbour hard feelings that could result in any social disorder. In recent years, there has been an increase in intermarriage between the two groups. However, government had exploited the cultural differences to create animosity between the Wayeyi and Hambukushu. The former votes for the opposition party, while the latter votes for the ruling party. When the tourism industry brings tenders for land concessions, government officials tend to favour community management committees that are dominated by Hambukushu, and this has caused tension.

Interviews with teachers about community relations indicated that the use of Setswana alone is not enough to facilitate social integration. Teachers feel that children have to learn about each other's language and culture in order to appreciate the other (see language awareness, as described by Hélot in Chapter 3). It seemed therefore that social integration can be achieved through acknowledgment of the existence of a multilingual and multicultural school and the development of a multilingual education curriculum. The use of Setswana as a national language is important for cross-cultural communication and does facilitate social integration, but only to some extent. Government's efforts to create monolingual schools in order to achieve social integration could only create a lingua franca, while ethnic identities remain unchanged as indicated in a study by Batibo and Smieja (2000). Optimal social integration calls for the support and nurturing of existing multilingual schools. Education plays a major role in nurturing unity in diversity and social cohesion.

Conclusions

The development of multilingual and multicultural schools in Botswana may be hampered by factors such as lack of resources, but it is also clear that the major impediment is lack of political will. Movements for linguistic revival coupled with parental desire for bilingual education, and supported by political debate may serve as the driving force for multilingual schools in the future. The road to the official support for multilingual schools may be long, but shifts in official discourse, the existence of some progressive policies, and international pressure continue to be a source of inspiration for implementation. The acquisition of education can no longer be viewed from a purely functional perspective. Sociocultural and power approaches need to be addressed in order to empower minorities for economic development and social cohesion.

This trend is important not only for the well-documented advantages of mother-tongue education, but also as a human right. If Botswana complies with the recommendations of CERD and accedes to internal pressures, then it will be more comparable with some of its neighbours (such as South Africa) who provide education in local languages during the early years of schooling. The Naro experiment should continue to inspire more use of local languages in schooling, and efforts in South Africa, Zambia, Namibia and other African countries should provide Botswana with the desire to do more. Africa needs more commitment towards the liberal model of providing education in local languages in order to address the development challenges facing its people today. Mulitilingual schools are not only good for education as a right, but also for the acquisition of the more widely spoken languages of the world.

Notes

1. 'Setswana' refers to the language spoken by the eight recognised tribes in Botswana. The term 'Tswana' refers to the cultures (inclusive of dialects) of these tribes. These terms are sometimes used interchangeably.
2. Those who are not ethnic Tswana – whose first language is not Setswana.

Summary

At independence, the government of Botswana imagined a monolingual society in which English would be the only language of education, the judiciary, and all other social domains. The government also imagined that Setswana would be the only language used in national life when dealing with the general population. The language-in-education policy and related legal instruments were put in place to create an ordinary citizen who is monolingual in Setswana and an educated one who is bilingual in Setswana and English.

In contrast to this view, the situation on the ground was that 99% of the population spoke one of the 26 unrecognized languages (Walter & Ringenberg, 1994). This population imagined a multilingual society and multilingual schools, thus creating a backlash between the Tswana political leaders and the numerical majority non-Tswana. This chapter describes government efforts in creating monolingualism and societal movements that counteracted this position and developed multilingualism and multiculturalism. Etsha 6 Primary School serves as an example of a school environment that represents the battlefield for and against monolingualism and reflects how this tension impacts on learning and social integration.

Moni ldivu ldi Wutswana, mona zindime za makumi a yiri ni wu vundja wuyiri (28). Mo ko mayiwa ishikoloni, zindime zii zimwe zari ku iyaaywa moni zikwere. Ati tuku tjhuturwa, Hurumente ka zi ranqi ku hwetwa moni iwayilisi, moni zikhwata indji ku iyaaywa ni zikwere, tana Shirwa indji Shikhuwa ngaho. Impampiri yinii yati ni ziira ngahoshi awatu wati shaka ku yaka zindime zao, indji ngahoshi Hurumente amati shaka ku zi bura. Yati ni ziira shi shikwere sha Etsha 6, ngahoshi wapundi wati shaka ku hweta zindime zao, hurumente ye kati wa tjika, indji ngahoshi wati shitirwa ku shikwere shi ku ha yuvwa naqa Shirwa indji Shikhuwa. (Shiyeyi)

Lefatshe la Botswana le na le diteme dile 28. Erile re tsaya boipuso, Goromente a kganela tiriso ya diteme tsotlhe tse di neng di dirisiwa mo dikolong ka nako ya Sekoloni, kwa ntle ga Setswana le Sekgowa fela. Pampiri e, e bolela maiteko a batho go boloka diteme tsa bone tse di nyelelelang, le jaaka Goromente a leka go di bolaya. E go bolelela se se dirafalang ko sekolong sa Etsha 6, jaaka bana ba rata go bua diteme tsa bone mme ba kganelwa, ba felele ba tholwa ke dithuto tsa bone ka ba sa utlwe sentle Setswana le Sekgowa. (Setswana)

Shango ye Botswana ina ndimi dzili 28. Kwakati ku wang'wa kuzwi busa, mbuso ubo u misa shingisiwa kwe dzimwe ndimi kuzhe kwe Itswana ne Ikhuwa. Nenguba bunji gwe bathu gu leba ndimi dzimwe, mbuso wakabe u alakana kuti ndimi idzedzi mbili ndidzo dzino zibga ne bathu banjinji, ngono kusaka jalo. Nkwalo iwoyu uno lakidza mazwimisilo e bathu bano lamba kuti ba ngondongedziwe ndimi ne tjilinje tjaba singa shake. Bana be ikwele tje Etsha 6 baka tungamila munja iwoyu se be shaka diyiwa ne lulimi gwabo mu ikwele, se basinga zibe kene hwa Itswana ne Ikhuwa. (Ikalanga)

Part 5

Negotiating Policies of Implementation

Chapter 11

Nichols *to* NCLB: *Local and Global Perspectives on US Language Education Policy*

NANCY H. HORNBERGER

Introduction

'Americans aren't used to receiving foreign aid, especially from a third world country such as Bolivia. But in the case of bilingual education, we may have a few things to learn from this poverty-stricken Andean country' (Dolson, 2004: 18). So begins California Department of Education Program Consultant David Dolson, in a recent piece reflecting on his return visit to a school in a Quechua-speaking Andean community he had first visited 25 years ago. Dolson goes on to highlight some of the educational innovations he observed there – new school buildings and modular furniture, world-class Quechua language arts readers and Quechua math textbooks for every child, abundant written material in Quechua and Spanish posted on the walls and in the classroom library and learning centers, fluently bilingual and well-trained teachers, and active involvement of parents in the school governing body. All of these are fruit of Bolivia's 1994 Educational Reform, with its key planks of bilingual intercultural education for all and popular participation in school governance (Hornberger & López, 1998).

I, too, have mused on the hope and example offered by multilingual language education policies, such as Bolivia's 1994 Education Reform and post-apartheid South Africa's 1993 Constitution, in creating ideological and implementational spaces for imagining multilingual schools – and on the possibility of putting such examples into practice in the United States and elsewhere (Hornberger, 2002). I have considered community and classroom challenges inherent in implementing the new ideologies that underlie multilingual language policies in educational settings and have proposed the continua of biliteracy framework as ecological heuristic for situating and addressing those challenges (Hornberger, 2003).

At this 10-year anniversary of the bold Bolivian and South African experiments in multilingual education, those directly involved are well aware of the many shortcomings thus far and the enormous challenges remaining ahead, but they are also perhaps more convinced than ever of the necessity and opportunity represented by what has been achieved so far. In both countries, national and international conferences convened in June and July of this year have taken a critical look back at the past 10 years, evaluating what has been accomplished and what remains to be done. In Bolivia, the Ministry of Education convened an international Latin American seminar to consolidate experiences and formulate recommendations on teacher professional development in bilingual intercultural education and the World Bank sponsored a five-country Latin American seminar on achievements and challenges in bilingual intercultural education (López & Küper, 2004). Both of these events were organized and coordinated by the consortial Andean regional postgraduate Program for Professional Development in Bilingual Intercultural Education (PROEIB Andes), housed at the University of San Simón in Cochabamba. Part of the impetus for these meetings was the need to take stock of the past 10 years of Bolivia's Education Reform, as the decennial educational policy-making National Congress of Education approaches (Anaya, 2004).

Similarly, 'Ten years of multilingualism in South Africa: Fact or fantasy?' was the theme taken up in July 2004 at the conference of the Southern African Applied Linguistics Association held at the University of Limpopo in South Africa. Classroom and community challenges faced at all institutional levels of implementation of the multilingual policy were candidly presented and discussed. These included the ongoing constraints on making the South African universities truly multilingual in ideology and practice, the shortcomings of assessment standards and criteria of the Revised National (K–12) Curriculum in relation to research understandings on second language acquisition and biliteracy (Heugh, 2004), the relative inaccessibility of and lack of specific focus on language statistics in education (Plüddemann *et al.*, 2004), and the ongoing threat to multilingual education posed by the common perception of English as language of access (Finlayson & Slabbert, 2004) – to name only a few. Yet, optimism and creativity were also readily in evidence, as for example in the newly-launched bilingual degree program at University of Limpopo (Joseph & Ramani, 2004) and the Home Language Project, a parent-based initiative that has successfully introduced one lesson per week of Nguni and Suthu mother-tongue/heritage language teaching in six formerly white Model C, but now multicultural, English-medium schools in the Johannesburg area (Owen-Smith *et al.*, 2004; Rodseth & Rodseth 2004). Another example is one teacher/researcher's balanced reading approach designed for her multicultural English-medium classroom of grade 1 and 2 Indian and Zulu students, which incorporated interactive reading and the valuing of the mother tongue (Wildsmith-Cromarty & Gounden, 2004).

In both national cases, the two broad areas of challenges I had highlighted in my 2002 paper (the popular demand for the language of power and the logistical complexities of working with multiple languages, literacies, and identities at the classroom level) – are ever-present and by no means resolved. Yet it is also true that there is accumulating evidence that they can be addressed. In direct response to the need for concrete answers to the logistical complexities of implementing bilingual intercultural education in the classroom, for example, the recently-concluded two-year Tantanakuy Project in Bolivia (co-sponsored by PROEIB Andes and the Government of Finland) produced several sets of self-learning modules for in-service professional development of classroom teachers. These include a set of modules on strategies for intercultural education in the classroom and another on working in multi-grade classrooms, which constitute 83% of Bolivian classrooms (*Proyecto Tantanakuy*, 2004: 2).

On the other hand, in regard to the challenges posed by the popular demand for the language of power, as exemplified in the recurring refrain of the Limpopo conference that South African parents choose English-medium schools, language policy expert and advocate Neville Alexander (2003) affirmed emphatically that his experience, and that of his colleagues at the Project for Alternative Education in South Africa (PRAESA) at University of Cape Town (Bloch & Alexander, 2003), is that what parents are choosing is NOT in fact the English medium of instruction, but rather the superior resourcing and academic preparation offered by the English-medium schools. Where schools can offer a well-resourced multilingual program taught by adequately prepared teachers, he said, parents are just as ready to choose those schools.

In both Bolivia and South Africa, there is a palpable sense of urgency among those involved, to take maximum advantage of the space afforded by the existing multilingual policies, before they foreclose. Just so, my own sense of urgency about the closing of ideological and implementational space for multilingual education in the US, as evidenced by the passage of Propositions 227 and 203 in California and Arizona, has only intensified in recent years, with passage of the Massachusetts version of the Unz initiative and the imposition of the most recent re-authorization of the Elementary and Secondary Education Act, euphemistically and misleadingly titled *No Child Left Behind* (NCLB, 2001). As Eugene Garcia tellingly and alarmingly put it in a recent AERA panel reviewing *Lau v. Nichols*, under the current English-only and anti-bilingual education conditions, 'We are quickly reaching pre-*Lau* and pre-*Brown* situations in schools' (E.E. Garcia, 2004).

So, what about *Lau*? In this anniversary year of landmark US Supreme Court decisions affirming the right to equal educational opportunity for all children irrespective of race or language origin, it behooves us to take a look at how well we are fulfilling those mandates. It is 50 years since the *Brown v.*

Board of Education ruling against racial segregation of students in public schools and 30 years since the *Lau v. Nichols* decision rejected the notion that equal provision necessarily equates to equal educational opportunity for English speaking and non-English speaking students alike. What kind of space did *Lau v. Nichols* create for multilingual schools in US language education policy? And what kind of spaces are left in the wake of anti-bilingual education initiatives and *NCLB*? In what follows, I would like to take a brief look back at *Lau* and then take up consideration of *NCLB*, with particular attention to the kind of ideological and implementational spaces created for multilingual schools in the US. I conclude with some international perspectives on where all this leaves us as we continue to imagine and construct multilingual schools for our learners.

Looking Back at *Lau v. Nichols*

Students of language policy and language rights in the United States have long recognized the deep-seated ambivalence that plays itself out in the waxing and waning of language tolerance across the history of our relatively young nation (Sapiens, 1978; Estrada, 1979; Grosjean, 1982; Ruiz, 1984a, 1984b; Perlman, 1990; del Valle, 2003: 9–87). Many remark on the striking resemblance between the earlier period of intolerance associated with the push for Americanization, beginning in 1880 and intensifying around the period of World War I (Ricento, 2003), and the current period of English-only and anti-immigrant sentiment beginning approximately one century later and intensifying around the turn of the millenium.

Furthermore, both of these assimilationist and language-restrictionist periods arose in the wake of increased numbers of immigrants that were perceived by the mainstream as 'different' – poorer and more uncultured, compared to previous immigrant groups. At the end of the 19th century, these were, for example, southern rather than northern Europeans, Asians recruited as indentured labor, and Puerto Ricans and Mexicans whose territories were annexed to the US. At the end of the 20th century, they were refugees from the wars in South-East Asia and Central America, as well as Asian and other immigrants benefiting from the 1965 Immigration and Naturalization Amendments which abolished the national origins quota system and permitted up to 20,000 entries per country per year (Wong, 1988: 196). In the earlier period, as in the more recent one, recurring anxieties fueling anti-immigrant sentiment include concerns that new immigrants: (1) are just too numerous, (2) slip through as undocumented immigrants or asylum seekers, (3) take jobs away from citizens, (4) contribute disproportionately to crime, (5) transform the demographic landscape, and (6) are not readily assimilating (Suárez-Orozco, 1996).

Yet, there have also been periods of relative language tolerance in US history, including nearly the whole first century of the republic (Kloss, 1977), as well as the intervening period from the early 1950s to the 1980s, when new discourses of language tolerance and language rights emerged. This new tolerance for, and interest in, languages other than English originated to some degree from a strategic need for translators and multilingual intelligence during World War II and intensified in the Cold War era, after the news-breaking 1957 Sputnik launch and ensuing media accounts of the foreign language (and other) achievements of the Russian educational system.

Even more significantly, however, it was the Civil Rights movement and Civil Rights law – emerging in 1954 with the US Supreme Court's school desegregation decision, *Brown v. Board of Education,* and punctuated at 10-year intervals thereafter by the 1964 *Civil Rights Act* (Title VI) and the 1974 *Equal Educational Opportunity Act* (EEOA) – that gave impetus to language rights. In the United States, it is on the terrain of civil rights that legal, political, and educational policy decisions supporting language rights rest, and, reciprocally, language rights is 'another pillar in the civil rights world, along with ... education, housing, and voting rights' (Del Valle, 2003: 4).

Brown v. Board of Education (1954) established, on the Constitutional basis of the 14th Amendment's Equal Protection Clause,[1] that segregation of students in public schools 'solely on the basis of race deprives children of the minority group of equal educational opportunities' (US Supreme Court 1954: Syllabus [e]). *Title VI* of the *Civil Rights Act* of 1964 and the *Equal Educational Opportunity Act* of 1974 respectively established, on a statutory basis, that:

(1) 'no person in the United States shall, on the ground of race, color, or national origin, be excluded from participation in, be denied the benefits of, or be subjected to discrimination under any program or activity receiving Federal financial assistance' (Section 601) and
(2) 'no state shall deny equal educational opportunity to an individual on account of his or her race, color, sex, or national origin, by ... the failure of an educational agency to take appropriate action to overcome language barriers that impede equal participation by its students in its instructional programs' (Section 1703 (f)) (Wong 1988: 372).

It was on the foundation of these precedents that the US Supreme Court rendered *Lau v. Nichols,* also in 1974, a decision that went beyond *Brown* in identifying and addressing disparate impact (Affeldt, 2004). *Brown* was about the need to avoid intentionally harming students, but *Lau* was about the need to avoid *un*intentionally doing so (Morán, 2004). While *Brown* had found that 'separate but equal' was not good enough to ensure equal educational opportunity, *Lau* found that 'equal' was in fact not necessarily 'equal.' *Lau* asserted, in fact, that 'there is no equality of treatment merely by providing students with the same facilities, textbooks, teachers, and curriculum; for students who do not understand English are effectively foreclosed from any meaningful education.'

The case was a suit brought against the San Francisco Unified School District by Kinney Kinmon Lau and 12 Chinese-American students (over half of them US-born) on behalf of approximately 1800 Chinese-speaking students in the District, charging that they were being denied an education because of a lack of special English classes with bilingual teachers (Wong, 1988: 378). Both the district court and the Ninth Circuit appeals court turned down the plaintiffs' claim, finding that the special needs of students did not create an additional obligation on the school district and characterizing such a claim as an 'extreme' extension of *Brown* (Del Valle, 2003: 237). Significantly, in its landmark decision reversing the lower courts and affirming the Chinese students' claim, the Supreme Court side-stepped the Constitutional issues and instead relied on Title VI of the Civil Rights Act. The Courts have consistently stopped short of granting language rights in and of themselves. It is in this sense that US policy toward minority languages can be characterized as 'swinging from tolerant to hostile with a pragmatic rather than an idealistic core' (Del Valle, 2003: 1).

Recently, even the pragmatism of civil rights claims is at risk, in light of the Supreme Court's decision in *Alexander v. Sandoval* (2001) that private individuals may not sue to enforce the disparate impact regulations of Title VI[2] (Del Valle, 2003: 71–76, 354; Rice, 2004: 34). In response, educational language rights advocates are turning to the Equal Educational Opportunity Act as a more viable alternative for claiming the right to bilingual educational programs that respond to language minority students' needs (Morán, 2004; Rice, 2004).

Establishment of language rights on a civil rights basis, or even on the claim to equal educational opportunity, is both a strong and a weak position. On the one hand, the appeal to civil rights is unassailable. On the other hand, basing language rights on non-language categories such as national origin, race, or equal educational opportunity leaves language itself vulnerable. Ruiz (2004) suggests that, with regard to orientations to language, *Lau* represented more continuity than change – it was about extending civil rights, not language rights, and left intact the language-as-problem orientation that favored implementation of quick, transitional bilingual education or indeed no bilingual education at all.

The *Lau v. Nichols* decision stopped short, not only with regard to side-stepping the issue of Constitutional language rights, but also by failing to specify any particular programmatic remedy (Wong, 1988: 379–380; Del Valle, 2003: 236–242; Rice, 2004: 5). Instead, the Court offered options: 'Teaching English to the students of Chinese ancestry who do not speak the language is one choice. Giving instructions to this group in Chinese is another. There may be others' (Wong, 1988: 379–380).

On the other hand, with these very words, *Lau* created ideological space for bilingual education, a space that was further reinforced by the Lau Remedies, authored in 1975 by a task force convened by the Office of Civil Rights and implemented for several years until the change in presidential administrations in 1980 (election of Reagan). Furthermore, the Lau Remedies, in conjunction with the Bilingual Education Act (Title VII of the Elementary and Secondary Education Act, originally passed by Congress in 1968 and reauthorized at multi-year intervals thereafter), created implementational space for bilingual education for more than 30 years. This implementational space ultimately even allowed space for ideological shift toward a *language as resource* view, as became evident in the 1994 reauthorization (Ruiz, 2004).

The backdrop for Texas Senator Ralph Yarborough's original introduction of what eventually became the Bilingual Education Act (BEA) was a growing awareness of the great disparity in educational achievement between Whites and Mexican-Americans. The 1960 census figures showed average years of schooling at 14 for Whites and 4.7 for Mexican-Americans (Wiley & Wright, 2004: 153). But, while the legislative discourse surrounding the enactment of the BEA included an interest in fostering bilingualism (Johnson, 2004: 82), the law as it was eventually passed had a compensatory thrust and an emphasis on transitional bilingual programs. Even so, it allowed space for the funding of programs using the native language in addition to English. For example,

> In 1970, 134 projects using 16 languages were funded (Liebowitz, 1980) [and] [f]our years later, 220 bilingual programs servicing 340,000 students were receiving Title VII funds, with more than 85% of the funds going toward Spanish programs (Kloss, 1977). (Wiley & Wright, 2004: 153)

In subsequent reauthorizations, while transitional bilingual programs remained a constant feature of Title VII, space and support for bilingual programs using and developing non-English languages alongside English waned and waxed, in accord with the political climate of the corresponding presidential administration (Wiley & Wright, 2004: 154). The 1974 reauthorization effectively curtailed the possibility of two-way programs by discouraging participation of English-speaking children and disallowing their learning of non-English languages in Title VII programs. The 1978 reauthorization lifted the ban on dual-immersion programs and on participation of English-speaking students. But it retained a deficit view of English language learners, modifying only slightly the original notion of 'limited English speaking' to 'limited English proficient' (LEP) to denote inclusion of all four domains of language skills (listening, speaking, reading, writing).

The 1984 reauthorization, under the Reagan administration, somewhat paradoxically and as the result of political bargaining and compromise, allowed for the first time some support for developmental bilingual (maintenance and dual language) programs. It also reserved 4% of Title VII funds for Special Alternative Instructional Programs (SAIPs) which, by definition, make no use of a non-English language. The 1988 reauthorization, also under Reagan, increased this reserved SAIP funding to 25% of the total.

At the time of the 1994 reauthorization under Clinton, developmental bilingual programs received an increased share of support (up to 25%), and dual-language education programs thrived in the ensuing years, having increased in number from about 30 in 1987 to 176 in 1994 and expanding to 261 in 1999, most of them receiving Title VII funding (Lindholm-Leary, 2001: 34–35). It was during this period, too, that the more positively connotative term 'English language learners' (ELLs) began to replace LEP in official usage (August & Hakuta, 1997), reflecting an ideological shift toward a language as resource view. *Lau v. Nichols* and the Bilingual Education Act did then create space for imagining and implementing multilingual schools – space that however appeared to be taken away overnight with passage of *NCLB* in December 2001.

Nichols in an *NCLB* era

With enactment of *No Child Left Behind* in 2002, bilingualism and bilingual education vanished (Wiley & Wright, 2004: 155), indeed were banished, from US educational policy vocabulary, closing up with one fell swoop both the ideological and the implementational spaces that had been created by the BEA. Symbolically, important name changes that abruptly removed all reference to bilingual education (see Table 11.1) reflected a shift

Table 11.1 Renaming bilingual education

English Language Learners (ELL)	became	Limited English Proficient (LEP)
Bilingual Education Act (Title VII)	became	Language Instruction for Limited English Proficient and Immigrant Students (Title III)
Office for Bilingual Education and Minority Language Affairs (OBEMLA)	became	Office of English Language Acquisition, Language Enhancement, and Academic Achievement for Limited English Proficient Students (OELA)
National Clearinghouse for Bilingual Education (NCBE)	became	National Clearinghouse for English Language Acquisition and Language Instruction Educational Programs (NCELA)

in ideological orientation, from the emerging language as resource orientation evident in the 1994 reauthorization back to the earlier orientation of language as problem.

In terms of the closing up of implementational space, *NCLB* does not allow for maintenance bilingual programs. It is, in fact, likely to discourage bilingual education and promote English-only approaches, owing to the combined effect of the large discretionary power accorded to states in the allocation of funding and the nature of the newly-defined accountability provisions (Wiley & Wright, 2004: 156). Competitive grant programs under the old Title VII have been replaced with formula grants to state education agencies, who define their own criteria and accountability systems for allocating funds within the constraints of *NCLB*. The accountability provisions specified in *NCLB* are in turn entirely English-oriented, with emphasis on development and attainment of English language proficiency, academic achievement measured through English-language tests in which LEP students must participate, and adequate yearly progress (AYP) mandated for LEP students.[3] These requirements put immense pressure on school districts to teach LEP students English as quickly as possible and to redesignate as many students as possible each year.[4]

On the other hand, despite the strong English-only orientation in the accountability requirements, it is also true that *NCLB* Title III does not explicitly outlaw bilingual education; in fact, it advocates neither for nor against bilingual education (Freeman, 2004: 26). It allows funding for transitional bilingual education programs (without referring to them by name) and, to some degree, for dual-immersion bilingual programs. Furthermore, there is more money available than before to be applied to this purpose; federal funding for LEP students has nearly doubled with *NCLB* (Wiley & Wright, 2004: 156).

This ambiguous implementational space leaves room to exploit *NCLB* to maintain and build developmental bilingual education programs. There is nothing in the law to prevent us developing the non-English language alongside the English language, as long as we do so in a way that meets all the English language and academic achievement accountability measures (R. Freeman, personal communication).

Such, for example, is the approach adopted in language policy development and bilingual program building in the School District of Philadelphia (SDP). In a recent paper analyzing the ongoing flow of discourse across federal policy, Pennsylvania commonwealth, and SDP discursive contexts, Johnson (2004) describes how one SDP grant writer who has worked on both Title VII and Title III grants sees *NCLB*'s emphasis on English language education for ELLs as not precluding one-way and two-way developmental programs in Philadelphia schools. Rather, this grant writer sees the accountability requirements for ELLs as 'a positive move toward forcing school districts to focus their attention and resources on education for English language learners.' If anything, Johnson reports, NCLB has enlivened this grant writer's passion, since more money per student is available and the requirement for scientifically-based research affirms and complements the SDP's reliance on research that favors dual language education (Johnson, 2004: 88).

From my perspective as researcher and observer of bilingual education in Philadelphia over the past 20 years, it is no accident that SDP language education personnel position themselves as wedges in the ambiguous implementational space left by *NCLB*. I would argue that this stance is built on a long tradition of research, practice and policy oriented toward imagining multilingual schools. This extends from the early efforts of Eleanor Sandstrom and others in founding the Potter Thomas bilingual program in 1968 under one of the first Title VII grants (Cahnmann, 1998) to the last Philadelphia School District Title VII five-year grant, awarded in 2000 to support the development of 10 dual-language programs in target schools in the major multilingual communities in the city (Freeman, 2004: 236). In her recent book, *Building on Community Bilingualism*, Freeman recounts how, as lead consultant for this grant, she worked with school-based language-planning teams in each school, encouraging them 'to take ownership of the planning and implementation of their programs and to hold themselves accountable for their students' performance' (Freeman, 2004: 237). Freeman also describes how, in Fall 2002, she undertook facilitation of a language policy formulation process in the SDP, at the request of the Philadelphia Association of Hispanic School Administrators (PAHSA). PAHSA had been challenged to come up with a language policy by the district's new chief executive officer appointed in the wake of the state takeover of the district in Spring 2002 (Freeman, 2004: 251). In this book, as in her earlier work, Freeman argues that:

> states, school districts, and schools in the United States have choices about the ways they organize their programs and practices to address their goals ... This book explains why [and] how school districts and schools can formulate policies and develop programs that enable English language learners AND English speakers to acquire English, achieve academically at school, AND maintain and develop expertise in languages other than English. (Freeman, 2004: viii)

In other words, the book is about how we can imagine and create multilingual schools, even in ambiguous spaces.

In his foreword to Freeman's book, Cummins points out that 'our collective reluctance to implement programs that are pedagogically and linguistically enriching for all students is an ideological choice' (Freeman, 2004:

iii). The implementational and ideological choices that educators make are, ultimately, what enable or disable the imagining of multilingual schools.

Furthermore, I believe those implementational and ideological choices can be used strategically as mutual reinforcements for each other. In my 2002 essay, I cited evidence from Chick and McKay (2001) in the South African case that suggested that ideological space opened up by top-down policies could contribute to the emergence of new discourses in implementational spaces at the grassroots level (Hornberger, 2002: 41). In like vein, Alexander affirms that:

> the fact that [the constitutional and legislative] instruments exist is of the greatest significance [in that they] represent democratic space for the legal and peaceful promotion of multilingualism and for mother tongue based bilingual education in South Africa. (Alexander, 2003: 15)

Ideological spaces carve out implementational ones. I think that perhaps it is also possible that implementational spaces carved out from the bottom up may reciprocally be a means for wedging open ideological spaces as they are being closed by top-down policies. It is my understanding that this is exactly what is happening, not only in Philadelphia, but also in California, Massachusetts, New York, and elsewhere in the United States, and certainly in many places around the globe.

To keep alive the promise of *Nichols* in a *NCLB* era, then, requires our concerted attention on continuing to implement our imagined multilingual schools from the classroom level up, even while English-only ideologies swirl around us. 'The litmus test for educational language planning in the United States in the "age of accountability" should not be one of defending the position of English, but one of acknowledging language diversity and developing it as a national resource' (Wiley & Wright, 2004: 163). I turn now to three recommendations to assist us in that endeavor.

Implementing *Nichols*-based Ideologies in Ambiguous *NCLB* Spaces: Three Recommendations

First, we need to recognize and celebrate that what may feel to us like stop-gap implementational measures to imagine and create multilingual schools in today's ideologically unfriendly national or global contexts are much more than that. They are in fact imaginative and creative moves that have a strategic role to play in shifting and expanding into more favorable ideological spaces.

Valdés has recently written, in her foreword to Roca and Colombi's anthology on Spanish as a heritage language in the United States:

> We are living in a moment when antibilingual education efforts have spread from California to Arizona to Colorado and more recently to

> Massachusetts. Teaching the mother tongue to young immigrant children, especially in Spanish, continues to be viewed by many as un-American and divisive. At the same time, the events of September 11 have once again made evident the importance of non-English language for national security. (Roca & Colombi, 2003: vii)

With Valdés and other colleagues, including those from the farthest reaches of our globe (such as PRAESA colleagues at the southernmost tip of Africa and Sami colleagues in the Arctic Circle, Quechua and Aymara colleagues in the high Andes and Aotearoa colleagues by the shores of the Pacific), I am more convinced than ever that we who imagine multilingual schools have the long-term advantage. Threat and fear and restriction can never prevail in the grand scheme of things, but a profuse and rich diversity of ways of speaking, meaning, thinking, valuing and being will.

Second, we need to grab hold of scientifically-based research that supports multilingual schooling, using it as systematic tool and guide for our multilingual classroom policy and practice. The Continua of Biliteracy model offers one research-based framework for that purpose (Hornberger, 2003). In the same vein, Hawkins (2004) has recently provided a synthesis of seven core notions that help us understand how classrooms work as complex social systems and as ecological spaces for the language and literacy development of English language learners. The core notions, which parallel and complement components of the continua framework, are:

(1) communities of learners/communities of practice (in relation to biliteracy contexts);
(2) Zone of Proximal Development/apprenticeship (in relation to biliteracy development);
(3) multiple social languages (in relation to biliteracy media);
(4) multiple literacies (in relation to biliteracy media);
(5) identities/positioning (in relation to biliteracy content);
(6) power/status (in relation to traditional power weightings in the continua);
(7) classroom as ecology (in relation to the continua of biliteracy as ecological framework).

These are just two examples of syntheses that attempt to bring together the vast research-based understandings on multilingual language and literacy learning into a usable form for policy, practice, and continuing research.

We know that, however robust in method and balanced in interpretation, research on bilingualism and bilingual education:

> will almost inevitably meet ideological and political arguments. The passionate politics surrounding immigration, social and political cohe-

> sion, and imagined threats to peace and prosperity, will pitch such research into the cauldron of political competition and controversy. However such political debates unequivocably need to be informed by research. (Baker, 2003a: 105)

We cannot abandon what we know from research and experience to be right and true just because it is unpopular. We do have choices and can exercise them.

Finally, it is high time for the US and other parts of the developed world to accept foreign aid from the developing world. I've alluded to the cases of South Africa and Bolivia, but there are many, many more. We can no longer afford to ignore the accumulating inspiration and insight available to us from the concrete experiences and experiments in multilingual education and multiliteracies pedagogy that are increasingly in evidence around the world.

Acknowledgements

I am grateful to Ofelia García and María Torres-Guzmán for envisioning and organizing the conference, Imagining Multilingual Schools: An International Symposium on Language and Education, which was held at Teachers College in New York City, from 30 September to 2 October 2004, at which this study was originally presented. I also thank Esther Ramani and Michael Joseph, who hosted my visit to SAALA 2004 in Limpopo, South Africa in July 2004, and Luis Enrique López, who hosted my visit to PROEIB Andes in Cochabamba, Bolivia in August and September 2004. An earlier version of this chapter appeared in *Working Papers in Educational Linguistics* 20 (2), 1–17 (2005)

Notes

1. '[N]or [shall any state] deny to any person within its jurisdiction the equal protection of the laws.'
2. A suit brought by Martha Sandoval, a driver's license applicant not proficient in English, against the state of Alabama, for relief in connection with the English-only policy of the Department of Public Safety.
3. 'Each state is required to develop English-language proficiency standards and assessments and define and develop "annual measurable achievement objectives" (AMAOs) for "increasing and measuring the level of LEP children's development and attainment of English proficiency" (US Department of Education, 2003: Part II, 5)' (Wiley & Wright, 2004:157). Additionally, all LEP students must be included in state assessment programs of academic achievement, regardless of how long they have been in the United States.
4. There are also serious concerns about the validity and reliability of the assessments themselves in relation to their use with LEP students, summarized as follows:

   > Inconsistent LEP classification, as well as the sparse population of LEP students in many states, threatens the validity of adequate yearly progress

> reporting. The LEP subgroup's lack of stability also threatens accountability, since students attaining English proficiency move out of the subgroup. The linguistic complexity of assessment tools may lower LEP student performance in areas with greater language demand. Finally, schools with larger numbers of LEP students with lower baselines may require greater gains. Thus, NCLB's mandates may unintentionally place undue pressure on schools with high numbers of LEP students. (Abedi, 2004: 4)

The pressures toward using large-scale assessment measures with LEP students have led to increased use of accommodations, but these too raise 'a number of thorny issues that are not easily resolved,' issues such as who should receive accommodations and what type and how we can ensure fairness 'so that accomodations enable English learners to demonstrate what they know without giving them an unintended advantage over other students' (Abedi *et al.*, 2004: 7).

Summary

In the anniversary year of landmark US Supreme Court decisions affirming the right to equal educational opportunity for all children irrespective of race or language origin, it behooves us to take a look at how well we are fulfilling the mandates of *Brown v. Board of Education* (1954) and *Lau v. Nichols* (1974). In an attempt to understand both what is happening and what could happen to promote and build on the multilingual resources present in US schools, this chapter takes a historical and comparative look at US language education policy at the federal level since 1974 and draws on ethnographic work locally in one urban school district and globally in multilingual contexts.

En un año aniversario de decisiones judiciales significativas de la Corte Suprema de los Estados Unidos afirmando los derechos de todo niño y niña a una educación sin prejuicio de su raza o lengua de origen, nos conviene mirar hacia atrás para ver hasta qué punto logramos los mandatos de Brown v. Board of Education de 1954 y de Lau v. Nichols de 1974. Aquí revisamos la política nacional educativa lingüística de los Estados Unidos desde el caso Lau v. Nichols (1974) hasta la ley No Child Left Behind (2001), prestando especial atención al grado en que las políticas permiten espacio ideológico y de implementación para imaginar y crear escuelas multilingües. Basándome en estudios etnográficos realizados en un distrito escolar local urbano y en contextos multilingües en otras partes del mundo, busco entender tanto lo actual cómo las posibilidades de promover e incrementar los recursos multilingües existentes en las escuelas estadounidenses. (Spanish)

Qayna wata 2004 Istadus Uniduspi phichqa chunka wata hatun kamachikuy Brown v. Board of Education nisqa ruwakusqanmanta hunt'akusqa. Kikillantaq, kimsa chunka wata hunt'akullasqataq wak kamachikuy Lau v. Nichols nisqa ruwakusqanmanta. Chaykunapi yuyaysapa abugadu wiraquchakuna llapa wawakuna iskwuylaman yaykunanpaq kamachisqanku, mana imapis paykunata hark'ananpaq – mana paqariyninpis mana rimayninpis hark'ananchu kanman.

Chaymantapacha kunankama, allintachu manachu chay kamachisqankuta hunt'achinchis, chayta kaypi rikusunchik. Kay qillqapi, hawamanta qhawarispa ukhumanta qhawarispa chay simi yachachina kamachikuykunata rikusunchik, Nichols nisqa kamachikusqanmanta NCLB (No Child Left Behind) nisqa kamachikusqankama qhawarisunchik. Rikusunchik imaynata ruwanku wakin yachay wasikunapi kay sispa llaqtapi, karu askha simiyuq llaqtakunallapitaq, chay ruwasqankumanta hap'isunchik yuyayninchikkunapi imaynan lliu simikunata sinchichasunchikman allinta, chayta. (Quechua)

Chapter 12

Cultural Diversity, Multilingualism and Indigenous Education in Latin America

LUIS ENRIQUE LÓPEZ

My commitment to more struggle recognizes neither boundaries nor limits; only those of us who carry our cause in our hearts are willing to run the risks.
Rigoberta Menchú, 1984: 236, 220

Introduction

Analyzing the situation of education in indigenous communities of Latin America takes us beyond pure pedagogical, cultural, and linguistic issues, since national policies that support the application of bilingual education in our region are mainly the result of indigenous suffering and struggle in a constant fight against racism and discrimination. If Paulo Freire (1973a) was right when, in the late 1960s and early 1970s he called our attention to the idea that education was not neutral and that every educational model or strategy responded to given underlying political orientations and expected outcomes, in Latin America the education of the native indigenous people has been at stake ever since our countries adopted the ideals of the early European liberals when immediately after independence our liberators claimed equality before the law.

For indigenous peoples of Latin America, ironically, the egalitarian ideal meant nothing but abuse, deprivation of their lands, neglect, and even forced invisibility, which in fact led to even worse conditions than those that they had enjoyed during colonial rule. It is worth recalling that the indigenous people in general were excluded from the process of independence and that the Latin American liberation process was most generally led by *criollo* political leaders – either Hispanic or mestizo. Inspired by the French Revolution, they adopted the underlying principles of classical European liberalism that portrayed the image of a uniform and homogeneous entity. Through the medium of Spanish and of the predominant Hispanic roots, they aimed at the construction of a single national culture, a single nation, and a unified country. Nearly 200 years after the formal ending of colonial rule, the relationship between indigenous and non-indigenous people in Latin America still resembles those most typical of colonial situations. To this date, all Amerindian societies live as subaltern communities (Spivak, 1988), even in those countries where they still constitute the majority of the population. Regardless of recent legal recognition of multilingualism and multiculturalism, language diversity is still perceived by a lot of people, and particularly by the social sectors in control of power, as problematic and as an impediment to national unity.

In spite of the unfavorable conditions under which they live, there are still over 40 million indigenous people in Latin America (González, 1994) who either admit their indigenous identity and/or speak an indigenous language. Although it is difficult to determine who is indigenous and who is not and what this category precisely defines,[1] there is a high correlation between speaking an indigenous language and being indigenous. Indeed non-indigenous Latin Americans who speak an indigenous language constitute real exceptions.

In Latin America the indigenous peoples represent approximately 10% of the total number of inhabitants of the region. This representation, however, is not uniform and varies from country to country. There are certain countries in which the indigenous peoples amount to less than 3% or even 1% of the total, as in the cases of Costa Rica and Brazil. But there are other countries where indigenous people constitute real demographic majorities. This is the case with Bolivia and Guatemala, the two Latin American countries with the highest indigenous presence.

Guatemala and Bolivia

Relatively recent national population censuses – 2002 for the case of Guatemala and 2001 for Bolivia – report that in Guatemala over 41% of the national population is indigenous, whereas in Bolivia this percentage rises to 62% of those over 14 years of age. Regardless of the unquestionable indigenous profiles of both Bolivia and Guatemala, no provision was made for any type of education in the pupils' mother tongue until the late 1960s or early 1970s. Throughout 300 years of colonial rule and more than 180 years of republican governments, the Amerindian people were forced to learn Spanish. On the other hand, the ruling classes never made any effort to learn the indigenous languages, except in the case of clerics and landlords in the highlands who needed to communicate with *their* peasants and who had the motivation to learn an indigenous language to exercise control in their new lands.

In this chapter, I use these two specific cases – Guatemala and Bolivia – to look at the implementation of indigenous bilingual education. To do this, I draw on observations of indigenous intercultural bilingual education (IBE) in Latin America that we have been carrying out at PROEIB Andes, in Cochabamba, Bolivia.[2] In my analysis I also take advantage of recent fieldwork in Guatemala and resort to interviews and to information collected while participating in informal talks and in a workshop (March, 2005) with indigenous professionals and leaders.

Particular emphasis will be given to the fact that indigenous leaders and organizations are now questioning some of the national policies that support and promote the implementation of intercultural bilingual education (IBE). In the Bolivian case in the early 1990s, the national government accepted the demands of indigenous leaders and organizations for a profound change in educational policy. As will be seen, most of the arguments presented in this chapter come precisely from these so-called *beneficiaries* of IBE.

Guatemala has a relatively long-standing history of indigenous bilingual education that dates back to the late 1960s when a pre-school experimental bilingual education project was put into practice with children belonging to the four most numerous Mayan communities: Kaqchikel, Kiche, Mam and Qeqchi (cf. Dutcher, 1995; Rubio, forthcoming). Bolivia's history in this field is more recent and dates back to the late 1970s and early 1980s when two pilot bilingual education projects were implemented, one in the Quechua region, and the other one in the Aymara area (cf. López, 2006). Quechua and Aymara are the two most widely spoken indigenous languages in this country.

In Guatemala 24 different languages are spoken, including Spanish; 21 of these languages belong to the Mayan linguistic family, and the other 2 languages (Garifuna and Xinca) form part of other linguistic families. Whereas Mayan languages in general are in good standing and in active use, Garifuna has only a few speakers in Guatemala, although there are many more in the neighboring Caribbean coasts of Belize, Honduras and Nicaragua. On the other hand, no more than 40 Xinca speakers survive and their language is at present at the verge of extinction.[3]

When bilingual education projects began in Guatemala, the country was undergoing internal violence and warfare. At that time, on average, indigenous boys achieved only two years of schooling and indigenous girls hardly completed grade 1. The Guatemalan governmental neglect of indigenous children and adolescents was an outcome of a hierarchically and racially structured society, which in many cases resembled Apartheid. In such a situation, and as Rigoberta Menchú explicitely stated, 'you had to keep your identity [and your language] hidden in order to resist' (Menchú, 1984:220). In spite of that, to this date approximately 5 out of 12 million Guatemalans speak a Mayan language, and most are bilingual in a Mayan language and Spanish. It is most probable that Spanish is the mother tongue of bilingual young Guatemalans. Mayan monolingualism represents only

13.5% of the population of three years or older and characterizes mainly rural population (Guatemala INE, 2003).[4]

Guatemala has one the of highest illiteracy rates in Latin America – 30% of adults cannot read and write alphabetic script. The illiteracy rate for the indigenous peoples is 47%, doubling that of the non-indigenous population. Almost 70% of adult indigenous women living in rural areas have not been given the chance to learn to read and write. Indeed the general formal education level of adult Guatemalans is still low and the national average hardly reaches grade 5. On average, indigenous adults complete only 2.6 years of schooling. Thanks to new educational policies implemented over the past decade, the situation has improved for all pupils under 18 years of age, although indigenous students still lag far behind Spanish monolinguals, precisely due to the limitations of official bilingual education in Guatemala (Rubio, forthcoming).

In Bolivia 33 distinct indigenous languages are spoken, but not all of them enjoy the same status. Languages such as Quechua and Aymara have millions of speakers (approximately 1.5 million Aymara speakers and slightly over 2 million Quechua speakers).[5] Certain other indigenous languages spoken in the Amazonian and Chaco lowlands have only about 100 speakers each but are nonetheless extremely vital; this is the case of the Araonas in the Amazonian basin. Other indigenous languages are almost extinct, like Guasarug'we with only 30 speakers in 2000 (cf. PROEIB Andes, 2001). Other indigenous people have decided to assimilate through interethnic marriage to a neighboring and linguistically related community; such was the case of the Pakawaras who in 2000 were down to only 21 speakers (PROEIB Andes, 2001). It is pertinent to highlight that the Pakawaras' decision to become assimilated into another indigenous community seems to be part of a conscious and deliberate strategy to continue being indigenous and is in fact a desire to resist mainstream Spanish-only assimilation.

Some 80% of the Bolivian population now speaks Spanish, but only about 40% of Bolivians are Spanish monolinguals. The remaining 60% are either monolingual in an indigenous language (12%), bilingual, trilingual or multilingual, speaking one or more indigenous languages (48%). Spanish has expanded significantly over the past fifty years. Before the National Revolution of 1952 Spanish monolingualism represented only 10% of the population. The 1952 revolution extended the Spanish-only-speaking school system into most rural areas of the country. However, the National Population Census of 2001 for the first time in history reports the presence of important numbers of urban speakers of indigenous languages. These new figures, which sometimes refer us to more than 50% of the population of certain Bolivian cities, reveal the bilingualism and multilingualism that characterize the most important Bolivian cities.

Although lower than in Guatemala, illiteracy is still high amongst indigenous Bolivians. The national illiteracy rate is 14.6%, but in rural areas (most of which are also indigenous areas) it increases to 26.2%. As many as 38% of indigenous women over 15 years of age have not had the opportunity to learn to read and write, and there seems to be a parallel situation regarding this type of knowledge amongst Guatemala's indigenous Mayan communities. In the year 2000, indigenous males in rural areas completed on average only 6.9 years of formal schooling – only 5.7 years in the case of rural indigenous women (Nucinkis, forthcoming). Nonetheless, one must recall that Bolivian indigenous women, and also men in certain societies, are excellent weavers of elaborate, complex and very detailed textiles that, amongst other things, imply an elaborate knowledge of arithmetic and geometry and which in many cases depict complex stories and different aspects of everyday life (cf. López, 2001).

In both Bolivia and Guatemala indigenous peoples have become more visible than ever in the last two decades. Their political presence has also acquired greater importance in national political life. In Guatemala this process began in the early 1990s and reached its peak with the Peace Accords of 1996 between the Guatemalan government and a 36 year-old guerrilla movement, now a conventional political party. In Bolivia the process started earlier, in 1982, when the country ended its long history of military dictatorships and when a democratic government, which involved leaders of important social and grassroots organizations and NGOs, took power. In both Guatemala and Bolivia well-known and socially-recognized indigenous professionals and leaders have reached high governmental positions. This is the case, for example, of the Vice presidency and the Ministries of Education and Indigenous Affairs in Bolivia, and of the Ministry of Culture and the Vice Ministry of Education in Guatemala. Almost one third of the Bolivian National Congress is now in the hands of indigenous representatives. A new constitution is being considered for 2006 that might conceive Bolivia as a plurinational state. Indigenous leaders and organizations have already begun campaigning at national level to guarantee their presence at the National Constitutional Assembly to be elected in early 2006. In so doing, they are appealing not only to politics of the conventional Latin American type, but also to indigenous social structure and networking.

The processes that Bolivia and Guatemala are undergoing form part of a relatively new and multidimensional phenomenon that, to a greater or lesser degree, affects every Latin American country from the South of the Rio Grande to Patagonia. In the late 1980s and early 1990s most of the region was involved in the reformation of their national legislation so as to recognize their indigenous origin and present populations. This recognition has implied further conceptual and pragmatic revisions of the multilingual and multicultural nature of all these countries.

Language and Bilingual Education Policies: Guatemala

Spanish is the official language of Guatemala, and the 1985 Constitution and the educational law of 1991 acknowledge the right of the indigenous peoples to education in their mother tongue (www.mineduc.gob.gt). However, the attempt to reform the Constitution as the result of the Peace Accords of 1996 failed, since the majority of the Guatemalan population voted against the changes that incorporated the recognition of indigenous rights, including the territorial officialization of all indigenous languages. To partially counteract this national failure to recognize their linguistic and cultural diversity and indigenous rights, a National Language Act was passed in 2003 (www.almg.org), a Vice-ministry of Bilingual Intercultural Education was created, and late that same year a new governmental decree declared the generalization of bilingual intercultural education (IBE).

Since 1979 bilingual education has been gradually extending, officially under an early-exit transitional strategy. The process started with only ten pilot schools. Today the National Directorate for Bilingual Intercultural Education is responsible for 2193 pre-schools and 1200 primary schools where educational materials in indigenous languages are distributed to the pupils of 13 different ethnolinguistic Mayan communities, although with a higher concentration in the four most widely spoken indigenous languages (Kachiquel, Kiche, Mam and Qeqchi). There is also an officially-funded but autonomous Mayan Language Academy – a recognized national body in matters related to Mayan language and culture. The Academy has regional branches in the 21 Mayan ethnolinguistic communities and these produce written materials (www.almg.org). There is no comparable institutional infrastructure for the other two indigenous ethnic communities (Xinca and Garifuna). Shortly after the Peace Accords were signed[6] in 1996 under diplomatic pressure from the international community, the Guatemalan Government organized a national educational reform commission whose members came both from government and civil society, including particularly well-known indigenous professionals and leaders. Some 50% of the commission members belonged to Guatemalan civil society. It was the first time in history that well-known indigenous leaders and intellectuals sat at an officially recognized discussion table with their[7] governmental counterparts in order to evaluate and profoundly revise national educational policies and curricula. The first educational reform proposal was published in 1998, and since then other initiatives have taken place in the areas of teacher training, development of educational materials, and project implementation (Comisión Paritaria, 1998). Intercultural education for all and bilingual intercultural education have been included in the Reform plans. Nonetheless, the discussions about the development of a new school curriculum took several years, since it was difficult for the parties involved to come to terms with new variables of linguistic and cultural diversity. The new proposal includes a three-tier or three-level curriculum: a national one, a regional one (determined by the corresponding sociolinguistic area) and a local one pertaining to each specific community and school. These new proposals, however, never reached schools, and the ideas behind this three-tier curriculum design and a simultaneous educational decentralization strategy appear to have been abandoned or at least put on hold. In early 2004 a new administration came into the Ministry of Education and in school year 2005 decided to implement only the general and national level school curriculum (concerned with Western knowledge and official Guatemalan history, culture and institutions)[8] for the first cycle of primary education – grades 1 to 3. Leaving aside general political declarations and including references to L1, L2 and even L3 learning for everybody, the new Guatemalan curriculum is no doubt monocultural in nature and takes into account only the Spanish language when it describes L1 competencies for all Guatemalan students (Guatemala Ministerio de Educación, 2005).

Nonetheless, the results of the most recent national exams provided evidence about the positive effects of bilingual education in the achievements of primary school children when comparing the results obtained by indigenous students in bilingual schools with those obtained by their peers in Spanish-only schools (Fernando Rubio, personal communication, March 2005). The new Minister herself is now referring to the need to revitalize bilingual education in the country and will launch a national campaign in support of it. The new monocultural curriculum, however, has already reached classrooms in indigenous communities. In the same vein, the Minister's concern is related solely to the area of language teaching, and the educational intercultural perspective adopted by the Peace Accords might be abandoned by the new authorities (interview, March 2005). In 2004 this new administration also promoted a national campaign to strengthen a single national Guatemalan identity, under the slogan of 'Proud of Being Guatemalan' (www.mineduc.gob.gt).

Discussions regarding the meaning and orientation of the new curriculum continue, since it has become difficult for educationalists and even for indigenous teachers to break away from the previous practice of imposing a single national curriculum from the center. An example of this is that the first textbooks for the new primary school curriculum were produced initially in Spanish and later translated, with minor adaptations, into the four most widely-spoken Mayan languages, as a result of the insistence of a policy of a one and only official textbook for everybody (interview with several indigenous educators involved in the process, March 2005).

Although the indigenous authors of such textbooks were advised not to go beyond translating the Spanish materials – a policy locally understood as 'contextualization' – they took it upon themselves to modify and culturally-adapt sections of these materials in order to make them more culturally appropriate.

The issue of textbook production in indigenous languages in Guatemala provides clear evidence of one of the most serious difficulties to be overcome in indigenous bilingual education in Latin America in general, and in other parts of the world. As in Guatemala, where there has been an explicit discursive shift favoring intercultural approaches to education within Guatemalan civil society, in Canadian Inuit education a lot of phraseology about a culturally-sensitive curriculum was produced and disseminated, but in the long run the tests and textbooks used with indigenous students were the same as for any other students in Southern Canada (Milloy, 1999).[9]

Officially, Guatemalan national bilingual education has also undergone a rhetorical move from transitional bilingual education into indigenous language maintenance and development, stressing the need to take education in the mother tongue beyond the first two grades of primary school.[10] However, it must be kept in mind that the average indigenous child in Guatemala completes only two or four years of schooling, and that there is also a pressing social need for them to also learn as much Spanish as possible in that same period.

Attempts have also been made to include bilingual intercultural education content in nationwide teacher education institutions, so as to raise teachers' critical awareness regarding the nature and implications of life and work in a multi-ethnic society. Regarding initial teacher education, 18 out of the approximately 80 public teacher-training centers offer specialization in bilingual education, although not all of the national indigenous languages are yet covered (Rubio, forthcoming).[11]

It is worth noting that, for the past decade, the Mayan indigenous movement has severely questioned the official bilingual education implementation strategies, and in 1994 began to implement their own Mayan educational model in a handful of schools (see Ogulnick, Chapter 7). This model incorporates previous and current bilingual education strategies but, unlike governmental plans, stresses indigenous traditional Mayan knowledge (e.g. in the area of mathematics). One of the most innovative aspects of the Mayan school movement is the importance placed on Mayan philosophy, spirituality, and way of life, as well as on community participation and involvement. Mayans consider that education should respond to their alternative development model which they regard as: 'Economic, sociocultural and political [... and] deep-rooted in their individual and collective identity' (CNEM, 2004: 68). Within this context, Mayan schools place strong emphasis on Mayan language and culture. By 2005, there were

56 Mayan schools, organized in two different but closely-connected school networks, both under the political and educational mandate of a single Mayan National Educational Council (Francisco Puac, personal communication, March 2005).

The differences between the official government model and that of the Mayan Council are important. On the one hand, while the Mayan proposal stresses local knowledge and language, the official model gives greater attention to the acquisition of Spanish language and the so-called Guatemalan culture, through an early-exit transitional scheme. On the other hand, while the government strategy promotes Spanish-only-education by grades 4 or 5, the Mayan model relates to the different levels of the educational system, including a good number of secondary schools.[12]

In fact, for them bilingual education could start at any level or grade and does not necessarily need to begin with either pre-school or grade one. This multilevel strategy is the result of an increasing interest from indigenous elders, parents and even Mayan school children who want to transfer to a Mayan school, after years of forced Hispanization, possibly as an expression of Mayan militancy. Nonetheless, because of unresolved structural complexities of Guatemalan society and the long history of negation and neglect of indigenous issues, neither the official school nor the Mayan one can assure at least primary education completion (six grades) for all indigenous children.

There might be a slight advantage for Mayan schools because of their community nature and involvement, which could indeed result in more years of schooling. However, these schools must negotiate official recognition and establish equivalencies with the governmental school system. To move forward in this direction Mayan schools claim that they adhere to the Peace Agreements and to the Educational Reform plans that emerged from them (Comisión Paritaria, 1998). They want to contribute to this process with curriculum orientations, plans and strategies that operationalize the ideals put forward by the Reform Commission, and thus give the transformation process feedback from local community and classroom-practice (ACEM, 2005).

The persistence of these two models might help to enrich national bilingual education policies since there is now greater concern in Guatemalan society about the need to improve the quality of educational plans for indigenous pupils. It seems that, at last, non-indigenous sectors have come to understand that national economic and social development is in doubt, precisely because of the limited access to education of most indigenous Guatemalans.

Language and Bilingual Education Policies: Bolivia

The linguistic situation is to some extent different in Bolivia,. The national Constitution does not grant official status to any of the languages spoken in the country, although *de facto* Spanish is the official language. In 2001, as a result of indigenous resurgence in the lowlands – an area with the largest ethnic and linguistic diversity comprising 36 different indigenous peoples and 30 different languages– a Presidential decree recognized all 33 of the country's indigenous languages[13] as official (López, 2006). However, no specific policies regarding application of this norm in the public sector followed, and the officialization act implied no more than a change in governmental rhetoric in the face of increasing indigenous social pressure. In fact, education constitutes the only domain where official language policies are being implemented by the Bolivian government. Increasingly, however, since the 1960s indigenous languages and cultures have enjoyed greater visibility and use in radio, television, videos and even in the cinema, as a result of increasing interest in the country in indigenous issues. For the past four years a weekly 8-page newspaper supplement in at least four languages has also been published and distributed nationwide.

The reformed Constitution of 1994 defines Bolivia as a multiethnic and multicultural country although reaffirming the unitary character of the nation (www.minedu.gov.bo). In that light, in 1994 a new education law was passed that adopted IBE as the official national strategy to be implemented with indigenous peoples, under a maintenance and development orientation. The new law also adopted the policy of intercultural education for all, with the idea that the traditional hierarchical organization of Bolivian society would change only if the educational system promoted a profound attitudinal change in all the learners, and particularly in the Spanish-speaking ones. The new law also opened up the possibility for Spanish-speaking pupils to learn an indigenous language at school, thus mainstreaming certain aspects of the bilingual education policy (cf. Hornberger & López, 1998).

As mentioned earlier, the 1994 Act incorporated demands that had been previously formulated by Bolivian indigenous and social organizations in general, dating back to 1982 and 1983 (cf. López, 2006). Unlike Guatemala, the Bolivian approach was to a certain extent bottom-up in the sense that the demands and the general philosophy were postulated by representatives of the indigenous peoples involved and of grass-roots organizations. It was not the Bolivian government who led the initiative in this field, although, as in Guatemala, the Ministry of Education had also previously conducted pilot projects in bilingual education – in the late 1970s, early 1980s and the 1990s. In fact, the most successful indigenous bilingual education pilot project implemented in Bolivia between 1990 and 1995 started when the national peasant union (Confederación Sindical Única de Trabajadores Campesinos de Bolivia or CSUTCB), other indigenous regional organizations,[14] and the rural teachers' union, jointly approached UNICEF and the Bolivian Ministry of Education. These unions participated in the design of the project, selected the teachers and professionals later to be appointed by the Ministry of Education, and exercised control over the activities of both government and the teachers in the communities where the project was carried out. When the new law was passed, indigenous leaders considered they had won one of their most important battles towards national recognition (cf. López, 2006).

The new law came into effect in 1996, when the educational reform reached the first approximately 1500 schools nationwide. Since then, all Bolivian rural schools have been incorporated into the reform. Of these, approximately 2800 are bilingual (22.2% of the total) covering the complete primary education level, which in Bolivia comprises eight years of schooling. Not all Bolivian rural schools, however, offer all three levels of primary education. Hence, a high number of indigenous pupils do not have the opportunity to complete their basic studies in their community of residence. In fact, 19% of all rural schools offer only the first three grades. Nevertheless, greater numbers of rural and indigenous children can now complete their primary education studies by moving to nearby communities and towns where the upper grades are offered. Completion rates have increased significantly and rapidly. In 2002, 48% of indigenous children had completed their first 8 years of schooling, compared to 37% who had done so in 1997. Indigenous girls living in rural areas are still more disadvantaged than boys, with only 43.2% completing primary school (8 grades), as opposed to 53.3% of the boys (Nucinkis, forthcoming).

In Bolivia, curricula and materials have been prepared for three of the most widely spoken indigenous languages in Bolivia – Quechua, Aymara and Guarani[15] – for the first six grades of schooling, and plans are under way to also introduce the new model of education in the numerically smaller groups in the lowlands. Bilingual education in the secondary level might be implemented as of 2006.

Almost half of all teacher education institutes (9 out of 20) have been transformed from Spanish-only teacher education centers into bilingual ones. A new national policy of popular participation in education has also been implemented, which entails the organization of four National Educational Indigenous Peoples' Councils. Such councils are responsible for the social scrutiny and control of the enforcement and implementation of the national educational and language policies. These indigenous councils are also the result of indigenous claims and demands, and were thus incorporated into the new national education policies.

Ten years after these new national language and educational policies were put into practice, indigenous leaders and organizations (including the Indigenous Councils mentioned above), have evaluated the implementation of IBE in the country in order to establish what was gained and what was lost when it became a national and official policy. In general, they considered that they erred in thinking that their sociopolitical situation would change radically with parliament and government new laws and regulations. The indigenous leadership is now convinced that, although legislation helps, it is not enough in situations where profound attitudinal changes are still needed in order to overcome racism and social and economic exclusion. In some indigenous communities, their leaders are questioning the application of the official model of IBE they themselves helped design.

Although as yet there is no indigenous social movement similar to that of the Maya schools in Guatemala, various indigenous leaders in Bolivia are now speaking of an educational strategy that should not only be intercultural and bilingual, but also productive and more deeply inserted into the indigenous ways of thinking, being, and feeling (cf. CEPOs, 2004). These new demands have arisen both amongst majority communities, such as the Quechua and Aymara ones, and also within numerically smaller linguistic communities. A common concern relates to the fact that, after 10 years of reform implementation, the Ministry of Education has failed to help implement local and decentralized curricula and the government's entire effort has been put into the design and implementation of the national common core the law envisaged.[16] Such evidence has made indigenous leaders concerned and even suspicious, leading them to conclude that the national government is interested only in resorting to one form and fund of knowledge (Moll & Greenberg, 1990) – the Western and hegemonic one.

The new Bolivian indigenous demands resemble the spirit of the Mayan school movement or of Colombian indigenous organizations that demand an education entrenched in their own development project or 'life plan' ('*plan de vida*') as they now call it. This might be the reason why they entitled their new education proposal as 'In line with indigenous education; towards ideological, political, territorial and socio-cultural self-determination' (cf. CEPOs, 2004). In this new context, in different indigenous Latin American communities it is now common for leaders to speak of their *own education* or *educación propia* – an endogenous model of education, which, contrary to what one could expect, does not respond to an isolationist or separatist motivation. Precisely due to the linguistic and cultural contact and conflict in which local knowledge has been historically constructed and reproduced, these indigenous leaders want their education to be intercultural and bilingual and thus flexible and open to other languages and funds or traditions of knowledge. But what is in question is the issue of social control of education and school management. They would like to see the school as an integral part of the indigenous community and not as an alien and isolated institution as is now the case. Furthermore, they want to intervene in curriculum decision-making.

An example of this comes from the Yuracares. The Yuracares speak an unclassified language and first came into contact with Spanish speakers less than 50 years ago when a protestant mission approached them in order to assimilate them to the Bolivian Spanish-only mainstream. Only 3500 Yuracares survive today in indigenous villages in the Amazon rainforest, although a good number of them live in tropical towns and intermediate cities. Part of the Yuracare community that appeared linguistically and culturally assimilated decided to return to 'the previous stage.' They now want their children to recover the ancestral language and culture and to restore its use in local community everyday life, and 500 of them have decided to return to the forest, claiming territorial rights under present Bolivian legislation, and have decided to open their own Yuracare schools. In 2004, they approached PROEIB Andes for help in systematizing their educational proposals and training their teachers so they could initiate their own community-run education project, which in their view should also receive complementary fiscal funds. They did not want official IBE as implemented by the Ministry of Education. Instead, they chose to organize their own Yuracare education, which would consist of what could be called a *dual educational system* – in the mornings they would replicate the best possible official Bolivian mainstream education, with educational reform textbooks and materials in Spanish, graduate teachers and even official supervision and support; in the afternoons they would construct a parallel and alternative educational system geared to linguistic and cultural recuperation under the direction of community-teachers they had already selected. The Yuracare proposal in a way resembles the Australian, two-way aboriginal model (cf. Harris, 1990) but it differs from it in that the Yuracares consider this new scheme better than the IBE official model, since they feel interculturalism can not really be reached or even attempted if the local indigenous culture and knowledge are not previously strengthened and repositioned both in the national context and even before the eyes of their own members. Such repositioning of indigenous languages and cultures is counter hegemonic to the colonial mentality in the country, including the absorption of certain colonial views by the indigenous peoples themselves.

Based on similar considerations, it is now common for Bolivian indigenous leaders to speak of the need for an intracultural orientation to education before moving into an intercultural one (Froilán Condori, personal communication 2004). Intraculturalism would foster confidence and belief in one's own cultural legacy and also contribute to the development of self-esteem and of a positive public image of the indigenous societies in question. As certain indigenous professionals in Guatemala now postulate, such intraculturalism might, to an extent, imply a conscious, political and strategic use of some type of indigenous essentialism (Rodrigo Chub, personal communication, March 2005).

Intercultural Bilingual Education Revisited

To understand why certain Bolivian indigenous leaders today question the educational model they earlier demanded and in fact helped design, or why Guatemalan Mayan leaders diplomatically express their reservations about official bilingual education implementation strategies, one has to refer to the pedagogical and political divide that Ministries of Education naturally establish. Ministries of Education generally understand IBE as an educational model contributing to better pupil achievement and improved pedagogical conditions in general, whereas indigenous leaders and organizations see IBE as well established in their historical struggle to survive as distinct societies and to end political and economic exclusion. IBE is thus perceived as a tool that facilitates access to power. Whereas for governmental decision-makers IBE positively influences learning outcomes, for indigenous organizations and indigenous leaders the most important contribution of IBE is related to the development of self-esteem and to the construction of social and personal indigenous identities in a context of struggle against colonial oppression and towards the appropriation of knowledge.

> IBE is a path towards our own education, and in the long run it will allow us to situate our struggle in the dispute of formal power. As an instrument of our liberation, IBE will permit us to construct an equitable and just society where those rights nowadays we can only dream with will be respected. We do not want an armed conflict; we postulate a struggle towards the appropriation of knowledge. (Walter Gutiérrez, President of the Bolivian Aymara council, interview October 2004)

Interviews conducted with the parents of indigenous children stress that one cannot see educational change in isolation, education is a right and as such is related to other rights that are equally important for indigenous well-being – territorial rights, the right to natural resources and one's language, knowledge, history, and ways of being and feeling. But just as imperative for indigenous people is learning a second language and gaining access to other funds of knowledge necessary for interacting with members of other societies (CEPOs, 2004).

Generally, when IBE becomes a national policy, the underlying political meaning and that content indigenous leaders attach to it are partially lost.

This does not mean, however, that everything is lost in the transition from a community demand to a governmental policy. In Latin America, official legal recognition is certainly an asset that every indigenous leader wants and indeed demands. But indigenous leaders resent the idea that IBE is understood and implemented as an isolated measure related to or affecting only the educational sphere. Their concern increases when IBE is seen as a model offered only to indigenous peoples. Guatemalan and Bolivian leaders make it explicitly clear that this should not be the case:

> We are not speaking of an educational model only for Mayas. Bilingual education needs to be extended also to Ladino [Spanish-only] schools and benefit Ladino children as well. We've always been bilingual or multilingual. And we know that there are advantages in speaking more than one language. It is up to you now to learn our languages and increase your linguistic capital. (Francisco Puac, personal communication, March 2005)

> IBE needs to be transformed into a two-way model: from an indigenous language into Spanish and from Spanish into an indigenous language. Everybody in Bolivia needs to learn our languages in so much as we have had to learn and use Spanish. Once and for all we need to eradicate monolingualism and monoculturalism if we want the political and social conditions of this country to improve and if we want our democracy to be inclusive of all and hence intercultural. (Walter Gutiérrez, personal communication, September 2004)

Nonetheless, both in Bolivia and Guatemala, indigenous leaders and organizations still support and defend the official IBE model, since they consider it superior to the monolingual and monocultural model that preceded it (CEPOs, 2004, Francisco Puac, personal communication). But, they now regard the type of IBE being implemented only as the official model of education for indigenous students. In Bolivia, 10 years after indigenous leaders and organizations managed to inscribe IBE in national legislation and policies, they now see the need to push the government forward, exercising the power they have so far gained by partially participating in IBE decision-making. Indigenous leaders clearly understand the power of their demands to the government. The white and mestizo minority in government also know that implementing IBE allows them to keep their privileges untouched, and they see this type of education as a partial reaction to the unresolved complex social and political situation they inherited. Both parties know what to expect and what they need to negotiate, as they try to re-interpret the multilingual and multicultural conditions of their society and as they give and take in the construction of new and more democratic relationships between the indigenous and non-indigenous sectors of the society.

The fact is that indigenous leaders and organizations are concerned not only with the education of their own indigenous children, but also with the education of all Bolivian and Guatemalan children. That is why they periodically show concern over the education offered to all members of the countries of which they are now part. In their view, IBE should be extended to the mestizo and white population and everyone should become aware of indigenous issues, including their ethnolinguistic identity, values and aspirations.

To foster the valuing indigenous languages, Spanish-speaking students should be taught at least the basics of the indigenous language most widely spoken in the region in which they live. Indigenous leaders consider that if power relationships and structures in these multilingual societies are to be transformed, the hegemonic population must also become bilingual and abandon its Spanish monolingualism and monoculturalism. Similarly, they are clearly aware that IBE will only improve and be sustained when offered also to those in power. Otherwise, IBE might remain only as a second-class educational model or even worse, as a type of education offered only to the poor. Hence, from their point of view, it is not only a matter of equity, but also and foremost, a question of equality since IBE is also seen as a path to a new and renowned citizenship.

In other words, language education in the multilingual societies of Latin America has to abandon the compensatory view from which it was originally approached. In times of democracy and of the emergence of indigenous voices, it has to be regarded as an educational model capable of contributing to the enrichment of every member of society. If in the late 1980s Latin American bilingual education began to move from an early-exit transitional strategy to a maintenance and development one, in this new century it might be necessary to experiment with an enrichment two-way bilingual education in which equal importance is given to the indigenous language, knowledge and world view, and to Spanish and Western knowledge in a context where every student benefits from IBE. However, mainstreaming IBE might not preclude indigenous leaders and organizations from looking for alternative educational models and strategies which although intercultural and bilingual might very well gradually aim at wider cultural pertinence in their struggle for increased political recognition and social emancipation.

The history of IBE to date leads us to believe that future indigenous demands will emphasize indigenous philosophy and knowledge, since what has most recently been at stake both in Guatemala and Bolivia is the controversy between different and conflicting funds of knowledge. And yet, as it has been repeatedly stressed:

> we cannot think of a model of isolation. We will not fall into the same trap of exclusion that the mainstream society exercised over us for centuries. It is very different to think of the need to recuperate and reinforce what is ours, because for us that is only the first step towards interculturalism. We are totally aware that we also need now to be in possession of Western Ladino knowledge but we want to exercise the right to choose and need to have the option to critically select what is most suitable for us. We are against a model of development that misinterprets our thoughts and knowledge, a model which only pursues economic accumulation as well as our assimilation into the hegemonic Western way of life. (Francisco Puac, personal communication, March 2005)

When IBE transcends the indigenous communities where it is now being implemented in Bolivia and Guatemala, new models and strategies will also have to be imagined, since IBE will have to respond to complex and diverse sociolinguistic settings, both in rural communities and in towns and cities. If IBE reaches urban schools, even in a weak form, the students will be introduced to alternative content portraying indigenous knowledge, values and social practices. Then, Latin America will be faced with the need to re-write its history and will simultaneously have to conceive diversity as a value in itself.

What Does This All Mean for Imagining Multilingual Schools?

In the first place, it means placing the language issue in ecological dynamics, where languages cannot be distanced from the history and concerns of speakers regarding their place in life and their future as members of distinct ethnolinguistic communities. Similarly, attention will need to be given to the history of the languages present in a given multilingual society since teachers and pupils have to engage in a process of critically revising the situation of language contact and conflict most typical of multilingual settings. Analyzing the factors that determine, for example, the disadvantaged situation of a given indigenous language *vis-à-vis* the dominant European language with which it converges will empower indigenous learners as well as make mainstream students aware of the historical factors that determine language oppression and hence decay and loss. Thus, an exclusive linguistic view of language that analyzes and describes language in isolation from its social context and the political and sociolinguistic complexities of multilingualism becomes thoroughly inappropriate.

Situating indigenous languages in a multilingual context of language learning and use is most certainly called for. Such an approach will allow us, on the one hand, to re-inscribe indigenous languages in the long-standing history of multiple language convergence and contact that has characterized language use in this part of the world. Let us not forget that when the Spanish invaders arrived they were amazed by the great linguistic diversity they came into contact with in most regions and contexts of the New World (López, 2001). On the other hand and linked to this previous argument, there is a need to break away from understanding bilingualism, or multilingualism for that matter, as a process of adding together two or more monolingualisms. If in academic Latin American circles this is no longer true, amongst bilingual education practitioners and teachers the myth prevails that languages are to be kept apart from one another, even in cases where the children are exposed to two or more languages from birth and when they code-switch or simultaneously resort to two or more of their languages to communicate with their peers in everyday life. If it is true that often such understanding arises from the need to revitalize a community's weaker language as well as to counteract Spanish linguistic hegemony, careful attention needs to be given to the multilingual nature of that same community. In other words, an ecological approach to language education would have to examine and at the same time respond to the way in which a given language is used in connection with other languages in a multilingual social setting.

Moreover, indigenous languages should not be dealt with in isolation and apart from the territories in which they are spoken and used. It is this situated and territorial view of language that allows us to restore and understand the relationship between language and culture, with languages closely related to their speakers' own values, knowledge, cultural practices, and even feelings.

Indigenous people approach life from a holistic or comprehensive perspective and tend to see different aspects of life as complementary to one another. In the same vein, multilingual communities and multilingual or bilingual schools must approach language education through this integral perspective. Hence, an epistemological move is also called for, since there is a need to break away from the positivist tradition that most generally dominates language teaching in favor of an interdisciplinary and more intuitive and emic approach. Thus, language learning will have to overcome its exclusive linguistic and pedagogical orientation, since it will be necessary to re-establish adequate relationships between learning and knowledge. As has been highlighted in this chapter, recent indigenous demands bring the ontology of knowledge into question, as also happens in indigenous communities in everyday life (cf. Stobart & Howard, 2002).

In additional, the dissimilar conditions enjoyed by the languages involved in indigenous bilingual education programs in Latin America confront us with a situation in which several tasks have to be carried out simultaneously with different corresponding objectives in mind. Indigenous languages need not only be used in line with specific pedagogical purposes, but also in order to contribute to their own good standing and development. In so doing, the relationship between ancestral orality and modern literacy as well as between school oracy and writing is immediately brought into question and requires the adoption of clear positions regarding the nature of the school as the par-excellence agency for the dissemination of alphabetic writing in Latin America.

At the same time, bilingual educators need to assume responsibilities that transcend language teaching, since they also have to engage in activities contributing to the indigenous language modernization, cultivation, and extended use. Bilingual educators do not only teach the indigenous language, but also transform it by using it in a context different from that in which it originally emerged and where it is traditionally used. This becomes more evident when one considers that the introduction of many of these communities and languages to alphabetic writing was rather recent (cf. Francis & Reyhner, 2002; López, 2001). In other words, bilingual educators must engage in a series of activities that go far beyond the classroom and teaching. They must simultaneously act as teachers, language planners, and language activists.

If this analysis is correct, many of the theories and models that language planners and language education specialists took to the indigenous communities need also be seriously revisited in close dialogue and interaction with their leaders and speakers in general. One of the issues under consideration is the transition–maintenance dichotomy. What might this opposition mean and imply in communities where children complete only 4 or 5 years of schooling? Should the issues underlying maintenance bilingual education be restricted only to program duration or does the question need to be understood more in relation to the quality of language education and in terms of the linguistic and sociolinguistic competencies and the critical language awareness (cf. Fairclough, 1992) that indigenous pupils should develop in the limited period of school time available in most rural areas of the region? Under such limitations, where should the emphasis be placed regarding second and/or third language teaching? Shouldn't perhaps more attention be given to strengthening the learners' linguistic, sociolinguistic and cultural competencies in their mother tongue? In cases like the ones discussed in this chapter, the answer might well be the latter since ample evidence is now available in the region regarding the indigenous pupils' abilities to transfer to their second language some of the key competencies developed through their first one (cf. Francis & Reyhner, 2002; López, 1998; Dutcher, 1995; Francis & Hamel, 1992). Proof of this transfer is that despite the fact that fewer hours per week are generally devoted to second language teaching, indigenous children in bilingual education programs maintain comparative gains in Spanish. At times, written production in Spanish could also surpass the level of oral proficiency in this language (cf. López & Jung, 2003).

> *He aprendido a leer y escribir en quechua desde primero de primaria hasta sexto curso. Más que todo hemos aplicado puro quechua. La EIB me gustó mucho. Pero en sí, yo no he podido dominar la lengua castellana. Cuando me vine de 8º de primaria a cursar 1º medio, aquí en Mizque, tuve muchos problemas. [Pero] ahora estoy bien, he aprendido el castellano y me dicen que soy un autodidacta. Estoy alegre y me siento bien, porque a la vez sé escribir y leer también en quechua. En mis estudios, ahora, estoy muy bien también. Estoy entre los mejores, porque desde el primero medio, siempre he tenido diplomas.* (Ramber Molina, Quechua student, April 2004)
> (I have learned to read and write in Quechua ever since I was in grade one and until grade six. Beyond it all we've studied real Quechua. I liked IBE a lot. But I really haven't been able to master Spanish. When I left the 8th of primary school to study 1st of secondary school here, in Misque, I had a lot of problems. But I'm now doing well, and I have also learned Spanish; they say that I'm an autonomous learner. I'm happy and I feel fine because I can also read and write in Quechua. I'm now doing very well in my studies. I'm amongst the best of my class; because from the first grade of secondary school onwards I have been given school prizes.)

In a context where language planning and IBE theoreticians, practitioners and activists adopted the suggestive and politically provoking notion of conflicting diglossia taken from Basque and Catalonian sociolinguistics (cf. Ninyoles, 1972; Hamel & Sierra, 1983) there might also be a need to evaluate what was gained and lost when these seminal ideas were applied to the specific sociolinguistic conditions of Indigenous America. IBE grew out of what were originally educational projects to foster the rapid dissemination of Spanish in all indigenous territories, but in a first instance the ideals of indigenous language maintenance and development, and later those of societal linguistic enrichment and extended bi- or multilingualism, relocated indigenous languages and cultures both in the indigenous territories and in mainstream society. In such a context, which was to some extent similar to the one experienced in Spain in the early 1970s when democratic rule was re-instituted, and language and educational planners adopted the notion of language normalization (Ninyoles, 1972). Through this concept Basques and Catalonians questioned the asymmetry that had historically favored Spanish and aimed at re-establishing the lost equilibrium between Spanish and the ancestral language of the Basque and Catalonian autonomous regions.

Similarly, in Latin America the introduction of IBE – particularly within the framework of the maintenance and development model – provided the appropriate framework for questioning the roles and functions that both Spanish and the indigenous languages were to play in a more culturally democratic society. All the efforts were directed towards modernizing the indigenous languages, developing writing-systems for them, and elaborating their lexicons so as to contribute to their standardization. Hence, IBE and the classroom where considered as media for socially and politically re-inscribing indigenous languages in the modern society, and for extending their use into new social domains and fulfilling new communicative functions. It was expected that the two languages – the indigenous one and Spanish – could be used alternatively throughout the primary school curriculum. The demands placed on the indigenous languages were vast, and a lot of effort was put into the intellectualization (cf. Garvin & Matthiot, 1968) of these languages – ironically to the detriment of the teaching of Spanish as a second language, which was in great demand in the indigenous communities in which IBE was implemented.

Two decades later, the time might have come to reconsider the notion of conflicting diglossia and to identify with the indigenous communities themselves the type of complementation they wish to establish between the two or three languages they speak or they would like their children to speak, read and write. Firstly, they might question the validity of the approach followed by IBE theoreticians and practitioners in line with indigenous language standardization, since they often claim that standardizing an indigenous language simultaneously implies neglecting the specific varieties they speak and which they generally regard as very close to their local and specific ethnic identity. Nonetheless, one must acknowledge the existence of political forces that see in unified writing systems and language standardization the means for indigenous national consolidation.

But, at the same time, the evolution of IBE ideology points us away from clear margins between tradition and modernity, which regarding the language issue will most certainly take us away from using indigenous languages only in traditional domains while languages of wider communication would be the only ones suitable in the so-called modern contexts. This is a boundary that indigenous leaders generally reject since in order to survive they have had to reposition themselves in 'the complex and fluid layers of interaction' (Howard *et al.*, 2002: 2) that nowadays characterizes communication in indigenous communities. In such a situation tradition and modernity complement each other and contemporary knowledge and other cultural elements could also be incorporated into the indigenous cultural matrix.

A few years ago, a well-known indigenous intellectual told me: 'I disregard the division you fellows establish between tradition and modernity.

We have also had our own modernity, the problem is that ours has been different from yours since it has been part of a different history' (Víctor Hugo Cárdenas, personal communication).[17] It is these other histories that we have to help re-construct and understand if we are to imagine multilingual schools in relocated multilingual societies.

This is particularly vital today when indigenous leaders and organizations submit their proposals to the mainstream society in appropriate and elaborate oral and written Spanish and, in cases such as the Guatemalan one, in books published by Mayan printing-houses. But when they need to do it before their peers, they analyze and present the issues in question in equally good Aymara, Maya, Quechua or Guarani, or at times also code-switching when they know that their interlocutors are bilingual.

When in the early 19th century indigenous leaders subscribed current legislation that recognized equality before the law and the right of all citizens to education, they constructed their own schools and initially paid their teachers so that, once schools were established and functioning, they could demand public teaching posts. Nowadays – also resorting to the national law, the written word and the hegemonic language – they claim their right to diversity and to being themselves in the framework of a plurinational state where schools are seen as the public agency responsible for promoting interculturalism and bilingualism/multilingualism. In so doing, they formulate proposals that go well beyond their specific ethnic interests in an attempt to mainstream their languages and cultures in a rejuvenated framework of an intercultural democracy. Indigenous leaders reiteratively remind the mainstream society that multiculturalism and multilingualism are not traits of the past, but rather features for the future that are related to competencies that all Latin Americans must develop in order to become citizens of the world. As they many times reaffirm, they have always had to adopt an intercultural and multilingual attitude in order to survive. The time might have come for non-indigenous individuals to learn from them and to become multilingual in order to cope with the new world that lies ahead of us in Latin America. To come to terms with these new political and societal conditions and challenges there is no other alternative than to imagine multilingual schools for a true multilingual and intercultural world.

Notes

1. The language variable can no longer be the only one to define indigenous identity, since because of colonial oppression in many cases individuals and/or communities who claim their indigenous identity no longer speak the ancestral language.
2. At our MA in intercultural bilingual education (IBE) specific attention is paid to the development of IBE in the region and specific emphasis is placed on the five

countries with the greatest presence of indigenous peoples in Latin America: Bolivia, Ecuador, Guatemala, Mexico, and Peru.

3. Xinca is an unclassified language spoken only in Guatemala. Contradictory data exists concerning the number of Xinca speakers. The 2002 national population census registers a population of approximately 16,000 thousand individuals who identify themselves as Xinca, but specialized studies refer to as few as 40 speakers.
4. Spanish monolingualism represents 65.5% of the total Guatemalan population of approximately 10 million people. The remaining 21% represent bilinguals or multilinguals.
5. Aymara and Quechua are also spoken in other countries of South America: Aymara in three (Bolivia, Peru and Chile) and Quechua in six (Peru, Bolivia, Ecuador, Argentina, Colombia and Chile). The total number of Aymara speakers is approximately 2.5 million and from 10 to 12 million people still speak Quechua. There are approximately 2.5 million Quechuas and 1.5 million Aymaras living in Bolivia.
6. The 1996 Peace Accords included a specific agreement entitled 'Accord on Identity and Indigenous Peoples Rights,' which considered mainstreaming intercultural bilingual education, the consolidation of Mayan education and the creation of a Mayan University. The Identity Accord was signed in 1995.
7. The population of Spanish-ancestry or non-indigenous Guatemalans in general is regarded as Ladino in Guatemalan society.
8. Throughout Latin America in general, official school curriculum content until recently used to regard indigenous societies only as part of the glorious historical pre-Hispanic legacy, reference was very seldom made to the present situation of these peoples.
9. I would like to thank Tove Skutnabb-Kangas for pointing out this reference to me.
10. Bilingual education in Guatemala is offered only in one grade in pre-school and in the first two grades of primary school; in other words, it is offered to children between the ages of 5 and 7 or 6 and 8.
11. Besides these 80 public teacher training institutes, there are more than 250 private institutions. Teacher education in Guatemala is still part of secondary education, starting after the first three grades of secondary education (the 9th grade). Discussions are being held to move teacher education forward to the level of higher education, as is the case in most Latin American countries.
12. In one of the Mayan Education networks under the supervision of the Mayan Educational Council – Asociación de Centros Educativos Mayas del Nivel Medio de Guatemala (ACEM) – 37 schools offer secondary education services throughout the country, following their model and strategies based on the ideals of multiculturalism, interculturalism and multilingualism. ACEM was founded in 2003 under the principles of 'a Mayan education towards the construction of a just, inclusive and intercultural society' (ACEM, 2005: 4). Some of the ACEM schools are private and others are funded by specific Mayan communities and also receive support from national and international NGOs.
13. Besides the 30 languages spoken in the lowlands three other languages (Aymara, Quechua and Uru) are spoken in the Bolivian highlands, the more densely populated region.
14. Within the general framework of this 5-year pilot project, the Guarani People's Assembly (Asamblea del Pueblo Guarani, or APG) played a determining role in the implementation of their IBE plans, in close relationship with their own indigenous development plan and exercised influence at national level.

15. Although Chiquitano has more speakers (approximately 120,000) than Guarani (80,000), official bilingual education began in the Guarani territory owing to the political pressure and to the level of organization of the Guaranis.
16. Bolivian curriculum regulations prescribe the existence of a national common-core curriculum and of a series of diversified branches. The national common-core considers the competencies that all Bolivian pupils should acquire whilst at school, and the diversified curriculum refers to local competencies and content, and thus is more closely related to the indigenous fund of knowledge.
17. An Aymara pedagogue and bilingual education specialist, Cárdenas, was elected Vice President of Bolivia for the period 1993–1997.

Summary

This chapter re-evaluates some underlying principles of intercultural bilingual education (IBE) in Latin America, based on a brief overview of the sociolinguistic contexts in which this type of education is implemented. Emphasis is placed on the cases of Bolivia and Guatemala, countries where indigenous peoples constitute real national majorities. Although intercultural bilingual education has evolved as a recognized national model, attention is paid to the emergence of recent alternative proposals, which according to their authors – indigenous leaders and organizations – search for even more cultural pertinence. The discrepancy results from the low importance given to indigenous knowledge in school curricula.

Thus, the new proposals of educación propia (own education) or endogenous education, which in spite of its denomination also include interculturalism and multilingualism under indigenous control and management. In the midst of such discrepancies, intercultural bilingual education is periodically reinvented through bottom-up indigenous proposals.

Esta comunicación reevalúa algunos supuestos de la educación intercultural bilingüe en América Latina, con base en una breve revisión de los contextos sociolingüísticos en los que este tipo de educación se desarrolla. Se enfatiza los casos de Guatemala y Bolivia, países latinoamericanos en los que las poblaciones indígenas constituyen mayorías nacionales. Frente al desarrollo de la educación intercultural bilingüe, se analiza el surgimiento de propuestas alternativas de líderes y organizaciones indígenas en busca de mayor pertinencia cultural. La divergencia surge, en parte, de la poca importancia que los currículos escolares prestan a los conocimientos indígenas. Por ello, emergen hoy propuestas de educación propia o endógena que, pese a su denominación, propone también la interculturalidad y el plurilingüismo, relacionando lo propio y lo ajeno, pero bajo el control y la gestión indígena. Así, periódicamente, la educación intercultural bilingüe se renueva y reinventa de abajo hacia arriba. (Spanish)

Chapter 13

Multilingualism of the Unequals and Predicaments of Education in India: Mother Tongue or Other Tongue?

AJIT K. MOHANTY

The Nature of Indian Multilingualism: A Closer Look

Linguistic diversity is a 'hallmark of India' (Bhatia & Ritchie, 2004: 794). But Indian multilingualism goes beyond a simple diversity of numbers which, in themselves, are quite overwhelming. There are 1652 mother tongues (1961 census) and a much larger number of dialects. These have been classified into 300 to 400 languages (five language families). There are 22 constitutionally recognized official languages (*Constitution of India*, VIIIth schedule, after the 100th constitutional amendment, December 2003) along with English (the associate official language). Some 104 languages are used for radio broadcasting and for adult literacy programs, and 87 are used for print media. It is not just the presence of a number of languages in different spheres of social life in India but the dynamics of the relationship between these languages and their users that make the ethos of language use in India quite distinct from that of dominant-monolingual societies. Of the several features that are characteristic of Indian multilingualism (Mohanty, 1991, 1994), the following seven are particularly relevant to understanding how multilingualism impacts on the social and individual processes (Mohanty, 2004):

(1) bilingualism at the grass-root level;
(2) maintenance norms;
(3) complementarities of languages;
(4) multiplicity of linguistic identities;
(5) bilingualism as a strategy for mother tongue maintenance;
(6) multilingualism as a positive force;
(7) early socialization for multilingual functioning.

Bilingualism at the grass-root level

Widespread use of two or more languages in different domains of daily life makes it possible for individuals and communities at the grass-root levels to communicate among themselves and with members of different speech communities. Despite linguistic diversity, communication across the country remains open and unimpaired (Khubchandani, 1978; Pattanayak, 1981). As Pattanayak (1984: 44) has said: 'If one draws a straight line between Kashmir and Kanyakumari and marks, say, every five or ten miles, then one will find that there is no break in communication between any two consecutive points.' This is because individual and community bilingualism at the local or regional levels can be seen as constituting the first incremental step towards concentric layers of societal multilingualism.

Maintenance norms

Language contact in dominant monolingual societies is associated with language shift. In such societies, bilingualism is a point in transition from monolingualism in native language to monolingualism in the dominant contact language. In India, minority languages in contact have tended to be maintained over generations. It has been held that, when Indian languages are in contact, language maintenance is the norm and shift is a deviation (Pandit, 1977). Such maintenance norms in India are supported by the multilingual ethos and the non-competing roles of languages in the lives of the common people. However, despite such strong maintenance norms, minority languages suffer marginalization and neglect owing to the hierarchical nature of the multilingualism that will be discussed later.

Complementarities of languages

The multilingual life style in India involves various patterns of language use in social interactions and in different domains of daily life. Complementarity of relationship between languages is achieved by smooth functional allocation of languages into different domains of use. Languages are neatly sorted into non-competing spheres of activities such as home, in-group communication, market place, religious rites, formal communication, entertainment, media, inter-group communication, and so on. For example, I use Oriya in my home, English in my work place, Hindi for television viewing, Bengali to communicate with my domestic helper, a variety of Hindi-Punjabi-Urdu in market places in Delhi, Sanskrit for my prayer and religious activities, and some conversational Kui with the Konds for my research in their community. These languages fit in a mutually complementary and non-competing relationship in my life. Under such conditions of multilingual functioning individuals naturally need and use different languages because no language is sufficient or suitable for meeting all the communicative requirements across different situations and social activities (Mohanty, 2004).

Multiplicity of linguistic identities

Bhatia and Ritchie (2004: 795) have said that '[m]ultiple languages and multiple language identities are defining features of Indian (and south Asian) bilingualism that reveal the dynamics of language usage and a constant negotiation of identities.' Typically, language users in India extend their identities beyond a particular language. This is possibly due to a high degree of flexibility in perception of languages and their boundaries (Khubchandani, 1983, 1986), which makes people move between languages with the patterns of identities changing under various social psychological conditions. Such multiple linguistic identities affect the dynamics of perceptions of mother tongues and linguistic boundaries (Mohanty, 1991, 1994).

Bilingualism as a strategy for mother tongue maintenance

Stable forms of bi/multilingualism in contact situations in India are a result of communities maintaining their languages, not by rejecting the contact language, but by linguistic accommodation (Bhatia & Ritchie, 2004). Becoming bilingual is an adaptive strategy for individuals and communities and this effectively stabilizes the relationship between individuals, communities and languages (Mohanty, 1994, 2003).

Multilingualism as a positive force

When mother tongues are healthily maintained along with bi/tri or multilingualism at the individual and community levels, social, psychological and educational benefits accrue to the minority groups. Our studies (Mohanty, 1982 a, 1982b, 1990; Mohanty & Babu, 1983; Mohanty & Das, 1987; also discussed in Mohanty, 1994, 2003; Mohanty & Perregaux, 1997) have shown that bilingual children:

> schooled as well as unschooled, have a distinct edge over their monolingual counterparts in terms of their cognitive and intellectual skills, metalinguistic and meta-cognitive task performance and educational achievement [in the case of schooled children]. (Mohanty, 2000: 110).

These studies were conducted among bilingual and monolingual Konds in Orissa (India) and it was possible to draw comparison samples from the same cultural and socioeconomic backgrounds, and at the same time to separate out the role of formal schooling from that of bilingualism *per se*. Community level bi/multilingualism has also been found to promote social integration in contact situations (Mohanty, 1987 reported in Mohanty 1994; Mohanty & Parida, 1993; Mohanty & Saikia, 2004; see also Skutnabb-Kangas, 1995 for a review of Mohanty, 1994). Reviews of cross-cultural studies on bilingualism including the Indian research (Mohanty & Perregaux, 1997) support the positive psychological and social role of multilingualism.

Early socialization for multilingual functioning

Given the grass-root level of multilingualism and the functional allocation of languages into different domains of daily activities, the processes of language socialization in India involve learning to communicate appropriately in a multilingual context. Such learning involves awareness and acceptance of functional separation of languages into different domains and contexts and interlocutor-specific differentiation of languages. The differentiation of languages also involves developing a hierarchy of preferences in patterns of language use. Studies (Mohanty, 2000; Mohanty *et al.*, 1999) among 2–9 year old children growing up in different regions of India under different contexts of linguistic heterogeneity show that Indian multilingual socialization involves development of:

(1) a progressive differentiation of languages;
(2 the norms of multiple language use and
(3) understanding and consistent use of the rules governing multilingual communication including a context-sensitive hierarchy of sociolinguistic preferences.

Regardless of their multilingual competence, the children show these developments by about 9 years of age, proceeding through three broad developmental periods – a period of language differentiation, a period of social awareness of languages, and a period of multilingual functioning (each period further divided into two stages). Thus, Indian multilingualism is supported by the early multilingual socialization through which children can be said to develop multilingualism as a 'first language.'

All these features make Indian multilingualism quite special and distinct from the presence of multiple languages in dominant-monolingual societies. In India, presence of many languages is natural and unmarked in all forms of social and individual communicative acts. Quite early in her/his development, the average Indian learns to easily accept the presence of many languages, to function smoothly and spontaneously with multiple modes of communication in different spheres of their activities, and to use a variety of languages as natural and flexible expressions of multiple identities. Thus, Indian multilingualism does not pose any threat or conflict for the individuals and the communities; languages are accepted as necessary and positive aspects of the social mosaic. These features add up to making multilingualism a positive phenomenon. They also ensure that the languages fall into neatly arranged pieces of coexistence which Pattanayak (1988), a leading Indian linguist, characterizes as 'the petals of the Indian lotus.'

Despite the multilingual ethos, however, a closer look at how languages are mutually related in the society shows a different picture. Nearly 80% of Indian languages are endangered. India is a multilingual country in which many languages coexist, many languages are maintained, but at the same time, many languages are also treated with neglect, discrimination and deprivation. In terms of their constitutional, legal, political, economic and educational status, Indian languages are hierarchical in the sense that some languages are privileged with access to power and resources while others are disadvantaged due to various forms of neglect. In practice, Indian multilingualism is characterized by unequal status of the languages (Mohanty, 2004).

The Other Side of Indian Multilingualism

Language and power: Multilingualism of the unequals

Chances of survival of minor, minority, and tribal languages in India are undeniably higher than in dominant-monolingual societies owing to the positive maintenance norms and the adoption of dominant contact languages by linguistic minorities along with native language maintenance in a form of stable bilingualism. However, such maintenance norms do not ensure equality of power and opportunities for speakers of all the languages. Particularly when it comes to minority and tribal languages, the very process of language maintenance is also the process of their marginalized survival, as I will show later in this chapter. Disabilities and disadvantages often associated with minor languages are not in any way inherent to these languages; they are social in origin and result from unequal treatment in the society. In fact, social, political, educational and economic conditions conspire to strengthen the association of the minor and tribal languages with the powerlessness and insufficiency that springs from the stark reality that the speakers of these languages are invariably disadvantaged to begin with. As a group they are usually poorer, belong to mostly rural and economically underdeveloped areas, and share many features of the disadvantaged populations.

Formal bases of language hierarchy

Often, linguistic hierarchy and inequality are institutionalized through various political and statutory processes. Of the large number of mother tongues (and languages) only some (22 by 2003) are given the status of constitutional recognition in terms of inclusion in the VIIIth schedule as 'scheduled languages'. English is given the status of an associate official language.[1] Table 13.1 lists all the constitutional languages and English with the percentage of the population who claim the language as their mother tongue.

Table 13.1 Constitutional (Official) languages and English (Associate Official language) in India

Scheduled languages	*Total no. of speakers*	*Percentage of population*
Hindi	329,505,517	38.93
Bengali	69,595,738	8.22
Telugu	66,017,615	7.80
Marathi	62,481,681	7.38
Tamil	53,006,368	6.26
Urdu	43,406,932	5.13
Gujarati	40,673,814	4.81
Kannada	32,753,676	3.87
Malayalam	30,377,176	3.59
Oriya	28,061,313	3.32
Punjabi	23,378,744	2.76
Assamese	13,079,696	1.55
Sindhi	2,122,848	0.25
Nepali	2,076,645	0.25
Konkani	1,760,607	0.21
Manipuri	1,270,216	0.15
Kashmiri	56,693	0.37
Sanskrit	49,736	0.01
Maithili	7,766,597	0.92
Bodo	1,221,881	0.14
Dogri	89,681	0.01
Santali	5,216,325	0.62
English	178,598	0.02
Total	*817,268,379*	*96.57*

Figures are based on mother tongue returns in the 1991 Census (which did not cover the state of Jammu and Kashmir). Hence, the figure for Kashmiri language is based on earlier census.

There are some other languages that are recognized for specific purposes such as state level official use, and some are acknowledged as mother tongues (often grouped under major language categories as in census reports). The rest are usually grouped under the 'other languages' category. The 1991 census of India lists 216 mother tongues with a minimum of 10,000 speakers. The mother tongues declared by fewer than 10,000 persons are all grouped under the 'other mother tongues' category, which includes nearly 9 million persons. Thus, more than 900 mother tongues go unlisted. Although these 'other mother tongue' speakers together constitute nearly 1% of the population, they seem to be powerless in the numbers game.

Educational neglect of languages is yet another notable instance of institutionalized linguistic inequality. Apart from the 22 constitutionally recognized official languages (Table 13.1), very few mother tongues find a place in the school curriculum (see below for details). The number of languages (as teaching languages and/or as school subjects) in Indian schools is declining over the years, almost down to half of what it was in 1970. Most of the tribal and minority mother tongues have no place in the educational system of India. The children who enter schools with these mother tongues are forced into a dominant language 'submersion' education with a subtractive effect on their mother tongues.

English and the power game

Linguistic accommodation, attitudes of mutual acceptance, and a 'true' multilingual worldview are seen as very characteristic of Indian multilingualism (e.g. Bhatia & Ritchie, 2004; Pattanayak, 1988). This has traditionally been reflected in a natural, mutually supportive, complementary and additive relationship between languages. However, this traditional relationship of sharing, coexistence and tolerance between languages seems to have been obliterated by the powerful presence of English as an international 'killer language' (Skutnabb-Kangas, 2000) in post-colonial India. In today's India, English is the language of power, used as an indication of greater control over outcomes of social activities.

In the colonial period, education in English was a means to social and economic resources, and now, it is also used to divide the society into the privileged and under-privileged classes. Public education, mostly in major regional state level languages and of poor quality, is seen as a disadvantage vis-à-vis education in English, and thus more and more people from the lower strata are forced to seek expensive English-medium private schools for their children. Over the post-Independence years, English has become the single most important predictor of socio-economic mobility. Failure in English alone accounts for more than 50% of the failures in high school examinations throughout the country. The privileged English-knowing elites (estimated to be less than 2% of the Indian population) seem to have an advantage since, with the positive attitudinal and environmental support for English, their children outperform the new aspirants. With the globalized economy, English education widens the discrepancy between the social classes. English has now become the most favoured first or second compulsory language in the school curriculum, pushing out the major state-level official and scheduled languages. Under the new dynamics of power relationship between languages, English has become a potent factor in the differential power equation. As English pushes the major languages, including Hindi, into positions of weakness, the minor and tribal mother tongues pushed further by the major languages, are rendered most powerless. Thus, multilingualism in India has yielded to a hierarchical 'pecking order' (Phillipson, 2001).

The hierarchical pecking order in action

The dominant status of English in official, educational, and economic spheres of Indian society is openly acknowledged. But what had perhaps not been anticipated, and hence has not been much discussed, is its power over the regional state languages and Hindi. This power of English over Hindi is augmented by the political processes by which acceptance of English is a strategy for keeping Hindi from being imposed as a national official and educational language. This is particularly true of the states in South India. In virtually all the non-Hindi states, English has continued to be the dominant language of governance, considerably weakening the position of the major regional or state languages. These languages, in turn, are also imposed on the minority, minor and tribal[2] languages.

In the educational sphere, projected as a global language of science, technology, and commerce, English has been seen as having a primary role despite statutory attempts to enforce regional state languages in schools. In Hindi majority states, as well as in non-Hindi states, an alarmingly-increasing proportion of the parents and students aspire to English-medium education as a road to power and success. This is weakening the already weak system of state-sponsored regional majority language schools that are imposed on tribal language communities, other linguistic minorities, and the poor and disadvantaged groups who cannot afford high-cost English-medium schools.

The hierarchical power relationship between languages is legitimated through a process of social transmission. Early language socialization, a life-long process of socially-constructed psychological processes of identity formation, reconciliation of dissonance, and perception of reality tempered by a fatalistic resignation, make linguistic communities legitimize the assigned roles for their language in the hierarchy. Most Indian children develop awareness of the higher social status of English compared to their own mother tongues, and schools contribute to such perceptions (Mohanty *et al.*, 1999). Even the speakers of the so-called non-standard varieties of major languages are disadvantaged because these varieties are considered inferior and even sometimes unacceptable for academic and formal use. Standard varieties are usually arbitrarily identified on the basis of the degree of *Anglicization* and *Sanskritization* of language. This perpetuates an elitist bias and increases the sharp discontinuity between school language and home language, and particularly for the disadvantaged groups adds further to their school failure. Thus, in the dynamics of power, languages and speech varieties are sorted into a hierarchical relationship with the dominant English language rendering even the major languages less powerful.

Pushed out of significant domains of power such as official and educational use, the major languages seem to remain confined to limited domains, and they in turn pressure the minority and tribal languages, pushing them into narrow domains of limited use and restricting the scope of their development. In the process, minority and tribal languages are marginalized. These languages are forced to adapt defensive survival strategies that I have characterized as 'anti-predatory strategies' (Mohanty, 2004).

Anti-predatory strategies and the cost of language maintenance

When animals of subordinate species are threatened by powerful predators, they engage in some anti-predatory behaviours to enhance their chances of survival. Such behaviours usually involve retreating to areas of lesser access and visibility and low resources. A similar pattern is quite evident in the maintenance of minor and tribal languages in contact with major languages in India. In face of pressures from dominant contact languages, these languages withdraw into domains of lesser socio-economic power and significance and their speakers usually adopt a form of bilingualism in which the tribal/minority languages are invariably restricted to domains of home and in-group communication and other less significant domains. These languages are pushed out of domains of power, such as education, official and formal use, trade and commerce, which are taken over by the dominant contact languages. In India, although language shift does not occur as a general pattern, there is considerable domain shrinkage for minority and tribal languages as a contact outcome. It seems that 'natural' bilingualism among the weaker and disadvantaged communities such as the tribals is a survival strategy that ensures smooth social functioning in the contact situations. But the cost of such survival and maintenance of languages is identity crisis, deprivation of freedom and capability, educational failure (due to inadequate home language development and forced submersion in majority language schools), marginalization, and poverty (Mohanty, 2000).

Minority group challenges to hierarchical multilingualism

There are several examples of minority and tribal language groups rising above the inequality inherent in hierarchical multilingualism through a process of struggle to assert their linguistic rights, a process characterized as 'assertive language maintenance' (Dorian, 2004). In December 2003, the Parliament of India passed the Constitutional (100th Amendment) Bill 2003 granting the status of scheduled official language to Bodo, language of the Bodo tribals of Assam. Along with Bodo, three other languages including Santhali (a tribal language) were also given official status as constitutional scheduled languages. The speakers of each of the new scheduled languages (Bodo, Dogri, Maithili and Santhali) have had a history of long struggle for assertion of their linguistic rights.

Particularly for the Bodos, there has been a process of agitation, armed conflict and political negotiation spanning a period of nearly four decades to assert their language rights. The Bodo movement began with a demand for Bodo-medium schools for the Bodo children, who were earlier forced to attend schools with Assamese as the teaching language. Through persistent and collective assertion of their linguistic, educational, and political rights, the Bodos have been able to reverse the process of marginalization of their language and culture. Our studies of linguistic identity, ethnolinguistic vitality, inter-cultural relations among the Bodos in Assam, and the positive benefits of mother-tongue-medium schooling for Bodo children (Saikia & Mohanty, 2004) show that it is possible for the minor and tribal languages to rise above the hierarchy in Indian multilingualism by collective assertion of identity. However, the Bodo situation is to be contrasted with the passive acceptance of marginalized status as a fait accompli by other tribal linguistic minorities, such as the Konds. It seems that the minor, minority and dominated languages need to reach a minimum threshold of ethnolinguistic vitality in order to show signs of assertive maintenance pressure and of striving for linguistic rights. Most of the tribal languages in India do not have the necessary economic and political support to reach the minimum level of vitality. They seem to have accepted their marginalized status by a clear dissociation between the perceived instrumental and integrative functions of languages.

In our sociolinguistic surveys of the Kond tribals in Orissa, India (Mohanty, 1994; Mohanty & Parida, 1993), the two languages (Kui, the indigenous language of the Konds, and Oriya, the majority language of the state of Orissa) were clearly separated in terms of their perceived instrumental value for education, employment, and economic benefits. The Konds agreed with their non-tribal Oriya contact group that Kui has no instrumental value, whereas Oriya was seen as instrumentally significant for education as well as economic mobility. The Konds accept the development of their language and culture as necessary for their maintenance and have a sense of pride in them. But, they do not consider educational use of Kui as beneficial for employment and economic opportunities. Thus, in a process of passive language maintenance, and perhaps resulting from anti-predatory strategy, most tribal linguistic communities such as the Konds are resigned to the status of their language and even to the fate of its speakers. Their language is the language of their identity, their group belongingness and pride, but its powerlessness is accepted as their destiny.

Multilingualism and Education in India

The systems of education in India – the public as well as the private – reflect the hierarchy of the power relations of societal multilingualism. Both school and higher education in India are dominated by English. English-medium instruction at all levels of education is the most preferred form despite the national policy of mother-tongue-medium education, and despite the research evidence that challenges the superiority of English-medium schools over mother-tongue-medium schools. Multilingualism is a social reality in India. Meaningful participation in the larger democratic socio-political and economic system of the country requires its people to develop oral and literacy skills in many languages. Therefore, educational practices need to promote multilingualism for all. The tribal and other linguistic minorities need to learn the majority regional language and languages of inter-regional and wider communication, beside their mother tongues. Similarly, the speakers of major languages need to learn at least one other language of national-level communication and a language for wider communication. Further, all educational programs in India must develop competence in English at some point or other. Thus, it is necessary to have multilingual education starting with mother tongue as a medium. In this context, the question, 'How well does the educational system in India meet the challenges of multilingualism?' is quite important.

Languages in Indian education: The beginnings

Prior to the modern education that started during the British rule, education in India was multilingual. In the earlier form, children began their education in the vernacular language, with each child learning to read, write and engage in arithmetic operations in his/her respective mother tongue. Later, following development of proficiency in the early subjects of instruction, the focus usually shifted to higher levels of scholarship which invariably involved learning a classical language such as Sanskrit. At higher levels of learning, the classical language became the medium of instruction (MI) in religious texts and philosophical discourse of various schools.

The distinction between language as a medium of teaching and language as a school subject began during the British rule. The language policy in British colonial education evolved around the Orientalist–Anglicist controversy (see Evans, 2002 for a discussion on the history of the 19th century language issues in Indian education). This centered on the role of English language vis-à-vis the vernacular and classical languages of India[3] as MI as well as curricular subject(s) in the government-sponsored education. Schools with English-medium instruction were promoted by British rule, and education in English was increasingly perceived as necessary for access to power and economic benefits. In any case, multilingual education in pre-Independence India usually stood for 'use of one language as medium, and two or more languages as subjects of study' (Koul & Devaki, 2000: 114). As the following discussion of the current status of languages in India shows, this notion of 'multilingual' education has hardly changed.

Education in multilingual India today: Policy and practice

By the end of British rule, English was well entrenched in Indian education and its essential role was widely accepted. The constitution of India accepted the principle of mother tongue medium instruction. Article 350A of the Constitution of India states that the state and the local authorities shall endeavor to 'provide adequate facilities for instruction in the mother tongue at the primary stage of education to children belonging to minority groups.' This constitutional provision still remains to be implemented in practice. Further, the question of the language of teaching at the secondary level was not resolved in the Indian constitution. So, the issue of languages in education continued to be examined and debated, and in 1957 the three-language formula was proposed for education.

The three-language formula was the official policy of the government of India which in 1957 recommended use of:

(1) regional language or mother tongue as the first teaching-language for five years;
(2) Hindi in non-Hindi areas and any other Indian language in Hindi areas as the second language (as a school subject) for 3 years (i.e. the 6th to 8th years in school);
(3) English as third language subject from the third year onwards.

This policy envisaged regional language or mother tongue being used as a MI in school. Further, the distinction between regional languages and mother tongue was not clear. This led to forced imposition of the majority regional language on the minority and tribal language groups. This policy was applicable to the government sponsored education only. The private educational institutions were free to introduce their own system in respect of languages. This eventually led to proliferation of English-medium private schools (which are ironically called 'public schools' in India, just like in Britain).

In 1964 the three-language formula was modified. Hindi was no longer compulsory for non-Hindi areas, and English could be taught either in place of Hindi or as a foreign language. According to this modified formula, the three languages to be studied as school subjects (regardless of the MI) were:

(1) mother tongue or regional language;
(2) Hindi or English;
(3) one modern Indian language or foreign language not covered under (1) and (2), and not used as MI.

In addition, for the tribal children this modification also proposed the use of the tribal language as the medium of teaching for the first two years and oral instruction in the regional language and use of regional language as MI from the third year onwards.

The three-language policy underwent several modifications, and different versions were applied depending on how the formula was interpreted in various states and school systems. Despite such variations, English became the most common second language subject in all the states, followed by either Hindi or Sanskrit as a third language subject.

With respect to minority languages, a significant policy recommendation was made in The Ramamurti Committee Report (Ministry of Human Resource Development, 1990). It recommended setting up minority-language-medium primary schools in areas with at least 10% minority language speakers. It also suggested having parallel sections in the same schools for instruction in the minority and the majority language medium so that the minority children are not segregated from the other children. Further, in areas with less than 10% minority-language speakers, appointment of minority-language teachers was recommended for teaching the minority children. These recommendations, however, mostly remained untranslated into practice.

It may be noted that in the Indian language policy, the mother tongues (which mostly refers to the languages of the tribal and other minority groups) were gradually differentiated from the regional majority languages. This resulted in use of some languages (outside those recognized as the scheduled languages in Indian constitution) as media of instruction. Further, from the policy perspectives in India, and in practice, use of different languages in a succession of phases, with mainly monolingual instruction through the medium of one language first, then another, and even a third, is sometimes considered multilingual education. For example, a regional language or in a few cases a minority mother tongue may be used as MI up to high school (10th year of school) level (with other languages taught as school subjects), and a different language such as English or Hindi or another majority language may be used as the medium for higher education. Finally, because of anomalous statutory provisions regarding privately-run educational institutions and also those run by minority religious groups, no uniform policy perspective ever emerged in respect to the role of languages in Indian education. On the whole, the three-language formula and other policy formulations have mostly remained political and ideological statements far removed from the actual practices, which were quite diverse.

Languages as media in Indian education today

The *Sixth All India Educational Survey* (NCERT, 1999) shows that only 41 languages are currently used in schools, either as MI or as a school subject. What is even more alarming is that this number has actually declined from 81 in 1970 to 67 in 1976 (Chaturvedi & Mohale, 1976), 58 in 1978, 44 in 1990, and 41 in 1998 (NCERT, 1999; also Pattanayak, 1997). It should be noted that the actual number of languages used as the language of teaching in schools (MI) is even smaller and is also declining. The sixth survey (NCERT, 1999) places the number of languages used as MI at 33 in primary level (i.e. the first five years of school), 25 in upper primary (6th and 7th years of school), 21 in secondary (8th to10th years of school) and 18 in higher secondary (11th and 12th years of school) levels of education. The corresponding figures in the earlier fifth survey (NCERT, 1990) were 43 in primary, 31 in upper primary, 22 in secondary and 20 in higher secondary levels of school education.

Further, use of minor languages (i.e. languages that are not recognized as official languages in the VIIIth schedule of the Indian constitution) and of tribal languages as languages of teaching (MI) is clearly decreasing. Although the three-language formula recommends use of mother tongue or regional language as the first language (language of teaching and as a school subject), in practice, mother tongues other than the major state languages or regional languages are left out. Koul and Devaki (2000, 2001) have shown that these languages are not used at all as media of instruction in higher secondary education. In any case, with less than 1% of the tribal children getting early education in their mother tongues, mismatch between school language and home language and the subtractive language development triggered by the forced 'submersion' are major educational issues.

English-medium schools in India

Unlike any other Indian language, English is used in all the states and Union Territories in India as a language of teaching (MI) at all levels of education. Thus, English language happens to be 'the most pervasive of all the media instruction (Koul & Devaki, 2001: 107). In a majority of the states in India, English is taught as a compulsory school subject by the 6th year of schooling, and it is gradually being moved to earlier grades – to the first year of schooling in some states. This is in contrast to the fact that (except in the Hindi-speaking states), Hindi is not taught as a compulsory subject, or is taught only as a third language from the 5th year onwards, in the schools in a majority of the states (Government of India, Ministry of HRD 2003). In some states (e.g. Tamil Nadu), Hindi is not a compulsory requirement in the school curriculum. Thus, in practice, English is better placed in school education in India than Hindi, the national language.

Evidently, the English language has impacted all aspects of Indian life. But its impact on education is perhaps the most crucial one. It is not only one of the most significant school subjects, but it is the most sought-after medium of schooling. It has given rise to a new basis of stratification of the Indian society – those educated in the more expensive privately run English-medium schools, and the less privileged others who go for the almost free regional-language-medium schools supported by the Government.[4] Since English-medium schools are 'market driven' the cost of privately-run schools is quite high. The fees for non-residential schools in India vary from less than 15 rupees (about US$0.30) to more than 15,000 rupees (about US$330) per month. The higher fees are for private English medium schools, and the schools in the lower end are usually state sponsored regional language or mother tongue schools. The increasing demand for English-medium schools has resulted in a large number of low quality English-medium schools charging lower schools fees than the better quality and prestigious ones. Such schools have proliferated in rural and semi-urban areas all over the country. Lured by the aspirations for Anglicization of children, parents from the lower economic strata struggle to meet the somewhat lower fees for the relatively inferior quality English-medium schools.

Our analysis (Mohanty, 1988) of the academic achievement of low socioeconomic status (SES) children in poor-quality English-medium schools show that these schools fail to promote adequate achievement among the children because the English language has no support in their home environment (unlike the higher SES children). Further, mother tongue development of all the children in these English-medium schools becomes restricted, since schools do not support it. The children from the tribal and other disadvantaged communities are clear losers in the process; their mother tongues have little scope for development outside their home, and their school language has little support outside the school. This has given rise to a new class of English-medium students with marginal success. Thus, the economics of choice of different forms of English-medium and regional language-medium schools, and the politics of language in school education, have provided the basis for a new social stratification of the literate groups:

(1) the privileged social class educated in high-cost English-medium schools;
(2) the less privileged social class educated in the low-cost English-medium schools;
(3) the under-privileged class educated in the regional language (also the mother tongue) medium schools; and
(4) the least privileged stratum, who are forced to be schooled in the medium of a regional language other than their home language.

The social cost of English-medium schooling in India is enormous and, it seems, the English educated élite has not cared to look critically at this issue.

Unfortunately, the question of English-medium schooling is pitted against mother-tongue-medium education creating an unnecessary duality and tension that ignores the possibility of bridging the language gap in the existing multilingual ethos of the Indian society. Schools where the language of teaching is English or a major regional language are thought of as better alternatives to schooling in mother tongue medium; the latter is considered unnecessary for further education in any major language. The possibility of additive development of other languages, along with mother tongue in a suitable form of multilingual education, has not been seriously considered in the Indian educational system. Bilingual or multilingual education is thought of only as a system in which multiple languages form part of the curriculum. Thus, a true form of multilingual education is yet to emerge in India.

In the following section I turn to an analysis of different modes of school education in India that deal with ways to develop multilingual competence. They do not use multiple languages for teaching school subjects other than the languages themselves and, hence, they are not multilingual education in the strict sense of the term (Anderson & Boyer, 1978). I have labeled them *nominal forms* of multilingual education.[5]

Nominal Forms of Multilingual Education in India Today

As has been mentioned, bilingual/multilingual education in the Indian context does not refer to the use of two or more languages as media of instruction, either simultaneously or successively. Rather, it refers to the use of two or more languages in education, usually as school subjects. In an informal sense, given the multilingual communicative ethos and the presence of different linguistic groups, Indian classrooms often become multilingual communicative contexts. Srivastava and Gupta (1984) have also discussed different patterns of informal bilingual / multilingual communication in the formal monolingual classrooms in the Indian schools.

Two types of nominal forms of multilingual education are described below: (1) *informal* multilingual education, and (2) *formal* multilingual education with a single or multiple MI.

Informal multilingual education

Support bilingual education

In some schools, the medium of school instruction needs to be supplemented or supported by another language. The lesson may be read in the medium of school instruction (MI) and explained/discussed/clarified in another language particularly when the MI is not the mother tongue (MT) of some or all of the students.

Partial bilingual education

Students provide answers in their mother tongues, but classroom interaction is conducted in a local language as MI. Sometimes, the teacher is not familiar with the students' MT (as when tribal children are taught by a non-tribal teacher who does not know the tribal language). In such cases a simplified register may be informally used for classroom communication, and the majority language is used as formal MI.

Formal multilingual education with a single MI

Majority language mother-tongue programs

A majority language MT is the MI, and other languages are taught as school subjects. These programs usually follow the three-language policy. But, their implementation in different states is quite different, particularly across Hindi and non-Hindi states (Viswanatham, 1999). In effect, these programs are forced submersion programs for minority and tribal language children whose MT is not the school MI.

Non MT-medium program

These programs are in a second-language medium with other languages taught as school subjects, such as in English-medium schools (sometimes also Hindi-medium schools) for children whose MT is not English (or Hindi) and where other languages are taught as school subjects.

Formal multilingual education with multiple languages as MI

In these programs usually two languages are used as MI either simultaneously or successively.

Simultaneous dual language MI

In some government-sponsored schools (e.g. Kendriya Vidyalaya), English is used as MI for mathematics, science and English subjects, and Hindi is used as the MI for teaching social studies and Hindi.

Successive dual language MI programs

A majority language MT is used as MI up to a certain level with other languages taught as school subjects. Thereafter, the students switch over to a second language MI. Sometimes primary and/or secondary level education is (are) in MT medium with English and/or Hindi and other languages taught as subjects. At a higher level is secondary education or university level, when the students switch to English (or Hindi) as the MI.

A program called the *Bilingual Transfer Model*, developed by the Central Institute of Indian Languages in Mysore, was specifically designed as a special type of successive dual language MI programs for the tribal groups. This program begins with use of tribal language as MI in the first year of schooling, along with oral communication in the regional language. Instructional time for the regional language is progressively increased as that for the tribal language is reduced so that, by the beginning of the fourth year of schooling, the child is ready for instruction in regional language only. Since most of the tribal languages do not have a writing system, the script of the regional language is modified and adapted for the tribal language for special transfer texts and for early reading instruction.

The two programs above are nominal forms of multilingual education because they are more focused on languages being taught as subjects rather than used as media of instruction. In most cases, use of languages is incidental to the nature of the programs, and as such, program outcomes cannot be linked to bilingual or multilingual education. Pattanayak (1997) has also referred to lack of any structured bilingual education programs in India.

Nominal forms of bilingual education in India. Conclusion

On the whole, education in India is only superficially multilingual, and it remains monolingual at an underlying level. The official *three-languages formula* is more abused and less used. Apart from the erratic manner in which it has been variously interpreted and used in different states and in school systems, it has also not addressed the real issues. Further, in spite of the multilingual predicaments that education in India has always faced, the relationship between societal multilingualism and communicative objectives of education has not been seriously attended to. This is true at the levels of social enquiry and policy formulations, as well as research. Even if the questions of the role of languages in education and multilingual education are extremely significant in the Indian society, there is still a dearth of a systematic, theory-driven empirical research on issues pertaining to multilingualism and multilingual education.

The Myth of English-medium /Second-language-medium Superiority

The hegemonic status of the English language and the instrumental benefits associated with it have led to the propagation of several myths about the success of English-medium education in India (Dua, 1994). English-medium privately-run schools that charge high fees are in a position to offer better physical facilities compared to the almost-free but poor-quality government-run regional or mother-tongue-medium schools. Further, the upper class bias in the student population of English-medium schools, associated with positive attitudinal and home-based support for English, has given the English-medium students added advantages. These conditions have led to a widespread belief in the superiority of English-medium schools over the mother-tongue-medium schools. This is also associated with the belief that early exposure to English results in improved English proficiency.

The available research evidence refutes these assumptions regarding English-medium schooling. Srivastava and his colleagues (1990) compared MT-medium and English-medium school students on measures of school achievements and self-concept. With the effect of intelligence separated out, there was no difference between the instructional media groups. The advantages of children from English-medium schools were attributed to variables related to the school climate, such as the criteria of selection and admission, the teaching methods, and the use of teaching aids and materials.

Another study (Patra, 2000) addressed the questions of MI and the early exposure to instruction in a second language. Patra compared Oriya mother tongue children from the 6th and 8th year classes in Oriya-medium and English-medium schools in Bhubaneswar, Orissa, on measures of mathematics, science, and language achievement. The two groups were matched for IQ, socioeconomic status and school climate. The mother-tongue-medium students did better than their English medium counterparts. In the second part of the study, Patra (2000) also compared Oriya-medium students in the 6th and 8th years of school with early and late exposure to teaching of English. The early-exposure group was taught English as school subject from the first year, and the late-exposure group from the 4th year of schooling. By the 8th year, there was no difference between the two groups. In other words, the late-exposure groups attained the same level of proficiency in English (as a second language) after four years of instruction, as the early-exposure group did after seven years. Thus, contrary to popular belief, early exposure to English (as a second language) does not enhance proficiency in English compared to late exposure. These findings clearly support Cummin's theory of linguistic interdependence.

A recent study (Saikia & Mohanty, 2004), examined the role of mother-tongue-medium schooling in school achievement of Bodo tribal children in Assam (India). Bodo children from Bodo (tribal mother tongue) medium and Assamese (regional majority language) medium schools were compared at the fourth year of schooling. The two groups were matched for SES, quality of schooling, and the ecological conditions of their villages. The tribal mother-tongue-medium children performed better than their non-MT medium counterparts in classroom achievement measures of mathematics and language, standard tests of minimum level of learning (in language and mathematics as school subjects), and class examination performance. Further, the performance of Bodo children in their mother-tongue-medium schools was comparable to that of the majority Assamese children in the Assamese-medium schools, in all but two of the mathematics achievements measures. This study shows the benefits of MT-medium instruction for tribal minority language children.

Thus, available Indian research questions the superiority of English (L2) medium over the MT medium schooling. It clearly shows that, when quality of schooling and student characteristics variables are controlled, MT schooling has a distinct advantage over schooling in a second-language medium (such as English or a regional majority language).

Imagining Multilingual Schools in India

Education in India has not responded to the challenges of its multilingual ethos. As I have shown in the first part of this chapter, the core of Indian multilingualism is in complementary relationship between languages and in the need to bridge the gap between the minor, minority, and tribal languages, and the languages of wider communication, including the regional and state level languages – Hindi and English. Multilingual education holds a central position in planning for a resourceful multilingualism that does not marginalize and deprive the minor, minority, and tribal language groups.

The existing educational programs in India hardly meet the criteria of multilingual education. Some school systems use two languages for teaching of different school subjects. The Kendriya Vidyalay schools of the Central Government located all over the country use a form of simultaneous dual language program of teaching. In these schools some school subjects (mathematics, sciences and English) are taught in English and the others in Hindi. Although at the surface level this program appears to be a bilingual one, its approach and objectives do not meet the requirements of a true multilingual program. It ignores any consideration of the mother tongues of the children. All the pupils, regardless of their linguistic background, have English and Hindi as instructional media. Further, use of English in teaching school subjects like mathematics and science reinforces the popular belief regarding English as the language of science and technology. The bilingual transfer program discussed earlier have claimed to be 'bilingual education'; but in reality they are soft assimilation programs that lead to a subtractive language learning and eventual loss of mother tongues. Both early-exit and late-exit transitional programs in different parts of the world have been shown to have the same characteristics of soft assimilation (Skutnabb-Kangas, 1984). In the context of Indian society, it is necessary to assess the extent to which the existing educational systems really support multilingualism. Skutnabb-Kangas and Garcia (1995) draw some general principles on the basis of which educational programs purporting to be bilingual or multilingual can be assessed. Unfortunately, the Indian programs of education do not support the weaker languages, nor do they promote a high level of bilingual proficiency.

Elsewhere (Mohanty, 2004), I have pleaded for a comprehensive language-in-education policy for empowerment of tribal and minority languages, along with the reappraisal of the role of English in Indian society. Multilingual education in India must be seen as a broad framework of education necessary for preserving the multilingual character of the society and for promoting multilingualism for all. It must be viewed not simply as a process of bringing the minority and tribal linguistic groups to the mainstream, nor as a process of enriching the majority alone.

Multilingual education in India can be imagined as a process that starts with development of MT proficiency which forms the basis for development of proficiency in all other languages with functional significance for specific groups. The theoretical foundation for such a system is well-developed and supported. It now needs to be implemented as multilingual schools developed within the context of Indian multilingualism. The question for these schools is not whether to use the mother tongue OR the other tongue. It is not about whether to use Hindi OR English. Multilingual education in India is about the mother tongue AND the other tongues as it develops multilingualism for all in Indian society.

Notes

1. The Indian Constitution initially granted this status to English for a period of 15 years only. But this privileged status to English has been extended for an indefinite period.
2. The indigenous or aboriginal communities are officially called 'tribes' in India, and referred to as 'scheduled tribes' in the Indian constitution. Specific tribes are identified as scheduled tribes on the basis of 'primitive traits', 'geographical isolation', 'distinct culture', 'economic backwardness' and 'limited contact with the outgroups'. So far, 573 notified or scheduled tribes are identified, and they constitute 8% of the total population. In this chapter, the term 'tribe' (rather than 'indigenous peoples') is used in its formal/official sense.
3. During the British rule, Sanskrit was usually referred to as a classical language, while all other Indian languages were labeled as vernaculars.
4. So strong is the link between English-medium education and perception of social class that the matrimonial advertisements published in newspapers emphasize English-medium education as a very positive point in the marriage negotiations.
5. The following discussion of different forms of multilingual education is based on Koul and Devaki (2001), who provide an exhaustive analysis.

Summary

Analysis of the nature of Indian multilingualism shows that, despite the strong maintenance norms, the hegemonic role of English gives rise to a socially legitimated and transmitted hierarchical pecking order in which mother tongues are gradually marginalized and pushed into domains of lesser power and resource in what can be characterized as a self-defensive anti-predatory strategy. Caught in the process of unequal power relationship between languages and lacking a clear multilingual framework, education in India is unable to balance the demands of the societal multilingualism and the dominant status of English.

The place of languages in Indian education and the various nominal forms of multilingual education are analyzed to show the cost of neglecting the mother tongues and tribal languages in education. Some studies interrogating the myth of English medium superiority and showing the benefits of mother-tongue-based multilingual education are discussed. It is argued that education must cater to the social needs of every child to develop from mother tongue to multilingualism and provide equality of opportunity through a language-shelter type of multilingual education that begins in mother-tongue medium and introduces other languages after at least three to five years of primary schooling.

भारतीय बहुभाषावाद की प्रकृति का विश्लेषण यह दर्शाता है कि सशक्त निर्वाह मूल्यों के बावजूद अंग्रेजी की प्रभुत्ववादी भूमिका ने सामाजिक बैधानिकता प्राप्त एक ऐसे वरीयता सोपान को जन्म दिया एवं प्रसारित किया है जिसमें मातृभाषाओं को हाशिये पर ले जा कर एक शक्ति-संसाधन क्षीण क्षेत्र में धकेला जा रहा है जिसे आक्रमण से बचने की आत्म-रक्षात्मक रणनीति के रूप में समझा जा सकता है। भाषाओं के मध्य असमान शक्ति संबंधों की प्रक्रिया मं उलझी और स्पष्ट बहुभाषावादी ढांचे के अभाव में भारत में शिक्षा सामाजिक बहुभाषावाद की मांगों और अंग्रेजी के प्रभावशाली स्थान के बीच संतुलन बनाने में असफल रही है। भारतीय शिक्षा पद्धति में भाषाओं का स्थान और बहुभाषावादी शिक्षा के अनेक किंतु नाममात्र के स्वरूपों का विश्लेषण शिक्षा में मातृभाषाओं एवं जनजातीय भाषाओं की कीमत को दर्शाने के लिए किया गया है। अंग्रेजी माध्यम की श्रेष्ठता के मिथक पर प्रश्न-चिन्ह लगाते और मातृभाषा पर आधारित बहुभाषावादी शिक्षा के लाभ पर किए गए कुछ अध्ययनों पर विमर्श किया गया है। यह तर्क दिया गया है कि शिक्षा को प्रत्येक बच्चे के मातृभाषा से बहुभाषावाद की ओर विकास की सामाजिक आवश्यकताओं की पूर्ति करना चाहिए और एक ऐसे भाषाई संरक्षण प्रकार के बहुभाषावादी शिक्षा द्वारा अवसर की समानता प्रदान करना चाहिए जो मातृभाषा माध्यम से आरंभ होती है और कम से कम तीन से पाँच वर्ष की प्राथमिक शिक्षा के बाद अन्य भाषाओं से परिचय कराती है।

(Hindi)

Biographies

About the Editors

Ofelia García is Professor at Columbia University's Teachers College in the Department of International and Transcultural Studies, and currently serves as the Coordinator of the Bilingual-Bicultural Education Program. She co-directs the Teachers College Center for Multiple Languages and Literacies (http://www.tc.edu/beta/cmll) with JoAnne Kleifgen. García has been Dean of the School of Education in the Brooklyn Campus of Long Island University and professor of bilingual education at The City College of New York. She is co-editor of *Spanish in Context* and was the editor of *Educators for Urban Minorities*. Among her books are: *The Multilingual Apple: Languages in New York City*, co-edited with Joshua Fishman (Mouton, 2nd edition 2001); *Policy and Practice in Bilingual Education: Extending the Foundations*, co-edited with Colin Baker (Multilingual Matters, 1995) and *English Across Cultures: Cultures Across English, A Reader in Cross-Cultural Communication*, co-edited with Ricardo Otheguy (Mouton, 1989). García has published numerous academic articles in the areas of bilingualism, sociology of language, US Spanish, the education of language minorities and bilingual education. She has been a Fulbright Scholar at the Universidad de la República, Montevideo (1996) and a Spencer Fellow of the US National Academy of Education (1985–88).

Dr Tove Skutnabb-Kangas of the Department of Languages and Culture, University of Roskilde, Denmark, and Åbo Akademi University, Department of Education, Vasa, Finland, is bilingual from birth in Finnish and Swedish. Her main research interests are in the areas of linguistic human rights, linguistic imperialism, bilingualism, multilingual education, language and power, the subtractive spread of English, and the relationship between linguistic (and cultural) diversity and biodiversity (also in practice, on an ecological smallholding, with her husband Robert Phillipson). Skutnabb-Kangas has been recipient of the 2003 Linguapax award and the 2003 Carl Axel Gottlund award. She has published over 30 authored or edited books and close to 400 book chapters and scientific articles, in some 30 languages. For CV and full list of publications, see http://akira.ruc.dk/~tovesk/.

María E. Torres-Guzmán is Associate Professor of Bilingual/Bicultural Education in the Department of International and Transcultural Studies at Teachers College, Columbia University. She has published extensively, and among her latest publications are: (co-authored with F. Etxeberría) 'Modelo B/Dual language programs in the Basque Country and the US' published in *International Bilingualism and Bilingual Education Journal* and (co-authored with S. Morales, A. Han and T. Kleyn) 'Self-designated dual-language programs: Is there a gap between labeling and implementation?' published in *Bilingual Research Journal*. Her two recent sole-authored articles are '*La lecture suivie n'est-elle qui lecture suivie?*' ('Are read alouds just read alouds?') for *Enjeux* 65 (2006) and 'Preparing teachers to recognize and confront symbolic violence in bilingual education' published in B.C. Wallace and R.T. Carter (eds) *Understanding and Dealing with Violence: A Multicultural Approach*.

About the Authors

Jim Cummins received his PhD in 1974 from the University of Alberta in the area of educational psychology. He is currently a professor in the Department of Curriculum, Teaching, Learning in the Ontario Institute for Studies in Education of the University of Toronto. His research has focused on the nature of language proficiency and second language acquisition, with particular emphasis on the social and educational barriers that limit academic success for culturally-diverse students. He has served as a consultant on language planning in education to numerous international agencies. His publications include: *Bilingualism and Special Education: Issues in Assessment and Pedagogy* (Multilingual Matters, 1984); *Bilingualism in Education: Aspects of Theory, Research and Practice* (with M. Swain; Longman, 1986); *Minority Education: From Shame to Struggle* (with T. Skutnabb-Kangas; Multilingual Matters, 1988); *Empowering Minority Students* (California Association for Bilingual Education, 1989); *Heritage Languages: The Development and Denial of Canada's Linguistic Resources* (with M. Danesi; Our Schools, Our Selves, 1990).

In September 1995, Cummins wrote (with Dennis Sayers) a volume analyzing the educational implications of the Internet: *Brave New Schools: Challenging Cultural Illiteracy through Global Learning Networks* (St Martin's Press). In May 1996, The California Association for Bilingual Education published *Negotiating Identities: Education for Empowerment in a Diverse Society*, which focuses on strategies for promoting academic development among culturally diverse students. In 1997, with David Corson he co-edited a volume on *Bilingual Education* as part of the Kluwer *Encyclopedia on Language and Education*. In October 2000, Multilingual Matters published his book *Language, Power and Pedagogy: Bilingual Children in the Crossfire. An*

Introductory Reader to the Writings of Jim Cummins, a collection of his academic papers over a 30-year period, edited by Colin Baker and Nancy Hornberger. Cummins is also co-author of Scott Foresman's *ESL: Accelerating English Language Learning, Lectura,* their Spanish reading program, and has been a contributor to their math, reading, and social studies programs. In the area of test development he is co-author of the *Bilingual Verbal Abilities Test* (Riverside Publishers).

Viv Edwards is Professor of Language in Education at the University of Reading where she is also Director of the National Centre for Language and Literacy. Her own interest in multilingualism derives from her family history in South Wales. Her great grandparents spoke very little English; her grandparents were bilingual with Welsh as their dominant language; her parents were bilingual with English as their dominant language and, like most of their generation, they used only English with their children. Viv is editor of the international journal, *Language and Education*, and has published widely in the area of learning and teaching in multilingual classrooms. Major publications include: *Oral Cultures Past and Present* (with T.J. Sienkewicz; Blackwell, 1991), *The Power of Babel* (Trentham 1995) and *Multilingualism in the English-speaking world* (Blackwell, 2004). She also co-edited *Literacy* (Volume 2 of the *Encyclopedia of Language and Education*, Kluwer, 1997) and *Multilingualism in the British Isles* (Longman, 1990).

Kathy Escamilla is Professor in the Division of Educational Equity and Cultural Diversity at the University of Colorado, Boulder. She has been in the field of bilingual education for over 30 years. She is a past President of the National Association for Bilingual Education. Currently, she teaches graduate courses in the areas of bilingual and multicultural education at the University of Colorado at Boulder. She maintains an active research agenda in the area of bilingual education, and is interested in questions related to education and Spanish-speaking Latinos. Her most recent research involves examining the impact of monolingual assessment systems on bilingual populations.

Feli Etxeberría Sagastume is Professor in Language Pedagogy in the Department of Methods, Evaluation and Research at the Universidad del País Vasco /Euskal Herriko Unibertsitatea. She has directed numerous research projects in the areas of language learning and teaching, bilingualism and education, and perceptions and values in language learning. She has also played a major role in the research project I+D, which examined the emergent models in systems and relations related to gender, the new socialization and politics of implementation of educational models (1996–2000) and the European Project of Socratic Programs (1993–1998).

Among her publications are *Language, Culture and Education in Bilingual Contexts; Minority Languages in Early Childhood Environments; The Case of Euskara; Perspectives on Psycho-Pedagogical Research, The Linguistic Dimension; The Functions of Language in Schooling*. She contributed to many national and international conferences.

Christine Hélot is Maître de Conférences at the Institut Universitaire de Formation des Maîtres in Alsace France, the post graduate-teacher education centre based in Strasbourg. She is a member of the research group LILPA EA 1339 (Linguistique, Langue, Parole) of the Université Marc Bloch in Strasbourg and is responsible within this group for a project centred on the issue of plurilingualism in primary schools. Prior to her post in France, she was a lecturer in Linguistics at the University of Ireland (Maynooth College) for 17 years. In 1988, she obtained her PhD from Trinity College Dublin for a thesis on infant bilingualism from a linguistic and sociolinguistic perspective. She has published numerous academic articles in the area of bilingualism and trilingualism in the family context, and bilingualism and plurilingualism in the school context and educational language policies and the development of bilingual education in France. Her present research focuses on educational policies in relation to children from ethno-linguistic background in France. She is involved in several European research projects on intercultural education and children's literature, on the inclusion of minority languages in teacher education and on language awareness. She is also responsible for the international exchange program at the IUFM of Alsace, and has developed student and teacher exchanges in numerous countries (Argentina, New Zealand, the USA, Canada, the UK, Spain, Finland, etc.). She is a member of the editorial board of *Language Policy* (Kluwer Academic publishers) and *Language and Education* (Multilingual Matters).

Nancy H. Hornberger is Professor of Education and Director of Educational Linguistics at the University of Pennsylvania, where she also convenes the annual international Ethnography in Education Research Forum. Professor Hornberger investigates language and education in culturally and linguistically diverse settings, using an approach that combines methods and perspectives from anthropology, linguistics, sociolinguistics, and policy studies. She gives special attention to educational policy and practice for indigenous and immigrant language groups, compared across national contexts. Dr Hornberger's particular focus is on Quechua-speaking populations in Peru and Bolivia and Cambodian and Puerto Rican populations in Philadelphia, but she has also visited and consulted with scholars, educators, and policymakers working with minority language groups in other parts of the world, including Brazil,

South Africa, Paraguay, New Zealand, India, Mexico, Norway, and Sweden. Twice recipient of the Fulbright Senior Specialist Award, Hornberger has also served as consultant under UNICEF and the United Nations Development Program. Author of several books and over 100 articles and chapters, her recent and forthcoming volumes include *Indigenous Literacies in the Americas: Language Planning from the Bottom up* (Mouton, 1996), *Continua of Biliteracy: An Ecological Framework for Educational Policy, Research, and Practice in Multilingual Settings* (Multilingual Matters, 2003), and *Heritage/Community Language Education: US and Australian Perspectives* (Multilingual Matters, 2005). Professor Hornberger co-edits an international book series on Bilingual Education and Bilingualism and serves on numerous international editorial advisory boards. She is General Editor for the forthcoming *Encyclopedia of Language and Education* (Springer).

Luis Enrique López is a Peruvian sociolinguist and educator. At present, he is Principal Advisor of PROEIB Andes, the regional German Technical Cooperation project (GTZ) for Intercultural Education in the Andean countries (Bolivia, Colombia, Chile, Ecuador, Perú and Argentina), at the Universidad Mayor de San Simón at Cochabamba, Bolivia. His post-graduate studies in applied linguistics and sociolinguistics are from the University of Lancaster, United Kingdom. His graduate work was carried out at Universidad Católica del Perú. López has specialized in the education of indigenous peoples of Latin America. He has also worked in Ecuador, Guatemala, Nicaragua, Paraguay, and Peru. His most recent books include *La educación intercultural bilingüe en América Latina: Balance y perspectivas* (Germany, 2002), *Educación intercultural bilingüe* (Guatemala, 2001), *Sobre las huellas de la voz* (Madrid, 1999) and *Abriendo la escuela* (Madrid, 2003). He is on the editorial board of *Language Policy* (US), *Linguas Indígenas* (Brazil), *International Journal of Intercultural Education* (United Kingdom), and *Prospects* (Switzerland). He was also a member of UNESCO's World Commission to study the world languages.

Teresa L. McCarty is the Alice Wiley Snell Professor of Education Policy Studies at Arizona State University. An educational anthropologist, she has been a bilingual curriculum developer, teacher, and coordinator of American Indian education programs at the local, state, and national levels. From 1989 to 2004, she was professor of Language, Reading and Culture at the University of Arizona, where she also served as department head, interim dean of the College of Education, and codirector of the American Indian Language Development Institute. A Kellogg National Fellow, her research and teaching focus on minority education, Indigenous language revitalization and maintenance, language planning and policy, and ethnographic methods in education. She has been the editor of *Anthropology and Education*

Quarterly, and is currently co-principal investigator on a national study of Native language shift and retention. Dr McCarty has published widely on Indigenous education, language planning and policy, and minority language rights. Her most recent books are *A Place To Be Navajo: Rough Rock and the Struggle for Self-Determination in Indigenous Schooling* and *Language, Literacy, and Power in Schooling*, both from Lawrence Erlbaum Associates.

Ajit K. Mohanty received his PhD in 1978 from the University of Alberta in Canada in the area of psycholinguistics. He is currently a Professor of Psychology and Chairperson in the Zakir Husain Centre for Educational Studies at Jawaharlal Nehru University, New Delhi. He has been a Professor, since 1983, and Chairperson at the Centre of Advanced Study in Psychology, Utkal University, India and President of the National Academy of Psychology, India (1997). Among his books are – *Bilingualism in a Multilingual Society;* and *Psychology of Poverty and Disadvantage*, co-edited with G. Misra. He has published extensively in the areas of psycholinguistics, multilingualism and reading processes and his work has focused on issues relating to education, poverty and disadvantage of linguistic minorities in multilingual societies characterized by unequal power relationship between languages. He has written (with Christian Perregaux) the chapter on 'Language acquisition and bilingualism' in the *Handbook of Cross-Cultural Psychology* (2nd edn). Ajit Mohanty is on the Editorial Boards of *International Journal of Multilingualism, Language Policy* and *Psychological Studies.* Mohanty has been a Fulbright Fellow in the University of Wisconsin in Madison, a Killam Scholar in the University of Alberta, a Senior Fellow of the Central Institute of Indian Languages and, a visiting scholar in the University of Geneva and University of Chicago.

Lydia Nyati-Ramahobo obtained her PhD in applied linguistics (language in education) at the University of Pennsylvania in 1991. She served as head of the Department of Primary Education at the University of Botswana from 1996 to 1999. She is currently Associate Professor and Dean of the Faculty of Education. Heı major publications include the book titled *The National Language: A Problem or Resource* (Pula Press), and papers on 'The language situation in Botswana' (in *Current Issues in Language Planning* 1 (2); 'From a phone call to the High Court: Wayeyi visibility and the Kamanakao Association's Campaign for Linguistic and Cultural Rights in Botswana' (*Journal of Southern African Studies* 28 (4). Nyati-Ramahobo is the co-founder of the Kamanakao Association, a pressure group for the linguistic and cultural rights of the Wayeyi tribe in Botswana. She is also founder and Secretary General of the RETENG: The Multi-cultural coalition of Botswana, which is an umbrella body of all associations in Botswana advocating for constitutional amendments to bring about equality in the provision of linguistic and cultural rights among the diverse ethnic groups of Botswana.

Karen Ogulnick is Associate Professor and Director of Programs of Teaching English to Speakers of Other Languages and Bilingual Education at C.W. Post College, Long Island University. She is the author of *Onna Rashiku (Like a Woman): The Diary of a Language Learner of Japan* (SUNY Press, 1998), *Language Crossings: Negotiating the Self in a Multicultural World* (Teachers College Press, 2000), and numerous journal articles and book chapters on the intersecting areas of language, identity, culture, and education. Her main research interests are minority language rights, bilingualism, multilingual education, language and gender and indigenous native language literacy. She has worked in a variety of educational settings ranging from the New York City public schools to teacher training in New York, Japan, Mexico, and Chile. She was a Fulbright Scholar in Chiapas, Mexico from 2002–2003, the recipient of a Mexico-North Transnational Research grant in 2004, and a Fulbright Senior Specialist in Chile in 2005.

Lynda Pritchard Newcombe grew up and lives in South Wales. She belongs to the first generation of her family to use English only as the language of the home, learning Welsh as an adult and, in due course, becoming a tutor of Welsh to adults. Her main publications are in the area of adult second-language learning. She has worked on various research projects involving the use of Welsh, including the *Twf* project reported in the chapter she has co-authored in this volume. She is presently a freelance tutor/researcher/writer.

Mary Eunice Romero is Assistant Professor of Multicultural and Indigenous Education at Arizona State University. Originally from Cochiti Pueblo in New Mexico, she has served as book review editor for *Anthropology and Education Quarterly* and co-principal investigator for the Native Language Shift and Retention Project, a study of the relationship between American Indian students' heritage-language proficiencies and their academic achievement. Prior to receiving her PhD in education from the University of California at Berkeley in 2001, Dr Romero served as the director of a program for gifted and talented students at an all-Native American junior high school and as principal investigator for a study of giftedness among the Keres-speaking Pueblos of New Mexico. She has worked extensively with New Mexico's tribal communities on Native language renewal and maintenance initiatives. Dr Romero is the recipient of the American Indian Leadership Fellowship from the W.K. Kellogg-UC Berkeley Partnership and the Katrin H. Lamon Resident Scholar Fellowship from the School of American Research. Her research interests include Indigenous language maintenance and renewal, American Indian education and policy, language socialization, second language learning, bilingual/multicultural education, and qualitative research.

Elana Shohamy is Professor of Language Education at the School of Education at Tel Aviv University. Her research focuses on issues of language assessment and language policies in multilingual societies. Her research in the past few years has been on the academic achievement of immigrants in schools, on the political and social implications of language tests and their effects on suppressing multilingualism as well as issues related to the study of Arabic in Israeli schools as a tool for co-existence. Her recent books include *The Languages of Israel: Policy, Ideology and Practice*, with Bernard Spolsky (Multilingual Matters, 1999) and *The Power of Tests: A Critical Perspective of the Uses of Language Tests* (Longman, 2001). Her latest book is entitled *Language Policy: Hidden Agendas and New Approaches* (Routledge, 2006).

Ofelia Zepeda is a member of the Tohono O'odham Nation of Southern Arizona, a professor in the Department of Linguistics, and affiliate faculty in the American Indian Studies Program and the Department of Language, Reading and Culture at the University of Arizona. The recipient of a MacArthur Fellowship for her work on American Indian language education, maintenance, and recovery, she has also published the first teaching grammar of O'odham, *A Tohono O'odham Grammar* (University of Arizona Press, 2003), and numerous articles and book chapters on the status of Native American languages, Indigenous language planning and policy, and Tohono O'odham linguistics. She is a co-founder and director of the American Indian Language Development Institute, an international teacher preparation program for educators of Native American youth. Dr Zepeda is also a published poet who writes in Tohono O'odham and in English. She has written two books of poetry, *Ocean Power: Poems from the Desert* (University of Arizona Press, 1995) and *Jewed I-hoi/Earth Movements* (Kore Press, 1997), and is the co-editor of *Home Places, An Anthology* (University of Arizona Press, 1995).

References

AANE (Assembly of Alaska Native Educators) (1998) *Guidelines for Preparing Culturally Responsive Teachers for Alaska's Schools*. Anchorage, AK: Alaska Native Knowledge Network.

AANE (Assembly of Alaska Native Educators) (2001) *Guidelines for Strengthening Indigenous Languages*. Anchorage, AK: Alaska Native Knowledge Network.

Abedi, J. (2001) Assessment and accommodations for English Language Learners: Issues and recommendations. *Policy Brief 4, CRESST, National Center for Research on Evaluation, Standards and Student Testing*. Los Angeles: UCLA Center for the Study of Evaluation.

Abedi, J. (2004) The No Child Left Behind Act and English language learners: Assessment and accountability issues. *Educational Researcher* 33 (1), 4–14.

Abedi, J., Hofstetter, C.H. and Lord, C. (2004) Assessment accommodations for English language learners: Implications for policy-based empirical research. *Review of Educational Research* 74 (1), 1–28.

ACEM (Asociación de Centros Educativos Mayas del Nivel Medio de Guatemala) (2005) *Cholb'al Q'ij. Agenda Maya 2005 (Año 5121)* [*Maya 2005 Year Book (Year 5121)*] Guatemala: Maya Na'oj.

Acuerdos de San Andrés (2003) *Biblioteca Popular de Chiapas*. Tuxtla Gutiérrez.

Ada, A.F. (1995) Fostering the home–school connection. In J. Frederickson (ed.) *Reclaiming Our Voices: Bilingual Education, Critical Pedagogy and Praxis* (pp. 163–178). Ontario, CA: California Association for Bilingual Education.

Adams, D.W. (1988) Fundamental considerations: The deep meaning of Native American schooling, 1880–1900. *Harvard Educational Review* 58 (1), 1–28.

Affeldt, J. (2004) Extending the protections of *Lau* to concepts of educational adequacy in California. Paper presented at the Annual Conference of the American Educational Research Association, San Diego.

Aikio-Puoskari, U. and Pentikäinen, M. (2001) *The Language Rights of the Indigenous Saami in Finland Under Domestic and International Law. Juridica Lapponica* 26. Rovaniemi: University of Lapland.

Aitchison, J. and Carter, H. (1988) *The Welsh Language in the Cardiff Region*. Aberystwyth: Department of Geography, Aberystwyth University.

Alexander, N. (2003) *Language Education Policy, National and Sub-national Identities in South Africa* (reference study). Strasbourg: Council of Europe.

Alridge, D.P. (2003) The dilemmas, challenges, and duality of an African American education historian. *Educational Researcher* 32 (9), 25–34.

Álvarez, F. (2002) El teatro Maya: Bravísima semblanza histórica, su situación actual y problemática. *Reencuentro* 33, 75–89.

Amrein, A. and Berliner, D. (2002) High stakes testing, uncertainty and student learning. *Educational Policy Analysis Archives* 10 (18). On WWW at http://epaa.asu.edu/epaa/v10n18. Accessed 3.2.2006.

Amrein, A. and Peña, R.A. (2000) Asymmetry in dual language practice: Assessing imbalance in a program promoting equity. *Education Policy Analysis Archives*, 8 (8). On WWW at http://epaa.asu.edu/epaa/v8n8.html. Accessed 3.2.2006.

Anaya, A. (2004) Lo que está en juego en el Congreso de Educación. *Pulso*. Lima, Peru. 10–16 September.

Anderson, B. (1983) *Imagined Communities*. London: Verso.

Andersson, T. and Boyer, M. (1978) *Bilingual Schooling in the United States* (2nd edn), Austin, TX: National Educational Laboratory Publishers.

Annamalai, E. (1998) Language choice in education: Conflict resolution in Indian courts. In P. Benson, P. Grundy and T. Skutnabb-Kangas (eds) *Language Rights*. Special volume. *Language Sciences* 20 (1), 29–43.

Annamalai, E. (2001) *Managing Multilingualism in India: Political and Linguistic Manifestations*. New Delhi: Sage.

Annamalai, E. (2003) Medium of power: The question of English in education in India. In J.W. Tollefson and A.B.M. Tsui (eds) *Medium of Instruction Policies: Which Agenda? Whose Agenda?* (pp. 177–194). Mahwah, NJ: Lawrence Erlbaum.

Anonby, S.J. (1999) Reversing language shift: Can Kwak'wala be revived. In J. Reyhner, G. Cantoni, R.N. St Clair and E.P. Yazzie (eds) *Revitalizing Indigenous Languages* (pp. 33–52). Flagstaff, AZ: Northern Arizona University.

Anzaldúa, G. (1987) *Borderlands/La Frontera: The New Mestiza*. San Francisco, CA: Aunt Lute Books.

Arendt, H. (1968) *Imperialism*. New York: Harcourt Brace Janovich.

Arratibel, N. (1999) *Helduen Euskalduntzean Eragiten Duten Prozesu Psikosozialak: Motibazioaren Errola*. Donostia/San Sebastián: Universidad del País Vasco.

Arviso, M. and Holm, W. (2001) Tséhootsooídi Olta'gi Diné bizaad b´hoo'aah: A Navajo immersion program in Fort Defiance, Arizona. In L. Hinton and K. Hale (eds) *The Green Book of Language Revitalization in Practice* (pp. 203–215). San Diego, CA: Academic Press.

Arzamendi, J. and Genesee, F. (1997) Reflections on immersion education in the Basque Country. In R.K. Johnson and M. Swain (eds) *Immersion Education: International Perspectives* (pp. 151–166). Cambridge: Cambridge University Press.

Atkins, J.D.C. (1887/1992). Barbarous dialects should be blotted out. In J. Crawford (ed.) *Language Loyalties: A Source Book on the Official English Controversy* (pp. 47–51). Chicago: University of Chicago Press.

August, D. and Hakuta, K. (eds) (1997) *Improving Schooling for Language-Minority Children: A Research Agenda*. Washington, DC: National Academy Press.

Azurmendi, M. José, Bachoc, E. and Zabaleta, F. (2001) Reversing language shift: The case of Basque. In J.A. Fishman (ed.) *Can Threatened Languages Be Saved?* (pp. 234–259) Clevedon: Multilingual Matters.

Baetens Beardsmore, H. (1995) The European school experience in multilingual education. In T. Skutnabb-Kangas (ed.) *Multilingualism for All* (pp. 21–68). Lisse: Swets and Zeitlinger.

Baetens Beardsmore, H. (1999) La consolidation des expériences en éducation plurilingue. In D. Marsh and B. Marland (eds) *CLIL Initiatives for the Millenium*. Jyväskylä: University of Jyväskylä, Finland.

Baker, C. (2001) *Foundations of Bilingual Education and Bilingualism*. Clevedon: Multilingual Matters.

Baker, C. (2003a) Education as a site of language contact. *Annual Review of Applied Linguistics* 23, 95–112.

Baker, C. (2003b) Language planning: A grounded approach. In J-M. Dewaele, A. Housen and L. Wei (eds) *Bilingualism: Beyond Basic Principles* (pp. 88–111). Clevedon: Multilingual Matters.

Baker, C. and Prys Jones, S. (1998) *Encyclopedia of Bilingualism and Bilingual Education*. Clevedon: Multilingual Matters.

Bakhtin, M. (1981) *The Dialogic Imagination: Four Essays*. M. Holquist (ed.) Translation by C. Emerson and M. Holquist. Austin, TX: University of Texas Press.

Barnhardt, R. and Kawagley, A.O. (2005) Indigenous knowledge systems and Alaska Native ways of knowing. *Anthropology and Education Quarterly* 36 (1), 8–23.

Baron, D. (2001) Language legislation and language abuse: American language policy through the 1990s. In R.D. Gonzalez and I. Melis (eds) *Language Ideologies: Critical Perspectives on the Official English Movement* (pp. 5–29). Mahwah, NJ: Lawrence Erlbaum Associates.

Batibo, H. and Smieja, B. (eds) (2000) *Botswana: The Future of Minority Languages*. Frankfurt: Peter Lang.

Bellinghausen, H. (2003) Traducen los acuerdos de San Andrés a diez lenguas indígenas de Chiapas. *La Jornada*, October 25.

Bellinghausen, H. (2004) La fiesta zapatista de la educación abre paso a una enseñanza verdadera. *La Jornada*, August 6.

Benson, C. (2000) The primary bilingual education experiment in Mozambique, 1993 to 1997. *International Journal of Bilingual Education and Bilingualism* 3 (3), 149–166.

Benson, Carol (2004) Do we expect too much of bilingual teachers? Bilingual teaching in developing countries. *International Journal for Bilingual Education and Bilingualism* 7 (2), 204–221.

Berliner, D. and Biddle, B. (1995) *The Manufactured Crisis: Myths, Fraud, and the Attack on America's Public Schools.* Reading, MA: Addison-Wesley Pub. Co.

Berque, J. (1985) *L'immigration à l'école de la République. Rapport au Ministre de l'Education Nationale*. Paris: La Documentation Française.

Bhabha, H.K. (1990) The third space: Interview with Homi Bhabha. In J. Rutherford (ed.) *Identity: Community, Culture, Difference* (pp. 207–221). London: Lawrence & Wishart.

Bhabha, H.K. (1994) *The Location of Culture*. New York: Routledge.

Bhatia, T.K. and Ritchie, W.C. (2004) Bilingualism in South Asia. In T.K. Bhatia and W.C. Ritchie (eds) *The Handbook of Bilingualism.* Malden, MA: Blackwell.

Bialystok, E. (2001) *Bilingualism in Development*. Cambridge: Cambridge University Press.

Biesele, M. and Hitchcock, R. (2000) Ju!'hoan language education in Namibia and its relevance for minority education in Botswana. In H. Batibo and B. Smieja (eds) *Botswana: The Future of Minority Languages* (pp. 237–265). Frankfurt: Peter Lang.

Bishop, R. (2003) Changing power relations in education: Kaupapa Māori messages for 'mainstream' education in Aotearoa/New Zealand. *Comparative Education* 39 (2), 221–238.

Black, B. and Valenzuela, A. (2004) Educational accountability for English language learners in Texas: A retreat from equity. In L. Skrla and J. Scheurich (eds) *Educational Equity and Parity: Paradigms, Policies, and Politics* (pp. 215–234). Albany: SUNY Press.

Blanchard, R.A., Charlie, P., DeGroat, J., Platero, P. and Secatero, S. (2003) Borderlands of identity: Revitalising language and cultural knowledge in a Navajo community living apart. In L. Huss, G. Camilleri, and K.A. King (eds) *Transcending Monolingualism: Linguistic Revitalization in Education* (pp. 193–224). Lisse: Swets and Zeitlinger.

Bloch, C. and Alexander, N. (2003) A luta continua! The relevance of the continua of biliteracy to South African multilingual schools. In Nancy H. Hornberger (ed.) *Continua of Biliteracy: An Ecological Framework for Educational Policy, Research, and Practice in Multilingual Settings* (pp. 91–121). Clevedon: Multilingual Matters.

BO n°4 (2002) Bulletin officiel. Hors Série du 29/8/2002. Paris: MEN-DESCO. On WWW at http://www.education.gouv.fr/bo/2002/hs4/default.htm. Accessed 3.2.2006.

Boal, A. (1979) *The Theatre of the Oppressed*. New York: Urizen Books.

Botswana Language Use Project (1998) *Languages of Botswana*. Gaborone: Botswana Bible Society.

Bourdieu, P. (1977) Economics of linguistic exchanges. *Social Science Information* 16 (6), 645–668.

Bourdieu, P. (1991) *Language and Symbolic Power*. Cambridge: Harvard University Press.

Bourne, J. (2003) Remedial or radical: Second language support for curriculum learning. In J. Bourne and E. Reid (eds) *Language Education* (pp 21–34). London: Kogan Page.

Bransford, J.D., Brown, A.L. and Cocking, R.R. (2000) *How People Learn: Brain, Mind, Experience, and School*. Washington, DC: National Academy Press.

Byrnes, H. (2005) Perspectives. *Modern Language Journal* 89 (2), 248–282.

Cahnmann, M. (1998) Over 30 years of language-in-education policy and planning: Potter Thomas Bilingual School in Philadelphia. *Bilingual Research Journal* 22 (1), 65–81.

Canagarajah, S. (2005) *Reclaiming the Local in Language Policy and Practice*. Mahwah, NJ: Lawrence Erlbaum.

Candelier, M. (2003a) *L'éveil aux langues à l'école primaire. Evlang, bilan d'une innovation européenne*. Bruxelles: De Boeck.

Candelier, M. (ed.) (2003b) *Janua Linguarum: La porte des langues. L'introduction de l'éveil aux langues dans le curriculum*. ECML, Strasbourg : Conseil de l'Europe.

Carder, M. (forthcoming) *A Model for Achieving Bilingualism in International Schools*. Clevedon: Multilingual Matters.

CNEM (Consejo Nacional de Educación Maya) (2004) *Uxe'al Ub'antajik le Mayab' Tijonik. Marco filosófico de la Educación Maya [Philosophical Framework of Mayan Education]*. Guatemala: Maya Na'oj.

Cenoz, J. (2001) The effect of linguistic distance, L2 status and age on cross-linguistic influence in third language acquisition. In J. Cenoz, B. Hufeisen and U. Jessner (eds) *Cross-linguistic Influence on Third Language Acquisition: Psycholinguistic Perspectives* (pp. 8–20). Clevedon: Multilingual Matters.

Central Statistics Office (2001) 2001 Population and Housing Census. Gaborone: Government Printer.

CEPOs (Consejos Educativos de Pueblos Originarios de Bolivia) (2004) *Por una educación indígena originaria. Hacia la autodeterminación ideológica, política, territorial y sociocultural [On the Way to an Indigenous Education. Towards Ideological, Political, Territorial and Socio-cultural Self-determination]*. La Paz: GIG.

Cerquiglini, B. (2003) *Les langues de France*. Paris: PUF.

Chaturvedi, M.G. and Mohale, B.V. (1976) *The Position of Languages in School Curriculum in India*. New Delhi: National Council for Educational Research and Training.

Chebanne, A. (2002) Minority languages and minority people: Issues on linguistic, cultural and ethnic death in Botswana. In I.N. Mazonde (ed.) *Minority in the Millennium: Perspectives from Botswana* (pp 47–55). Gaborone: Lents we la Lased.

Chebanne, A. and Nyati-Ramahobo, L. (2003) 2001 Population and Housing Census Dissemination Seminar, September 8–11, 2003. Gaborone: Central Statistics Office.

Cheng, L., Watanabe, Y. and Curtis, A. (eds) (2004) *Washback in Language Testing: Research contexts and methods*. Mahwah, NJ: Lawrence Erlbaum and Associates.

Chick, K. and McKay, S. (2001) Teaching English in multiethnic schools in the Durban area: The promotion of multilingualism or monolingualism? *Southern African Linguistics and Applied Language Studies* 19 (3&4), 163–178.

Chilora, H. (2000) School language policy, research and practice in Malawi. Paper presented at the Comparative International Education Society Conference. San Antonio, March.

Chow, P. and Cummins, J. (2003) Valuing multilingual and multicultural approaches to learning. In S.R. Schecter and J. Cummins (eds) *Multilingual Education in Practice: Using Diversity as a Resource* (pp. 32–61). Portsmouth, NH: Heinemann.

Churchill, S. (1986) *The Education of Linguistic and Cultural Minorities in the OECD Countries*. Clevedon: Multilingual Matters.

Churchill, W. (1994) *Indians are Us? Culture and Genocide in Native North America*. Monroe, ME: Common Courage Press.

Churchill, W. (1997) *A Little Matter of Genocide: Holocaust and the Denial in the Americas, 1492 to the Present*. San Francisco, CA: City Lights Books.

CIA *The World Factbook*. On WWW at http://www.cia.gov/cia/publications/factbook/geos/pp.html. Accessed 3.10.2006.

Clyne, M. (1991) *Community Languages: The Australian Experience*. Cambridge: Cambridge University Press.

Colinet, J-C. and Morgen, D. (2004) Les langues regionales de France: Etat des lieux à l'automne 2002. In MEN DESCO *Enseigner en classe bilingue* (pp 261–275). Alsace: Actes de l'Université d'Automne, IUFM Alsace. On WWW at http://www.eduscol.education.fr. Accessed 3.2.2006.

Colorado State Legislature (2000) SB00-186. *Education Reform Bill*.

Comisión Paritaria de Reforma Educativa (1998) *Diseño de Reforma Educativa* [Educational Reform Proposal]. Guatemala: MINEDUC.

Common European Framework of Reference for Languages (2002) On WWW at http://www.coe.int/T/E/Cultural_Co-operation/education/Languages/Language_Policy/Common_Framework_of_Reference/1cadre.asp#TopOfPage. Accessed 3.2.2006.

Cook, R. (Revd) (2003) Challenges and breaking through in minority languages: Seven years of language development efforts in Botswana. Paper presented at the Mother Tongue workshop, held at the University of Botswana, February 21–22.

Cornejo, J. and Enríquez, E. (2002) En México, al menos once lenguas indígenas en riesgo de desesaparecer. *La Jornada*. February 22.

Coste, D. (2001) *'La notion de compétence plurilingue': Actes du séminaire: L'enseignement des langues vivantes, perspectives*. Paris: Ministère de la Jeunesse de l'Education et de la Recherche, DES. On WWW at http://www.eduscol. education.fr/DOO33/langviv-acte3.htm. Accessed 3.2.2006.

Costo, R. and Costo, J.H. (eds) (1987) *The Missions of California: A Legacy of Genocide*. San Francisco, CA: Indian Historian Press.

Craig, B.A. (1996) Parental attitudes toward bilingualism in a local two-way immersion program. *Bilingual Research Journal* 20 (3&4), 383–410.

Crawford, J. (1999) Life in a politized climate: What role for the educational researcher? Linguistic Minority Research Institute. Conference on the Schooling of English Language Learners in the Post-227 Era, Sacramento, California. On WWW at http://ourworld.compuserve.com/homepages/jwcrawford/LMRI.htm. Accessed 3.2.2006.

Crawford, J. (2000) *At War with Diversity: US Language Policy in an Age of Anxiety*. Clevedon: Multilingual Matters.

Crawford, J. (2002) Census 2000: A Guide for the Perplexed. On WWW at http://ourworld.compuserve.com/homepages/JWCRAWFORD/census02.htm. Accessed 3.2.2006.

CSAP (1998) *Colorado Student Assessment Program: Final Technical Report*. Monterey, CA: CTB/McGraw-Hill.

Cummins, J. (1981) The role of primary language development in promoting educational success for language minority students. In California State Department of Education (ed.) *Schooling and Language Minority Students. A Theoretical Framework*. Sacramento, CA: California State Department of Education.

Cummins, J. (1984) *Bilingualism and Special Education: Issues in Assessment and Pedagogy*. Clevedon: Multilingual Matters.

Cummins, J. (2000) *Language Power and Pedagogy: Bilingual Children in the Crossfire*. Clevedon: Multilingual Matters.

Cummins, J. (2001) *Negotiating Identities: Education for Empowerment in a Diverse Society* (2nd edn). Ontario, CA: California Association for Bilingual Education.

Cunningham, G. (2000) *Assessment Reform Network Message*. On WWW at ARN-L@LISTS.CUA.EDU. Accessed 10.30.2000.

De Goumoëns, C., De Pietro, J-F. and Jeannot, D. (1999) Des activités d'éveil au langage et d'ouverture aux langues à l'école: Vers une prise en compte des langues minoritaires. *Bulletin Suisse de Linguistique Appliquée* 69/2, 7–30.

De la Torre López, A. (1998) Chanob Vun ta Batz'i K'op ta Sna Jtz'ibajom: An alternative education in our native languages. *Cultural Survival Quarterly* (Spring), 44–45.

Del Valle, S. (2003) *Language Rights and the Law in the United States: Finding Our Voices*. Clevedon: Multilingual Matters.

Dewitte, P. (ed.) (1999) *Immigration et intégration, l'état des savoirs*. Paris: La Découverte.

Dolson, D.P. (2004) Foreign Aid: A language lesson from Bolivia. *Language Magazine* (July), 18–21.

Dorian, N.C. (2004) Minority and endangered languages. In T.K. Bhatia and W.C. Ritchie (eds) *The Handbook of Bilingualism*. Malden, MA: Blackwell.

Dua, H.R. (1994) *Hegemony of English*. Mysore: Yashoda Publications.

Dunbar, R., Skutnabb-Kangas, T., Id Balkassm, H., Nicolaisen, I., Magga, Ole H. and Trask, M.M. (forthcoming) Education of Indigenous children and violations of Articles II(b) and II(e) of the UN Genocide Convention: Expert paper written for the United Nations Permanent Forum on Indigenous Issues. New York: United Nations.

Durán, R.P., Durán, J., Perry-Romero, D. and Sánchez, E. (2001) Latino immigrant parents and children learning and publishing together in an after-school setting. *Journal of Education for Students Placed at Risk* 6 (1&2), 95–113.

Dutcher, N. (1995) *The Use of First and Second Languages in Education. A Review of International Experience. Pacific Islands Discussion Paper Series Number 1: East Asia and Pacific Region-Country Department III*. Washington, DC: The World Bank.

Early, M., Cummins, J. and Willinsky, J. (2002) From literacy to multiliteracies: Designing learning environments for knowledge generation within the new economy. Proposal funded by the Social Sciences and Humanities Research Council of Canada.

Edwards, V. (2001) Community languages in the United Kingdom. In G. Extra and D. Gorter (eds) *The Other Languages of Europe* (pp. 243–60). Clevedon: Multilingual Matters.

Edwards, V. (2004) *Multilingualism in the English-speaking World: Pedigree of Nations.* Oxford: Blackwell.
Edwards, V. and Pritchard Newcombe, L. (2003) Evaluation of the efficiency and effectiveness of the *Twf* Project, which encourages parents to transmit the language to their children. Cardiff: Welsh Language Board.
Edwards, V. and Pritchard Newcombe, L. (2005a) Language transmission in the family in Wales: An example of innovative language planning. *Journal of Language Problems and Language Planning* 29 (2), 135–50.
Edwards, V. and Pritchard Newcombe, L. (2005b) When school is not enough: Initiatives in intergenerational language transmission in Wales. *International Journal of Bilingualism and Bilingual Education* 8 (4), 298–312.
Encuesta Sociolinguistica (1996) Departamento de Educacón, Universidad e Investigación.Vitoria: Gobierno Vasco.
Escamilla, K., Aragon, L., Grassi, E., Riley-Bernal, H., Rutledge, D. and Walker, D. (2000) *Limited English Proficient Students and the Colorado Student Assessment Program (CSAP): The State of the State.* Denver: Colorado Association for Bilingual Education.
Escamilla, K., Mahon, E., Riley-Bernal, H. and Rutledge, D. (2001) *Limited English Proficient Students and the Colorado Student Assessment Program (CSAP): The State of the State, 2000–2001.* Denver: Colorado Association for Bilingual Education.
Escamilla, K., Chavez, L., Fitts, S., Mahon, E. and Vigil, P. (2002) *Limited English Proficient Students and the Colorado Student Assessment Program (CSAP): The State of the State, 2001–2002.* Denver: Colorado Association for Bilingual Education.
Escamilla, K., Mahon, E., Riley-Bernal, H. and Rutledge, D. (2003a) High-stakes testing, Latinos and English language learners: Lessons from Colorado. *Bilingual Research Journal,* 27 (1), 25–49.
Escamilla, K., Chavez, L., Fitts, S., Mahon, E. and Vigil, P. (2003b) *Limited English Proficient Students and the Colorado Student Assessment Program (CSAP): The State of the State, 2002–2003.* Denver: Colorado Association for Bilingual Education.
Escobar, M. (1985) *Paulo Freire y la educación liberadora.* México: SEP/Caballito.
Escobar, M. (1998) *Educación alternativa, pedagogía de la pregunta y participación estudiantil.* México: UNAM.
Espi, M.J. (1988) Adquisición de segundas lenguas en situación de lenguas en contacto. Un análisis psicosocio-lingüístico. Unpublished doctoral thesis. San Sebastián: University of the Basque Country.
Estrada, L. (1979) A chronicle of the political, legislative and judicial advances of bilingual education in California. In R.V. Padilla (ed.) *Bilingual Education and Public Policy in the United States* (pp. 97–108). Eastern Michigan University: Bilingual Bicultural Education Programs.
Ethnologue: Languages of the World (2005) Statistical summaries. On WWW at http://www.ethnologue.com/ethno_docs/distribution.asp?by=size. Accessed 3.2.2006.
Etxeberría, F., Dendaluze, I., Bereziartua, J., Picabea, I. and Mendia, P. (2002) Percepción y autovaloración de la adquisición bilingüe. Presented at the Second International Symposium on Bilingualism. University of Vigo, Galicia, Spain.
EUSTAT (2004) Vitoria, Euscadi. On WWW at http://www.eustat.es. Accessed 3.2.2006.
Evans, S. (2002) Macaulay's minute revisited: Colonial language policy in nineteenth-century India. *Journal of Multilingual and Multicultural Development* 23 (4), 260–281.
Extra, G. and Yagmur, K. (2004) *Urban Multilingualism in Europe. Immigrant Minority Languages at Home and at School.* Clevedon: Multilingual Matters.

EZLN (2003) Speeches at Oventic. August 8.

Fairclough, N. (ed.) (1992) *Critical Language Awareness*. New York: Longman.

Ferdman, B.M. (1999) Ethnic and minority issues in literacy. In D.A. Wagner, R.L. Venezky and B.V. Street (eds) *Literacy: An International Handbook* (pp. 95–101). Boulder: Westview.

Fillmore, L.W. (2005) Promises to keep: The education of bilingual children under No Child Left Behind. Presentation at the National Association for Bilingual Education Annual Conference, San Antonio, January 21.

Finlayson, R. and Slabbert, S. (2004) LiEP and a rights-based approach to education: How possible is this? Paper presented at the International Conference of the Southern African Applied Linguistics Association (SAALA), University of Limpopo.

Fishman, J.A. (1972) *The Sociology of Language*. Rowley: Newbury House.

Fishman, J. (1991) *Reversing Language Shift: Theoretical and Empirical Foundations of Assistance to Threatened Languages*. Clevedon: Multilingual Matters.

Fishman, J.A. and Lovas, J. (1970) Bilingual education in sociolinguistic perspective. *TESOL Quarterly* 4, 215–222.

FOMMA (Fortaleza de la Mujer Maya) website (2004) At www.fomma.org. Accessed 3.2.2006.

Fordham, S. (1990) Racelessness as a factor in Black students' school success: Pragmatic strategy or Pyrrhic victory? In N.M. Hidalgo, C.L. McDowell and E.V. Siddle (eds) *Facing Racism in Education* (reprint series 21; pp. 232–262). Harvard: Harvard Educational Review.

Francis, N. and Hamel, R.E. (1992) La redacción en dos lenguas. Escritura y narrativa en tres escuelas bilingües del Valle del Mezquital [Writing in two languages. writing and narrative in three bilingual schools of the Mezquital Valley]. *Revista Latinoamericana de Estudios Educativos* 22, 11–36.

Francis, N. and Reyhner, J. (2002) *Language and Literacy Teaching for Indigenous Education: A Bilingual Approach*. Clevedon: Multilingual Matters.

Freeman, R.D. (2004) *Building on Community Bilingualism*. Philadelphia: Caslon Publishing.

Freeman, Y.S., Freeman, D.E. and Mercuri, S.P. (2005) *Dual Language Essentials for Teachers and Administrators*. Portsmouth, NH: Heinemann.

Freire, P. (1973a) *Education for Critical Consciousness*. New York: Seabury.

Freire, P. (1973b) *Pedagogy of the Oppressed* (rev. edn; M.B. Ramos, trans.). New York: Continuum.

Gaglioti, F. (1999) Aboriginal bilingual education axed in Australia's Northern Territory. *World Socialist*, 10 April. On WWW at www.wsws.org/articles/1999/apr1999/educ-a10.shtml. Accessed 3.2.2006.

Gajo, L. (2001) *Immersion, Bilinguisme et Interaction en classe*. Paris: Didier.

Garcia, E.E. (2004) Undoing the promise of *Lau*: Proposition 227, 203, and the new restrictions on access to equal opportunity. Paper presented at the Annual Conference of the American Educational Research Association, San Diego.

García, M.E. (2004) Rethinking bilingual education in Peru: Intercultural politics, state policy and indigenous rights. *International Journal for Bilingual Education and Bilingualism* 7 (5), 348–367.

García, O. (1992) Societal bilingualism and multilingualism. Unpublished document, City University of New York, New York.

García, O. (1997) Bilingual education. In F. Coulmas (ed.) *The Handbook of Sociolinguistics* (pp. 405–420). Oxford: Basil Blackwell.

García, O. (2006) Lost in transculturation: The case of bilingual education in New York City. In M. Pütz, J. Fishman and J. Neff-van Aertselaer (eds) *Along the Routes to Power: Explorations of the Empowerment Through Language* (pp. 157–178). Berlin and New York: Mouton de Gruyter.

García, O. and Baker, C. (1995) *Policy and Practice in Bilingual Education*. Clevedon: Multilingual Matters.

García, O. and Bartlett, L. (forthcoming) A speech community model of bilingual education: Educating Latino newcomers in the United States. *International Journal of Bilingual Education and Bilingualism.*

García, O., Bartlett, L. and Kleifgen, J. (forthcoming) From biliteracy to pluriliteracies. In P. Auer and L. Wei (eds) *Handbooks of Applied Linguistics* (Vol. 5): *Multilingualism.* Berlin: Mouton de Gruyter.

García, O. and Traugh, C. (2002) Using descriptive inquiry to transform the education of linguistically diverse U.S. teachers and students. In L. Wei, J-M. Dewaele and A. Housen (eds) *Opportunities and Challenges of (Societal) Bilingualism* (pp. 311–328). Berlin: Walter de Gruyter.

García Huidobro, J.E. (1985) La educación popular. In P. Latapi and A. Castillo (eds) *Lecturas Sobre Educación de Adultos en América Latina*. México: CREFAL.

Gardner, R.C. (1985) *Social Psychology and Second Language Learning*. London: Edward Arnold.

Garvin, P. and Matthiot, M. (1968) The urbanization of the Guarani language. In J. Fishman (ed.) *Readings in the Sociology of Language* (pp. 365–374). Berlin: Mouton de Gruyter.

Gee, J.P. (2001) Identity as an analytic lens for research in education. In W. G. Secada (ed.) *Review of Research in Education* 25 (99–126). Washington, DC: American Educational Research Association.

Genelot, S. (2002) Evaluation quantitative du cursus Evlang (Rapport de recherche du programme Evlang remis à la Commission Européenne). On WWW at http://jaling.ecml.at-pdfdocs-evlang-evlang4.pdf. Accessed 3.2.2006.

Gochicoa, E. (1996) *Función social y significado de la educación comunitaria. Una sociología de la educación no formal*. México: UNICEF.

Gonzáles, J.M. (1975) Coming of age in bilingual/bicultural education: A historical perspective. *Inequality in Education* 19, 5–17.

González, F.M. and Pérez, P.E. (1998) Indigenous rights and schooling in highland Chiapas. *Cultural Survival Quarterly* (Spring), 41–43.

González, M.L. (1994) How many indigenous people? In G. Psacharopoulos and H. Patrinos (eds) *Indigenous People and Poverty in Latin America: An Empirical Analysis* (pp. 21–39). World Bank Regional and Sectorial Studies. Washington, DC: The World Bank.

González, M. (2002) The Zapatistas: The challenges of revolution in a new millennium. In T. Hayden (ed.) *The Zapatista Reader* (pp. 430–451). New York: Nation Books.

Goodz, N. (1994) Interactions between parents and children. In F. Genesee (ed.) *Educating Second Language Children: The Whole Child, The Whole Curriculum, The Whole Community* (pp. 61–81). Cambridge: Cambridge University Press.

Gordon, B. (2001) On high-stakes testing. *Division Generator* (Autumn), 1–4.

Gottlieb, M. (2001) *The Language Proficiency Handbook: A Practitioners Guide to Instructional Assessment.* Springfield, IL: Illinois State Board of Education.

Government of India, Ministry of HRD (2003) *Selected Information on School Education in India.* New Delhi: Government of India.

Greene, M. (1988) *The Dialectic of Freedom.* New York: Teachers College Press.

Greene, M. (2000) *Releasing the Imagination: Essays on Education, the Arts, and Social Change*. San Francisco, CA: Jossey-Bass Publishers.

Gregory, E. and Williams, A. (2000) *City Literacies: Learning to Read across Generations and Cultures*. New York: Routledge.

Grosjean, F. (1982) *Life with Two Languages: An Introduction to Bilingualism*. Cambridge, MA: Harvard University Press.

Gruffudd, H. (2000) Planning for the use of Welsh by young people. In C. Williams (ed.) *Language Revitalisation* (pp. 173–207). Cardiff: University of Wales Press.

Guatemala Instituto Nacional de Estadística (2003) *Características de la población y de los locales de habitación censados* [*Characteristics of the Population and of the Houses included in the Census*]. Guatemala: INE & UNFPA.

Guatemala Ministerio de Educación (2005) *Curriculum Nacional Base* [*Basic National Curriculum*]. Guatemala: DICADE.

Gundaker, G. (forthcoming) Hidden education among enslaved African Americans. In H. Varenne (ed.) Searching for education in everyday life. anthropological explorations into hidden processes of deliberate change. Unpublished manuscript.

Gutiérrez, K., Baquedano-López, P. and Alvarez, H. (2001) Literacy as hybridity. In M. de la Luz Reyes and J.J. Halcón (eds) *The Best for Our Children* (pp. 122–141). New York: Teachers College Press.

Hamel, R.E. (1994) Indigenous education in Latin America: Policies and legal frameworks. In T. Skutnabb-Kangas and R. Phillipson (eds) *Linguistic Human Rights: Overcoming linguistic discrimination* (271–287). Berlin: Mouton de Gruyter.

Hamel, R.E. (ed) (1997) Linguistic human rights from a sociolinguistic perspective. *International Journal of the Sociology of Language* 127 (entire issue).

Hamel, R.E. and Sierra, M.T. (1983) Diglosia y conflicto intercultural: la lucha por un concepto o la danza de los significantes [Diglossia and intercultural conflict: struggles towards a concept or the dance of the signifiers]. *Boletín de Antropología Americana* 8, 89–110.

Hamers, J. (1992) Comportement linguistique et développement bilingue. In F. Etxeberría and J. Arzamendi (eds) *Bilingüismo y adquisición de lenguas*. Bilbao: Universidad del País Vasco.

Hamers, J. and Michel, B. (2000) *Bilinguality and Bilingualism*. Cambridge: Cambridge University Press.

Harding, S. (1998) *Is Science Multicultural? Postcolonialisms, Feminisms, and Epistemologies*. Bloomington: Indiana University Press.

Harmon, D. (1995) The status of the world's languages as reported in the *Ethnologue*. *Southwest Journal of Linguistics* 14 (1&2), 1–28.

Harmon, D. (2002) *In Light of Our Differences: How Diversity in Nature and Culture Makes Us Human*. Washington, DC: The Smithsonian Institute Press.

Harris, S. (1990) *Two Way Aboriginal Schooling: Education and Cultural Survival*. Canberra: Aboriginal Studies Press.

Harvey, D. (2005) *The New Imperialism*. Oxford: Oxford University Press.

Hasselbring, S. (2000) *A Sociolinguistic Survey of the Languages of Botswana: Sociolinguistic Studies of Botswana Languages Series* (Vol. 1). Gaborone: Tasalls Publishing and Books.

Hasselbring, S., Segatlhe, T. and Munch, J. (2001) *A Sociolinguistic Survey of the Languages of Botswana: Sociolinguistic Studies of Botswana Series* (Vol. 2). Gaborone: Tasalls Publishing and Books.

Haviland, J.B. (1981) *Sk'op sotz'leb: El Tzotzil de San Lorenzo Zinacantán*. Mexico: Universidad Nacional Autónoma de México.

Hawkins, E. (1984) *Awareness of Language: An Introduction.* Cambridge: Cambridge University Press.

Hawkins, M.R. (2004) Researching English language and literacy development in schools. *Educational Researcher* 33 (3), 14–25.

Heller, M. (1982) Negotiations of language choice in Montreal. In J. Gumperz (ed.) *Language and Social Identity* (pp. 108–118). Cambridge: Cambridge University Press.

Heller, M. (1995) Language choice, social institutions, and symbolic domination. *Language in Society* 24, 373–405.

Heller, M. (2002) *Eléments d'une sociolinguistique critique.* Paris: Didier.

Hélot, C. (2003) Language policy and the ideology of bilingual education in France. *Language Policy* 2, 255–277.

Hélot, C. (2005) Bridging the gap between prestigious bilingualism and the bilingualism of minorities: Towards an integrated perspective of multilingualism in the French education context. In M. Ó Laoire (ed.) *Multilingualism in Educational Settings.* Tübingen: Stauffenburg Verlag.

Hélot, C. and Young, A. (2002) Bilingualism and language education in French primary schools: Why and how should migrant languages be valued? *International Journal of Bilingual Education and Bilingualism* 5 (2), 96–112.

Hernández-Chávez, E. (1994) Language policy in the United States: A history of cultural genocide. In T. Skutnabb-Kangas and R. Phillipson (eds) in collaboration with M. Rannut *Linguistic Human Rights: Overcoming Linguistic Discrimination* (pp. 141–158). Berlin: Mouton de Gruyter.

Heugh, K. (2000) *The Case Against Bilingual and Multilingual Education in South Africa.* Cape Town: PRAESA.

Heugh, K. (2004) SLA, assessment and transformation in the new (revised) curriculum: Where are we? Paper presented at the International Conference of the Southern African Applied Linguistics Association (SAALA), University of Limpopo.

Hinton, L. and Hale, K. (eds) (2001) *The Green Book of Language Revitalization in Practice.* San Diego, CA: Academic Press.

Holm, A. and Holm, W. (1995) Navajo language education: Retrospect and Prospects. *Bilingual Research Journal,* 19 (1), 141–167.

hooks, b. (1990) *Yearning: Race, Gender and Cultural Politics.* Boston: South End Press.

Hornberger, N.H. (2002) Multilingual language policies and the continua of biliteracy: An ecological approach. *Language Policy* 1 (1), 27–51.

Hornberger, N.H. (ed.) (2003) *Continua of Biliteracy: An Ecological Framework for Educational Policy, Research, and Practice in Multilingual Settings.* Clevedon: Multilingual Matters.

Hornberger, N.H. and King, K. (1999) Authenticity and unification in Quechua language planning. In S. May (ed.) *Indigenous Community-Based Education* (pp. 160–180). Clevedon: Multilingual Matters.

Hornberger, N.H. and López, L.E. (1998) Policy, possibility and paradox: Indigenous multilingualism and education in Peru and Bolivia. In J. Cenoz and F. Genesee (eds) *Beyond Bilingualism: Multilingualism and Multilingual Education* (pp. 206–242). Clevedon: Multilingual Matters.

Horstman, P.M. and Jackson-Dennison, D. (2005) Perspectives on the implications of Proposition 203 and the *Flores* decision for Navajo language use in Arizona schools. Presentation at the Arizona Language Minority Rights Research Roundtable of Arizona, Arizona State University, Tempe, January 28.

Horton, M. (1997) *The Long Haul: An Autobiography.* New York: Teachers College Press.

Howard, E.R. and Loeb, M.I. (1998) *In Their own Words: Two-way Immersion Teachers Talk about their Professional Experiences* (ERIC Digest EDO-FL-98-14). Washington, DC: ERIC Clearinghouse on Languages and Linguistics. On WWW at http://www.cal.org/ericcll/digest/intheirownwords.html. Accessed 3.2.2006.

Howard, E.R., Sugarman, J. and Christian, D. (2003) *Trends in Two-Way Immersion Education: A Review of the Research. Baltimore, MD: Center for Research on the Education of Students Placed at Risk* (CRESPAR), Johns Hopkins University. Online at www.csos.jhu.edu/crespar/techReports/Reports63.pdf. Accessed 3.2.2006.

Howard, R., Barbira-Freedman, F. and Stobart, H. (2002) Introduction. In H. Stobart and R. Howard (eds) *Knowledge and Learning in the Andes: Ethnographic Perspectives. Liverpool Latin American Studies. New Series* 3 (pp. 1–13). Liverpool: Liverpool University Press.

Hull, G. and Schultz, K. (2001) Literacy and learning out of school: A review of theory and research. *Review of Educational Research* 71 (4), 575–612.

Hull, G. and Schultz, K. (eds) (2002) *School's Out! Bridging Out-of-school Literacies with Classroom Practice.* New York: Teachers College Press.

ICSU (2002) Science education and capacity building for sustainable development. S. Malcom, A.M. Cetto, D. Dickson, J. Gaillard and Y. Quéré. *Science for Sustainable Development* 5. Paris: International Council for Science.

INED: Institut National d' Etudes Démographiques (1999) *Enquête familles.* On WWW at http://www.ined.fr. Accessed 3.2.2006.

Irvine, J. (1998) Ideologies of honorific language. In B. Schieffelin, K.A. Woolard, and P. Kroskrity (eds) *Language Ideologies: Practice and Theory* (pp. 51–67). New York: Oxford University Press.

Jiménez, A. (2004) Reconocen a asociación que rescata y difunde cultura y lenguas Mayas. *La Jornada,* October 24.

Jiménez, R.T. (2003) Literacy and Latino students in the United States: Some considerations, questions and new directions. *Reading Research Quarterly* 38, 122–128.

Johnson, D.C. (2004) Language policy discourse and bilingual language planning. *Working Papers in Educational Linguistics* 19 (2), 73–97.

Johnson, F. and Wilson, J. (2005) Tséhootsooí Diné Bi'ólta', Diné language immersion school. Presentation at the National Association for Bilingual Education Annual Conference, San Antonio, January 21.

Joseph, M. and Ramani, E. (2004) Cummins' four quadrants: A pedagogic framework for developing academic excellence in the new bilingual degree at the University of the North. Paper presented at the international Conference of the Southern African Applied Linguistics Association (SAALA), University of Limpopo.

Juan, M.J.B. (2003) Modern nomad. *100°* (September), 26–30.

Kachru, B.B. (1986) *The Alchemy of English: The Spread, Functions and Models of Non-Native Englishes.* Oxford: Pergamon.

Kamanā, K. and Wilson, W.H. (1996) Hawaiian language programs. In G. Cantoni (ed.) *Stabilizing Indigenous Languages* (pp. 153–156). Flagstaff: Northern Arizona University Center for Excellence in Education.

Karmani, S. (2005a) Islam and English in the post-9/11 era: Introduction. *Journal of Language, Identity and Education* 4 (2), 87–102.

Karmani, S. (2005b) Petro-linguistics: The emerging nexus between oil, English, and Islam. *Journal of Language, Identity and Education* 4 (2), 85–86.

Kazombungo, J. (2000) Ghanzi District Farm Workers' Project: Successes and problems. Report on a three-day conference on the Education for Remote Area Dwellers: Problems and Perspectives. Gaborone: University of Botswana Research and Development Unit and Regional San Project of the Working Group on Indigenous Minorities in Southern Africa (WIMSA).

Khubchandani, L.M. (1978) Distribution of contact languages in India. In Joshua A. Fishman (ed.) *Advances in the Study of Societal Multilingualism*. The Hague: Mouton.

Khubchandani, L.M. (1983) *Plural Languages, Plural Cultures*. Hawaii: East–West Centre.

Khubchandani, L.M. (1986) Multilingual societies: Issues of identity and communication. *Sociolinguistics*, XVI (1), 20–34.

King, L. (ed.) (1998) *Reflecting Visions: New Perspectives on Adult Education for Indigenous Peoples*. Waikato: University of Waikato.

Kloss, H. (1977) *The American Bilingual Tradition*. Rowley, MA: Newbury House.

Kloss, H. (1998) *American Bilingual Tradition*. Washington, DC: Center for Applied Linguistics and Delta Systems.

Komarek, K. and Keatimilwe, G. (1988) Language competence and educational achievement in primary schools in Botswana: Part II. *Aligemeine Bildung, Wissenchaft und Sprot. Journal of the Deutsche Gesellschaft fur Technische Zusammenharbeit* (GTZ).

Kotler, P., Armstrong, G., Saunders, J. and Wong, V. (1999) *Principles of Marketing* (2nd European edn). London: Prentice Hall Europe.

Koul, O.N. and Devaki, L. (2000) Multilingual education in India: Concepts and strategies. In O.N. Koul and L.Devaki (eds) *Linguistic Heritage of India and Asia* (pp. 110–129). Mysore: Central Institute of Indian Languages.

Koul, O.N. and Devaki, L. (2001) Medium of instruction across levels of education in India. In C.J. Daswani (ed.) *Language Education in Multilingual India* (pp. 104–116). New Delhi: UNESCO.

Kourtis-Kazoullis, V. (2002) DiaLogos: Bilingualism and the teaching of second language learning on the Internet. Unpublished doctoral dissertation, University of the Aegean, Primary Education Department, Rhodes.

Krashen, S.D. (1985) *The Input Hypothesis: Issues and Implications*. London: Longman.

Krashen, S.D. (1992) Sink-or-swim success stories and bilingual education. In J. Crawford (ed.) *Language Loyalties: A Source Book on the Official English Controversy* (pp. 354–57). Chicago: University of Chicago Press.

Krashen, S.D. (2003) *Explorations in Language Acquisition and Use*. Portsmouth, NH: Heinemann.

Krashen, S.D. (2004) *The Power of Reading: Insights from the Research* (2nd edn). Portsmouth, NH: Heinemann.

Krashen, S.D. Stephen Krashen's mailing list. On WWW at http://sdkrashen.com/mailman/listinfo/krashen_sdkrashen.com. Accessed 3.2.2006.

Krauss, M. (1998) The condition of Native North American languages: The need for realistic assessment and action. *International Journal of the Sociology of Language* 132, 9–21.

Krauss, M., Maffi, L. and Yamamoto, A. (2004) The world's languages in crisis: Questions, challenges, and a call for action. In O. Sakiyama, F. Endo, H. Watanabe and F. Sasama (eds) *Lectures on Endangered Languages* 4 (pp. 23–27). Osaka: The Project 'Endangered Languages of the Pacific Rim'.

Kress, G.R. and Leeuwen, T.V. (1996) *Reading Images: The Grammar of Visual Design*. London: Routledge.

Lambert, W.E. (1974) Culture and language as factors in learning and education. In F.E. Aboud and R.D. Meade (eds) *Cultural Factors in Learning and Education*, Bellingham, WA: 5th Western Washington Symposium on Learning.
Lambert, W.E. (1980) The social psychology of language. In W.H. Giles, P. Robinson and P.M. Smith (eds) *Language: Social Psychological Perspectives* (pp. 415–424). Oxford: Pergamon.
Lang, J. (2001) *L'évolution des dispositifs d'enseignement des langues et cultures d'origine.* On WWW at http://www.education.gouv.fr/discours/2001/evolangue.htm. Accessed 3.2.2006.
Lasagabaster, D. (2001) Bilingualism, immersion programmes and language learning in the Basque Country. *Journal of Multilingual and Multicultural Development* 22, 401–425.
Laughlin, R. (1975) *The Great Tzotzil Dictionary of San Lorenzo Zinacantán.* Washington, DC: Smithsonian Institution Press.
Laughlin, R. (2002) The Mayan renaissance: Sna Jtz'ibajom, The house of the writer. *Cultural Survival Quarterly* 17 (4), 8–10.
Laughlin, R. (2004) Maya literacy project taking its lessons to Mexican universities. *Cultural Survival Quarterly* (Winter), 65.
Lave, J. and Wenger, E. (1991) *Situated Learning: Legitimate Peripheral Participation.* Cambridge: Cambridge University Press.
Le Monde (2004) Faut-il rendre l'apprentissage de l'anglais obligatoire dès le CE2? *Le Monde* 22 November.
Legendre, J. (2004) *Rapport d'information sur l'enseignement des langues étrangères en France.* N° 63. Online at www.senat.fr/rap/r03-63/r03-0631.pdf. Accessed 3.2.2006.
Lenhart, F. (2003) *Dialogue on English Language Acquisition: Conference with the Field.* Denver, CO: Colorado Department of Education.
Leoni, L. and Cohen, S. (2004) Bringing students' identity to the fore of literacy. Paper presented at the Conference on Cultural Diversity and Language Education, University of Hawaii, September.
Levin, T., Shohamy, E. and Spolsky, B. (2003) Academic achievement of immigrant students in Hebrew and mathematics: Report (in Hebrew) submitted to the Ministry of Education, Jerusalem, Israel.
Liebowitz, A.H. (1980) *The Bilingual Education Act: A Legislative Analysis.* Washington, DC: National Clearinghouse for Bilingual Education.
Lindholm-Leary, K.J. (2001) *Dual Language Education.* Clevedon: Multilingual Matters.
Lomawaima, K.T. and McCarty, T.L. (2002) When tribal sovereignty challenges democracy: American Indian education and the democratic ideal. *American Educational Research Journal* 39 (2), 279–305.
Lomawaima, K.T. and McCarty, T.L. (2006) *To Remain an Indian: Lessons in Democracy from a Century of Native American Education.* New York: Teachers College Press.
López, L.E. (1998) La eficacia y validez de lo obvio: Lecciones aprendidas desde la evaluación de procesos educativos bilingües [The efficacy and validity of the obvious. Lessons learnt from the evaluation of bilingual educational processes]. *Revista Iberoamericana de Educación* (Madrid) 17, 51–90.
López, L.E. (2001) Literacies and intercultural education in the Andes. In D. Olson and N. Torrance (eds) *Literacy and Social Development: The Making of Literate Societies* (pp. 201–224). Oxford: Blackwell.
López, L.E. (2006) *De resquicios a boquerones: Análisis de la educación intercultural bilingüe en Bolivia* [*From Fissures to Craters: Analysis of Intercultural Bilingual Education in Bolivia*]. La Paz: Plural.

López, L.E. and Jung, I. (2003) 'Hay se termina este chiquitito cuentito'. Informe de un estudio piloto comparativo sobre la relación entre el habla y la escritura en el aprendizaje de una segunda lengua['That's where that little story ends'. Report on a pilot comparative study on the relationship between speech and writing in second language learning]. In I. Jung and L.E. López (eds) *Abriendo la escuela* [*Opening up the School*]. Madrid: Ediciones Morata.

López, L.E. and Küper, W. (2004) *La Educación Intercultural Bilingüe en América Latina: Balance y Perspectivas* (2nd edn). La Paz-Cochabamba: Cooperación Técnica Alemana (GTZ)-PINSEIB-PROEIBAndes.

Lowell, A. and Devlin, B. (1999) Miscommunication between Aboriginal students and their non-Aboriginal teachers in a bilingual school. In S. May (ed.) *Indigenous Community-Based Education* (pp. 137–159). Clevedon: Multilingual Matters.

Luke, A. (2005) Evidence-based state literacy policy: A critical alternative. In N. Bascia, A. Cumming, A. Datnow, K. Leithwood and D. Livingstone (eds) *International Handbook of Educational Policy* 2, 661–677. Amsterdam: Springer.

Lukusa, S.T. (2000) The Shekgalagadi struggle for survival: Aspects of language maintenance and shift. In H. Batibo and B. Smieja (eds) *Botswana: The Future of Minority Languages* (pp. 55–78). Frankfurt: Peter Lang.

Mackey, W.F. (1972) A typology of bilingual education. In J.A. Fishman (ed.) *Advances in the Sociology of Language* 2, 413–432. The Hague: Mouton and Co.

Maffi, L. (2000) Language preservation vs. language maintenance and revitalization: Assessing concepts, approaches, and implications for language sciences. *International Journal of the Sociology of Languages* 142, 175–190.

Maffi, L. (2001a) Introduction. In L. Maffi (ed.) *On Biocultural Diversity: Linking Language, Knowledge and the Environment* (pp. 1–50). Washington, DC: The Smithsonian Institute Press.

Maffi, L. (ed.) (2001b) *On Biocultural Diversity: Linking Language, Knowledge and the Environment*. Washington, DC: The Smithsonian Institute Press.

Magga, O.H. and Skutnabb-Kangas, T. (2003) Life or death for languages and human beings: Experiences from Saamiland. In L. Huss, A. Camilleri Grima and K. King (eds) *Transcending Monolingualism: Linguistic Revitalisation in Education* (pp. 35–52). Lisse: Swets and Zeitlinger.

Magga, O.H., Nicolaisen, I., Trask, M., Dunbar, R. and Skutnabb-Kangas, T. (2005) Indigenous children's education and indigenous languages. Expert paper written for the United Nations Permanent Forum on Indigenous Issues. New York: United Nations.

Malete, L. (2003) School attendance and drop out rates by age, gender and region: 2001 Census. 2001 Population and Housing Census Dissemination seminar, September 8–11. Gaborone: Central Statistics Office.

Marainen, J. (1988) Returning to Sami identity. In T. Skutnabb-Kangas and J. Cummins (eds) *Minority Education: From Shame to Struggle* (pp. 179–185). Clevedon: Multilingual Matters.

Marcos (1998) Above and below: Masks and silences. *Communiqué*, July 18.

Martin, I. (2000a) Aajjiqatigiingniq: Language of instruction research paper. A report to the Government of Nunavut. Department of Education, Iqaluit, Nunavut, Canada. Unpublished. Ian Martin's Nunavut reports on WWW at http://www.gov.nu.ca/education/eng/pubdoc/ENG%20LOI%20Report.pdf. Accessed 3.2.2006.

Martin, I. (2000b) Sources and issues: A backgrounder to the discussion paper on language of instruction in Nunavut Schools. Manuscript. Department of Education, Nunavut.

Maslow, A. (1968/1999) *Towards a Psychology of Being* (3rd edn). New York: John Wiley and Sons.

May, S. (ed.) (1999) *Indigenous Community-based Education*. Clevedon: Multilingual Matters.

May, S. (2003) Misconceiving minority language rights: Implications for liberal political theory. In W. Kymlicka and A. Patten (eds) *Language Rights and Political Theory* (pp. 123–152). Oxford: Oxford University Press.

McCarty, T.L. (1993a) Federal language policy and American Indian education. *Bilingual Research Journal* 17 (1 & 2), 13–34.

McCarty, T.L. (1993b) Language, literacy, and the image of the child in American Indian classrooms. *Language Arts* 70, 182–192.

McCarty, T.L. (2002) Between possibility and constraint: Indigenous language education, planning, and policy in the United States. In J.W. Tollefson (ed.) *Language Policies in Education: Critical Issues* (pp. 285–307). Mahwah, NJ: Lawrence Erlbaum.

McCarty, T.L. (2003) Revitalising indigenous languages in homogenising times. *Comparative Education* 39 (2), 147–163.

McCarty, T.L. (2005a) Introduction: The continuing power of the 'Great Divide'. In T.L. McCarty (ed.) *Language, Literacy, and Power in Schooling* (pp. xv–xxvii). Mahwah, NJ: Lawrence Erlbaum.

McCarty, T.L. (2005b) The power within: Indigenous literacies and teacher empowerment. In T.L. McCarty (ed.) *Language, Literacy, and Power in Schooling* (pp. 47–66). Mahwah, NJ: Lawrence Erlbaum.

McCarty, T.L. (ed.) (2005c) *Language, Literacy, and Power in Schooling*. Mahwah, NJ: Lawrence Erlbaum.

McCarty, T.L., Romero, M.E. and Zapeda, O. (2006) Reclaiming the gift: Indigenous youth counter-narratives on native language loss and revitalization. *American Indian Quarterly* 30 (1&2), 28–48.

McCarty, T.L. and Watahomigie, L. (1999) Indigenous community-based education in the USA. In S. May (ed.) *Indigenous Community-Based Education* (pp. 79–94). Clevedon: Multilingual Matters.

McLaughlin, M. and Shepard, L. (1995) *Improving Education Through Standards Based Reform*. Washington, DC: National Academy of Education.

McNamara, T. (1997) Policy and social considerations in language assessment. In B. Grabe (ed.) *Annual Review of Applied Linguistics* 18, 304–319.

McQuillan, J. and Tse, L. (1996) Does research really matter? An analysis of media opinion on bilingual education, 1984–1994. *Bilingual Research Journal* 20 (1), 1–27.

MEN (2003) *Qu'apprend-on à l'école élémentaire: Les Nouveaux Programmes*. Paris: CNDP: XO Editions.

Menchú, R. (1984) *I Rigoberta Menchu: An Indian Woman from Guatemala*. London: Verso.

Menken, K. (2000) What are the critical issues in wide-scale assessment of English Language Learners? *Issues in Brief* 6. Washington, DC: National Clearinghouse for Bilingual Education.

Mignolo, W. (2000) *Local Histories/Global Designs: Coloniality, Subaltern Knowledges, and Border Thinking*. Princeton, NJ: Princeton University Press.

Milloy, J.S. (1999) *A National Crime: The Canadian Government and the Residential School System 1879–1986*. Winnipeg: University of Manitoba Press.

Milon, J. (1989) Discourse in primary English in Botswana. Report submitted to the German Foundation for International Development, Gaborone.

Ministry of Human Resource Development (1990) *Report of the Acharya Ramamurti Committee for Review of the National Policy on Education.* New Delhi: Government of India.

Modiano, N. (1973) *Indian Education in the Chiapas Highlands.* New York: Holt, Rinehart, and Winston.

Mohanty, A.K. (1982a) Cognitive and linguistic development of tribal children from unilingual and bilingual environment. In R. Rath, H.S. Asthana, D. Sinha and J.B.P. Sinha (eds) *Diversity and Unity in Cross-Cultural Psychology* (pp. 78–86). Lisse: Swet & Zeitlinger.

Mohanty, A.K. (1982b) Bilingualism among Kond tribals in Orissa (India): Consequences, issues and implications. *Indian Psychologist* 1, 33–44.

Mohanty, A.K. (1987) Social psychological aspects of assimilation/integration in a language contact situation. Paper presented in the Thematic Panel on Language and National Integration. XII Indian Social Science Congress, Mysore, India.

Mohanty, A.K. (1988) SES, home environment and academic achievement of grade VI students in English medium schools. Unpublished paper, CAS in Psychology, Utkal University, Bhubaneswar, India.

Mohanty, A.K. (1990) Psychological consequences of mother tongue maintenance and multilingualism in India. In D.P. Pattanayak (ed.) *Multilingualism in India* (pp. 54–66). Clevedon: Multilingual Matters.

Mohanty, A.K. (1991) Social psychological aspects of languages in contact in multilingual societies. In G. Misra (ed.) *Applied Social Psychology in India* (pp. 54–66). New Delhi: Sage.

Mohanty, A.K. (1994) *Bilingualism in a Multilingual Society: Psychosocial and Pedagogical Implications.* Mysore: Central Institute of Indian Languages.

Mohanty, A.K. (2000) Perpetuating inequality: The disadvantage of language, minority mother tongues and related issues. In A.K. Mohanty and G. Misra (eds) *Psychology of Poverty and Disadvantage.* New Delhi: Concept.

Mohanty, A.K. (2003) Multilingualism and multiculturalism: The context of psycholinguistic research in India. In U. Vindhya (ed.) *Psychology in India: Intersecting Crossroads.* New Delhi: Concept.

Mohanty, A.K. (2004) Multilingualism of the unequals: The 'killer language' and anti-predatory strategies of minority mother tongues. Keynote address, International Conference on Multilingualism, Southern African Applied Linguistics Association, University of the North, South Africa, July 13–15.

Mohanty, A.K. and Babu, N. (1983) Bilingualism and metalinguistic ability among Kond tribals in Orissa, India. *The Journal of Social Psychology* 121, 15–22.

Mohanty, A.K. and Das, S.P. (1987) Cognitive and metalinguistic ability of unschooled bilingual and unilingual tribal children. *Psychological Studies* 32, 5–8.

Mohanty, A.K., Panda, S. and Mishra, B. (1999) Language socialization in a multilingual society. In T.S. Saraswathi (ed.) *Culture, Socialization and Human Development* (pp. 125–144). New Delhi: Sage.

Mohanty, A.K. and Parida, S. (1993) Bilingualism and attitude towards language and cultural maintenance and integration in a tribal-nontribal contact situation. Unpublished report, CAS in Psychology, Utkal University, Bhubaneswar, India.

Mohanty, A.K. and Perregaux, C. (1997) Language acquisition and bilingualism. In J.W. Berry, P.R. Dasen, and T.S. Saraswathi (eds) *Handbook of Cross-Cultural Psychology*: (Vol. 2) *Basic Processes and Human Development* (pp. 217–253). Boston: Allyn & Bacon.

Mohanty, A.K. and Saikia, J. (2004) Bilingualism and intergroup relationship in tribal and non-tribal contact situations. Paper presented in the XVII International Congress of International Association for Cross-Cultural Psychology, Xian, China, August 2–6.

Moll, L. and Greenberg, J. (1990) Creating zones of possibilities: Combining social contexts for instruction. In L. Moll (ed.) *Vygotsky and Education. Instructional Implications and Applications of Sociohistorical Psychology* (pp. 319–348). Cambridge: Cambridge University Press.

Moll, L., Amanti, C., Neff, D. and González, N. (1992) Funds of knowledge for teaching: Using a qualitative approach to connect homes and classrooms. *Theory into Practice* 31 (2), 132–141.

Mombert, M. (2001) Enseigner la langue de l'ennemi. In G. Zarate (ed.) *Langues, xénophobie, xénophilie dans une Europe multiculturelle* (pp. 15–25). CRDP de Basse Normandie.

Morán, R. (2004) *Lau*, bilingual education, and the role of the courts in shaping language policy. Paper presented at the Annual Conference of the American Educational Research Association, San Diego.

Mühlhäusler, P. (1990) 'Reducing' Pacific languages to writings. In J.E. Joseph and T.J. Taylor (eds) *Ideologies of Language* (pp. 189–205). London: Routledge.

Mühlhäusler, P. (1996) *Linguistic Ecology: Language Change and Linguistic Imperialism in the Pacific Region*. London: Routledge.

Myers-Scotton, C. (1993) Elite closure as a powerful language strategy: The African case. *International Journal of Sociology of Language* 103, 149–163.

Nagengast, C. and Vélez-Ibañez, C.G. (eds) (2004) *Human Rights: The Scholar as Activist*. Washington, DC: Publications of the Society of Applied Anthropology.

Nahmad, S. (1998) Historical and contemporary policies of Indigenous education in Mexico. *Cultural Survival Quarterly* (Spring), 59–60.

NAW (National Assembly for Wales) (2003a) *Welsh in Schools*. Cardiff: Statistical Directorate, National Assembly for Wales.

NAW (National Assembly for Wales) (2003b) *Iaith Pawb: A National Action Plan for a Bilingual Wales*. Cardiff: NAW.

NCERT (1990) *Fifth All India Educational Survey*. New Delhi: National Council of Educational Research and Training.

NCERT (1999) *Sixth All India Educational Survey*. New Delhi: National Council of Educational Research and Training.

NCLB (No Child Left Behind) (2002) Pub.L.No. 107–110. On WWW at www.senat.fr/rap/r03-063/r03-063.html. Accessed 3.6.2006.

Nettle, D. (1999) *Linguistic Diversity*. Oxford: Oxford University Press.

Nettle, D. and Romaine, S. (2000) *Vanishing Voices: The Extinction of the World's Languages*. Oxford: Oxford University Press.

New London Group (1996) A pedagogy of multiliteracies: Designing social futures. *Harvard Educational Review* 66, 60–92.

Nical, I., Smolicz, Jerzy J. and Secombe, M.J. (2004) Rural students and the Philippine bilingual education program on the island of Leyte. In J.W. Tollefson and A.B.M. Tsui (eds) *Medium of Instruction Policies: Which Agenda? Whose Agenda?* (pp. 153–176). Mahwah, NJ: Lawrence Erlbaum.

Nicholls, C. (2001) Reconciled to what? Reconciliation and the Northern Territory's bilingual education program, 1973–1998. In J. Lo Bianco and R. Wickert (eds) *Australian Policy Activism in Language and Literacy* (pp. 325–41). Melbourne: Language Matters.

Nicholls, C. (2005) Death by a thousand cuts: Indigenous language bilingual education programmes in the Northern Territory of Australia, 1972–1998. *International Journal of Bilingual Education and Bilingualism* 8 (2 & 3), 160–177.

Nicolau, S. and Valdivieso, R. (1992) Spanish language shift: Educational Implications. In J. Crawford (ed.) *Language Loyalties: A Source Book on the Official English Controversy.* Chicago: University of Chicago Press.

Ninyoles, J.L. (1972) *Lenguaje y Poder Social [Language and Social Power].* Madrid: Cátedra.

Nieto, S. (2001) *Language, Culture and Teaching: Critical Perspectives for a New Century.* Mahwah, NJ: Lawrence Erlbaum.

Noddings, N. (1984) *Caring: A Feminine Approach to Ethics and Moral Education.* Berkeley: University of California Press.

Noddings, N. (1992). *The Challenge to Care in Schools: An Alternative Approach to Education.* New York: Teachers College Press.

Norton, B. (formerly Peirce Norton) (2000) *Identity and Language Learning: Gender, Ethnicity and Educational Change.* London: Longman.

Nucinkis, N. (forthcoming) Situación de la educación intercultural bilingüe en Bolivia. In L.E. López (ed.) *La educación intercultural bilingüe bajo examen* [*Intercultural Bilingual Education under Examination*]. La Paz: Plural Editores.

Nyati-Ramabobo, L. (1997) Language in education and the quality of life in Botswana. In D. Nteta and J. Hermans (eds) *Poverty and Plenty: The Botswana Experience* (pp. 251–269). Gaborone: Botswana Society.

Nyati-Ramahobo, L. (2001) Language situation in Botswana. *Current Issues in Language Planning* 1 (2), 243–300.

Nyati-Ramahobo, L. (2002) From the phone call to the high court: Wayeyi visibility and the Kamanakao Association's campaign for linguistic and cultural rights in Botswana. *Journal of African Studies* 28 (4), 685–709.

Nyati-Ramahobo, L. and Chebanne, A. (2005) The development of minority languages for adult literacy in Botswana: Towards cultural diversity. *Journal of Education with Production* 30, 2005.

Ortiz, J. (2003) Man ordered to speak English to daughter. On WWW at http://www.cbsnews.com/stories/2003/10/15/national/main578064.shtml. Accessed 3.2.2006.

Ovando, C., Collier, V. and Combs, M.C. (2003) *Bilingual & ESL Classrooms: Teaching in Multicultural Contexts* (3rd edn). New York: McGraw-Hill.

Owen-Smith, M., Moabelo, C. and Msibi, F. (2004) The Home Languages Project: The teachers present, the experts respond. Paper presented at the International Conference of the Southern African Applied Linguistics Association (SAALA), University of Limpopo.

Pahl, K. and Rowsell, J. (2005) *Understanding Literacy Education: Using New Literacy Studies in the Classroom.* San Francisco: Sage.

Pandit, P.B. (1977) *Language in a Plural Society: The Case of India.* Delhi: Dev Raj Channa Memorial Committee.

Pardo, M.T.(1993) El desarrollo de la escritura de las lenguas indígenas en Oaxaca. *Iztapalapa* 13 (29), 109–134.

Patra, S. (2000) Role of language of instruction in the multilingual school system of India. Unpublished doctoral dissertation, Utkal University, Bhubaneswar.

Patrinos, H.A. and Panagides, A. (1994) Poverty and indigenous people in Mexico. *Akwe:kon Journal* 11 (2), 71–77.

Pattanayak, D.P. (1981) *Multilingualism and Mother Tongue Education.* Delhi: Oxford University Press.

Pattanayak, D.P. (1984) Language policies in multilingual states. In A. Gonzalez (ed.) *Panagani (Language Planning, Implementation and Evaluation)* (pp. 75–92). Manila: Linguistic Society of the Philippines.

Pattanayak, D.P. (1988) Monolingual myopia and the petals of Indian lotus: Do many languages divide or unite a nation? In T. Skutnabb-Kangas and J. Cummins (eds) *Minority Education: From Shame to Struggle* (pp. 379–389). Clevedon: Multilingual Matters.

Pattanayak, D.P. (1997) *Language Curriculum for Teacher Educators.* New Delhi: National Council of Teacher Education.

Pavlenko, A. and Blackledge, A. (2004) *Negotiation of Identities in Multilingual Contexts*. Clevedon: Multilingual Matters.

Pavlenko, A. and Norton, B. (in press) Imagined communities, identity, and English language learning. In J. Cummins and C. Davison (eds) *International Handbook of English Language Teaching*. Dordrecht: Springer.

Peate, M.R., Coupland, N. and Garret, P. (1998) Teaching Welsh and English in Wales. In W. Tulasiewicz and A. Adams (eds) *Teaching the Mother Tongue in a Multilingual Europe* (pp. 87–100). London: Cassell.

Pecos, R. and Blum-Martínez, R. (2001) The key to cultural survival: Language planning and revitalization in the Pueblo de Cochiti. In L. Hinton and K. Hale (eds) *The Green Book of Language Revitalization in Practice* (pp. 75–82). San Diego: Academic Press.

Peirce, B. Norton (1995) Social identity, investment, and language learning. *TESOL Quarterly*, 29 (1), 9–31.

Pennycook, A. (1994) *The Cultural Politics of English as an International Language.* London: Longman.

Pennycook, A. (1998) *English and the Discourses of Colonialism*. London: Routledge.

Pérez, B. (2004) *Becoming Biliterate: A Study of Two-Way Bilingual Immersion Education.* Mahwah, NJ: Lawrence Erlbaum.

Perlman, J. (1990) Historical legacies: 1840–1920. *Annals of the American Academy of Political and Social Science* 508, 27–37.

Perregaux, C., De Goumoens, C., Jeannot D. and De Pietro, J-F. (2003) *Education et Ouverture aux Langues à l'école.* Neuchâtel: Conférence Intercantonale de l'Instruction Publique de la Suisse Romande et du Tessin (Sécrétariat Général).

Phillipson, R. (1992) *Linguistic Imperialism*. Oxford: Oxford University Press.

Phillipson, R. (2001) Global English and local language policies: What Denmark needs. *Language Problem and Language Planning* 25 (1), 1–24.

Phillipson, R. (2003) *English-Only Europe? Challenging Language Policy.* London: Routledge.

Phillipson, R. (2005) *English, a Cuckoo in the European Higher Education Nest of Languages?* On WWW at www.palmenia.helsinki.fi/congress/bilingual2005/Phillipson.pptrogram.ppt. Forthcoming in European *Journal of English Studies.*

Phillipson, R. and Skutnabb-Kangas, T. (1994) English, panacea or pandemic. English only? in Europe/in Europa/en Europe. *Sociolinguistica* 9 (International Yearbook of European Sociolinguistics), 73–87.

Phillipson, R. and Skutnabb-Kangas, T. (1996) English only worldwide or language ecology? *TESOL Quarterly* 30 (3), 429–452.

Phillipson, R. and Skutnabb-Kangas, T. (1999) Englishization as one dimension of globalization. In D. Graddol and U.H. Meinhof (eds) *English in a Changing World. AILA Review* 13, (pp. 19–36). Oxford: The English Book Centre.

Plüddemann, P., Braam, D. and October, M. (2004) Language mapping using GIS: Work-in-progress from the Western Cape. Paper presented at the International Conference of the Southern African Applied Linguistics Association (SAALA), University of Limpopo.

Posey, D.A. (1999a) Introduction: Culture and nature: The inextricable link. In D.A. Posey (ed.) *Cultural and Spiritual Values of Biodiversity. A Complementary Contribution to the Global Biodiversity Assessment* (pp. 3–18). New York: United Nations Environmental Programme (UNEP).

Posey, D. (ed.) (1999b) *Cultural and Spiritual Values of Biodiversity. A Complementary Contribution to the Global Biodiversity Assessment*. New York: United Nations Environmental Programme (UNEP).

PROEIB Andes (Programa de Formación en Educación Intercultural Bilingüe para los Países Andinos) (2001) *Estudios sociolingüísticos y socioeducativos de las tierras bajas de Bolivia* [*Sociolinguistic and Socioeducational Studies of the Bolivian Lowlands*]. Cochabamba. Mimeo.

Proyecto Tantanakuy (2004) La realidad de las unidades educativas multigrado. Cochabamba, Bolivia: Proyecto Tantanakuy (Cuadernillo de Aprendizaje: Escuelas Multigrado, No. 1). *Quarterly* 29 (1), 9–31,

Ramirez, J.D., Yuen, S. and Ramey, D. (1991) Final report: Longitudinal study of structured English immersion strategy, early exit and late-exit transitional bilingual education programs for language minority children. US Department of Education Contract No. 300-87-0156. San Mateo, CA: Aguirre International.

Rao, A.G. (2005) Gepatralingva edukado por indighenoj [Mother-tongue education for indigenous peoples]. *Monato*, September. On WWW at http://www.esperanto.be/fel/2005/008714.php.

Rassool, N., Edwards, V. and Bloch, C. (in press) Language and development in multilingual settings: A case-study of knowledge transfer and teacher education in South Africa. *International Review of Education*.

Rebuffot, J. (1993) *Le point sur l'immersion au Canada*. Anjou, Québec: Centre Educatif et Culturel.

Reimer, F.J. (1996) Literacy classes in Thimbukushu: The local context of literacy and BCC's organization of support. Report of Botswana Christian Council (BCC), Etsha 6.

Republic of Botswana (1997) Towards prosperity for all: Vision 2016. Gaborone: Government Printer.

RERS (2003) *Repères et recherches statistiques*. Paris: MEN/DESCO A1.

Reyhner, J. and Eder, J. (2004) *American Indian Education: A History*. Norman: University of Oklahoma Press.

Rice, R. (2004) Where we were and where we are going: Remembering Brown v. Board of Education, *Lau v. Nichols*, and *Castañeda v. Pickard*. *NABE News* 27 (3), 4–6, 34.

Ricento, T. (2003) The discursive construction of Americanism. *Discourse and Society*, 14 (5), 611–637.

Rivera, C. and Stansfield, C. (2000) *An Analysis of State Policies for the Inclusion and Accommodation of English Language Learners in State Assessment Programs during 1998–99*. Washington, DC: The George Washington University Center for Equity and Excellence in Education.

Roberts, C., Byram, M., Barro, A., Jordan, S. and Street, B. (2001) *Language Learners as Ethnographers*. Clevedon: Multilingual Matters.

Roca, A. and Colombi, M.C. (eds) (2003) *Mi Lengua: Spanish as a Heritage Language in the United States, Research and Practice*. Washington, DC: Georgetown University Press.

Rodseth, W. and Rodseth, V. (2004) Developments in the Home Language Project (HLP) since SAALA 2002. Paper presented at the International Conference of the Southern African Applied Linguistics Association (SAALA), University of Limpopo.

Romero, M.E. (2001) Indigenous language immersion: The Cochiti experience. Presentation at the 22nd Annual American Indian Language Development Institute, University of Arizona, Tucson, June 9.

Rubagumya, C.M. (ed.) (1990) *Language in Education in Africa: A Tanzanian Perspective*. Clevedon: Multilingual Matters.

Rubio, F. (forthcoming) Educación bilingüe en Guatemala. Situación y desafíos. In L.E. López (ed.) *La educación intercultural bilingüe bajo examen [Intercultural Bilingual Education under Examination*]. La Paz: Plural Editores.

Ruiz, R. (1984a) Language teaching in American education: Impact on second language learning. A synthesis report for the National Institute of Education.

Ruiz, R. (1984b) Orientations in language planning. *NABE Journal* 8 (2), 15–34.

Ruiz, R. (1988) Orientations in language planning. In S. McKay and S. Wong (eds) *Language Diversity: Problem or Resource?* (pp. 3–25). Cambridge, MA: Newbury House.

Ruiz, R. (2004) From language as a problem to language as an asset: The promise and limitations of *Lau*. Paper presented at the Annual Conference of the American Educational Research Association, San Diego.

Said, E. (1993) *Culture and Imperialism*. New York: Alfred Knopf.

Saikia, J. and Mohanty, A.K. (2004) The role of mother tongue medium instruction in promoting educational achievement: A study of Grade IV Bodo children in Assam (India). Unpublished manuscipt. Zakir Husain Centre for Educational Studies, JNU, New Delhi.

Sapiens, A. (1978) Language and education policy affecting the Chicano in California: A historical perspective. Unpublished manuscript.

Schmidt, A. (1990) *Loss of Austria's Aboriginal Language Heritage*. Canberra: Aboriginal Studies.

Schools for Chiapas (2004) *Schools for Chiapas Newsletter*. September.

Seidman, I. (1998) *Interviewing as Qualitative Research: A Guide for Researchers in Education and the Social Sciences* (2nd edn). New York: Teachers College Press.

Shohamy, E. (2001) *The Power of Tests*. Longman: Pearson.

Shohamy, E. (2003) Implications of Language Education Policies to language study in schools and universities. *Modern Language Journal* 87 (2), 278–281.

Shohamy, E. (2004) How 'real' are multilingual schools given overt and covert educational language policies? Paper presented at the Conference on Imagining Multilingual Schools: An International Symposium on Language in Education, New York.

Shohamy, E. (2006) *Language Policy: Hidden Agendas and New Approaches*. London: Routledge.

Sigüán, M. (2001) *Bilingüismo y Lenguas en Contacto*. Madrid: Alianza Editorial.

Sigüán, Mi. and Mackey, W.F. (1986) *Educación y Bilingüismo*. Madrid: Santillana.

Sims, C.P. (2001) Native language planning: A pilot process in the Acoma Pueblo community. In L. Hinton and K. Hale (eds) *The Green Book of Language Revitalization in Practice* (pp. 63–73). San Diego: Academic Press.

Skourtou, E., Kourtis-Kazoullis, V. and Cummins, J. (in press) Designing virtual learning environments for academic language development. In J. Weiss, J. Nolan and V. Nincic (eds) *Handbook of Virtual Learning*. Dordrecht: Kluwer Academic Publishers.

Skutnabb-Kangas, T. (1981) *Tvåspråkighet*. Lund: Liber Läromedel. (English translation: Skutnabb-Kangas, T. (1984) *Bilingualism or Not: The Education of Minorities*. Clevedon: Multilingual Matters.)

Skutnabb-Kangas, T. (1984) *Bilingualism or Not: The Education of Minorities*. Clevedon: Multilingual Matters.

Skutnabb-Kangas, T. (1988) Multilingualism and the education of minority children. In T. Skutnabb-Kangas and J. Cummins (eds) *Minority Education: From Shame to Struggle* (pp. 9–44). Clevedon: Multilingual Matters.

Skutnabb-Kangas, T. (1990) *Language, Literacy and Minorities*. London: The Minority Rights Group.

Skutnabb-Kangas, T. (1995) Review of *Bilingualism in a Multilingual Society: Psychosocial and Pedagogical Implications* by Ajit K. Mohanty. *TESOL Quarterly* 29 (4), 775–780.

Skutnabb-Kangas, T. (2000) *Linguistic Genocide in Education or Worldwide Diversity and Human Rights?* Mahwah, NJ: Lawrence Erlbaum.

Skutnabb-Kangas, T. (2004a) The one common feature in multilingual schooling: Politics and emotions rule while research results are invisibilised. Paper presented at the International Symposium on Language in Education: *Imagining Multilingual Schools*, Teachers College, Columbia University, New York, 30 September to 2 October.

Skutnabb-Kangas, T. (2004b) The right to mother tongue medium education: The hot potato in human rights instruments. Opening plenary at the 2nd Mercator International Symposium, Tarragona, Spain, 27–28 February 2004. On WWW at http://www.ciemen.org/mercator/pdf/simp-skuttnab.pdf. Accessed 3.02.06.

Skutnabb-Kangas, T. (2004c) Endangered linguistic and cultural diversities and endangered biodiversity: The role of educational linguistic human rights in diversity maintenance. Keynote address at the Cultural Diversity and Linguistic Diversity conference, Diyarbakir/Amed, 20–25 March. On WWW at http://www.pen-kurd.org/Diyarbakir-seminar/tove-endangered-linguistic-and-cultural-diversities.html. Accessed 3.02.06

Skutnabb-Kangas, T. and Cummins, J. (eds) (1988) *Minority Education: From Shame to Struggle*. Clevedon: Multilingual Matters.

Skutnabb-Kangas, T. and García, O. (1995) Multilingualism for all: General principles? In T. Skutnabb-Kangas (ed.) *Multilingualism for All* (pp. 221–256). Lisse: Swets and Zeitlinger.

Skutnabb-Kangas, T., Maffi, L. and Harmon, D. (2003) *Sharing A World of Difference. The Earth's Linguistic, Cultural, and Biological Diversity*. Paris: UNESCO Publishing. Available at www.terralingua.org/UNESCO%20publication.pdf. Accessed 3.2.2006.

Sna Jtz'ibajom (1996) *Lo'il maxil: Relatos Tseltales y Tzotziles: sk'op ya'yej jtseltal sok jtzotziletik*. Gobierno del Estado de Chiapas, Tuxtla Gutiérrez.

Sna Jtz'ibajom (2003) *Sts'unbal jts'ibtik: Nuestras semillas literarias, cuentos infantiles*. San Cristóbal de las Casas, Chiapas: Fray Bartolomé de las Casas.

Sna Jtz'ibajom website (2004) At http://www.mnh.si.edu/anthro/maya/. Accessed 3.2.2006.

Solway, J. and Nyati-Ramahobo, L. (2004) Democracy in process: Building a coalition to achieve political, cultural and linguistic rights in Botswana. *Canadian Journal of African Studies*.

Spack, R. (2002) *America's Second Tongue: American Indian Education and the Ownership of English, 1860–1900*. Lincoln: University of Nebraska Press.

Spivak, G.C. (1988) Can the Subaltern Speak? In C. Nelson and L. Grossberg (eds) *Marxism and the Interpretation of Culture* (pp. 271–313). Chicago: University of Illinois Press.

Spolsky, B. (1974) Navajo language maintenance: Six-year-olds in 1969. In F. Pialorsi (ed.) *Teaching the Bilingual* (pp. 138–149). Tucson: University of Arizona Press.

Spolsky, B. (2002) Prospects for the survival of the Navajo language: A reconsideration. *Anthropology and Education Quarterly* 33 (3), 139–162.

Spolsky, B. (2004) *Language Policy*. Cambridge: Cambridge University Press.

Spring, J. (1996) *The Cultural Transformation of a Native American Family and Its Tribe 1763–1995: A Basket of Apples*. Mahwah, NJ: Lawrence Erlbaum.

Spring, J. (1998) *Education and the Rise of the Global Economy*. Mahwah, NJ: Lawrence Erlbaum.

Sridhar, K. K. (1996) Societal multilingualism. In S.L. McKay and N.H. Hornberger (eds) *Sociolinguistics and Language Teaching* (pp. 47–70). Cambridge: Cambridge University Press.

Srivastava, A.K. (1990) Multilingualism and school education in India: Special features, problems and prospects. In D.P. Pattanayak (ed.) *Multilingualism in India* (pp. 37–53). Clevedon: Multilingual Matters.

Srivastava, R.N. and Gupta, R.S. (1984) Media of education in higher education in India. In J.B. Pride (ed.) *Languages for the Third World Universities* (pp. 1–22). New Delhi: Bahri Publications.

Stavenhagen, R. (1995) Cultural rights and universal human rights. In A. Eide, C. Krause and A. Rosas (eds) *Economic, Social and Cultural Rights: A Textbook* (pp. 63–77). Dordrecht: Martinus Nijhoff Publishers.

Stiles, D.B. (1997) Four successful indigenous language programs. In J. Reyhner (ed.) *Teaching Indigenous Languages* (pp 148–262). Flagstaff, AZ: Northern Arizona University.

Stobart, H. and Howard, R. (2002) (eds) *Knowledge and Learning in the Andes: Ethnographic Perspectives. Liverpool Latin American Studies. New Series* 3. Liverpool: Liverpool University Press.

Stora, B. (2004) Algérie 1954–2004: Le douloureux héritage. *Politis* 823, pp. 10–11.

Street, S. (1990) La educación de adultos en México: Los planificadores teorizan su práctica. *Revista Latinoamericana de Estudios Educativos*, XX (3), 41–56.

Suárez-Orozco, M.M. (1996) Unwelcome mats. *Harvard Magazine* (July–August), 32–35.

Summer Institute of Linguistics (2005) *Ethnologue of World Languages*. On WWW at http://www.ethnologue.com. Accessed 3.2.2006

Thomas, J. (Chief), with Boyle T. (2001) *Teachings from the Longhouse*. Toronto: Stoddart (originally published 1994).

Thomas, W. and Collier, V. (2002) Summary of findings across all research sites. A national study of school effectiveness for language minority students' long-term achievement. Final Report: Project 1.1. Santa Cruz, CA: Center for Research on Education, Diversity and Excellence, University of California.

Tippeconnic, J.W.III and Faircloth, S.C. (2002) Using culturally and linguistically appropriate assessments to ensure that American Indian and Alaska Native students receive the special education programs and services they need. *ERIC Digest* EDO-RC-02-8. Charleston, WV: ERIC Clearinghouse on Rural Education and Small Schools.

Tirado, M. (2001) Left behind: Are public schools failing Indian kids? *American Indian Report*, September, 12–15.

Tollefson, J.W. and Tsui, A.B.M. (2004) The centrality of medium of instruction policy in sociopolitical processes. In J.W. Tollefson and A.B.M. Tsui (eds) *Medium of Instruction Policies: Which Agenda? Whose Agenda?* (pp. 1–18). Mahwah, NJ: Lawrence Erlbaum.

Toohey, K., Manyak, P. and Day, E. (2006) ESL learners in the early school years: Identity and mediated classroom practices. In J. Cummins and C. Davison (eds) *International Handbook of English Language Teaching*. Dordrecht: Springer.

Torres, L. (1997) *Puerto Rican Discourse: A Sociolinguistic Study of a New York Suburb*. Mahwah, NJ: Lawrence Erlbaum.

Torres-Guzmán, M.E. (2003) Preparing teachers to recognize and confront symbolic violence in bilingual education. In B.C. Wallace and R.T. Carter (eds) *Understanding and Dealing With Violence: A Multicultural Approach* (pp. 201–225). Thousand Oaks, CA: SAGE Publications.

Torres-Guzmán, M. and Etxeberría, F. (2005) Modelo B-dual language programs in the Basque Country and the US. *International Journal of Bilingualism and Bilingual Education*.

Torres-Guzmán, M.E., Morales, S., Han, A. and Kleyn, T. (2005) Self-designated dual-language programs: Is there a gap between labeling and implementation? *Bilingual Research Journal* 29 (2)

Trujillo, A. (1999) *Comunidad y educación bilingüe intercultural en Chiapas*. Mexico: CONECULTA.

Tsui, A.B.M. (2004) Medium of instruction in Hong Kong: One country, two systems, whose language? In J.W. Tollefson and A.B.M. Tsui (eds) *Medium of Instruction Policies: Which Agenda? Whose Agenda?* (pp. 97–116) Mahwah, NJ: Lawrence Erlbaum.

UNESCO (2001) *Atlas of the World's Languages in Danger of Disappearing*. Paris: UNESCO

United Nations Committee on the Elimination of all Forms of Racial Discrimination (CERD) 2002. CERD sixty-first session. 5–23 August. Geneva.

United Nations Development Programme (2004) Human development report 2004. On WWW at http://hdr.undp.org/reports/global/2004/. Accessed 3.2.2006.

US Department of Education (2003) The growing numbers of limited English proficient students (1992/93–2002/03). On WWW at http://www.ed.gov/about/offices/list/oela/index.html. Accessed 3.2.2006.

Valdés, G. (1997) Dual-language immersion programs: A cautionary note concerning the education of language-minority students. *Harvard Educational Review* 67, 391–429.

Valdés, G. and Figueroa, R. (1994) *Bilingualism and Testing: A Special Case of Bias*. Norwood, NJ: Ablex Publishing Corporation.

Valenzuela, A. (1999) *Subtractive Schooling: US-Mexican Youth and the Politics of Caring*. Albany: State University of New York Press.

Varenne, H. (forthcoming) On education as movement in everyday life. In H. Varenne (ed.) Searching for education in everyday life: Anthropological explorations into hidden processes of deliberate change. Unpublished manuscript.

Varro, G. (2003) *Sociologie de la mixité: De la mixité amoureuse aux mixités sociales et culturelles*. Paris: Belin.

Vermes, G. and Boutet, J. (eds) (1987) *France, Pays Multilingue* (Vols 1 & 2). Paris: L'Harmattan.

Vesely, R. (2000) *Multilingual Environments for Survival: The Impact of English on Xhosa-speaking Students in Cape Town*. Cape Town: PRAESA.

Villarreal, A. (1999) Rethinking the education of English language learners: Transitional bilingual education programs. *Bilingual Research Journal* 23 (1), 11–45.

Visser, H. (2000) Language and cultural empowerment of the Khoesan people: The Naro Experience. In H. Batibo and B. Smieja (eds) *Botswana: The Future of Minority Languages* (pp. 193–216). Frankfurt: Peter Lang.

Viswanatham, K. (1999) An anatomy of three language formula. *International Journal of Dravidian Linguistics* 28 (2), 89–108.

Walter, S.L. and Ringenberg, K. (1994) Language policy, literacy and minority languages. *Policy Studies Review* 13 (3–4), 341– 365.

Warner, S.L. No'eau (1999) *Kuleana:* The right, responsibility, and authority of indigenous peoples to speak and make decisions for themselves in language and culture revitalization. *Anthropology and Education Quarterly* 30 (1), 68–93.

Warner, S.L. No'eau (2001) The movement to revitalize Hawaiian language and culture. In L. Hinton and K. Hale (eds) *The Green Book of Language Revitalization in Practice* (pp. 133–144). San Diego: Academic Press.

Warschauer, M., Knobel, M. and Stone, L. (2004) Technology and equity in schooling: Deconstructing the digital divide. *Educational Policy* 18 (4), 562–588.

Wildsmith-Cromarty, R. and Gounden, R. (2004) A balanced reading approach for grade one and two English L1 (first language) and EAL (English additional language) learners. Paper presented at the International Conference of the Southern African Applied Linguistics Association (SAALA), University of Limpopo.

Wiley, T.G. and Wright, W.E. (2004) Against the undertow: Language-minority education policy and politics in the 'Age of Accountability.' *Educational Policy* 18 (1), 142–168.

Williams, E. (1998) Investigating bilingual literacy: Evidence from Malawi and Zambia. *Education Research* 24. London: Department for International Development.

Williams, E. (2004) Attracting the Welsh worm. *Cambria* 6 (5), 50–1.

Williams, R. (2004) The fight for the language. *Cambria* 6 (4), 14–16.

Wilson, W.H. (1998) I ka 'olelo Hawai'i' ke ola [Life is found in the Hawaiian language]. *International Journal of the Sociology of Language* 132, 123–237.

Wilson, W.H. (1999) The sociopolitical context of establishing Hawaiian-medium education. In S. May (ed.) *Indigenous Community-Based Education* (pp. 95–108). Clevedon: Multilingual Matters.

Wilson, W.H. and Kamanā, K. (2001) Mai loko mai o ka 'i'ni: Proceeding from a dream. The 'Aha Punana Leo connection in Hawaiian language revitalization. In L. Hinton and K. Hale (eds) *The Green Book of Language Revitalization in Practice* (pp. 147–176). San Diego: Academic Press.

WLB (Welsh Language Board) (n.d.) *Developing Bilingualism in Children: Advice for Health and Childcare Professionals in Wales*. Cardiff: Welsh Language Board.

Wong, S.C. (1988) Educational rights of language minorities. In S.L. McKay and S.C. Wong (ed.) *Language Diversity: Problem or Resource? A Social and Educational Perspective on Language Minorities in the United States* (pp. 367–386). Cambridge, MA: Newbury House.

Woolard, K.A. (1998) Introduction: Language ideology as a field of inquiry. In B. Schieffelin, K.A. Woolard and P. Kroskrity (eds) *Language Ideologies: Practice and Theory* (pp. 3–47). New York and Oxford: Oxford University Press.

Young, A. and Hélot, C. (2003) Language awareness and or language learning in French primary schools today. *Language Awareness* 12 (3 & 4), 236–246.

Zentella, A.C. (1997) *Growing up Bilingual: Puerto Rican Children in New York*. Boston, MA: Blackwell Publishers.

Zepeda, O. and Hill, J. (1992) The condition of Native American languages in the United States. In R.H. Robins and E.M. Ehlenbeck (eds) *Endangered Languages* (pp. 135–155). New York: Berg.

Zinn, H. (2003/1980) *A People's History of the United States, 1492–Present*. New York: Perennial Classics.

Zozula, K. and Ford, S. (1985) *Keewatin Perspective on Bilingual Education*. Rankin Inlet: Keewatin Board of Education.

Index

Authors

Subjects